THE SCYTHIANS

the
SCYTHIANS
NOMAD WARRIORS OF THE STEPPE

BARRY CUNLIFFE

OXFORD
UNIVERSITY PRESS

OXFORD
UNIVERSITY PRESS

Great Clarendon Street, Oxford, OX2 6DP
United Kingdom

Oxford University Press is a department of the University of Oxford.
It furthers the University's objective of excellence in research, scholarship,
and education by publishing worldwide. Oxford is a registered trade mark of
Oxford University Press in the UK and in certain other countries

First Edition published in 2019

Impression: 2

Published in the United States of America by Oxford University Press
198 Madison Avenue, New York, NY 10016, United States of America

British Library Cataloguing in Publication Data
Data available

Library of Congress Control Number: 2018967284

ISBN 978–0–19–882012–3

Typeset by Sparks—www.sparkspublishing.com

Printed in Great Britain by
CPI Group (UK) Ltd, Croydon CR0 4YY

PREFACE

MANY years ago as a young undergraduate at Cambridge I came across a brief reference, in a series of essays written by Gordon Childe, to horsemen who had moved westwards from the Pontic steppe and had established themselves in Hungary at the end of the Bronze Age. I was surprised to find that none of my teachers at Cambridge had any interest in, or indeed much knowledge of, the subject so I decided to follow it up, as far as I could, from published sources and to make it my own. That which we discover for ourselves we cherish. So began a lifelong fascination with the warrior nomads of the steppe.

Some years later, in the early 1970s, I managed to arrange a brief study trip to Hungary, then still under Soviet control, the first of many visits to Eastern Europe to meet colleagues and to establish academic links. It was in the National Museum in Budapest, looking in awe at two great gold stags, brought to northern Hungary by horsemen from the steppe, that the brilliance and energy of the Scythian world first really struck home. Thereafter I have dogged the footsteps of the Scythians, in the Ukraine and the Crimea, and across Central Asia as far as Mongolia. I have also made pilgrimages to two of the world's greatest collections of Scythian art, in the State Hermitage Museum in St Petersburg and the Museum of Historical Treasures in Kiev. This book is my homage to these remarkable people.

For the most part the story told here is presented as a straightforward narrative but a small collection of end matter has been added: a list of Scythian kings, a brief timeline, and a Gallery of Objects in which ten selected items, which best illustrate Scythian life, are presented—chosen because they are frequently referred to in the text. There is also a section offering a Guide to Further Reading for those who, I hope, might wish to begin to dig deeper into the detail.

To an educated Greek, the Scythians were one of the four great peoples of the barbarian world. They were well known. Scythian archers were frequently depicted on Attic Black-Figured pottery and historians like Herodotus recorded stories from their

v

history exploring, with undisguised delight, their unusual behaviour and beliefs. Nowadays Scythians are seldom in our consciousness. They are hardly represented in our museum collections and only rarely are they the subject of temporary exhibitions. Recently, in 2017, the British Museum has hosted a brilliant exhibition, *Scythian Warriors of Ancient Siberia*, from the State Hermitage Museum, St Petersburg. Before that one has to go back to the *Frozen Tombs* exhibition of 1978. America has been rather better served but even so the wonders of Scythian culture are seldom seen in the West.

There are many reasons for this. The difficulty and expense of mounting international displays must rank large. But there are also cultural reasons. The Scythians were largely nomads, constantly on the move and frequently covering large distances. They left no cities or monumental architecture. For most people in the world today, leading sedentary, urban lives, nomadism is difficult to comprehend; it is much easier to empathize with Greeks and Romans, or even Egyptians or Aztecs. The Scythians are 'other', alien and therefore a little unnerving—best left on the margin where they belong. Yet to the Greeks it was just this that made them so fascinating. And rightly so. I hope that this book will go some way in making the world of the Scythian nomads a little more accessible and understandable and will encourage at least some readers to explore for themselves the wonders of Scythian culture and the breathtaking steppe landscape in which they lived.

Barry Cunliffe
Oxford
April 2018

CONTENTS

1

DISCOVERING
THE SCYTHIANS

I N April 1698 a tall young man, 26 years old, untidily dressed and with hands scratched and scarred through hard work, decided to take time off from studying shipbuilding in the Deptford and Greenwich yards on the Thames to visit Oxford with a small group of friends. The party stayed in the Golden Cross Inn in Cornmarket, where they evidently had a convivial evening, and the next morning set out to visit the Ashmolean Museum, then in Broad Street. The museum had been opened fifteen years earlier, under the patronage of Elias Ashmole, to house his 'cabinet of curiosities' inherited from the collector John Tradescant. The visit to the museum was brief but the group had attracted notice and by the time they left to cross the road to visit Trinity College chapel a large crowd had gathered. Irritated by the attention the young man decided to return to London to immerse himself once more in the intricacies of shipbuilding. He was Peter Alexeyevich, Tzar of Russia, later to be known as Peter the Great.

Peter was an intellectual and a man of action. He had realized that for his country to grow in the modern world it would have to become a great sea power. Since its few ports on the icebound White Sea were far from adequate he set his heart on establishing a navy on the Black Sea—an ambition which meant confronting the Ottomans, who then controlled the region. Later in his reign he was to turn his attention to the Baltic and the Caspian Sea, involving Russia in wars with Sweden and Persia. It was his early realization of the importance of sea power that led him to take a deep

 1

1.1 Peter the Great, Tzar of Russia (r. 1682–1725) dedicated his life to transforming his country from the medieval backwater in which he was born to a forward looking state embracing western ideals of culture, government, and military prowess. His intellectual curiosity led to him amassing a collection of scientific curiosities and antiquities. This 'cabinet of curiosities' was first displayed in the Kunstkamera in the new capital of St Petersburg. Later the collection was transferred to the Hermitage.

interest in shipbuilding. In 1697 he travelled incognito to western Europe with a small delegation, known as the Grand Embassy, to learn about the West and to establish new alliances. His interest in maritime technology led him to spend time in Amsterdam in the shipyards of the Dutch East India Company, as well as in the London dockyards. Later he visited Malta to study the Knights of St John and their fleet, and even considered the possibility of setting up a Russian naval base on the island.

It was in Amsterdam, in 1697, that Peter's other great interest, in collecting scientific curiosities and antiquities, began to develop. There he met the great Dutch collector, Jacob de Wilde, whose collection of scientific instruments, antiquities, coins, and medals he is said later to have acquired. It was this fascination with curiosities that drew him, on that spring day, to visit Ashmole's museum in Oxford. Like many educated men of the time Peter became an eclectic collector of curiosities, amassing works of fine and applied art, artefacts, items of oriental culture, and *naturalia*, especially human malformations, which were eventually displayed in the Kunstkamera (Cabinet of Curiosities)—a grand structure built on the banks of the Neva in St Petersburg, opened in 1727, two years after Peter's death. The collection remained there until December 1859 when it was moved to the Winter Palace, but on the orders of Tzar Alexander II it was transferred the next year to the Hermitage. One part of Peter's collection, to which he was particularly attached, was a group of artefacts, mainly of gold, which came from Siberia. It was handed over to the Academy of Sciences in 1723, eventually passing to the Hermitage, where it is still displayed as The Siberian Collection of Peter the Great.

Siberia was a vast region sparsely populated by nomadic tribes. Russian conquest had begun in 1581–2 under Ivan IV (The Terrible) and by the middle of the seventeenth century under official encouragement the flow of Russian settlers had increased, attracted by the many economic opportunities which the virgin territory had to offer.

 2

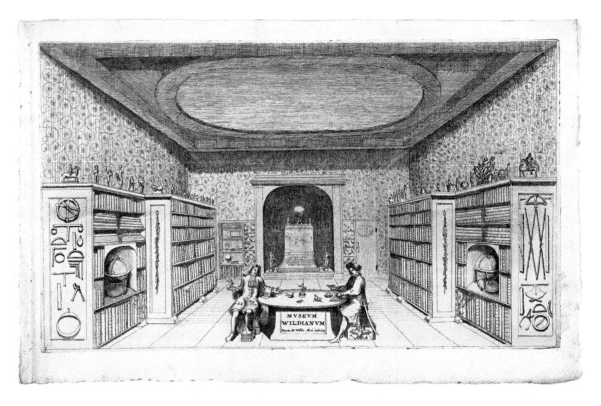

1.2 During his travels in Western Europe Peter spent time in Amsterdam, where he met many scholars and collectors. Among them was Jacob de Wilde, collector-general for the Admiralty of Amsterdam, who had amassed a considerable personal collection of scientific instruments and antiquities. The two men first met in de Wilde's library on 13 December 1697. The occasion was recorded by de Wilde's daughter, Maria, in an engraving published in 1700 (Tzar Peter is on the right).

Rumours that there were gold artefacts to be found in ancient grave mounds soon began to circulate and it was not long before the commanders of the communities of Tomsk and Krasnoyarsk began to organize bands of mound-diggers (*bugrovshchiki*) to dig into the many kurgans (burial mounds) scattered about the landscape in search of treasure. One report, sent from Tobolsk to Tzar Alexey in 1670, speaks of much gold and silver being dug out of 'Tartar' graves by the Russians.

Six years earlier a Dutchman, Nicolaas Witsen, had spent a year in Russia as part of the Dutch embassy and, developing a deep interest in the country and its culture, had begun to collect artefacts emanating from Siberia. He continued to do so through Russian agents long after he had returned home. 'How civilized must have been the people who buried these rarities', he wrote. 'The gold objects are so artfully and sensibly ornamented that I do not think European craftsmen could have managed

 3

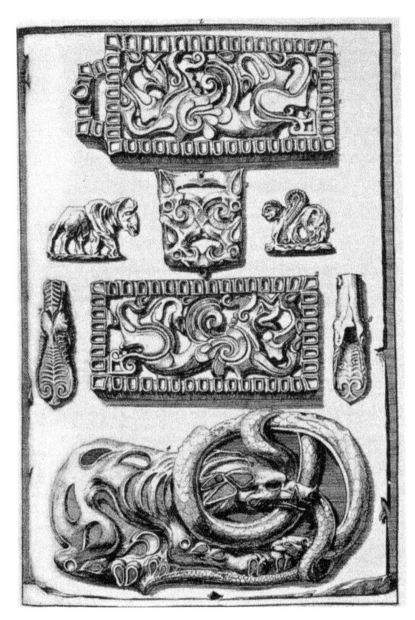

1.3 Peter also met the Dutch collector Nicolaas Witsen, who had built up a significant collection of antiquities from Siberia. On Witsen's death in 1717 Peter tried to acquire it but without success. The engraving showing a selection of Witsen's Siberian antiquities is taken from his *Noord en oost Tartaryen*, 2nd edn. (Amsterdam, 1785).

better.' Witsen was a prominent citizen in Amsterdam, serving as mayor of the city on thirteen occasions between 1682 and 1706. In 1697 it was he who organized a four-month attachment for the young Tzar Peter in the shipyards of the Dutch East India Company, and introduced him to other scientists and collectors in the city. Peter will have been well aware of Witsen's collection of Siberian antiquities and tried to acquire it after his death in 1717, but apparently without success.

By this time Peter was himself an avid collector of Siberian gold artefacts. His main supplier was Prince Matvei Petrovich Gagarin who, as governor of Siberia, lived at Tobolsk, the capital of the province. On one occasion we hear of Gagarin ordering that poor peasants sheltering in a monastery should be sent out to dig into

1.4 Gold belt buckle sent to Peter the Great by M. P. Gagarin, governor of Siberia, from Tobolsk in 1716, dating from the fourth or third century BC, now in the State Hermitage Museum, St Petersburg. This is one of a pair of plaques which made up the belt buckle. The scene is set beneath the Tree of Life and centres on a goddess, wearing a tall pointed hat, comforting a dead hero. The gorytos (quiver) hanging on the tree symbolizes the marriage between the goddess and the hero, completing the cycle of birth, death, and rebirth (p. 279).

mounds to find gold and silver. The first package he sent to the tzar contained ten items. The second, sent in 1716, was more substantial, comprising 172 objects. It was accompanied by a note: 'Your Majesty has instructed me to search for the old objects buried in the land of ancient treasures. According to this instruction of Yours, I am sending You as many gold objects as it has been found. Descriptions of these object and details of their number and weight are enclosed to this letter. Your Majesty's humblest slave, Matvei Gagarin.' A third batch, sent a year later, included sixty gold objects and two of silver. Gagarin had been a faithful agent diligently collecting for his master but soon fell from favour and in 1721 was publically hanged 'for abuse of authority'. But he was not the only supplier of antiquities. Already, in 1715, a Siberian mine owner, Alexis Demidov, had presented Peter with twenty gold objects and more will have arrived from other sources.

Peter's fascination with Siberian gold artefacts stemmed from his collector's instincts for accumulating curiosities, but the flow of antiquities also provided material to help him forward his ambition to write a history of Russia and its peoples. The artefacts were research data and had to be preserved from unscrupulous peasants whose natural inclination was to melt them down and sell the gold, but if they were to be used to write history it was also necessary to learn something of their context. Thus, in 1718, a decree was issued to bring an end to the plundering of graves. It threatened death to anyone found 'searching for gold stirrups and cups'. Instead, local officials were ordered to collect 'from earth and water ... old inscriptions, ancient weapons, dishes, and everything old and unusual'. Information about the context should be recorded and 'all objects found be drawn'. It was an enlightened attitude, far in advance of Western European practices at the time, but very difficult to enforce. Peter realized this and had already decided to be more proactive in gathering new knowledge.

Expeditions to Siberia: The Pioneers

The idea of sending a scientific expedition to Siberia was clearly in Peter's mind when, in 1716, he was spending some time in Danzig (now Gdańsk). There he visited the natural scientist and collector, Johann Philipp Breyne, whose work had gained international acclaim, winning him election as a Fellow of the Royal Society in London. In addition to examining Breyne's natural history collection Peter also sought his advice on setting up a Siberian expedition. Breyne recommended that the tzar should entrust the venture to a German medical doctor, Daniel Gottlieb Messerschmidt, who had helped him build his own collection. Messerschmidt was invited to St Petersburg, and in November 1718 was charged to travel to Siberia to study the geography, natural history, medicine, medical herbs, diseases, peoples, languages, monuments, and

1.5 The expansion of Russia between 1505 and 1783. Besides the exploration and settlement of Siberia, Peter was intent on extending Russia's frontiers to the Baltic and to the Black Sea so that the country could develop an effective way to become a world power. In the north he was successful, conquering territories belonging to Sweden, but on the Black Sea, although his forces took the fortress of Azov (on the Sea of that name) in 1696, it was regained by the Turks. The Khanate of Crimea did not become Russian until 1783 at the time of the expansion driven by Catherine the Great.

 7

antiquities; to 'make a description of everything remarkable'; and to 'collect rarities and medical plants'. Preparation for this daunting task took some time but he finally set out in March 1719 for Tobolsk on what was to be a seven-year expedition. In the report, written on his return after Peter's death, he explained his brief more fully: 'I shall look for herbs, and flowers, roots, birds, and so on … and also for ancient burial objects … portrayals of people and animals, Kalmyk mirrors. I was ordered to announce in the towns and regions that everybody must bring me such herbs, roots, and flowers and ancient burial things … and if any of them are found worthy, the burial objects shall be paid for generously'. In the event he acquired few items of gold, suggesting to him that most of the readily accessible graves had already been robbed. As an enquiring scientist, however, he decided to test this for himself by excavating a number of burial mounds. Although he found little that he considered to be of value, his were the first scientifically driven excavations in Russia—the beginning of modern archaeology.

Messerschmidt returned to St Petersburg in March 1727. His patron, Tzar Peter, had died two years earlier and there was now little enthusiasm for this kind of work, but the records and collections he brought back were assigned to the Kunstkamera, now under the control of the Imperial Academy of Sciences, which had been established in 1724/25. No further resources were made available to him and he died in poverty in 1735 at the age of 50.

The Academy's interests lay elsewhere, with the exploration of the eastern extremities of Asia and the sea passages to China and Japan. In 1725 it had sponsored the First Kamchatka Expedition led by the Dane, Vitus Bering, after whom the strait between Asia and America was named. The second expedition, which set out in 1733 and was to last for ten years, was a vast enterprise involving some 3,000 people, its task to explore eastern Asia, to map the entire Arctic coast of Siberia, and to chart America's north-west coast and islands. The man chosen to oversee the geographical and historical aspects of the work was a 28-year-old German, Gerhard Friedrich Müller, who had for five years served as secretary to the Academy. His brief was to 'describe Siberia's civil history, its antiquities, and the manners and customs of the people'.

Müller is best known for his ethnographic observations, but having been closely involved with Messerschmidt's archaeological collection when it arrived at the Kunstkamera he took a particular interest in burial mounds, amassing a collection of his own, mostly restricted to bronze artefacts since very little gold was now being recovered. Times had changed. 'I saw a lot of people in Siberia', he explained, 'who used to do this (grave robbery) for a living but in my time nobody was doing it because all the graves that could have held treasures had already been dug.' Nonetheless his collection was considered to be of scientific value and was bought by the Academy of Sciences in 1748 to be added to the existing Siberian collection housed in the Kunstkamera.

Broadening Horizons: The Black Sea

By the middle of the eighteenth century educated people with access to the Siberian collection were becoming familiar with the distinctive animal art of Siberia so vividly depicted on metalwork recovered from the kurgans scattered across the steppe. The Russian military advance to the Black Sea during the reign of Catherine the Great (1762–1796) brought many more kurgans into the Russian sphere and their potential for producing spectacular finds was not lost on the Russian elite now commanding the new territories. One such was General Alexei Petrovich Melgunov (1722–1788), governor of Novorossiysk, a province of the Ukraine. In 1763 he opened several kurgans at Litoy in the vicinity of Kirovograd, finding in one of them a rich burial of the late seventh or early sixth century BC. It was accompanied by a short iron sword (*aki-nakes*) in a gold scabbard decorated with fantastic animals. Such weapons are typical

1.6 At the end of the eighteenth century silver mines were being developed at Zmeinogorsk in the Barnaul District in the Altai Mountains of Siberia. One of the mining engineers was Petr Frolov, who was also an avid collector. Among the antiquities he accumulated were bone and wooden carvings dug out of local kurgans. This bone plaque from the Frolov collection, showing a tiger, dates from the fifth to third centuries BC.

 9

1.7 The expansion of the Russian empire at the time of Catherine the Great brought much of the Pontic steppe within the Russian domain. Early travellers and settlers were impressed by the massive kurgans (burial mounds) which littered the countryside. The first to be excavated, at Litoy near Kirovograd, in 1763 was under the auspices of General Melgunov, governor of the region. The engraving shows the Perepyati-cha kurgan (published in 1879).

of the Scythians, but at the time little was known of them and the sword was ascribed to the Sassanians. The grave also produced the silver legs of a stool which can now be identified as coming from the Urartian region of Asia Minor. Melgunov's finds were displayed in the Kunstkamera in St Petersburg where they caused a minor sensation, reminding the world of the riches to be had from the great kurgans of the Pontic steppe and raising the intriguing question of the relationship between the animal art represented in the Siberian collection and the similar art found in the kurgans in Russia's newly won Black Sea territories. By comparison with the kurgans of Siberia those in the Pontic steppe were massive and could not fail to impress. One of the largest, Chertomlÿk, near the city of Nikopol in the Ukraine, nearly 20m high and 50m in diameter, is first mentioned in 1781. In this new-found enthusiasm for the Scythians, Herodotus' *Histories*, written in Greek in the fifth century BC, which gives an extended account of the Scythian lifestyle, was translated into Russian.

The wonders of the Pontic–Caspian region had begun to be more widely appreciated following a programme of fieldwork commissioned by Catherine II and carried out by the natural scientist Peter Pallas in 1793–4. His findings were published at the end of the century in German, and later in English translation as *Travels through*

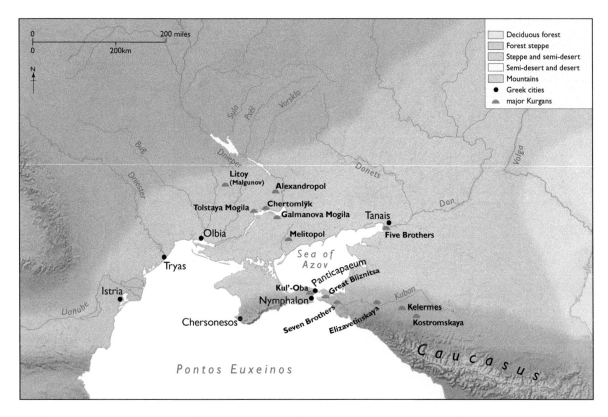

1.8 The Pontic steppe and the northern Black Sea coast. The map shows the principal Greek colonies and the larger and more important of the Scythian kurgans.

the Southern Province of the Russian Empire (1802–3). One of his observations was of the remains of the Greek colony of Olbia in the estuary of the Bug—a discovery which stimulated classical scholars to begin to consider the intriguing question of the interaction between the Greeks and the native Scythians—a relationship already known to them through the *Histories* of Herodotus.

The civilizing influence of the Russian state, coming after centuries of stultifying Ottoman rule, brought with it many benefits and not least a new intellectual curiosity, one manifestation of which was the foundation of museums in the flourishing port cities of the Black Sea: Nikolaev in 1806, Theodosia in 1811, Odessa in 1825, and Kerch in 1826. These provided the inspiration for collecting and for excavation. The earliest of the excavations—which can fairly be said to have kick-started Scythian studies— was carried out at the kurgan of Kul'-Oba in 1830 by a team of amateurs and museum professionals from the museum at Kerch at the eastern extremity of the Crimean peninsula. The excavators found a stone-built tomb, probably constructed by Greek

 11

1.9 (*Opposite top*) The Alexandropol kurgan in Dnipropetrovsk region, excavated between 1853 and 1857, is one of the largest kurgans on the Pontic steppe, measuring 21 m high with a circumference of 320 m. It is shown here in an engraving made before the excavation.

1.10 (*Opposite middle*) The kurgan of Solokha as it appeared before the excavations of 1912 and 1913.

1.11 (*Opposite bottom*) The excavation of 1912–13 in progress at the kurgan of Solokha. The principal central grave had been robbed in antiquity but a side grave remained intact.

masons resident in the nearby town of Panticapaeum. It dated to the fourth century BC and contained the bodies of a Scythian king, his wife, and a servant, accompanied by a number of gold items. Among the objects recovered were several depicting Scythians, most notably a gold vessel showing bearded, long-haired Scythians wearing trousers, heavy fur coats, and pointed hoods, together with their spears and shields and bow and arrow cases (Gallery, no. 1). In one scene a warrior is shown in the act of stringing his recurved bow. In a second scene a man is bandaging the leg of a colleague, while a third shows a man attending to the tooth of another person. Also from the tomb was a gold appliqué plaque showing two men firing their short bows. Here, for the first time, were vivid images of Scythians as they would have been known to their Greek neighbours. For the fascinated Russian intelligentsia the Scythians of the Pontic steppe could at last begin to be appreciated as a real people. But to add to the excitement, from beneath the floor of the tomb came a massive gold plaque, which had once decorated a shield or the case for a bow and arrows,

1.12 The Kul'-Oba kurgan, in the vicinity of Kerch on the Crimean peninsula, as it is now presented.

 13

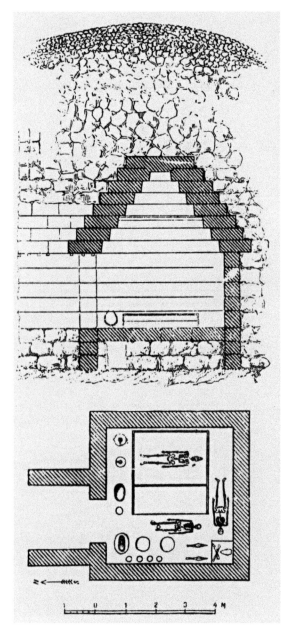

1.13 Contemporary plan of the Kul'-Oba kurgan showing the burial chamber as excavated. The masonry architecture reflects Greek influence and the tomb may, indeed, have been designed by a Greek architect from the nearby town of Panticapaeum.

depicting a stag with legs folded beneath and antlers streaming across its back. It is a masterpiece of animal art matching the vitality of similar, well-known pieces in the Siberian collection.

In 1831 the finds from Kul'-Oba were sent to the Hermitage and put on display before a wondering public. So impressed was the Imperial Court that it granted 2,000 roubles to fund the continuation of the excavation. Seeing the new finds, and in particular the golden stag, many will have begun to wonder how these Pontic Scythians, enjoying close contacts with the Greeks, related to their contemporaries living a nomadic existence thousands of kilometres away in Siberia.

More excavations followed thick and fast. Between 1853 and 1856 the massive kurgan of Alexandropol, 21 m high, was examined. It was found to have been totally robbed, but around the central grave the excavators found fifteen horse burials, their bridles decorated in gold and silver. Those who knew their Herodotus would have been reminded of his descriptions of the slaughter of horses to accompany dead leaders in their graves. Some years later, in 1863, the excavators, who had taken on the challenge of the Chertomlýk kurgan were rewarded with an intact burial chamber of the fourth century BC. One of the stunning discoveries from the tomb was of a gold-hilted iron sword contained in a richly decorated gold sheath depicting a battle between Greeks and Persians and a griffin attacking a stag. The scabbard is almost certainly of Greek workmanship, demonstrating the presence of Greek craftsmen working in the Black Sea colonies to serve the demands of the Scythian elite.

Other kurgan excavations were to follow. In the Taman Peninsula, on the east side of the Strait of Kirch which gives access to the Sea of Azov, the great Bliznits kurgan was examined between 1864 and 1868. Among the various grave goods recovered an Iranian seal and an Egyptian amulet showed the extent of the exchange networks then in operation. Immediately to the east, the

Kuban region yielded further important discoveries. Excavations began in 1875 on a group of kurgans known as the Seven Brothers. The great mound of Kostromskaya was examined in 1897 and work on kurgans in the vicinity of the village of Kelermes took place from 1903 to 1909. Unlike the burials in the Ukraine, which had mostly been robbed, many of those examined in the North Caucasus were intact.

The last of the spectacular excavations to be undertaken, before the First World War and the Russia Revolution brought the luxury of archaeological excavation to a temporary end, was at the kurgan of Solokha on the banks of the river Dnieper in Ukraine. Work began in 1912. Although one burial chamber had been robbed, another was found intact, producing a remarkable collection of grave goods including a now-famous gold comb which depicts a battle between a foot soldier and two horsemen, one whose horse has just been killed (Gallery, no. 5). They wear a mixture of Greek and Scythian armour, a conflation of styles reflected again by the Greek bronze helmet and greaves with which the dead king in the burial chamber had been provided.

Putting it All Together

The eight decades of kurgan digging in the Ukraine and North Caucasus had provided an astonishing array of material reflecting the life of the Scythian elite in the Pontic region and their burial practices which quite eclipsed the old Siberian Collection. The Scythians had burst into the popular imagination and scholars around the world were intrigued. The animal art of the nomads was surprising, even shocking, to those used to the familiar harmonies of the classical world, but it was the coexistence of these bar-barians with the Greek colonists living on their shores and the cultural interaction of the two different worlds that really caught the imagination. Many were drawn to write about it, among them a young Cambridge scholar, Ellis Minns, who after graduating spent three years in Russia studying the antiquities, art, and history of the country. Returning to a comfortable academic life in Cambridge he devoted himself to writing a massive tome, *Scythians and Greeks*, which was published in 1913. It was this book that introduced the Scythians to the English-speaking world and it remains a seminal text.

The other great name in the pioneering years of Scythian studies was the Russian born Mikhail Rostovtzeff. Rostovtzeff left Russia during the 1917 revolution, living for a short while in Oxford before leaving, in 1920, to make a new life for himself in America. From 1925 until his retirement in 1944 he taught ancient history at Yale. Before leaving Russia his interests had included the anthropology and archaeology of South Russia and the Ukraine and in his brief interlude in Oxford he devoted himself to preparing material for two books, *Iranians and Greeks in South Russia*, published in 1922, and *Skythien und der Bosporus*, which appeared three years later. In both ventures

he received the friendship and active encouragement of Ellis Minns. Thus it was that in the second decade of the twentieth century Scythian studies came of age. In 1923 a special journal, *Skythica*, was launched in Prague. One of the papers in the first volume, 'Central Asia, Russia and the Animal Style', was contributed by Rostovtzeff.

Meanwhile in Siberia

The Russian fascination with Siberia in the eighteenth century led, as we have seen, to state organized expeditions. As the potential of the region became better known and Russian authority was established, educated men gravitated to the area to settle and to work. One such was Petr Frolov, a trained mining engineer who, in 1793, was sent to the silver mine at Zmeinogorsk in the Barnaul District, situated in the Altai Mountains of Siberia. He worked in the mines until 1830 developing new machinery to improve efficiency, and among his many achievements built the first cast iron railway in Russia, designed to move ore from the mine to the smelting works two kilometres away. To while away the long Siberian winters he engaged in a wide range of cultural activities, collecting antiquities, geological samples, manuscripts, and scientific instruments. In 1823, in partnership with the explorer and ethnographer, F. V. Gabler, he founded the Barnaul Mining Museum. Among the artefacts he was able to acquire from the local peasants were bone and wood carvings, mostly in Siberian animal style, which had been dug out of the kurgans. They dated from the fifth to third centuries BC. What was remarkable was the unusual state of preservation of these organic materials.

By the mid nineteenth century Barnaul had become a thriving cultural centre, its energy deriving from the rich deposits of copper and silver in the nearby mountains. One person attracted there was the German-born Vasily Radlov, who, as a young man, became a schoolteacher in the city. Radlov developed an interest in the ethnography and folklore of the region and went on to become an expert in the Turkic languages. Later in life he played a part in the establishment of the Russian Museum of Ethnography and eventually, in 1884, became director of the Asiatic Museum in St Petersburg. During his years in Barnaul he would have become familiar with the wooden animal carvings from the Altai kurgans on display in the museum and, no doubt, heard stories about their discovery. In 1865 he decided to explore the kurgans for himself, choosing two for excavation, one near the village of Katanda and the other on the Berel River. In both he found that the ground beneath the mound of stones of which the kurgan was constructed was permanently frozen and it was this that had preserved all the organic material buried with the deceased in the wooden burial chamber below. Among the objects he recovered were wooden carvings, some of them covered with gold sheet, fur clothing, and Chinese silk. It was

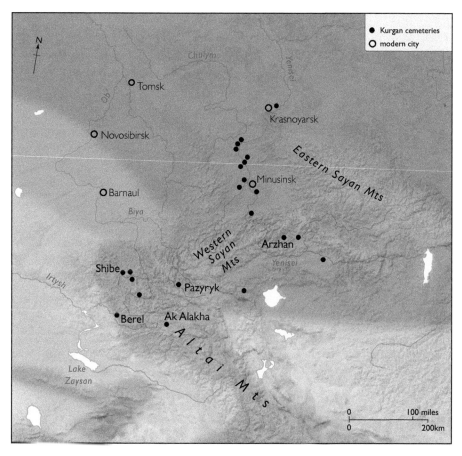

1.14 The Altai–Sayan Mountains were the home of nomadic pastoralists and the region has produced many burials of the Scythian period. A number of them were exceptionally well preserved by permafrost (the freezing of the ground beneath the mound) which has ensured that the organic component of the deposit has not decayed.

an astonishing series of discoveries throwing entirely new light on nomadic life in the late first millennium BC. Coming at the time when the kurgans of the Pontic steppe were beginning to be explored, it provided a stark reminder of the vast area across which nomadic animal art had once extended, raising many questions, not least how the remarkable cultural connectivity which must have existed throughout the steppe related to the movements of people.

Surprisingly, it was not until the 1920s that Radlov's discoveries were followed up, when a new expedition from the Archaeological Section of the Russian Museum at Leningrad (as St Petersburg was renamed after the Revolution), under the leadership of Sergei Rudenko (1885–1969), was sent to make an archaeological survey of the High

 17

Altai. In 1927 a frozen tomb at Shibe dating to the first century BC was examined by one of the team, Mikhail Griaznov (1902–1984). Here the body of the deceased was very well preserved together with horse gear, gold appliqués, and emblems cut from bark. Two years later, at Pazyryk in the eastern Altai, Griaznov opened a kurgan in a barrow cemetery that the expedition had discovered earlier in 1924. The preservation in the Pazyryk kurgan was exceptional. The timbers of the burial chamber and several layers of logs that had been piled above and around the chamber to deter robbers were perfectly preserved as were the ten mares buried with the dead man. Although the main grave had been robbed, what remained firmly established the importance of the cemetery, but it also made clear that there were many technical difficulties to be overcome when dealing with delicate organic materials preserved in permafrost conditions.

After the excavation of kurgan 1 at Pazyryk in 1929 work on the frozen tombs came to a halt. Both Rudenko and Griaznov were removed from their posts during Stalin's Great Terror, which began with a purge of the intelligentsia. Rudenko was arrested for wasting time on pointless investigations while Griaznov was charged with working with nationalists in Ukraine. Both were eventually reinstated and Rudenko returned in 1947 to Pazyryk, where over the next three years he excavated seven kurgans with spectacular results. The well-preserved mummified and tattooed bodies that were recovered together with the elaborately dressed horses, wooden carvings, and brightly coloured carpets, appliqué felts, and silks caught the imagination. Rudenko published a popular, but thorough, account of his work in 1953—a work widely disseminated in

1.15 The cemetery of Pazyryk was discovered during an expedition in the 1920s. The first kurgan, excavated in 1929, covered a timber burial chamber set in a grave pit. The timber construction and the contents of the chamber were preserved by the permafrost conditions.

1.16 The excavation of kurgan 1 at Pazyryk exposed a log-built burial chamber with the body of the deceased interred in a massive larch tree-trunk coffin which had been opened sometime in antiquity when the grave was robbed.

1.17 Archaeologists returned to Pazyryk in 1947 and over the next two years excavated more kurgans. The photograph shows the removal of logs roofing the burial chamber beneath kurgan 5.

 19

its English edition, *The Frozen Tombs of Siberia*, published in 1970. Pazyryk had gained its place in the history of archaeology, bringing the rich culture of the Altai nomads, with its striking animal art and complex rituals, to the attention of the whole world.

Having finished his excavations at Pazyryk Rudenko moved to the Central Altai. In 1950 he excavated two frozen tombs at Bashadar and two more at Tuekta in 1954. Since then work has continued in the region. In 1993 the well-preserved body of an elite female was found buried in a kurgan at Ak-Alakha on the Ukok plateau close to the border with China. She was partially tattooed and was finely dressed for burial wearing an elaborate headdress nearly a metre high. Dendrochronological analysis of timbers from the tomb chamber show that the burial took place in the fifth century BC. In 1998 a new programme of work was initiated at the cemetery of Berel in the Kazakh Altai where Radlov had first dug more than 130 years before. Here some twenty-four kurgans have now been excavated dating mainly from the fourth and third century BC. They vary in their elaboration from quite simple constructions to rich, well-furnished tombs such as kurgan 10, with its ten sacrificed horses decked out with elaborate saddles and harness buried beside the timber burial chamber. The value of the more recent work is that excavation techniques have improved and excavators are now far more aware of the need to have dedicated conservation facilities on hand to prevent the rapid deterioration which sets in immediately the bodies and artefacts are removed from the frozen ground.

It is no exaggeration to say that the frozen tombs of Siberia have revolutionized our understanding of the first millennium BC nomads of the Altai region. The occupants of the graves physically confront us as real people whose lives we can visualize from seeing the totality of their organic belongings and whose beliefs come alive through the evidence of their complex burial rituals. The ability to study the tattooed skin of a nomad princess or the stomach contents of her horse can add so much more to our understanding of the past than having to rely only on metal artefacts and dry bones. The evidence from the Altai kurgans will feature large in discussions throughout this book.

But perhaps the greatest surprise arising from the excavations in the Altai was that a vibrant animal art existed in the region so similar to the Scythian animal art of the Pontic steppe that the two must have been part of the same cultural continuum. Russian archaeologists refer to this as Scythian–Siberian animal art and some see it as representing a distinct culture. But the very use of the term raises a myriad of questions. Where and when did the art originate? Does its use over a large area imply a degree of ethnic identity? Can the name Scythian be used to embrace the whole region or has it to be restricted to the people of the Pontic steppe? These are some of the questions to which we shall return.

After the Revolution

In the years following the Revolution of 1917 attention turned from the graves of the rich to the lives of the ordinary people. Settlements began to be excavated and attempts were made to define regional groupings based on archaeological evidence: the elite were no longer thought worthy of study. But following the end of the Second World War attention turned again to the great kurgans of Ukraine and the Caucasus. It had long been recognized that in the distant past grave robbers had managed to plunder most of the central burials but, as excavations in the earlier twentieth century had shown, the major Scythian tombs often contained burials placed off centre which had been missed and in some of the plundered burials robbers had overlooked items hidden beneath floors or tucked away in side chambers. There was also much to learn about the ritual activities which had taken place around the main burial.

The first of the spectacular post-war discoveries was made when a robbed kurgan under threat from development was examined near Melitopol in Ukraine. Here, in a hidden recess, a *gorytos* (a case for holding a bow and its arrows hung by a warrior's side) was discovered. It had been covered with a gold sheet decorated in repoussé depicting animals in combat and scenes from the life of Achilles. A few years later, in 1969–70, the kurgan at Gaymanova mogila was excavated producing a silver-gilt cup decorated with figures of Scythian warriors in repoussé (Gallery, no. 3). The next year the excavation of Tolstaya mogila showed that, although the tomb had been pillaged in antiquity, a surprising amount of gold had been missed, including ornaments, a gorytos, a sword in a highly decorated gold scabbard, and a magnificent gold pectoral (a neck ornament that hangs across the chest) depicting lively scenes in two registers. The upper shows Scythians engaged in peaceful pastoral activities while the lower is composed of incidents of violent conflict between wild and domesticated animals (Gallery, no. 9). The gold from these three tombs is all likely to have been produced in workshops in Greek colonies fringing the Black Sea to satisfy the Scythian elite. Its discovery greatly excited art historians and reinvigorated the debate about the Greek/ barbarian interaction.

Meanwhile other kurgan excavations were adding more details about burial ritual. Between 1981 and 1986 the famous Chertomlÿk mound was re-examined by a Russian–German expedition. One of the unexpected results was the discovery of horse and human bones scattered around the base of the mound providing, for the first time, direct evidence for a practice described in vivid detail by Herodotus which involved sacrificially killing a group of riders and their horses and securing their bodies with wooden stakes to give them rigidity so that they could be set up in riding positions around the grave (below, pp. 306–7). Another result of the excavation was

the observation that the mound was built largely of turves cut from the steppe. The excavators estimated that to build Chertomlÿk would have required the stripping of 75 hectares of grassland—a colossal input of labour. What did such an act imply? Clearly it expressed the power of the dead men's lineage to coerce labour, but was it symbolic of his pasture in the other world? (See below, pp. 304–5.)

While these large set-piece excavations were going on less dramatic work was in progress as new infrastructure projects threatened to destroy or damage archaeological sites. One irrigation project in Ukraine in 1960–1 alone required the examination of a hundred kurgans. Nor were settlements neglected. As a nomadic people the Scythians had left little trace of permanent settlement but it has long been known that some very large defended enclosures (*gorodišče*) found in the steppe zone and forest steppe were occupied in the Scythian period. One, at Kamenskoe on the Lower Dnieper, was intermittently excavated between 1937 and 1950. It covers some 12 sq km and the excavations show that the occupants were heavily involved in iron production. An even larger enclosure at Bel'sk on the River Vorskla, a tributary of the Dnieper, extended to some 35 sq km. Excavation began in 1958, and since 1992 the work has been carried out by a Ukrainian–German team. Occupation lasted from the seventh to the third century BC, during which time the occupants were engaged in producing a wide range of commodities. It is also highly likely that the Scythian elite resided there for at least part of the year. These *gorodišče* raise many questions about the workings of Scythian society to which we will return (pp. 129–35).

Far to the East

Great excitement had been generated by the remarkable array of finds from frozen tombs excavated in the Altai at Pazyryk and elsewhere, not only because of the excellent preservation of the organic items but also because of the cultural implications of the finds. It was clear for all to see that the belief systems displayed by the Altai burial rituals and the energetic animal art enlivening objects of everyday use bore striking resemblances to those of the Scythians living on the Pontic steppe—so similar that archaeologists began to accept a close link between them, some referring to a Scythian–Siberian cultural continuum stretching across 3,500 km of steppe.

Much further to the east, in the Minusinsk Basin and the Tuva region of the Sayan Mountains—regions linked together by the north-flowing Yenisei River—discoveries of prehistoric nomadic culture, mainly from burials, were prompting further speculation. In the Minusinsk Basin—an expanse of rich steppe surrounded by high mountains—it was possible to trace an unbroken cultural tradition extending from the middle of the second millennium to the late first millennium BC, rooted in the

Late Bronze Age Andronovo cultural continuum found extensively across the steppe of central Asia. From about the fourteenth century BC a local culture, known as the Karasuk culture, began to crystallize out which, by the end of the tenth century, had evolved into the Tagar culture, dominated by a horse-riding elite using a highly distinctive set of horse gear, weapons, and other artefacts. What is important here is that the archaeological evidence suggests that the changes were largely indigenous, evolving over a period of time, and were not caused by significant influxes of new people. In other words, in the Minusinsk Basin we can trace the emergence of nomadic elites for whom horse-riding was both a way of life and a mark of status. More to the point they were beginning to adopt representations of animals, drawing on a tradition that can be traced back to the second millennium in the Altai–Sayan region. It was this love of animal forms that was to pervade the art of the steppe throughout the later first millennium.

Further upriver the Yenisei is joined by a tributary, the Uyuk, which flows through a remote steppe basin with a floor of lush grassland pasture giving way to alpine meadows on the flanks of the surrounding mountains. It was, and still is, an idyllic environment for nomadic pastoralists. Toward the centre of the basin, near the village of Arzhan, is a massive kurgan, 110 m in diameter and up to 4 m high, surrounded by a vertical stone wall. It had once been covered with a thick layer of large stone blocks which had helped to maintain permafrost conditions in the ground beneath but the layer had been stripped off to provide construction material in the decades following the Second World War, making the delicate archaeological remains beneath increasingly vulnerable to decay. The potential importance of the site was recognized by the archaeological community and in 1971 Mikhail Griaznov (who had dug the first Pazyryk barrow 44 years earlier) began an excavation which was to last until 1974. We will consider the kurgan in some detail below (pp. 95–100). Suffice it to say that it was a royal burial, with the king and his consort laid together in the central chamber and their favourite retainers and horses buried immediately around them. This royal tomb was set within a vast timber construction built of larch logs, arranged in a radial fashion, each segment being divided into chambers. Within the chambers were groups of horses with their grooms. Since the trapping associated with the horses suggest that many of them had been brought in from considerable distances, they must represent the power of the king to command the allegiance of entourages from far away. The burial had much in common with elite burials on the Pontic steppe but what was astonishing was its early date. A number of radiocarbon assessments leave little doubt that burial took place in the late ninth century BC, thus pre-dating by more than a century the earliest of the royal graves on the Pontic steppe. The excavation of Arzhan 1, then, showed that all the elements of the Scythian

 23

cultural system—a royal warrior burial accompanied by sacrificed retainers, the allegiance of mounted warriors from afar, and the prevalence of a highly distinctive animal art—were already present in the Sayan Mountain region of Siberia soon after the beginning of the first millennium BC. For the excavator, Mikhail Griaznov, this was strong evidence to support the idea that Scythian culture originated in the Altai–Sayan region and spread westwards.

The great Arzhan kurgan was one of several in the region but it was not until 1998 that work began on another, this time led by a Russian–German team. The first season involved making a geographical survey. Trial excavations began in 2000 and between 2001 and 2003 the mound was completely excavated revealing another royal burial. While Arzhan 1 had suffered from grave robbing, Arzhan 2 was intact and yielded an impressive array of gold, much of it decoration from clothes. Dating to the seventh century, the burial shows that elite nomadic culture was still flourishing in the Sayan region at the time that the historical Scythians were beginning to raid Asia Minor and were settling in the Pontic region.

Between East and West

The tract of steppe stretching between the Black Sea region and the Altai–Sayan Mountains—most of it within the boundaries of modern Kazakhstan—was also home to nomadic pastoralists who buried their dead beneath kurgans. Those who lived on the southern border of the region, in what is now Uzbekistan and Turkmeni-stan, are known historically from their various engagements with the Persian empire. They were generally referred to as Sakā, renowned for their horse-riding skills and distinguished by their tall pointed hats. The famous relief carved in a rock face at Bisitun, Iran, dating to 520–19 BC, which shows the Persian leader, Darius, trium-phant over nine rebel kings, depicts a bearded Sakā king, in the dress of a horseman, resplendent in just such a hat.

In 1969 a farmer ploughing his fields near Issyk not far from Almaty in southern Kazakhstan discovered an embossed gold plaque on the edge of a kurgan. The find was reported to the authorities and the excavation which followed showed that, while the central tomb had been plundered by grave robbers, they had missed a second burial chamber to the side of the mound, dating to the fourth century BC, which contained a body, probably of a young man, wearing clothes covered with gold appliqué and a tall, pointed, gold-trimmed headdress. The 'golden man', or 'golden princess' as some would prefer, caused a sensation and has now been adopted as one of the symbols of the Kazakh state.

1.18 The great relief carved into the cliff at Bisitun, Iran, shows a procession of captives being brought before the triumphant Persian king Darius. The last in the line is Skuka, king of the Saka, wearing a long, belted coat and trousers typical of nomad dress. His tall pointed hat was characteristic of the Saka. (See also Fig. 2.4.)

 25

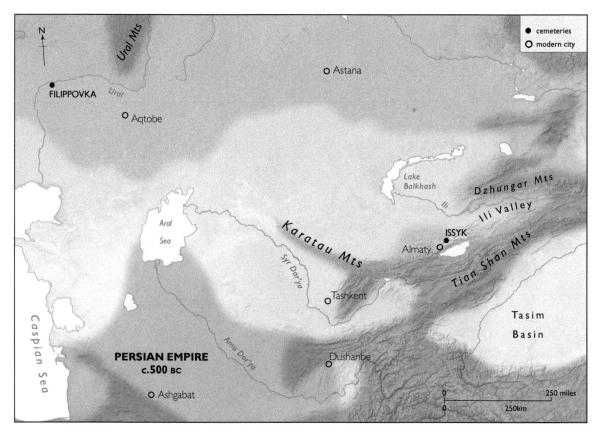

1.19 The map of the Central Asian steppe showing the expanse of the open steppe (in green) and some of the more significant Scythian burials.

The Issyk burial is not alone. It lies in a region of particularly rich pasture—the Semireče (Seven-River region) between the Tian Shan Mountains and Lake Balkhash—where kurgans proliferate. They have been the subject of a systematic programme of excavation but most had been robbed in antiquity. The concentration of kurgans does, however, show that the Semireče was a centre of nomad power in the second half of the first millennium BC.

A second region with an unusual concentration of kurgan burials lies at the southern end of the Ural Mountains between the Ural River and its tributary, the Ilek. This is the vital corridor linking the Pontic steppe and the Kazakh steppe where the grassland narrows between the southern end of the Urals and the desert region around the Caspian. Among the many cemeteries examined by both Russian and Kazakh workers, that of Filippovka in the Orenburg region, stands out. Excavations

26

in 1986–90 and 2004–7 have between them explored twenty-six kurgans, mostly dating to the fifth–fourth century BC, providing a detailed insight into the variety of ritual practices associated with burial. Many burials were accompanied by items of gold reflecting a vigorous animal art. Most Russian archaeologists agree that Filippovka dates to the formative period of the Sarmatian peoples—horsemen who were to oust the Scythians from their Pontic homeland and eventually to confront the Roman empire.

What is in a Name?

The horse-riding nomads of Eurasia in the first millennium BC have come into sharp focus as the result of a succession of excavations beginning in the eighteenth century. These peoples were named by various ancient writers who had heard stories of them or even, in rare cases, encountered them, but to assign these ethnic names to archaeologically defined communities is difficult for many reasons. Nomads by their very nature were always on the move, often crossing considerable distances in a very short time. Dominant elites, moving into new pastures, would have acquired followers who, thereafter, might have assumed their new leader's affiliations. Elsewhere discrete bands joining larger confederacies might have retained their identity and clan name whilst also embracing that of the leading overlord. On the steppe mobility reigned and ethnicity was a mobile concept. An ancient writer, brought up in a world of cities and states, would have found the complexity of nomad behaviour and affiliation difficult to comprehend. There would have been a tendency to treat the situation as static when in reality it was ever changing.

An archaeologist, viewing the wealth of evidence deriving largely from burials, cannot fail to be impressed by the broad cultural similarities stretching across the steppe from the Sayan Mountains of Siberia to the Lower Danube valley. It is possible to glimpse sudden transcontinental movements and far-flung connectivities counterbalanced by distinct regional developments and to contain the whole within a broad chronological framework. This great continuum of mobile horse-riding communities dominating the steppe from the ninth to the third century may share a Scythian–Siberian culture, but to fully appreciate its nuances one must remember that it was made up of many different groups with different names, only some of which, like Sakā and Scythian, are recorded in the historical sources. It was a society in which movement, often rapid and over considerable distances, was a way of life. At best all archaeologists can hope to do is to glimpse a few frames of this fast-moving kaleidoscope.

2

THE SCYTHIANS AS OTHERS SAW THEM

FOR someone used to life in a civilized community, like the city states of Greece, the kingdoms of Asia Minor, or the empires of Assyria or Persia, those living beyond the frontiers were 'Other'—people different from us, foreigners. To the Greeks they were barbarians, aliens who made incomprehensible sounds like 'bar bar'. Yet the Other, by their very nature, were worthy of attention. They commanded valuable resources such as gold, tin, furs, and horses and they had worthwhile skills, like their ability to use the bow and to fight in close formation on horseback, which could be learned or their horsemen hired. And for the more thoughtful these uncomplicated barbarians, as they were perceived to be, were a source of endless interest simply because of their otherness. They were a reminder of the deep fascination of the little-known outer world and a refreshing contrast to the complexities and perversions of civilized society.

Lands of Mists

By the eighth century BC Greeks from the Aegean world were making regular journeys into the Black Sea. Much later the sea was to be known as the *Euxine*—the hospitable sea—but in the early days, when its moods were unknown and the inhabitants of its shores were regarded as dangerous savages, it was the *Pontos Axeinos*—the 'unfriendly, dark sea'—a term first used in the fifth century by the poet Pindar, who was no lover of oceans. Little is known of the early Greek explorations. A few ships making brief

landings on the alien shores will have left few archaeological traces. Later, when friendly natives were encountered, regular seasonal visits developed to encourage a little lucrative trade. If successful, these places would, in time, have become trading enclaves with Greeks overwintering, creating permanent settlements which might eventually grow into fully fledged colonies. According to the ancient author Pseudo-Scymnus, the first colony was founded at Sinope on the southern (Asia Minor) shore of the sea. Strabo later described the site as 'beautifully equipped both by nature and human foresight, for it is situated on the neck of a peninsula and has on either side harbours and roadsteads and wonderful tuna fisheries …'. He claimed that the first settlement was developed by the native Kimmerians and was later refounded by colonizers from Miletos. One of its sister colonies, Trapezus, further along the same coast, was, according to Eusebius, founded in 756 BC. How much reliance can be placed on these traditional stories is debatable. The earliest pottery so far found at Sinope is of the late seventh century but there would be nothing at all surprising if settlement had begun many decades earlier.

Stories of strange people who lived in the lands of mists on the north shores of the sea were circulating in the eighth-century Greek world and were known to both Hesiod and to Homer, who referred to the nations as *Hippemolgi* (mare-milkers) and *Galactophagi* (curd-eaters)—appropriate descriptions of nomadic pastoralists who grew no grain. Other stories may have originated from these early encounters like that of gold-rich Colchis where Jason and his followers ventured to find the Golden Fleece. It may have been from these early travellers' tales that Herodotus, composing his *Histories* in the fifth century, heard the story of the 'wandering Scythians' who 'once dwelt in Asia' and, driven out by the Massagetae, entered 'the land of the Kimmerians', thus arriving on the Pontic steppe, the region they still inhabited at the time when Herodotus was doing his research. The historian goes on to relate what he understood to have happened next. In the face of the Scythian threat the Kimmerians were in discord. The elite—the 'Royal tribe'—wanted to stay and fight; the rest of the people thought it best to leave. Dissent led to a civil conflict in which the Royal tribe was slain, and their bodies were buried near the River Tyras (Dniester). 'Then the rest of the Kimmerians departed and the Scythians on their arrival took possession of a deserted land' (*Hist*. iv. 11). We will return to the fate of the Kimmerians later (below, pp. 106–7). Herodotus, looking back on these events, reminded his readers that there were still traces of the Kimmerians to be seen, Kimmerian forts, and place names like Kimmeria (the Crimea) and the Kimmerian Bosphorus, the strait leading from the Black Sea to the Sea of Azov.

These ethnic dislocations were playing out at the end of the eighth century when the Greeks were first beginning to explore the Black Sea. Stories based on current

events and observations of native behaviour merged with fanciful tales and specula-
tions: it was an enticing mix. When, in the mid seventh century, the Greek city states
encircling the Aegean began to experience social tensions caused by demographic
growth, the Black Sea offered attractive prospects for entrepreneurial colonization.
The nomads of the misty shores were soon to become close neighbours.

Crossing the Caucasus

Herodotus adds one further observation on the Kimmerians: that they fled into Asia
Minor keeping to 'a route that led along the sea shore', the implication being that at
least some of the survivors of the internal conflict made their way eastwards, at first
along the Black Sea coast following the coastal route into Asia Minor, the intention
being to seize new land to settle or to find gainful employment as mercenaries in the
internecine struggles now being played out in the region. En route, Herodotus says,
they settled on the peninsula of Sinope. In the same section (*Hist.* iv. 12) he adds that
'the Scythians followed them but missing their route poured into Media. For … the
Scythians held the Caucasus on their right …'. That northern nomads were active in
the territory of the Medes at this time is confirmed by other sources which refer to
the intruders as Scythians. What is less convincing is that they did so in pursuit of the
Kimmerians. A more likely reading of the events of the second half of the eighth century is that the advance of horse-riding nomads coming from Central Asia involved
many groups of varying allegiances driven by different aspirations: one group moved
westwards into the Pontic steppe; others skirted the western shore of the Caspian
Sea to establish themselves in the territory of the Medes, roughly modern Kurdis-
tan. Thereafter, those identified as Kimmerian and Scythians remained active in Asia
Minor until about 630 BC, but they kept to separate spheres and there is no record of
them ever coming into confrontation.

The last twenty years of the eighth century saw the Assyrian empire at its strong-
est and most extensive. Under Sargon II (r. 721–705) it had expanded from its original
focus in the Tigris and Euphrates valleys northwards into the fringes of the mountain ranges of Anatolia, westwards to the Taurus Mountains, and south-westwards
to include the lands between the coast of the Mediterranean and the Syrian Desert.
The Medes and Mannaeans occupied the mountain region to the east; the kingdom
of Urartu, with its capital of Tushpa on Lake Van, flanked the north, centred in what
is now Armenia; while further west in Asia Minor were the kingdoms of Phrygia and
Lydia. It was a time of tension with Urartu and the Assyrians contesting their border
region. For the steppe nomads the rivalries of the powerful polities and the consequent social disruption created tempting opportunities.

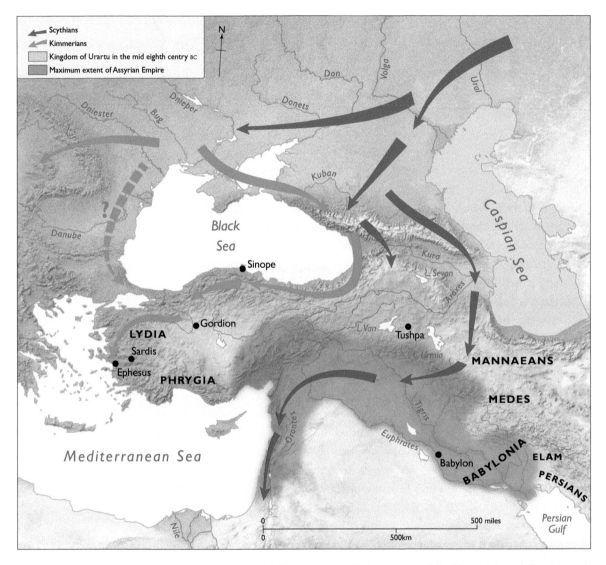

2.1 Historical sources record the movements of Kimmerians and Scythians in the eighth and seventh centuries BC. Some of these peoples crossed the Caucasus and played a significant part in the conflict between the kingdom of Urartu and the Assyrians.

Some sense of the uncertainties of the time can be gathered from events recorded in contemporary Assyrian cuneiform tablets augmented by Greek sources compiled two centuries later. The first mention of the Kimmerians in Asia Minor comes in 714, when an Assyrian spy reported that Kimmerians were on the northern frontier of Urartu. Another report records their success in 707 in a conflict with the Urartian

 32

king Rusa I, who later, perhaps as a consequence of a defeat at their hands, committed suicide. Thereafter there is silence for about thirty years. It may be that during this time the Kimmerians made some accommodation with the Urartians, perhaps serving as mercenaries. In any event Kimmerians are later reported to be supporting Rusa II (r. 680–639) on the frontier at Shupria near the headwaters of the Tigris. This may have been the same band that, in 677, had rampaged across Phrygia destroying the capital city of Gordium. The Assyrian texts record that the Kimmerians were led at this time by a king named Dugdamme.

The Greek sources now take up the story as the force moved westwards towards the Mediterranean. Their first target was the kingdom of Lydia, where they launched an attack on the capital, Sardis. The first onslaught was beaten off by the Lydian king, Gyges, but in 652 Sardis was taken and Gyges was killed. They then turned their attention to the rich coastal region, destroying the Greek city of Magnesia and raiding other Greek cities along the coast. In one of these raids the Kimmerians attempted to burn down the famous temple of Artemis at Ephesus.

According to the Greek texts these raids were under the command of king Lygdamis, who must be the Dugdamme of the Assyrian texts, the Λ being a Greek scribal error for the Δ. Dugdamme then led his forces into Cilicia threatening Assyrian interests, but there, to the relief of the Assyrians, he died painfully of natural causes said to be gangrene of the genitals. Thereafter nothing more is heard of Kimmerians in Asia Minor.

While the Kimmerians were active in territories to the north and west of Assyria, the Scythians based themselves on the north-eastern frontier in the lands of the Mannaeans and Medes, favouring the highly fertile pasturelands around Lake Urmia—land ideal for maintaining the large herds of horses on which they were entirely dependent. Little is known of their activities at this time but one incident is revealing. Sometime in the 670s the Scythian king Bartatua asked the Assyrian king Esarhaddon to send him one of his daughters to be his wife. Rather than being an act of arrogant bravado on the part of the Scythians it is more likely to reflect the careful diplomacy of the period.

Throughout the middle decades of the seventh century, while Assyria was still strong, it is likely that the Scythians maintained peaceful relations with their horse-riding neighbours, the Medes and Mannaeans, and with the Assyrians, but the situation was inherently unstable. With the founding of the Neo-Babylonian dynasty in 626 and the rapid rise of Babylonian power, the Assyrian empire began to fragment. This provided the opportunity for the Scythians, sometimes working in concert with the Medes, to raid widely throughout the old Assyrian domain, feeding off the carcass of the decaying empire.

 33

There are several different versions of these events recorded by Greek writers, the best known being the account given by Herodotus. The essence of the story is that the Scythians, led by their king Madyes, overthrew the Medes and began a twenty-eight-year rule of Asia 'during which time their insolence and oppression spread ruin on either side'. Having established themselves, they set out to invade Egypt but were bought off by the pharaoh Psammetichus. On their return to Asia Minor they plundered the temple of Aphrodite Urania at Ashkelon. By this time the Medes had grown in strength and had opened negotiations with the Scythians. The Scythian elite were invited to a great feast at which they succumbed to the delights of alcohol and were promptly slaughtered by their hosts. Those who survived fled back to their homeland where they met opposition from the younger generation—the children of their wives and slaves they had left behind. But the returning warriors overcame their opponents by using whips, a symbol of their superiority over slaves. A different version of the story, recorded by Pompeius Trogus, tells of two Royal Scythian youths, Plynos and Scolopitus, who, exiled from their homeland, led an expedition to Cappadocia where they raided for many years. Eventually they were killed by trickery and their wives took up arms, becoming the first Amazons.

Herodotus' version of events, drawn from tales that would have been circulating for nearly two centuries before he encountered them, has a ring of truth to it. The break-up of the Assyrian empire provided the opportunity for young Scythians to leave their homeland somewhere around Lake Urmia, between the Zagros Mountains and the Caspian Sea, and to range widely across the remnants of empire, some bands returning home several years later to a less than friendly reception.

Echoes of these events are also to be found in the Hebrew literature, preserved in the Old Testament in Genesis and the prophets Jeremiah and Ezekiel. In Genesis, written in the eighth or seventh century, various 'people of the north' are listed, including the people of Gomer, cognate with the Assyrian Gimmirai (Kimmerians), and the Ashkenaz (Ashguzai in Assyrian), who were the Scythians. The prophet Jeremiah conjures up the fearsome vision that God will send these violent northerners to punish the people of Israel:

> Thus saith the Lord, behold a people cometh from the north country … They lay hold on bow and spear, they are cruel and have no compassion; their voice is like the roaring sea and they ride upon horses; set in array, as a man for war against thee, O daughter of Zion…. Go not forth into the field nor walk by the way; for there is the sword of the enemy and terror on every side.
>
> (Jeremiah 6:22–3, 25)

Jeremiah was written in the late seventh or early sixth century at just the time that the Scythians raiders were making their way south through the Levant towards Egypt. For those in their path the prophecy must have suddenly become very real.

We have summarized the stories contained in the Greek and Assyrian sources. At best they are a fragmentary record of what must have been a complex interaction between incoming bands of predatory nomads and the sedentary states south of the Caucasus over a period of a century or more. The sources seem confident enough to distinguish between two ethnic groups, Kimmerians and Scythians, implying that they were active in different spheres. There is no need to dismiss any of this but in all probability the flow of nomad horsemen from the steppe started earlier than the texts would allow and it would certainly have been a lot more complex. We will return to the archaeological evidence for the nomad presence later (pp. 103–9).

Greeks living along the Aegean coast of Asia Minor will have heard stories of the Scythians and their brief dominance in Asia after the collapse of the Assyrian rule. They would have been more directly aware of the devastation wrought by the Kimmerian horsemen on their homelands a few generations before. There may have been physical reminders of it still evident. Who would not have recalled when visiting the temple of Artemis at Ephesus the attempt of the Kimmerians to burn it? Indeed there may have been traces of the fire still remaining on the temple stonework. One effect of these events is recorded on an inscription dating to 283 BC found on the island of Samos. It refers to a still-ongoing dispute between Samos and the city of Priene on the mainland over a seaside region that was abandoned by its inhabitants during a Kimmerian attack four hundred years earlier.

It was the Greeks of these coastal cities who were to organize the colonial ventures which established trading enclaves and settlements around the Black Sea at the interface with the Pontic steppe, the original homeland of the Kimmerians and the Scythians. Those who knew their history may have wondered at the game the Fates were playing.

The Black Sea Adventure

The Greek colonization of the Black Sea littoral was the result of a number of factors but the one driving force was the rise in population in the Greek cities scattered around the Aegean.

In normal circumstances animal communities reproduce at such a rate that, if unconstrained, the population increases exponentially until the holding capacity of the environment is overstepped and can no longer provide sustenance for the growing population. At this point tensions appear within the community leading to

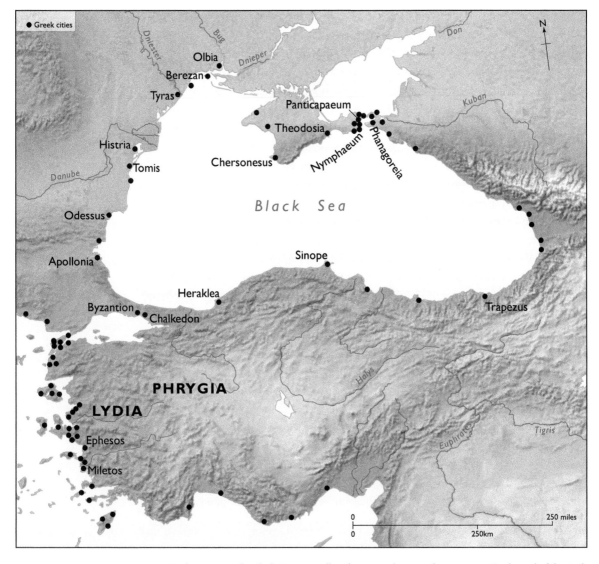

• Greek cities

Dniester

Bug

Dnieper

Don

N

Olbia
Berezan
Tyras
Histria
Danube
Tomis
Odessus
Apollonia
Byzantion
Chalkedon
Heraklea

Panticapaeum
Theodosia
Chersonesus
Nymphaeum
Phanagoreia

Kuban

Black Sea

Sinope

Trapezus

PHRYGIA

LYDIA

Halys

Ephesos

Miletos

Euphrates

Tigris

0   250 miles
0   250km

2.2 Greek interest in the Black Sea was well underway in the seventh century BC. By the end of the sixth century colonies had been established around the entire coast with a particular concentration along the Kerch Strait linking the Black Sea to the Sea of Azov.

unusual behaviour in order to keep the numbers down, and sectors of the community migrate from the home base to establish themselves in new ecological niches. So it is with humans. As the population moves towards the holding capacity various constraints kick in. The age of marriage may rise; communities may practice infanticide or senilicide; and warfare is likely to become more prevalent. Warfare is an effective system that has the potential both to increase the territorial holding of the successful contestants and to thin out excess population. At the same time tranches of the community may decide, or be persuaded, to seek a new life overseas.

Many of the Greek cities had comparatively restricted fertile hinterlands which were intensively cultivated, the more marginal tracts to the point of exhaustion. Over-cropping by goats on the mountainsides also led to soil erosion. As the urban population increased there was little scope for improving local productivity and communities had to rely more and more on imports of food. At the same time social stress intensified. In such conditions it is understandable that young men, tiring of increasing restrictions imposed by the society in which they had been brought up, were prepared to join others of like mind to seek new lands abroad. In consequence the Greek city states began to organize overseas colonial expeditions.

The new colonies served a multitude of functions, the most important being that they relieved social tension at home by providing an outlet for the dissatisfied and the antisocial. Colonies also syphoned off excess population. Some overseas enclaves began as trading entrepôts, others as settlements of farmers cultivating the land around the newly founded city, but the trading centres might soon attract settlers who wished to farm and so the differences became obscured. Once established, a colony could serve as a valued trading partner for its mother city, providing a ready market for manufactured goods which could be traded on to the indigenous native population. In return they could gather foodstuffs for export, either produced by the colonists themselves or acquired from the indigenous population, and rare raw materials such as metals and furs and the ever-valuable slaves arriving from further inland along the existing trading networks. The essence of the Greek colonial model was symbiosis. To be successful the colony had to have the agreement of the indigenous people and to live in harmony with them. The return to the native population was considerable, not least access to a range of exotic goods and a ready market for their surplus produce. The patronage of the foreigners could also be a powerful tool in social negotiations and local power struggles.

The first Greek colonies in the Black Sea were set up on the southern, Asiatic, shore at Trapezus and Sinope possibly as early as the mid eighth century. If they were as early as this, they would have been forerunners of the main wave of colonization to follow, traditionally ascribed to the organizing powers of the Ionian city of Miletos. The early date claimed for the initial settlement at Sinope is supported by the report that it had to be refounded by the Miletians after an attack and occupation by the Kimmerians sometime around 700 BC. Thereafter, until about 530 BC, the setting up of colonies around the shores of the sea continued at some pace: in all, Miletos is credited with founding ninety cities. If this figure even approximates to the truth, it

 37

would imply that Miletos must have been serving as the agent for the disenchanted who swirled around the Aegean in search of purpose and fortune. So large a colonizing force could hardly have been recruited from its own meagre hinterland.

Although the sending out of colonial ventures was probably a near continuous process spread over almost two centuries, it is possible to identify three surges in activity. The first was underway in the middle of the seventh century. It was at this time that Histria was established on a narrow peninsula close to the mouth of the Danube and the island (or peninsula) of Berezan was settled. Berezan lies close to the wide estuary into which the rivers Dnieper and Bug flow and was admirably sited to command trade along these river routes leading deep into the steppe and the forest steppe. A little later Apollonia was founded on an island just off the coast of what is now Bulgaria. These establishments, on restricted peninsulas or islands were trading enclaves (*emporia*). They had no agricultural land (*chora*) to support farming communities.

The next wave of colonization got underway soon after 600 and involved settlers establishing themselves to farm (*apokia*). Tomis, to the south of Histria, was founded at this time. Existing communities received incomers and began to acquire land for them. Such was the case with Berezan, where land on the mainland was opened up, and it was not long before a new town was created at Olbia in the midst of it, not far from the pioneering island market. Attention also turned to the Taman and Kerch Peninsulas which commanded the Kimmerian Bosphorus—the seaway which led from the Black Sea to the Sea of Azov giving access to the river Don which flowed into it. So attractive was the area that in the brief period 580–60 nine new colonies were set up, five on the European side and four on the Asian side. All were ports, and prominent among them was Panticapaeum directly overlooking the strait. Not only were the land and sea productive but the opportunity to trade with the Scythians inhabiting the region was irresistible.

A third wave of colonization began after about 560 and lasted for some thirty years, encouraged, at least in part, by the Persian incursion into western Asia Minor and the consequent disruption which this caused. While many new colonies were established by the Greek cities of the Aegean, extending now all around the shores of the Black Sea, some of the existing colonies sent out pioneer communities of their own to found new settlements. Everywhere the immigrant Greek population grew, especially on the Kerch and Taman Peninsulas. That the process of settlement was complex is shown by the city of Chersonesos on the southern shore of the Crimean peninsula. According to Greek tradition the initial settlement was founded in the fifth century by colonists sent from Herakles, a town established on the southern shore of the Black Sea in 554 by Boeotians and Megarians. Excavations have shown, however, that a large settlement already existed on the site of Chersonesos and was

flourishing in the last decades of the sixth century. Details of this kind hint at the fluidity of the situation. While flagging settlements could be revived by newly arrived pioneers, successful colonies would need to expand, bringing more and more coastal territories under Greek sway.

The flood of Greeks into the Black Sea in the seventh and sixth centuries brought the urban world of the Aegean face to face with the nomadic world of the steppe. For the most part the two communities coexisted in harmony. While the equilibrium may have been unstable, the trading advantages to both were such that it was in everyone's interest that peaceful, ordered relations were maintained.

Confronting the Persians

At the time that the Scythians were active in Asia Minor a small state came into existence in Persia in what is now the Iranian province of Fars, on the eastern flank of the Persian Gulf at the southern end of the Zagros Mountains. According to tradition the first king, Achaemenes, ruled in the seventh century establishing the dynasty named after him. The great Assyrian empire that had dominated the Near East finally collapsed in 612 when the Medes and Babylonians, with Scythian help, sacked Nineveh. In the half-century of uncertainty which followed, the power of the Achaemenids (Persians) began to grow and with the accession of King Cyrus in 539 the world was set to change. In an astonishingly short period of less than three decades Cyrus had created a great empire stretching from the Aegean to the fringes of the Indus valley.

The northern frontier of the new empire was conveniently delimited by natural features along much of its length. It extended to the southern shores of the Black Sea, the Caucasus mountains, and the southern shores of the Caspian. But further east between the Caspian and the Pamir Mountains there was no clear natural boundary, just an expanse of desert (the Karakum, Kyzylkum, and Muyunkum deserts) interspersed with extensive marshlands and lakes and crossed by two great rivers, the Oxus (Amu Darya) and the Jaxartes (Syr Darya), eventually giving way to desert steppe and steppe to the north. The southern part of this great open region was occupied by horse-riding nomads known to the Persians as Sakā—a name which Herodotus recorded to be the same as Scythian. The Persians recognized two distinct groups, the Sakā Tigrakhauda (the Sakā of the pointed hats), who occupied the marshland areas, and the Sakā Haumawargā (the haoma-consuming Sakā), who lived mainly in the plains and deserts. Haoma is a plant which suitably prepared can produce an inebriant with other beneficial properties. The Persian expansion absorbed the Sakā Haumawargā, who were incorporated into the provinces of Sogdiana and Chorasmia, but the Sakā Tigrakhauda retained a degree of freedom as a vassal state.

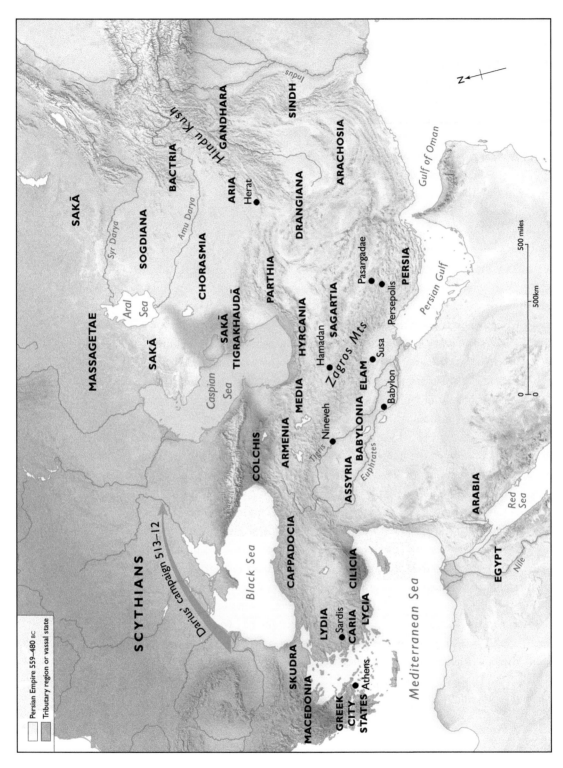

2.3 The Persian Empire grew rapidly between 559 and 480 BC, confronting the Sakā along much of its northern frontier. Darius' campaign of 513–12 against the Pontic steppe Scythians may have been intended to establish a Persian-controlled corridor around the north side of the Black Sea.

Beyond the Syr Darya and probably extending to the Caspian Sea were the Massagetae, a people who, so Herodotus believed, resembled the Scythians: 'They fight both on horseback and on foot…. They use bows and lances but their favourite weapon is the battleaxe. They also used much gold in their personal decoration and that of their horses' (*Hist.* i. 215). The Massagetae were at this time led by a queen, Tomyris, and it was Cyrus' intention to bring them within the empire. Diplomacy failed, however, so in 530 BC he crossed the river and invaded their territory. It was during the ensuing hostilities that, according to Herodotus, Cyrus was killed. His body was brought back to the Persian capital, Pasargadae, where his tomb still survives.

Cyrus' achievement in creating such a huge empire was remarkable and further extensions were made by his son Cambyses (r. 530–522) and by Darius (r. 521–486). But there were inherent instabilities in so vast an edifice. Before Darius could assume power he had to put down a contender, Gaumata, leader of a rebellion which broke out in the recently conquered territories. His success is dramatically displayed in a relief carved from a cliff face at Bisitun in Iran which shows the triumphant king, one foot upon the body of his dead adversary, confronting nine rebel kings, hands bound behind them, roped together by their necks. The last of the line is King Skunkha, leader of the Sakā Tigrakhauda, distinguished by his tall pointed hat. As a composition designed to strike terror in the heart of anyone thinking of opposing the authority of Darius it could hardly have been more effective.

2.4 Darius fought a successful campaign against Gaumata, a contender for the throne, whose body is seen here under the right foot of Darius on the famous relief at Bisitun, Iran, dating to 520–19. The nine kings who had joined the rebellion, including Skuka, the king of the Sakā (last in the line) were brought in chains to Darius.

41

Although the relationship with the nomadic tribes on the Central Asian frontier was at times troubled, both sides could benefit. At the capital Persepolis one of the reliefs on the wall of a large hypostyle hall known as the Apadāna shows ambassadors from all corners of the empire bringing offerings to the Persian king. Among them is a deputation of Sakā, distinguished by their tall pointed hats. One of the gifts they are leading is a sturdy horse—a reminder of their contributions to the Persian cavalry. Sakā horsemen also served in the Persian army as mercenaries. Diplomatic gifts will have flowed the other way, introducing into the world of the nomads Persian artistic motifs and values to be selectively incorporated into their own repertoires (below, pp. 170–6).

The Persians in Europe

Darius recognized three distinct groups of Sakā, the two Central Asian groups already mentioned and a third group, the 'Sakā beyond the Sea'. These were the Scythians who lived on the Pontic steppe with whom the Persians were to engage in 513/512 when Darius launched his European campaign.

Having reached natural boundaries to north, south, and east, the only direction left for the Persians to expand was to the west where lay the evident attraction of the wealthy cities of Greece. But before turning his attention to the Greeks Darius decided to campaign against the European Scythians. His reasons for this are obscure. It may be that he was intending to try to conquer the entire Pontic steppe, thus creating a broad corridor linking to the Caspian Sea and the Persian territory beyond. As a strategy it was not without its advantages for by doing so he would have been able to control the whole of the Black Sea and the Greek colonies around it.

Whatever his ultimate intention, his first requirement was to create a base on the European shore of the sea, on the south bank of the Danube. To do this he ordered an Ionian naval force to sail to the Danube mouth to build a bridge across the river. This they did, choosing a suitable location two days upstream. The Danube at this time formed the southern boundary of Scythian territory. While this was in progress he built a bridge over the Bosphorus and led his army across, setting foot in Europe for the first time. His onward march took him through Thrace northwards toward the Danube, meeting little opposition except from the Getae, whom he defeated and 'forthwith enslaved'. At the Danube the Persians crossed the river and, on Darius' orders, the bridge was dismantled. The plan was for the army to march against the Scythians while the Ionian naval detachment supported them by sea.

The response of the Scythians to the attack was to fall back, driving off their herds, burning the forage, and blocking up the wellsprings. By doing this they drew the Per-

sian army deeper and deeper into the deserted land, always staying one day's march ahead. Eventually, when the Persians were dangerously far from the Danube, the Scythians began harrying the army with surprise attacks while sending ambassadors to the Ionians, who had been left to guard the Danube crossing, with the intention of trying to persuade them to defect, thus cutting off the Persians' retreat. Herodotus, whose narrative we have been following, adds an intriguing detail at this point. The Scythian horsemen, he says, were at a disadvantage because their horses were frightened by the braying of the asses and the appearance of the mules accompanying the Persians. They were totally unused to such creatures.

The stand-off continued until at last a confrontation of the two armies seemed about to happen, but before the armies could engage a hare started up between them and the Scythian cavalry rushed off in pursuit leaving the Persians astonished and frustrated. According to Herodotus, Darius turned to one of his officers and said, 'These men do indeed despise us utterly.' An amusing anecdote which may even be true, it nicely characterizes the stark cultural differences between the two forces, the one stolid, controlled, and over-trained, the other whose whole being was mobility and spontaneity.

It was at this point that Darius decided to abandon the campaign and to retreat under cover of darkness, leaving his sick and wounded and his braying asses and mules to deceive the Scythian scouts. When the Scythians realized what had happened they divided their force, the main part tracking the retreating Persians while the other group sped to the Danube crossing in a last attempt to persuade the Ionians to destroy the bridge and to pull back leaving the Persians stranded. In the event, this did not happen and Darius and his dispirited army crossed safely from Scythia to the comparative safety of Thrace.

Twenty years later, in 492, the Persian armies entered Thrace and Macedonia again, this time intent on breaking the power of Athens, but their failure at Marathon in 490 and at Salamis and Plataea in 480–479 brought the Persian adventure in Europe to an end.

The sixth century BC was a time when the steppe nomads came increasingly in touch with the sedentary, urban world of Greece and Persia. For the Central Asian nomads it was contact with the Persians that made the greatest impression but it was a diffuse encounter enacted over the limitless desert and desert steppe. Those occupying the Pontic steppe, on the other hand, faced the Greek world across a confined coastal interface, their interaction carefully articulated through the port colonies. The brief Persian intrusion into the region in 513/512, though it generated stories rich in character and incident, can have had little, if any, lasting effect. The rhythms of coexistence driven by commerce provided a steadying influence. And so it was

 43

that the Greek world was able to observe at leisure the fascinating life of the Scythian nomads.

Recording the World of the Other

The Greek cities of the Aegean coast of Asia Minor became great centres of learning, particularly in the sixth and fifth centuries BC, in no small part due to their geographical position at the interface between the maritime world of the Aegean and the Mediterranean and the land-based kingdoms and empires of the Near East. They were hubs through which knowledge from Asia, Egypt, and the Mediterranean flowed and where it could be brought together by keen minds eager to understand and explain the world around them. Principal among these cities was Miletos, which, as we have seen, was instrumental in organizing the colonial expeditions sailing for the Black Sea. Here lived the early philosopher scientists, Thales (c.624–546), Anaximander (c.610–545), and Anaximenes (c.585–528), each striving to understand the nature of the universe. They were developing their ideas, debating with their fellows in the stoas of Miletos, and avidly picking up new information from the visitors flocking to the city when the fever of colonization was at its height. These were heady times for anyone with an enquiring mind. From what he learned of geography Anaximander is credited with drawing the first world map.

The advance of the Persians under Cyrus had, by 530 BC, engulfed much of Asia Minor including the Greek cities of its Aegean coast. A level of resistance to foreign occupations was ever present but the social and economic life of the citizens had not greatly changed. It was in these uneasy times that Hecataeus (c.550–476), born in Miletos twenty years before the Persian occupation began, grew up. He came from a wealthy family and travelled widely, devoting himself to writing books on geography and history. He almost certainly knew Anaximenes, providing a link with the old order. One of his books, *Journey around the Earth*, described what was then known of Europe, Asia, and Africa. He had heard of the Celts in the west of Europe, perhaps gathering his information from travellers coming from the colony of Massalia (Marseilles) in the western Mediterranean and he knew of the Scythians, hearing about these mare-milking nomads from visitors arriving from the Black Sea colonies. The book no longer exists but scraps of its content are referred to in later works providing tantalizing clues as to its original scope and content. Apart from his writings, Hecataeus' main claim to fame was that in 500, at the time when the Ionian cities were planning to rebel against the Persians, he argued unsuccessfully against the venture. Six years later, after the rebellion had been defeated, he helped to negotiate favourable terms with the Persian authorities.

Other Greeks were also taking an interest in distant lands and their people. One was Hellanikos of Lesbos (*c.*490–405), who wrote a number of books, including *Babarika Nomina* in which there was a section on *Skythika*. Some of the material he used seems to have come from the writings of Hecataeus but only fragments survive and it is impossible to be certain.

A far more important source, important not least because the text survives in full, is the justly famous *Histories* of Herodotus of Halicarnassus (*c.*484–425). The book opens with the author introducing himself and then telling his reader what to expect:

> The purpose is to ensure that the traces of human actions are not lost through time and to preserve the memory of the important and remarkable achievements of both Greeks and non-Greeks. Among the subjects covered is, in particular, the course of hostilities between Greeks and non-Greeks.

His principal theme was the conflict between the Greeks and the Persians between 490 and 470 but he sets the story in the broadest of contexts emphasizing, as all good historians should, the geographic and ethnographic setting of his narrative. His evident love of all the esoteric data at his fingertips leads him to offer an encyclopaedic view of the world full of fascinating detail and anecdote, this background accounting for at least two thirds of the book.

His early life, probably spent in or around the Dorian city of Halicarnassus, would have brought him into contact with travellers offering information about distant lands and it seems probable that he himself travelled to Egypt, Mesopotamia, and the northern shore of the Black Sea. At some stage, around 447, he left home for good, spending a few years in Athens and then, in 443, joining a colonial expedition organized by Athens to found a city at Thurium in southern Italy. His *History*, written over many years, was completed by about 430 and became widely known, though not universally appreciated, by his near contemporaries. Thucydides would write him off as a mere storyteller but in the more mellow assessment of the orator, Cicero, he was the 'Father of History'.

There has been, and continues to be, much debate about the acuity of his judgement in using his disparate sources but it is clear from asides in the text that he was conscious of the difference between what he regarded as valid sources and mere hearsay and was prepared to say so. He also observed things for himself and interviewed informants in the course of his travels. It was probably at the Greek port of Olbia on the north shore of the Black Sea that he gathered much of his information about the Scythians and their country which makes up so much of Book IV of his *History*. In the early twentieth century, his Scythian ethnography was considered by some scholars to be a stereotype of the barbarian 'Other', created to reassure his Greek

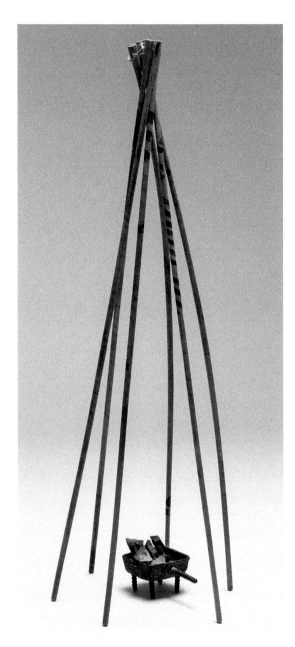

2.5 Pazyryk kurgan 2. Six wooden poles wound with birch-cherry bark formed a framework supporting a cover of felt. Within this small tent-like structure was a bronze brazier containing heated stones on which hemp seeds had been thrown. The Scythians inhaled the fumes as part of the purification rituals concluding the process of burial.

audience of their unique identity. But as archaeological data began to accumulate, mainly from the excavation of Scythian burials, the veracity of many of his observations has become apparent. His famous description of Scythian burial ritual can be matched detail by detail with the excavation data (below, Chapter 11). To give just one example, in describing the purification rituals following burial he says:

> They make a booth by fixing in the ground three sticks inclined towards one another and stretching around them woollen felt which they arrange so as to fit as close as possible: inside the booth a dish is placed on the ground into which they put a number of red-hot stones and then add some hemp seed.
>
> (*Hist.* iv. 73)

He relates how they then went inside the booth and inhaled the fumes 'shouting for joy' at the effects of the drug. Tent poles and bronze basins full of burnt stones and charred hemp seeds found in excavations, notably at Pazyryk, show that the practice was widespread throughout the steppe (below, p. 306).

Elsewhere he mentions Gelonus, a vast city 'surrounded by a high wall thirty furlongs [about 6 km] each way, built entirely of wood' (*Hist.* iv. 108). That such a place could have existed was thought to be pure fantasy until the discovery, in the 1970s, of a huge fortification at Bel'sk in the valley of the Dnieper with ramparts extending around a circumference of 33 km (below, pp. 133–4). Another example of Herodotus vindicated.

To write his Scythian ethnography Herodotus must have had access to a variety of sources in addition to his own observations and interviews conducted during his visit to Olbia. He certainly knew of the works of Hecataeus and may have had access to Hellanikos but he made his own judgements. In one instance Hecataeus (quoted by a late source) notes that the Melanchlaeni and Issedones were Scythian people, while

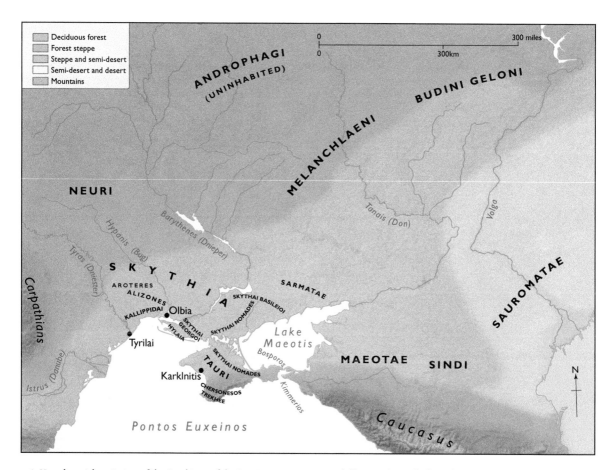

2.6 Herodotus' description of the Scythians of the Pontic steppe mentions different tribes, which can be placed approximately in the modern landscape.

Herodotus says they were different from the Scythians. It is a small detail but hints that Herodotus was assessing evidence for himself rather than simply following others.

As a source for Scythian ethnography, Herodotus is invaluable and we will have cause to return to his descriptions many times in later chapters. He also provides some historical facts and an, albeit sketchy, outline of the many different nomadic tribes of the Pontic steppe and Central Asia.

There is one further text which should be mentioned, a work called *On Airs, Waters, and Places* ascribed to Hippocrates, the Greek doctor who presided over the famous medical school on the island of Kos in the fifth century. It is one of many treatises belonging to the school but is unlikely to have been composed by Hippocrates himself. There are internal hints that its unknown author, usually referred to as Pseudo-Hippocrates, may have come from Knidos. The second part of the work, chapters 17–22, gives an intriguing and detailed account of Scythians 'dwelling around Lake Maeotis' (the Sea of Azov). It deals with their physical characteristics, way of life, gender issues, and health owing little to earlier or contemporary accounts and giving every impression of being based on close personal observation. Its particular value lies in the light which it throws on attitudes to gender in Scythian society (pp. 218–20).

The ethnographic accounts of the steppe nomads given by Herodotus and Pseudo-Hippocrates provide an unusually vivid account of a barbarian people observed and researched by their Greek contemporaries. Through writings such as these and through daily contact in the north Pontic coastal colonies the Scythians became familiar to the Greek world. For Ephoros, writing in the mid fourth century, the Scythians were one of the four great barbarian peoples of the known world, the others being Celts, Persians, and Libyans.

A View of the Scythian World and Beyond, c.400 BC

Herodotus had a clear view of the land occupied by the people he considered to be Scythians. It was 'level, well-watered, and abounding in pasture' and was crossed by eight major rivers, each of which he names, all flowing into the Black Sea. At the western extremity was the Ister (Danube), while the eastern limit of Scythian territory lay on the Tanais (Don). He believed the Borysthenes (Dnieper) to be the greatest and most productive of the rivers of the steppe.

> It has upon its banks the loveliest and most excellent pastures for cattle; it contains an abundance of the most delicious fish; its water is most pleasant to taste; its stream is limpid while all the other rivers near it are muddy; the richest harvests spring up along its course and where the ground is not sown, the heaviest crops of grass; while salt forms in great plenty about its mouth without human aid.
>
> (*Hist.* iv. 53)

His eulogy is probably based on personal observations made when visiting Olbia, situated on the river estuary. From there he probably travelled inland to explore the Scythian steppe.

Between the Danube and the Don Herodotus mentions seven distinct groups of Scythians, giving some indication of their locations in relation to the rivers. That there is some doubt about the identification of the rivers, combined with the fact that the distances he gives may have been subject to scribal error (and anyway his grasp

of the exact geography is not strong), makes it difficult to place them with any degree of precision. That said, the broad picture is reasonably clear. Around Olbia the Callipedae were to be found: they were 'Graeco-Scythian', presumably the result of intermarriages between the Greek settlers and the indigenous population. Further inland were the Alazonians, who, like the Callipedae, were cultivators, growing wheat, millet, lentils, garlic, and onions. Yet further inland still there was another, unnamed community who 'grow grain not for their own use but for sale'. Then come the Neuri, whose 'customs are like the Scythians'. Beyond them the land was unpopulated. The emphasis on cultivation and the possibility that some of these farming communities may have been exporting their surplus grain through the port of Olbia to the Greek world show that nomadism was not universal among the Scythians. In this western part of the Scythian world the forest steppe was well suited to cultivation: mixed farming had been practised here well before the advent of the Scythians.

To the east of the Dnieper were Scythian pastoralists who called themselves Olbiopolites. They occupied a large territory extending northward upriver, eleven days' sail. Further on was a desolate unoccupied land and beyond that lived cannibals. East of the pastoralists were nomadic Scythians extending as far as the river Gerrhus, on the opposite side of which were the Royal Scythians—'the bravest of the Scythian tribes, which look upon all the other tribes as their slaves'. Their domain appears to have extended eastwards to the Don. The identity of the Gerrhus has been much debated but with no convincing resolution. To the north of the Royal Scythians were the Melanchlaeni (Black Robes), whom Herodotus believed to be a different race from the Scythians. Way to the north-east, in a region occupied by hunters and gatherers, he tells us there existed an enclave of Scythians who had broken away from the Royal Scythians and had migrated to these distant lands.

Although the information available to Herodotus was patchy and no doubt incorrect in part, and his cognitive geography of the steppe region was vague, the picture which is given is of a high degree of ethnic unity stretching from the Danube to the Don and from the shores of the Black Sea deep into the forest zone. He is also very well aware that throughout this region the economic base of the different tribes ranged from pure nomadism to settled agriculture. The existence of a super tribe of Royal Scythians is also interesting. It is a reminder that in mobile nomadic-centred societies like the Scythians elite families could impose their will on less powerful tribes. The social and economic diversity which Herodotus describes across Scythia was probably the result of the fusion of incoming nomadic Scythians and the indigenous population. The direct descendants of the invading elite—the Royal Scythians—by extending their authority over the local people embraced them within a single ethnicity while allowing their diverse economies to continue.

Beyond the River Don lay the Sauromatae, who were regarded by Herodotus as being 'beyond the land of the Scythians'. They 'speak the language of Scythia but have never spoken it correctly'. According to a story which he relates, the Sauro-matae were the result of the intermarriage of Amazons, women who had escaped from their Greek captors in Cappadocia, and Scythians living on the shores of the Sea of Azov, who at some later stage decided to find a new home east of the Don. The story—probably little more than a convenient myth—had the advantage of explain-ing the similarities between Scythians and Sauromatae while accounting for social differences such as the high status of women among the Sauromatae. Sauromatian territory, completely treeless, stretched north for fifteen days' journey up to the forest zone where the Budini lived.

Beyond the Sauromatae the land becomes 'rugged and stony', giving way to 'lofty mountains'—a description suggesting to some commentators that he was referring to the southern end of the Urals where the steppe narrowed. Here lived the Argip-paeans 'who are said to be ... bald from birth and to have flat noses and very long chins'. Nothing is said of their language, but they wore the same type of clothes as the Scythians. Up to this point, Herodotus says, the land and the people were well known because the Scythians and Greek traders from the coastal ports journeyed through these regions, though they had to take interpreters able to speak the seven different languages encountered. The one Greek traveller known by name who is said to have explored this region is the semi-legendary poet Aristeas, whose poem *Arima-spea* mentions a journey far to the east. He is reported to have been absent from home for seven years. Herodotus, who knew of the poem, said that Aristeas got as far as the land of the Issedones.

> Above them dwelt the Arimaspi, men with one eye. Still further the gold-guarding Griffins and beyond them the Hyperboreans .... All of these nations (except the Hypeboreans), beginning with the Arimaspi, were continually encroaching upon their neighbours. Hence the Arimaspi drove the Issedonians from the country, while the Issedonians pushed out the Scythes; and the Scythes, pressing upon the Kimmerians, who dwelt on the shores of the Black Sea, forced them to leave the land.
>
> (*Hist.* iv. 13)

Where exactly these semi-mythical people lived it is difficult to say but they probably extended across what is now the Kazakh steppe as far east as the Altai Mountains. It is tempting to link the gold-guarding Griffins with the nomads of the Altai, whose burial rites proclaim the easy availability of gold and whose art frequently includes fabulous griffin-like beasts. What is particularly interesting about the observations

 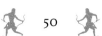

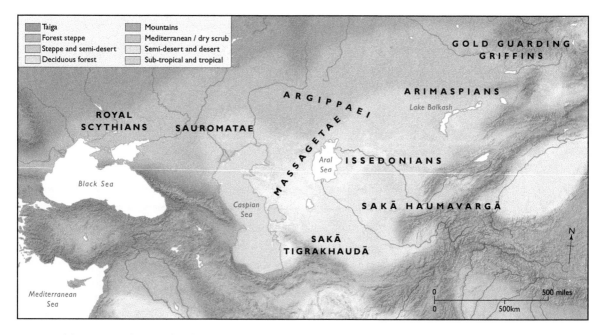

2.7 Beyond the river Don the nomadic tribes of Central Asia received only a brief mention in the ancient sources but those recorded can be broadly located.

of Aristeas is his description of the relentless mobility of the various tribes and the dislocation which this caused.

To the south of the Kazakh steppe, between the Caspian Sea and the Pamir Mountains, were the deserts and desert steppe of Central Asia, the home of the Sakā and the Massagetae. The name Sakā was used by the Persian sources as interchangeable with Scythians (above, p. 39), while the Massagetae, who were neighbours of the Issedonians, were according to Herodotus also regarded by many to be of the Scythian race. Clearly, different observers had different views on ethnicity. Herodotus was specific in his definition of Scythians; others were less so. But what is evident, particularly from the archaeological data, is that there was a broad similarity in the culture of the nomads from the Altai to the Danube and, given the mobility of the times, it is simpler to regard them as belonging to a broad cultural continuum.

Fascinating and valuable though Herodotus' description of the Scythians and related nomads is, it is, at best, a snapshot, blurred in part, of a moment in time. He was observing people in a period of rapid change as the original nomad influx of the Archaic period gave way to more settled societies coming to terms with the Greek presence around the northern Pontic coast. The social and economic changes which

 51

were to transform Scythian society between the eighth and third century will be discussed later (below, Chapter 5).

The Scythians through the Eyes of the Athenians

While the citizens of the Greek colonies around the north Pontic coast were in daily contact with Scythians and interacted with them in many ways, including sometimes through marriage, the Greeks living in the Aegean region, far removed from the steppe, will have been much less familiar with these northern barbarians, learning of them from sailors who traded with the Black Sea or perhaps coming across actual Scythians brought into the Greek world to serve as slaves.

In the fifth century, following the Persian Wars, Scythian slaves began to be imported in some quantity and later writers like Polybius and Strabo praised their quality. In 414/413 a Scythian slave was priced at 144 drachmas—a high price to pay. Unlike the Greek world, Scythian society did not depend on slaves, but early contacts with the Greeks showed that there was a real economic advantage to be had in rounding up and selling on unwanted humanity. Once the principle had been established, it is likely that the Scythian elites organized slave-raiding expeditions into the forest steppe, bringing their spoils to towns like Olbia to sell to Greek merchants. It may, indeed, have been this upsurge in activity that led to a new phase of growth at Olbia in the 470s. In return for slaves the Greeks offered a range of consumer goods, among which wine was much in demand, as the distribution of wine amphorae across the steppe region bears witness. That a high percentage of the amphorae came from Chios suggests a direct link with the wine producers of that island, and it is no coincidence that Chios soon gained a reputation as a thriving slave market.

2.8 Mounted Scythian archers, distinguished by their long pointed hats, shown here on a Greek Black-Figured vase of the sixth century, found in Italy and now in the Vatican Museum, Rome.

In fifth-century Athens the image of the Scythians would have been familiar. More than 600 Attic Black-Figured pots incorporate depictions of them, showing them as aliens, differently dressed, often bearded, and usually carrying a bow. They appear in a variety of different contexts, suggesting that whenever a foreign barbarian was required the Scythian stereotype would suffice. But Scythians were also present in Athens in person, employed by the state as an urban police force. How

2.9 Archers in Scythian dress, one named Kimerios, shown in action on a Greek Black-Figured vase of c.570 BC from Chiusi, Italy.

this came to be is a matter of speculation but from the mid sixth century detachments of mounted Scythian archers were used to strengthen the Greek hoplite army and it may have been that the Scythian archer police were recruited from among the veterans of these forces. According to the limited textual evidence available, they were public slaves who served as watchmen and guards whose task it was to keep the general public in order. One account speaks of them rounding up recalcitrant citizens and herding them in to vote using short ropes dipped in red paint so that the unwilling could be identified by red marks on their clothes. In the Assembly the chairman could ask them to remove anyone speaking for overlong; they could also make arrests. In Aristophanes' *Lysistrata*, a magistrate orders the Scythian police force to arrest Lysistrata. That foreign slaves could be used as a civil police force may at first sight

2.10 An archer in Scythian dress on a Greek Red-Figured plate of c.530–490 BC from Vulci, Italy.

 53

seem curious but the explanation may be that it was unthinkable for a Greek to lay hands on another Greek. When restraint was necessary a magistrate would resort to ordering specially designated slaves to perform the distasteful task for him.

In Greek drama the Scythian archer police are depicted as figures of fun. Lysistrata resists arrest, requiring additional Scythian archers to attempt to restrain her. Women join in to support her and in the melee which ensues Lysistrata has to call off her friends to protect the demoralized police, who are now cowering on the ground. In another of his plays, *Thesmophoriazusae*, Aristophanes has his Scythian policeman distracted from his duty by a dancing girl and mocks him mercilessly for his otherness—his unusual appearance and his almost incoherent Greek. While a lumbering, stupid police force is always an easy target for a playwright (witness Gilbert and Sullivan), Aristophanes is deliberately ridiculing the Scythian archers because they are foreign barbarians.

Another stereotype of the Scythian is as a drunkard. That Scythians preferred to drink their wine undiluted was, to the Greeks, uncivilized behaviour. The point is explicitly made in a poem by Anacreon:

> Let's not fall
> Into riot and disorder
> With our wine like the Scythians
> But let us drink in moderation
> Listening to lovely hymns.

In *Lysistrata*, when the leader of the Scythian policemen tells one of his men to pay attention and stop looking for a tavern, the Athenian audience will have recognized the joke. Drunkenness was not solely the weakness of the Scythians. In the Graeco-Roman world the Celts' love of wine was legendary and the Germans were also noted for their lack of moderation. Drunkenness was part of the caricature of the barbarian.

That 'Scythians' carried with it an element of contempt was evident when, in the fourth century, Aeschines tried to denigrate his political opponent Demosthenes by saying that he was descended from a Scythian. Demosthenes' maternal grandfather, Gylon, had been exiled to the Crimea and there had married a Scythian woman. Their child, Kleoboule, who married a Greek, was Demosthenes' mother. The fact that Aeschines believed this to be a valid cause for insult is an interesting reflection on Greek values.

But this is not to say that all Scythians were derided in Athens, as the case of the philosopher Anacharsis demonstrates. Anacharsis grew up in, or in the vicinity of, the Greek colony of Olbia. His father Gnurus was a Scythian and his mother was Greek; he was probably a member of the royal house. In the late sixth century he set

out on his journeys and spent some years in Athens, where he gained a reputation as a skilled philosopher and was sufficiently revered to be given Athenian citizenship. Among the many wise utterances ascribed to him two will give some flavour of his widely reported wit: 'Laws are spiders' webs which catch little flies but cannot hold big ones' and, about democracy, 'Wise men speak, fools decide'. For such wisdom he is seen as a forerunner of the Cynics. Brought up in the cosmopolitan world of Olbia where he acquired a level of Greek culture, he was readily accepted in Athens, but when he returned home he was felled by an arrow shot by his brother. Herodotus used the story to illustrate his contention that 'the Scythians have an extreme hatred of all foreign customs particularly those in use among the Greeks'. While this may have been true in the sixth century, over the years the frontier communities learnt to appreciate each other's values.

The Athenian acceptance of educated Scythians like Anacharsis raises the question of how many more Scythians were living in Athens other than the much-mocked police force. Scythians were certainly in evidence in the Kerameikos, the graveyard just outside the city. In the grave precinct of Dionysios of Kollytos two statues of Scythian archers were discovered not far from a deposit containing eighty bronze arrowheads. It is possible that the precinct contained the burial of a deceased Scythian, perhaps a valued retainer in the service of his master Dionysios. The burial is a reminder that Athens may have had a Scythian community active across the social spectrum.

Later Encounters

During the fourth century BC the kingdom of Macedonia, beyond the northern border of Greece, grew to be a polity of considerable strength. Under King Philip II (r. 360–336 BC) its armies advanced northwards through Thrace, reaching as far as the River Danube, where they encountered Scythians under the leadership of King Ateas (c.429–339 BC). In his early life Ateas had fallen out of favour with the Royal Scythians but had established a powerful kingdom of his own in the Pontic coastal zone between the Danube and the Dniester. Like Philip, he too was interested in the region to the south of the Danube, and in the late 340s the two kings were cooperating in campaigning against the Histriani of Thrace. But in 339 the relationship soured when Ateas refused to send Philip help to support his advance on Byzantium. Finally the two former allies confronted each other in battle on the Danube estuary. The Macedonians emerged triumphant: Ateas, who was 90 if tradition is correct, was killed and Philip wounded. As reparations the Macedonians returned home with 20,000 Scythian women captives and a large number of horses. Three years later, in 336, in

55

2.11 Tombs of the Macedonian elite were found in the great burial mound at Vergina in northern Greece. Tomb II is believed to be that of Phillip II. In the antechamber was found a Scythian gorytos (arrow quiver) made in gold and two greaves associated with the cremated remains of a female, probably his Scythian wife or concubine.

the theatre of Aigai (Vergina) in Macedonia, Philip was assassinated and his body was buried in the royal cemetery nearby.

In 1977, in one of the most spectacular archaeological discoveries of the century, the Macedonian royal cemetery was discovered and Philip's tomb was excavated. In the antechamber the cremated remains of a young woman was found buried together with a gold-covered Scythian gorytos for carrying a bow and arrows, a number of arrows, and two gilded bronze greaves (leg armour), the left shorter and narrower than the right. A careful analysis of the bones showed that the young woman, aged about 30, had been an experienced horse rider and that she had broken her left leg, leaving it deformed. A plausible explanation of the discovery is that the woman in the antechamber was a Scythian princess, the daughter of Ateas, who had become Philip's seventh wife or concubine. She had died and had been buried in his tomb ready to accompany him to the other world, a custom widely practised among the Scythians.

Philip's engagement with the Scythian world was brief and of little moment but it was a reminder to his successor, Alexander, of the formidable power that the Scythians could still wield. It may have been this awareness that prompted Alexander to keep well clear of them and to concentrate his efforts on conquering the Persian

2.12 The exile of the Roman poet Ovid to Tomis on the Black Sea coast is recorded in his well-known laments complaining about the indignity of living among barbarians. His plight is depicted in Eugene Delacroix's *Ovid among the Scythians*, painted in 1859.

empire. Even in Central Asia, where he could have confronted the Sakā, he wisely chose instead to turn south to the richer pickings of India.

In the centuries following Philip's success against the Scythians in the Danube estuary the nomads of the steppe continued the natural rhythm of their lives, with pressures from the east generating a constant flow of nomads thrusting further and further to the west. In such uncertain times the Greek cities of the north Pontic region declined, some into desolate ruins.

South of the Danube the cities along the western shore of the Black Sea still maintained a precarious existence. Some sense of the life in one of them, Tomis, founded in the sixth century BC, is captured in the lament, *Tristia*, written by the Roman poet Ovid. Ovid was 50 years old when, in AD 8, he was exiled to Tomis by the emperor Augustus, who could no longer tolerate the poet's louche behaviour and risqué verses. Tomis (modern Constanţa) was close to the Danube mouth in an area then

settled by Sarmatians, a nomadic horse-riding people who had moved westwards from a homeland to the east of the Don and would soon confront the Roman empire. Ovid hated the place:

> The Scythian marshes lie behind, a handful of names in a region scarcely known. Further there is nothing but uninhabited cold. Ah, how near I am to the ends of the earth.
>
> (Tristia iii. 4)

Tristia was written for his friends back home in Rome in the hope that they would intercede with the emperor on his behalf: it is drenched in self-pity and no doubt exaggerated. Of the town's inhabitants he writes, 'They are more cruelly savage than wolves …. They keep off the evils of cold with animal skins and baggy trousers … and have shaggy faces hidden by long hair.' He goes on to observe that those who still spoke some Greek did so with grotesque accents and laments, 'I, the Roman poet— forgive me Muses—am forced to speak Sarmatian …. The place is hateful and nothing could be sadder on earth.' The emperor did not relent and Ovid died at Tomis after ten years of exile.

While his account may lack objectivity, it captures something of the frontier-like quality of life in the old Greek colonies and the attitudes of the Graeco-Roman world to the barbarians. The intellectual enthusiasm with which Herodotus and Pseudo-Hippocrates had written about the Scythians in the fifth century BC was now replaced with disdain tinged with fear. A century and a half later the Sarmatians would pour across the Roman frontier—a prelude to the barbarian onslaught which was to follow.

3

LANDSCAPES
WITH PEOPLE

OMMUNITIES exist in landscapes and landscapes help form communities. This is particularly true of the Scythians, whose natural habitat was the Eurasian steppe. They were the inheritors of traditions stretching back for more than three thousand years during which time people had learned to adapt to the steppe environment in all its subtle variations, developing their subsistence strategies to suit the many regional differences. They had also to contend with climate change which, even if only of minor amplitude, in so fragile an ecosystem would have had a major dislocating effect. Nor should we forget the impact of population growth. The holding capacity of the steppe was limited. When a population outgrew the available resources migration provided the only readily available safety valve. Steppe society existed, then, in a state of unstable equilibrium: so delicate was the balance that the slightest trigger could upset the system and set everything in motion.

The nomadic communities of the steppe occupied a territory between hunter-gatherers to the north and sedentary agriculturalists to the south and there would, inevitably, have been extensive contacts across the ill-defined boundaries between them. As the sedentary polities developed into more complex states and empires, contact increased, driven largely by the demand of the south for commodities. So it was that across the Black Sea, the Caucasus Mountains, and the Central Asian deserts trade networks developed along which new ideas, behaviours, and desires flowed to infect nomad society. These interactions served both partners well, but they introduced a dynamic that could drive change.

 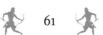

3.1 The landscape of the steppe.

The predatory nomad bands that were to emerge quite suddenly at the beginning of the first millennium BC and to spread rapidly throughout the steppe were a phenomenon new to Eurasia. They were forged during the second millennium through an interplay of all these disparate factors.

The Steppe Corridor

The steppe corridor is a remarkable phenomenon. It is the largest expanse of temperate grassland in the world, stretching in an almost continuous swathe from Manchuria in the east to the Great Hungarian Plain in the west—a distance of 8,000 km. It mostly lies between the latitudes of 40° and 50°N. The temperature range within this zone is warm enough to allow grass and shrubs to grow but is too dry to favour tree growth. To the south the vegetation gradually thins, creating a roughly parallel zone of desert steppe, beyond which the open desert is reached. To the north the steppe merges with the forest steppe. As the density of trees increases, the forest steppe eventually gives way to forest proper—the light covering of spruce and other conifers that make up the *taiga* of Russia and the deciduous woodland that characterizes much of the European peninsula.

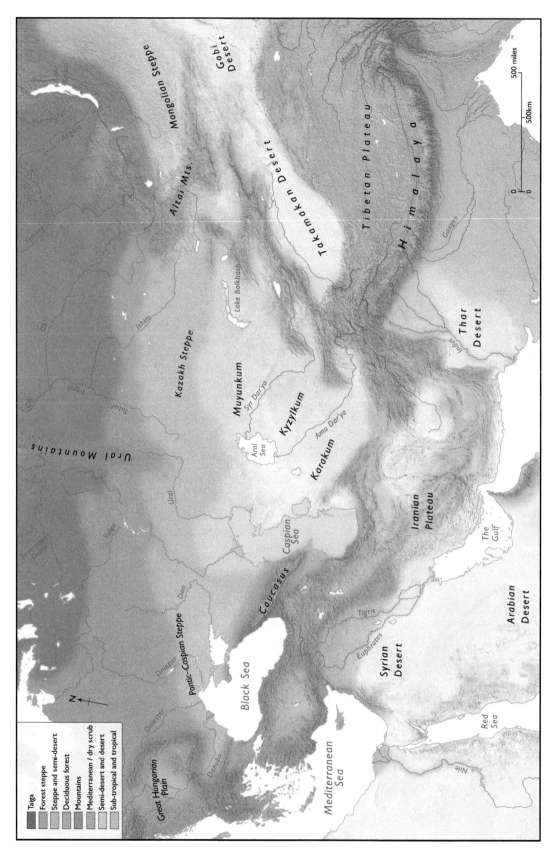

3.2 The ecological zones of Eurasia were largely determined by latitude. Between the forests of the north and the deserts of the south lay the great swathe of steppe grassland extending from Manchuria to the Great Hungarian Plain. This was the natural home of the horse.

The steppe zone, then, is the creation of latitude but it is moderated by another less obvious factor: proximity to the Atlantic. The wind system and currents of the ocean create a predominantly east-moving air stream, damp and mild enough to ameliorate the climate of the European peninsula that creates conditions in which the deciduous forest will thrive. The moderating effect of the Atlantic system extends eastwards about as far as the Volga River, allowing deciduous forests to extend this far in place of *taiga*. It also means that the western steppe and forest steppe are moister and warmer than comparable regions further east, their pastures accordingly being lusher. This creates what is known as the steppe gradient. As one travels from the east to the west the climate changes from cold and dry to warm and damp. It was a reality well understood by those who inhabited these regions and provided an ever-present incentive to migrate. A community living in the cold high steppe of Mongolia subjected to cycles of intense cold had three options to improve its life: to move south into China, to move south-west into India, or to move due west towards Europe. All three options were taken at different times throughout history but the first and second meant crossing into different ecological zones. By choosing to move westwards along the steppe corridor the migrants had the great advantage of staying within an environment with which they were familiar, and one that facilitated fast movement. It was for this reason that the history of Eurasia was dominated by constant flows of people from east to west along the steppe and why so many of them, from the Yamnaya culture of the early third millennium BC to the Mongols of the thirteenth century AD, ended their travels at the most westerly extremity of the steppe zone: the Great Hungarian Plain.

For the most part the steppe corridor is gently undulating land broken only by the great rivers flowing across it, some northwards into the Arctic Ocean, others south-wards into the Caspian Sea and the Black Sea. But at two points mountain ranges hinder east–west progress. The greatest obstacle is offered by the Altai Mountains separating the eastern, or Mongolian, steppe from the Kazakh steppe to the west, but lush valleys and passes provide ways through. The other intrusion is the south end of the Ural Mountains. It was less of a barrier but it caused the zone of grassland steppe to narrow between the forest steppe flanking the end of the mountain range and the desert steppe fringing the Caspian and Aral seas. To the east of the Urals lies the Central, or Kazakh, steppe while to the west is the Western, or Pontic–Caspian steppe, which extends along the Danube valley to the *puszta* of Hungary.

Although, on the map, the distances along the steppe corridor look formidable in terms of ancient travel, the relatively level, open land facilitated speed. In the thirteenth century AD it is claimed that a Mongol dispatch rider, setting out from Kara-korum in the Mongolian steppe, changing horses whenever necessary, could reach

Hungary within a month. Even at the more leisurely pace of 25 km a day the journey could be accomplished comfortably within the year. The very nature of the steppe encouraged movement. On a horse, with nothing but swaying grass extending to the horizon, why not go riding forever onwards? The German traveller, J. G. Kohl, visiting the Ukraine in 1841 nicely summed up the character of the steppe, which by this time was beginning to come under cultivation:

> It is a mystery how a man could think of settling as a farmer in the steppe whose whole nature cries out against this abuse, whose whole land is movement, whose soil abhors deep-rooted plants, favouring instead mobile cattle-breeding, where winds carry everything before them far and wide and whose flatness invites everything to move across it in haste.
>
> J. G. Kohl, *Russia and the Russians, in 1842* (English edn., 1843)

This desire to constantly move on is noted by other travellers writing of the steppes: the sheer monotony of it all, the endless swathes of gently moving grass, and the great open skies offer no distraction to onward movement, while the line of the horizon is always there to entice the rider forward.

The steppe is not an easy environment in which to exist. Temperatures in the summer can rise to 45° C and in the winter fall to −45° C, but with 200–500 mm of rain a year sufficient rich grass grows to sustain flocks and herds through the spring and summer months so long as the animals are kept constantly on the move. For the winters there are the river valleys offering shelter and water, while bushes, some trees, and the all-important reed, phragmites, provide fodder to overwinter the livestock.

Maintaining the well-being of the flocks and herds within the constraints of the environment drove everything. For some it meant that the entire community had to be constantly on the move as the animals roamed. But others, particularly those living near mountains, could practise vertical transhumance: the men took the stock to the mountain pastures while the rest of the family remained at a home base. These were but two of the multitude of survival strategies that developed to make steppe life possible. Yet at all times existence was precarious and the lifestyle could be forced to change almost overnight.

The Ever-changing Climate

Comparatively minor changes of climate in an ecozone like the steppe, bringing about only slight or short-term changes, can have a disproportionate effect on the lives of pastoral nomads. Minor oscillations in climate normally occur in the region on a fairly regular cycle, a decade or so of moderate weather being followed by one or

two severe winters before normal conditions return. At such a periodicity it is possible for communities to cope and to ride out the worst, but if the interval shortens or the number of harsh winters multiplies then massive social disruption can follow. Recent events in Mongolia provide a frightening illustration of the magnitude of the damage that can be done. Mongolian herders always fear the *dzud*—an unusually dry summer followed by a severe winter. One is bad enough, but between 1999 and 2002 there were three in succession as the result of which eleven million animals died. A decade later the *dzud* hit again, in two successive years, 2009 and 2010. In some regions temperatures plummeted to −45° C and stayed at that level for fifty consecutive days. This time eight million animals died, with 9,000 families—20 per cent of the rural population—losing all their livestock. In the face of catastrophes of this magnitude people leave the land, giving up their traditional livelihood, and migrate to the city. Only five years later, in 2015–16, the next *dzud* hit, killing one million animals and the following winter was equally as severe. In these conditions, especially if the period between the *dzuds* decreases as the consequence of global climate change, it is difficult to see how the traditional nomadic lifestyle of Mongolia can continue. Mongolia is an extreme case because its steppe uplands are particularly cold and dry but it illustrates how prone steppe communities are to even minor fluctuations in the climate.

Sudden changes in weather conditions were nothing new in Mongolia. A recent dendrochronological study, using stunted Siberian pine found in the Khangai Mountains, allowed climatic fluctuations to be charted in some detail during the late twelfth and early thirteenth century AD. By counting tree rings back from the present day precise dates can be arrived at for the more ancient growth and by measuring the width of the individual ring, representing a year's growth, the growing conditions can be assessed. What the study showed was that there was a long period of intense drought accompanied by exceptional cold from AD 1180 to 1190, followed by a phase of heavy rainfall and mild temperatures from AD 1222 to 1225. This change corresponds with major social and political events. In the late twelfth century the Mongols were split between feuding factions but in 1206 they were unified by Chinggis Khan into a formidable fighting force which, from about 1210, expanded exponentially, conquering large areas of northern China and Central Asia. While it is possible that there was no direct cause and effect linking the environmental change and historical events, a plausible scenario would be to suggest that the social fragmentation of the last decades of the twelfth century were exaggerated by the intense period of dry, cold weather. With the rapid amelioration of the climate about 1211 grassland flourished, increasing the biomass available for horses and other livestock. This would have made life much easier and could have provided the conditions for a charismatic leader like Chinggis Khan to unify the disparate tribes and build a massive force of horsemen fired with ambitions for adventure and conquest. It would have been quite impossible to amass the forces required (remembering that each rider needed five horses) without there being sufficient rich pastures able to support them. At the very least, we can suppose that the fluctuation in climate facilitated, and may have triggered, a major event in the history of Eurasia.

By studying dendrochronology and pollen sequences recorded from peat deposits and lake sediments one can build up a picture of climatic fluctuations across much of the steppe region and identify periods of major change. An example of an event which affected Europe and much of the western steppe was the Piora Oscillation, a period of extremely cold winters which began about 4200 BC and lasted until about 3800 BC. One of the effects of this climatic downturn was to bring to an end the system of sedentary agriculture which generated tells (high mounds created by successive settlements) in many parts of the Balkans and in the middle and lower Danube valley. At the same time groups of pastoralists crossed the Volga and moved westwards into the Pontic steppe, establishing what archaeologists call the Sredni Stog culture. The increase in the percentage of horses used for meat and milk noted at this time is probably because horses are better able to survive harsh winters caused by a climatic downturn than are cattle and sheep. Another part of the same general movement saw herders move from the Dnieper valley to the Danube delta, some penetrating as far west as the Tisza valley in what is now Hungary. They were characterized by the use of kurgan burials and distinctive stone mace-heads shaped like horses' heads. In archaeological terminology the people are called the Suvorovo-Novodanilovka culture.

These westerly movements of herding communities into areas previously inhabited by settled agriculturalists between 4200 and 3800 BC were almost certainly driven by climatic factors. They were a prelude to similar movements that were to dominate the next 5,000 years.

A little later, c.3500–3000 BC, pollen sequences from the valleys of the Don and Volga and from the north Kazakh steppe show that the whole of the Pontic–Caspian region was now experiencing a dryer and generally cooler climate, conditions which allowed the steppe grasslands to expand significantly at the expense of forest. The dryer pastures meant that herding communities had to keep their flocks and herds moving and thus to range over greater areas. To achieve this there developed a more mobile lifestyle with entire families now being constantly on the move. This new mobility was made possible by the ox-drawn covered wagon—a cumbersome four-wheeled affair—which was used for transporting household equipment and those unable to follow on horseback. Extensive nomadism of this kind required coopera-

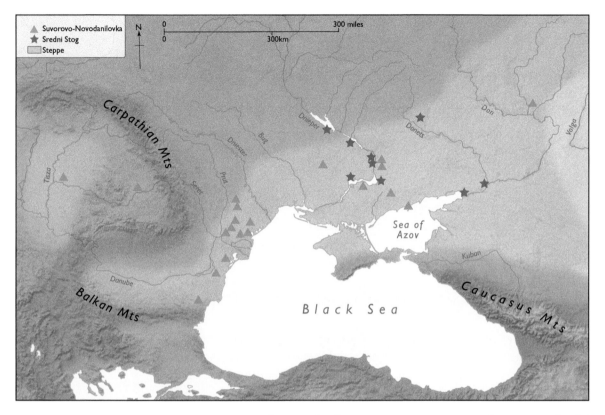

3.3 Over time steppe nomads migrated to the west, sometimes impinging on the territories of settled farming communities in Eastern Europe. Among the earliest to be identified were people called by archaeologists the Suvorovo-Novodanilovka culture who entered the Danube region c.4200–3900 BC.

tion and agreements over the use of pasture as well as complex networks of exchange, which created an appearance of cultural unity spreading across the steppe from the Urals to the Danube delta. The phenomenon is known as the Yamnaya culture. It was not long before internal pressures led to the expansion of the Yamnaya communities westwards into the Great Hungarian Plain.

Another period of cool, dry weather began around 2500 BC. It reached a peak of aridity in about 2000 BC, again causing grassland to expand at the expense of forest. At the same time the extent of the marshlands along the river valleys became far more restricted. This climatic downturn particularly affected the steppe regions east of the Urals, while the more westerly areas still benefited to some extent from the ameliorating effects of the Atlantic airstream. It was in this region, at the south-eastern end of the Urals between the rivers Tobol and Ui, that the distinctive Sintashta culture emerged. Driven by the need to protect the valley marshlands, so necessary

LANDSCAPES WITH PEOPLE

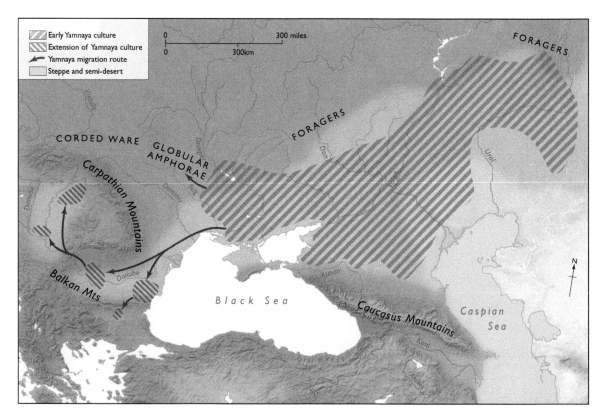

3.4 By 3300–3000 BC pastoral nomads of the Yamnaya culture had established themselves throughout the Pontic–Caspian steppe and between 3100 and 2600 BC groups had moved west along the Danube valley and into the Carpathian Basin.

to provide fodder for animals through the winter, communities built large defended villages that overlooked the river valleys, thereby creating a more sedentary base for society and allowing hierarchies to emerge. In the Sintashta culture elite status was displayed by the use of the chariot—a light platform carried on two spoked wheels and pulled by a pair of horses. Such a construction involved the investment of much skill, not only in carpentry but also in training horses to work as a pair. Some writers have argued that the appearance of chariots and defended settlements imply an increase in warfare. While this may be so, the chariots are probably more a reflection of an elite who required a way to display their skills in competition and in the leisure activity of the hunt. This does not, of course, exclude the possibility that the competitive tendencies of the chariot teams may sometimes have led them into physical conflict with neighbours.

69

Sufficient will have been said to show that in ecozones like the steppe region even comparatively slight or short-lived climate events can have major effects on the life-styles of pastoral societies leading to changes in social systems and encouraging people to move, usually westwards, to seek lusher pastures. Climate change, however, is only one of many factors that, interacting together, create history.

The Horse

Steppe societies have always been dependent on the horse, whose natural habitat was the open grassland. In the Early Holocene, following the Last Glaciation, various species of equine roamed the steppe. The more numerous and most powerful was *Equus caballus*, the ancestor of modern domesticated horses, short with stout legs, dun-coloured, and with a stiff upstanding mane. Its closest modern relative is the Przewalski's horse, a wild horse taken into protective captivity in the nineteenth century and now running free again in the nature reserves of Mongolia and Kazakhstan. Other species were *Equus hydruntinus*, a smaller beast once living in the Pontic–Caspian steppe which became extinct in the fourth millennium BC and *Equus hernionas*, the Onager, an ass-like equid native of the semi-arid land around the north and east side of the Caspian Sea.

As herbivores wild horses thrive on the steppe. They grow thick coats in the winter as protection from the severe cold and are able to kick their way through the snow cover to get to the grass beneath—a skill which sheep and cattle have failed to master—giving the horse the capability of surviving on the open steppe without human intervention. In the wild the natural social unit is the harem herd composed of a single stallion and his entourage of mares. They are accompanied by their foals and fillies until such time that the foals approach maturity, when they are driven off by the stallion. One of the mares emerges as the leader of the herd while the stallion is its protector. The young males driven from the harem herds join up to form bachelor bands until they can challenge and oust old stallions or lure away mares to join them.

Hunters and gatherers attempting to exist on the steppe would soon have learned the behaviour of wild horses sufficient to track them and arrange ambushes in the wooded river valleys where they came to drink. In this way the small *E. hernionas* and *E. hydruntinus* were soon hunted to extinction, leaving only the larger and faster *E. caballus* to be the main meat provider. In some of the late Mesolithic hunting groups in the Dniester region more than 50 per cent of the animal bones were of horse, and food refuse at some sites in the Caspian Depression was composed almost exclusively of equid remains. Without the wild horse a hunter-gatherer existence on the more open steppe, where other animals were scarce, would have been impossible.

3.5 Wild Przewalski's horses living in their natural habitat on the Mongolian steppe.

The practice of domesticating cattle, sheep, and goats began to spread to the Pontic steppe from farming communities in the west from about 5200 BC. The advantages of having a ready supply of milk and meat to hand was evident to neighbouring hunter-gatherers and soon they began to develop flocks and herds of their own by acquiring beasts in sufficient numbers to create breeding populations through exchange transactions or by raids. But on the harsh steppe cattle, sheep, and goats had to be provided with water and fodder during the long winter period. Hunters, used to the behaviour of wild horses, were well aware of the animal's superiority in being able to fend for itself. The advantages of domesticating horses would have been self-evident. The herd behaviour of cattle and horses is very similar and, since cattle were managed by controlling the lead cow, herders would have come to realize that all that was needed to begin to domesticate horses was to capture the lead mare. The rest of the herd would stay close and could be lured into contact with humans by offers of fodder. The stallion might object but he could be kept at bay for as long as he could tolerate the isolation.

The earliest evidence suggestive of horse domestication comes from the middle Volga region from burials dated about 4800 BC. Here offerings of horsemeat were treated in the same way as were offerings of beef and mutton placed in graves, the implication being that there was no perceived difference between the animals, all now being domesticated.

 71

More direct evidence of the human/horse relationship was discovered at a large herder settlement at Botai in the forest steppe region of northern Kazakhstan occupied between 3700 and 3000 BC. Of the huge quantity of animal bones recovered 99.9 per cent was of horse, the rest being from a range of wild animals. Although it remains a probability that a large number of the horses consumed at Botai were wild animals killed during the hunt, there is strong evidence that some horses had by this time been domesticated. Analysis showed that animal fats (lipids) found in the fabric of some of the pots used for cookery had come from milk, the implication being that docile mares were being kept near the settlement for milking. The process would have required that foals be taken to a tethered mare to encourage lactation before milking could begin: this had to be done up to six times a day. The discovery of dung within the settlement is another indication that some horses were being stabled. Complete carcasses were also sometimes found within the habitation area. Since it is highly unlikely that a whole beast would have been brought home from a hunt without first being jointed, this too supports the idea that there were domesticated horses in or near to the settlement. The evidence taken together is impressive and leaves little doubt that the Botai herders relied on at least some domesticated horses.

Archaeologists studying the horse bones have made one further observation of considerable significance. A careful investigation of the first premolar teeth from a sample of the horses showed that 26 per cent displayed patterns of wear of the kind most likely to have been made by a bit. If horses had been bitted, then the implication is that they were being ridden.

The Botai community emerges, then, as one whose entire existence was dependent on the horse. Not only did the domesticated herd provide the meat and milk so necessary for existence but the horses trained for riding would have greatly facilitated the hunting of wild horses as well as the rounding up of the domesticated herd at such times that that was necessary.

Botai was unusual in its near total dependence on horses. In other herding societies in which sheep and cattle were kept in some number, a man on horseback would have brought great advantages. Supported by a well-trained dog, he could have ranged over distances of up to 60 km a day caring for much larger flocks and herds. Suddenly the scale of the world had changed.

Exactly where and when horse riding began is impossible yet to say but it must have been somewhere on the Pontic–Caspian steppe, probably in the latter half of the fifth millennium. It was a huge step forward. The symbiotic relationship between horse and human was to become a decisive force in human history for the next seven millennia. It opened the way for two major advances: the use of teams of horses pull-

ing chariots, like those first developed at Sintashta about 2100 BC, which could be used in complex warfare, and the consequent creation of bands of horsemen working in concert with devastating effects. These nomad hordes were soon to dominate life on the steppe and threaten the sedentary communities of Europe.

The Late Bronze Age Continuum: 1800–1200 BC

The first two centuries of the second millennium saw regional differences gradually become less distinct across the steppe as increased connectivity led to the development of a continuum of broadly similar cultures. There were multiple causes for this but the development of horse riding and the growing importance of copper metallurgy were among the more important. The horse provided an impetus for greater mobility, stimulating interaction between widely dispersed communities, while a greatly increased demand for bronze tools and weapons led both to the extensive copper-mining operations at Kargaly in the south Urals near Orenburg and at Karaganda near Uspenskyi in central Kazakhstan and to the mining of tin in the Zeravshan in Uzbekistan. Since the two metals occurred only in restricted locations networks of exchange developed to facilitate distribution. Another factor added to the developing connectivity: the growing demand for raw materials and horses by the consuming states in Mesopotamia and Iran. For them the steppe zone had become a significant supplier.

In the period 1800–1200 BC two broad cultural zones can be distinguished: the Pontic–Caspian steppe from the Ural Mountains westwards to the Dnieper, was occupied by the Srubnaya (Timber-Grave) culture, while the Urals eastward to the Altai and Tien Shan Mountains, extending as far south as the Amu Darya river, were occupied by broadly similar cultural groupings known as the Andronovo continuum. In both regions a more settled way of life emerged. What led to this widespread shift in subsistence strategy is a matter of debate, but the change to a cooler and more arid climate between 2500 and 2000 BC may have been a deciding factor, driving communities to establish ownership of the tracts of marshland flanking rivers so necessary for the winter fodder that resulted in the setting up of permanent settlements nearby.

In the Pontic–Caspian steppe many hundreds of small Srubnaya settlements are known, extending across the steppe and forest steppe. A detailed study of a discrete landscape in the Samara valley, a tributary of the Volga, showed that the permanent settlement of Barinovka on the Samara was associated with a number of herding camps along a nearby tributary extending up to 12 km upstream but no further. This gives some idea of the size of the territory worked by this particular community.

It was for some time believed that the shift to permanent settlements was the result of the development of cereal growing as an adjunct to the herding economy.

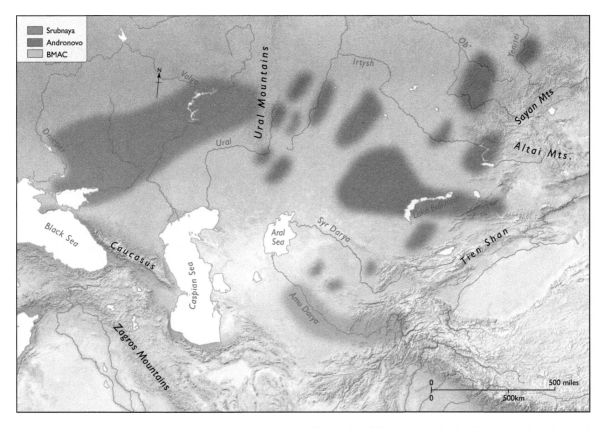

3.6 In the Late Bronze Age the nomadic peoples of the steppe can be divided into two broad cultural complexes, the Srubnaya in the Pontic–Caspian steppe and the Andronovo in Central Asia. The BMAC (Bactria Margiana Archaeological Complex) were sedentary communities who served as middlemen facilitating exchanges between the nomads and the developed states to the south.

But while cereals are found on some Srubnaya sites, especially in the more westerly part of the region, work in the Samara valley has shown that this was not invariably the case. The settlement site of Krasnosamarskoe, where occupation deposits were thoroughly analysed, showed that there was no trace of cultivated grain. Pits did, however, produce abundant remains of *Chenopodium* and *Amaranthus,* wild plants that yield high volumes of nutritious seeds. Gathering these from wild stands would have provided a welcome supplement to a diet of meat, milk, and blood. A study of human

3.7a/b (*Opposite*) In the microcosm of the Samara Oblast, on the Volga river, where intense fieldwork has been carried out, a dense pattern of Srubnaya settlements has been identified concentrated along the river valleys.

 74

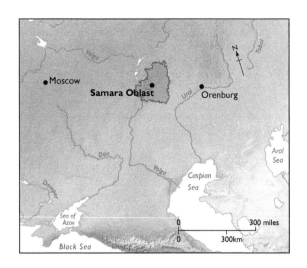

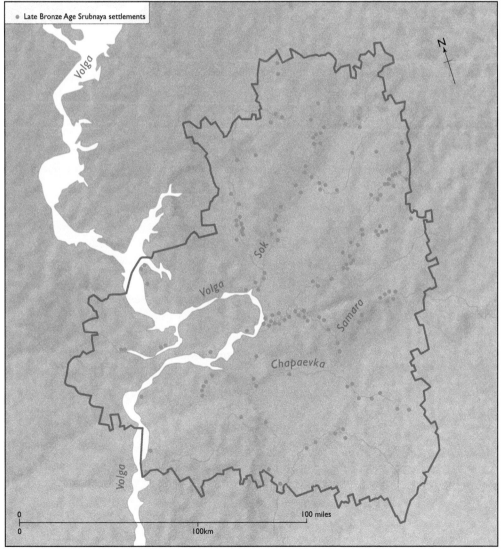

Late Bronze Age Srubnaya settlements

skeletons from twelve cemeteries in the Samara region showed that there was almost no dental decay present of the kind usually associated with cereal consumption, adding further support to the conclusions that here, in the eastern part of the Srubnaya zone, cereal growing was of little or no significance.

To the east of the Urals, in the region of the Andronovo continuum, permanent settlements representing communities of 50–250 individuals were widespread. Cattle, sheep or goats, and horses were reared providing the basic food needs, while cereals were present but seem to have been a comparably minor component of the diet. There was, however, much variation within the Andronovo continuum, which is hardly surprising given the size of the region and the different ecozones represented within it.

Standing back from the mass of archaeological detail reflecting life on the steppe throughout the second millennium one is impressed by the broad similarity of lifestyle that had developed between the Altai and the Danube. It was a distinctive steppe culture easily distinguishable from the sedentary states of the south and the hunter-gatherers of the forest zone to the north. Although communities now lived in permanent settlements, the well-being of the flocks and herds dominated existence, the horse providing the mobility to husband them. There may well have been small-scale folk movements caused by population pressure but no major migratory events can be detected, nor is there much evidence in the burial record for great differences in wealth or power. It was from this level playing field, in more senses than one, that the predatory nomad warrior elites soon to dominate the steppe were to emerge.

The Final Bronze Age and the Roots of Change: 1200–850 BC

The comparative stability of the lifestyle enjoyed by the Andronovo and Srubnaya communities began to be disrupted around 1200 BC by another change in the climate as increasing aridity gripped the land. The effects were widespread, extending from Central Asia to the east Mediterranean. In the steppe the decline of the forests in the river valleys combined with increased annual flooding disrupted settlement patterns and economic strategies. In the Samara valley the number of settlements declined with a greater concentration now appearing in the lower parts of the valley where woodland survived. At the same time the communities began to cultivate grain—wheat, barley, and millet—reflecting the increase of cereal growing now evident across the steppe.

It has been suggested that another consequence of the increasing aridity was that flocks and herds, instead of being restricted to grasslands within easy reach of the settlement, were now driven to more remote pastures in order to enable the livestock population to expand. This may, in some regions, have created competition for territory, resulting in conflict and possibly outright warfare. These processes, developing at different rates in different regions, led to an increase in transhumant pastoralism across much of the steppe region.

At its extreme eastern limit the Andronovo culture reached the Minusinsk Basin, an area of elevated steppe surrounded by mountains, the eastern Sayan to the north, the western Sayan to the south, and the Kuznetskiy Alatau and Abakan ranges to the west. The basin was formed by the upper reaches of the Yenisei River but also includes the Chulym River, a tributary of the Ob. It was a favoured environment— fertile and protected by mountains.

The settlement history of the region was continuous from the Andronovo period to the succeeding Karasuk period that began in the fourteenth century BC and lasted to the middle of the ninth century. The change between the Andronovo and Karasuk cultures was gradual, with many of the Andronovo traditions continuing into the later period. The transition coincided with the onset of a more humid and cooler climate which led to a much lusher vegetation cover that improved and extended areas of grazing. This had two effects: flocks and herds increased in size and more complex patterns of seasonal transhumance developed with flocks of sheep and goats being taken away from the lowland steppe to fatten on the mountain pastures. Horses also increased in number, in part to manage the more extensive systems of husbandry. That horse riding was widely practised is reflected in the number of distinctive three-holed sidepieces from the bridle now appearing in the archaeological record.

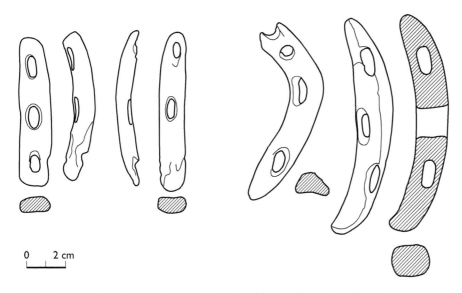

3.8 Bone cheek pieces from bridles of the Karasuk period found in the Minusinsk Basin.

 77

Alongside the expanding productivity came a steep rise in population, some estimates suggesting a tenfold increase over the 500-year period. The population increase led to a more hierarchical social structure expressed in the arrangement and elaboration of tombs. The elite were buried in stone-built cists set in large circular burial enclosures up to 100 m in diameter. While the grave goods were still comparatively modest—pottery vessels, food offerings, and bronze knives—the social effort required to build the large grave structures marked them out as belonging to individuals of importance. The burial evidence also showed that society was strongly patriarchal.

The enclosed Minusinsk Basin, well protected and increasingly fertile, provides a microcosm of the changes taking place in favoured areas in and around the Altai–Sayan Mountains in the Final Bronze Age (*c*.1200–850 BC). Similar developments can be seen in other steppe regions, notably in eastern Kazakhstan, but the enclosed upland environments tended to intensify them. In the Minusinsk Basin, in the ninth century BC, the economic and social changes underway during the Kasusuk period culminated in the creation of a very different kind of society, known archaeologically as the Tager culture, one in which horse-riding elites began to dominate life and to change the course of history. The significance of these developments for the emergence of the Scythians will be considered in the next chapter.

In the Pontic steppe the effects of climate change are also apparent. Here, in the Late Bronze Age up to the twelfth century BC the climate had been moist and cool, allowing for a growth in population on the steppe and expansion onto the more open grassland with the scattered communities living in permanent settlements. Two

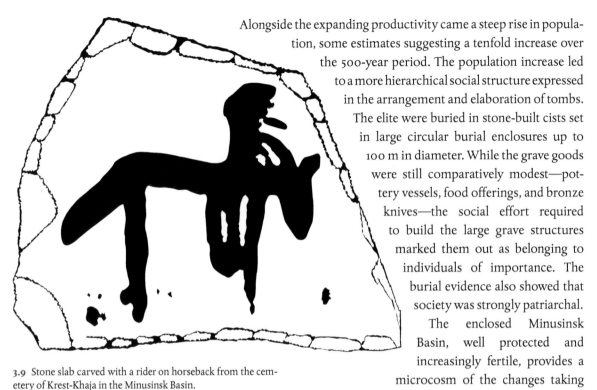

3.9 Stone slab carved with a rider on horseback from the cemetery of Krest-Khaja in the Minusinsk Basin.

3.10 (*Opposite*) The Yenisei River threads through the Sayan Mountains linking expanses of steppe. In the Minusinsk Valley many settlements and cemeteries of the Late Bronze Age Karasuk culture have been identified, indicating a dense population.

 78

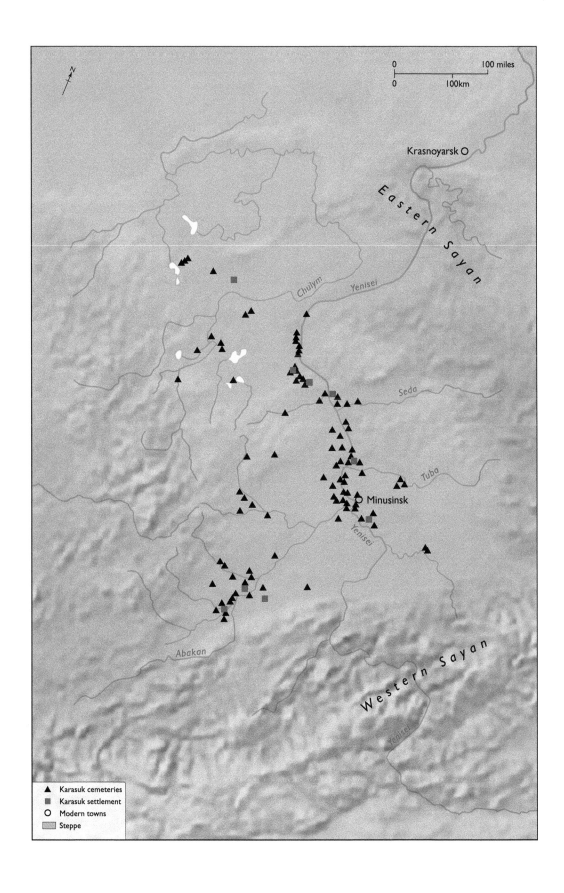

Krasnoyarsk O

E a s t e r n   S a y a n

Chulym

Yenisei

Seda

Tuba

O Minusinsk

Yenisei

Abakan

W e s t e r n   S a y a n

Yenisei

0 _____ 100 miles
0 _____ 100km

N

▲ Karasuk cemeteries
■ Karasuk settlement
O Modern towns
▢ Steppe

3.11 The elaborate burials of the Karasuk culture indicate the emergence of an elite. These graves are from the cemetery at Anchil Chon in the Minusinsk Valley.

broadly contemporary cultural groups can be defined archaeologically, the Srubnaya culture occupying the region east of the river Don and the Sabatinovka culture located largely between the Don and the Danube. A major change in climate becomes apparent in the eleventh century when the Pontic–Caspian region and the Kazakh steppe began to experience a far more arid climate manifest in the fall in the level of the Black Sea and Caspian Sea and a significant shift to the north in the ecological boundaries of the steppe zone. The overall effect of this change was that the comparatively settled economy based on cattle breeding and agriculture gave way to a more nomadic style of cattle breeding; horse riding became increasingly important; and, over time, the population declined. The communities of the Belozerka culture, which followed the Sabatinovka culture in the late eleventh century in the region between the Don and the Danube, abandoned the open steppe for the river valleys and coastal region. Based on the number of known settlements it has been suggested that there may have been a tenfold decrease in population.

3.12a/b (*Opposite*) Settlement on the Pontic steppe. The upper map shows the situation in the fourteenth to twelfth century BC, when two cultural groups can be distinguished. The lower map shows the situation in the twelfth to tenth century BC, when the population seems to have considerably diminished, moving away from the open steppe to concentrate in the river valleys.

 80

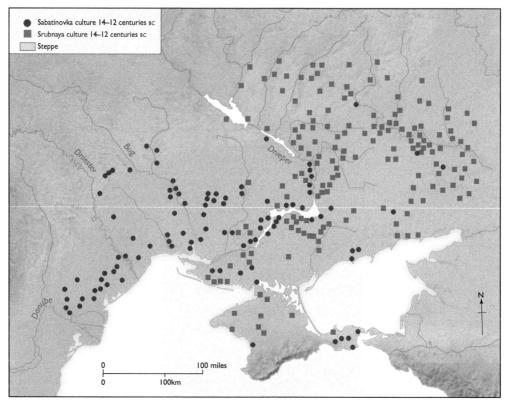

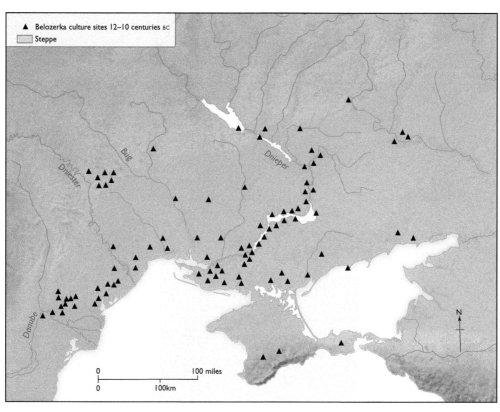

Broadly contemporary changes in climate across Eurasia had varied effects in different regions. While in the Minusinsk Basin the population was increasing dramatically, in the Pontic–Caspian it was decreasing at about the same rate. This was a period of destabilization with communities everywhere attempting to adjust to changing environmental conditions and to the consequent demographic imbalances.

The New Dynamic

Different communities living in the great expanse of the steppe developed a broadly similar culture based on the care of flocks and herds rather than on the intensive growing of cereals. The constraints of the landscape determined the specific strategies adopted but changes in climate, even quite small changes, forced people to adapt, often quite quickly. By the beginning of the first millennium BC a greater degree of mobility was apparent throughout the steppe, with transhumance playing an increasing part in daily life. Horses and horsemanship accordingly became more prominent. In the more ecologically favoured regions, such as the upland valleys and plains of eastern Kazakhstan and in the Altai–Sayan region, these changes encouraged a rise in population, putting strains on society and requiring new systems to evolve to alleviate the tensions now being felt. The steppe gradient—the physical reality that the grass was always greener in the west—introduced another dynamic. It was the interaction of these complex factors coming together at the beginning of the first millennium BC that created the conditions for the emergence of highly mobile predatory nomad hordes. Out of this melee the Scythians were born.

4

ENTER THE
PREDATORY NOMADS

THE brief period of two centuries, from the mid ninth to the mid seventh century, saw a dramatic transformation in steppe society. At the beginning of the period a patchwork of different communities, culturally rooted in their traditional territories, characterized the vast steppe corridor. Variations in ecology and climate affected different regions in different ways, in some facilitating growth in population, in others nudging populations to modify their pastoral strategies. All these communities are historically anonymous, known only by the names ascribed to them by archaeologists. By the end of the period the archaeological evidence suggests that bands of predatory horsemen were ranging widely over considerable areas. Historical texts speak of Kimmerians on the Pontic steppe with Scythians thundering in from Central Asia to oust the Kimmerians from their homeland and to rampage through Asia Minor. To untangle what was going on during these two crucial centuries is a challenge, not least because there are considerable gaps in the evidence and reliable radiocarbon data are few but, that said, it is possible to examine in detail the cultural transformations underway in certain regions and to construct at least the skeleton of a narrative that embraces the archaeological evidence while making sense of the brief historical references.

One matter of nomenclature needs to be clarified at the start: the use of the name Scythian. As we have seen (above, pp. 30–5) the ancient Greek writers used it specifically to refer to people who were settled on the Pontic steppe and whom they believed came from the east. They also knew of many other nomadic groups by name which they distinguished from the Scythians. Archaeologists, on the other hand,

have tended to be impressed by the cultural similarities spanning huge areas from the Altai Mountains to the Great Hungarian Plain. In particular they note similar styles of elite burials, the use of the bow and arrow in fighting from horseback, and a highly distinctive animal art—three characteristics which some Russian archaeologists have referred to as the Scythian triad. Others have preferred simply to stress the similarities between the culture of the Scythians of the Pontic steppe and that of the communities of the Altai–Sayan region, referring to the cultural continuum as the Scythian–Siberian culture. These nomenclatures nicely focus on the central issue: just how connected did the culture of the steppe become in the period from the mid ninth to mid seventh century? Do the similarities we perceive represent, as many would believe, a highly mobile situation with massive displacements of horse-riding hordes spreading rapidly across the grasslands, jostling each other for position? These are the issues we shall address in this chapter.

One River, Two Innovative Communities

The valley of the Yenisei River, which rises in the eastern Sayan mountains and flows across the vastness of Siberia to the Arctic Ocean, can fairly claim to be the birthplace of the horse-riding hordes that were to dominate the steppe. Threading its way between the mountain ranges the river provided a corridor of communication between the different communities occupying its basin and upland plateaus where rich grasslands flourished and where the enclosing mountain slopes provided summer pastures for the transhumant population and their animals. Two regions are of crucial importance to the debate, the Minusinsk Basin which has already been mentioned (above, pp. 77–9) and, further upriver, the Uyuk hollow in the region of Tuva close to the northern border of Mongolia. The significance of the Minusinsk Basin is that intensive archaeological research allows the social and economic development of the region to be traced throughout the first millennium BC. The Tuva region is less well known but the thorough excavation of aristocratic burials at Arzhan, the earliest dating to about 800 BC, offers a vivid insight into the coercive power of the elite at an early stage in the development of a rigid hierarchical system.

The study of pollen samples recovered from the Minusinsk Valley and the Uyuk hollow in the Tuva region showed that the cool conditions which had characterized the Karasuk culture started to change in the ninth century as the temperature began steadily to rise, while at the same time the climate became increasingly more

4.1 (*Opposite*) The Yenisei River flows through the Sayan Mountains of southern Siberia. The Uyuk Hollow in Tuva where the cemetery of Arzhan was located was upriver from the Minusinsk Valley, where burial mounds of the Tagar culture proliferate.

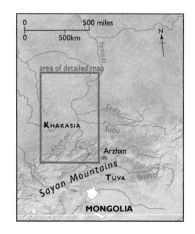

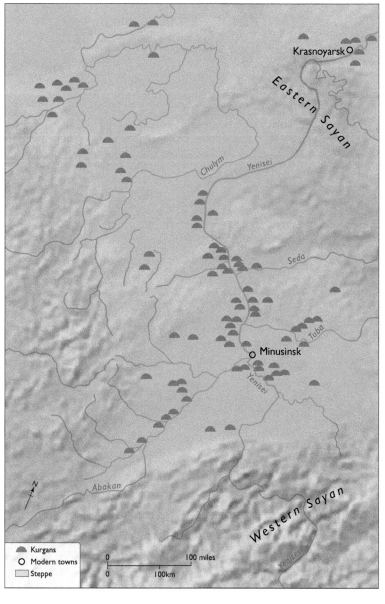

area of detailed map

Khakasia

Seda

Tuba

Abakan

Arzhan

Sayan Mountains

Tuva

Yenisei

MONGOLIA

0   500 miles

0   500km

N

Yenisei

Krasnoyarsk O

Eastern Sayan

Chulym   Yenisei

Seda

Tuba

O Minusinsk

Yenisei

Abakan

N

Western Sayan

Yenisei

Kurgans

O Modern towns

Steppe

0   100 miles

0   100km

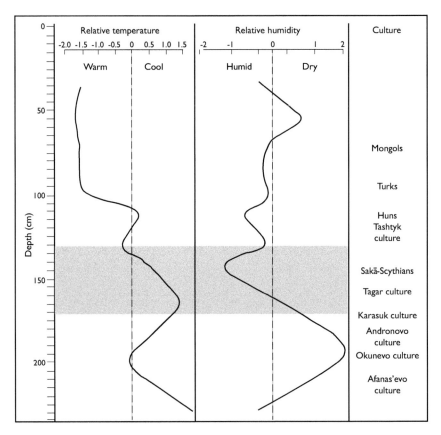

4.2 Palaeoclimatic chart showing the onset of warmer and more humid conditions at the beginning of the first millennium BC.

humid. These changes heralded an improvement of the grassland resources, generating a higher biomass capable of supporting a growing population, and mark the beginning of the archaeologically defined Tagar culture, which developed from the long-established Karasuk culture. Four phases of the Tagar culture are recognized, named after individual sites: Bainovo, late 10th–8th centuries; Podgornova, 8th–6th centuries; Saragash, 6th–3rd centuries; and Tes, 2nd century BC–1st century AD. The changes between the phases are comparatively slight and represent the gradual evolution of indigenous communities rather than significant influxes of new people.

The funerary monuments provide the bulk of the archaeological data. Burials were placed in rectangular pits set within square enclosures bounded by stone slabs and covered with mounds. The graves were originally stone cists, a characteristic of the preceding Karasuk culture, but were soon replaced with log-lined chambers

 88

roofed with multiple layers of logs. The enclosures within which the grave pits were set tended to become larger over time and concomitantly the number of burials placed in each pit increased. The barrows covering the burials also increased in size, occasionally reaching up to 20 metres in height. By the sixth century BC social stratification had led to the considerable elaboration of some of the burials. The Bolshoi Salbykskii mound, in the Salbyk valley, was 11 metres high, while the enclosure wall contained huge vertical stone slabs standing 6 metres in height, each weighing up to 50 tons. The construction of such a mound implies that the lineage of the deceased wielded considerable coercive power.

The grave goods buried with the dead in the Tagar period attest an assured and skilled bronze casting tradition rooted in the Late Bronze Age. Prominent among the offerings were weapons: bows and arrows (represented now by bronze arrow-

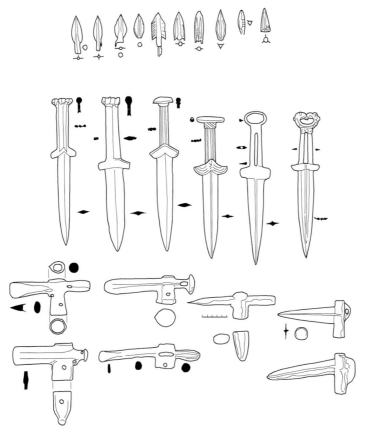

4.3 A selection of offensive weapons of the Tagar period from the Minusinsk Valley—bilobate and trilobate arrowheads, daggers, and battleaxes—all types which became widespread among the Scythians.

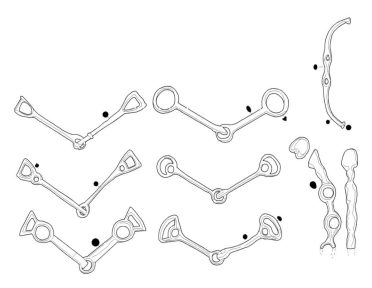

4.4 Tagar period bridle fittings, bits, and cheek pieces from the Minusinsk Valley.

heads), daggers, and battleaxes. The arrowheads are of various forms, both bilobate and trilobite, the former being the earlier. Daggers, with handle and blade cast as one, often have butterfly-shaped guards and flat or ring-shaped pommels. The battleaxes were cast with short tubes, set at right angles to the blade, to facilitate the attachment of the handle. Other items found in graves include ring-handled knives, bronze cauldrons, circular bronze mirrors, bone combs, and a variety of wooden vessels.

Horse gear features large in the repertoire. In about 800 BC the bone cheek pieces of the Karasuk type were replaced by bronze cheek pieces with two or three perforations for rein attachments. Bits were two-linked with ends terminating in rings or stirrup-shaped openings and there was also a variety of strap junctions and decorative pendants. The amount of horse gear recovered and the numerous rock carvings depicting horses leave little doubt that riding now played a significant part in the life of the community.

Finally there is the animal art which pervades Tagar culture: isolated animals cast in bronze for attachment to fabric or wood, animals integrated with the casting of other objects like mirrors, rattles, or battleaxes, and petroglyphs carved on the stone slabs retaining the burial mounds. The animals depicted include felines (possibly snow leopards), argali sheep with recurved horns often standing in characteristic pose with feet together, and recumbent deer with feet tucked beneath the body, head raised, and antlers splaying out behind. Less often there are depictions of horses,

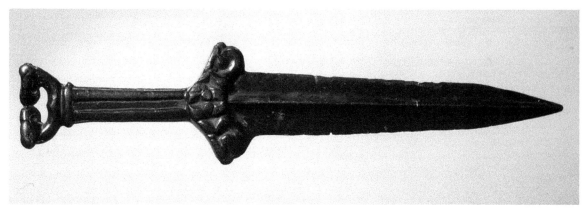

4.5 (*Top left*) Finial terminal in the form of an argali ram dating to the Tagar period. Collected in the Krasnoyarsk region by G. F. Müller in 1735.

4.6 (*Top right*) The head of a bronze battleaxe from a Tagar period kurgan near Mount Barsuchikha, Krasnoyarsk region.

4.7 (*Bottom*) Dagger of the Tagar period from the Krasnoyarsk region. The pommel is in the form of two wolves' heads nose to nose.

4.8 Bronze plaque in the form of a recumbent stag from the Minusinsk region. Collected by V. V. Radlov in 1863.

boars, and birds. It is a rich repertoire created by people who regularly observed these animals in their natural habitats and were confident enough to distil the essentials of a beast into semi-stylistic form befitting the animal's place in their belief system. This kind of animal art is found at its earliest on the famous deer stones—standing stones elaborately carved with deer motifs—that are found in the Sayan and Altai Mountains extending into northern Mongolia, where they are dated to the Final Bronze Age (c.1300–700 BC). That the deer stones sometimes depict belts with weapons attached suggests that they might have been made to commemorate a particular person. If so, the deer carved on them could represent body tattoos proclaiming status, like those found on the human bodies preserved in the later Altai burials. An alternative explanation might be that the stags symbolize the departing soul: there is ample room for speculation. What is important to the present debate is that the lively animal art of the Tagar culture, which quickly spreads across the steppe and is so prevalent in the

4.9 Late Bronze Age deer stone from Ushkin Uver, Hövsgöl Aimag, Mongolia. The stone represents a warrior. His weapons are shown attached to his belt, indicated by two horizontal lines towards the bottom of the pillar.

art of the Pontic steppe Scythians, originates in the Bronze Age culture of the Altai–Sayan Mountains and is most likely to be a manifestation of a deeply rooted shamanistic belief system. A petroglyph, clearly of a shaman, has been found carved on a rock at Georgievskaya in a Tagar period context.

The well-researched archaeological record of the Minusinsk Valley provides clear evidence of a community developing, little disturbed by influences from outside, over a period of a millennium and a half. By the ninth century BC a change in climate to wetter and warmer conditions had increased the holding capacity of the land. This resulted in an increase in popula-

4.10 Two petroglyphs of the Tagar period depicting a shaman, (*left*) from Georgievskaya and (*right*) from Boyaru in the Minusinsk Valley.

 93

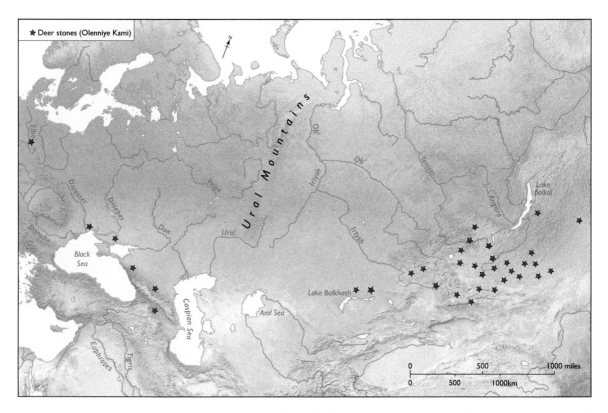

4.11 Deer stones originate in Mongolia where they occur in some number, but examples are found extending westwards across the steppe.

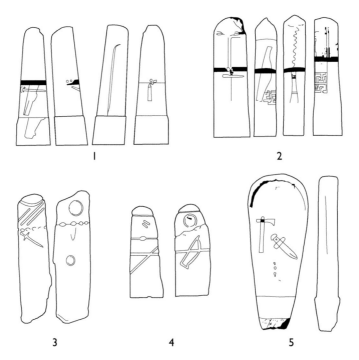

4.12 Simplified deer stones from across Eurasia: 1 Olbia; 2 Belogradec, Bulgaria; 3 Sosnovka, Tuva; 4 Gumarevo, Orenburg region; 5 Novo Mordova, middle Danube region.

tion and a more mobile form of pastoralism that led in turn to the development of a strongly hierarchical society with powerful leaders able to command the allegiance and resources of increasingly large groups of followers. Invigorating it all was the horse, providing mobility, speed, and the facility for men to work together as a horde: humans had learnt from their horses how to become herd animals.

The Chieftains of Arzhan

Further up the Yenisei River system, 60 km to the north-west of the city of Kyzyl, a minor tributary of the Yenisei, the River Uyuk, winds its way across a lush upland plateau. The marshy river valley with its tall grass and reeds provides ample winter fodder for flocks and herds while the surrounding mountain slopes offer fresh grass in the spring and early summer. These ideal conditions have long provided a congenial environment for pastoral communities dependent for their well-being on flocks of sheep and, of course, horses. The attraction of the Uyuk Valley to past communities is demonstrated by the large number of kurgans scattered throughout the landscape. The distribution is particularly dense near the village of Arzhan, where two of these kurgans have now been excavated, Arzhan 1 by the veteran archaeologist M. Gryaznov in 1971–4 and Arzhan 2, 9 km away, by a Russian–German team in 2001–3. It is no exaggeration to say that these two excavations have totally transformed our ideas about Scythian origins.

Arzhan 1 was a massive kurgan, 110 metres in diameter and up to 4 metres in height. It was enclosed by a stone wall and covered by large stone slabs forming a platform. The complex internal structure focused around a central grave pit 5 metres square, set within a grave chamber 8 metres square. The grave pit, lined and roofed with logs, contained the bodies of an old man and a younger woman placed in wooden coffins and once arrayed with gold, turquoise, and coloured fabrics. The grave had been robbed at some time in antiquity leaving only fragments as clues to its former splendour. The bodies had originally been laid on a thick bedding composed of fifteen to twenty horse tails. Within the grave chamber, and arranged around the central grave pit, were eight human burials, presumably retainers sacrificed to accompany the dead leader into the afterlife. At the eastern end of the chamber were six of his horses, their bridles decorated in gold.

Around the central grave chamber a complex timber structure had been built. It was constructed of horizontally laid larch logs from trees 100 years old, carefully trimmed with their bark removed and arranged to create seventy or so roughly rectangular chambers. Within them were placed a range of offerings, most notably about 150 horses, many of them with saddle and bridles. The horses were arranged

95

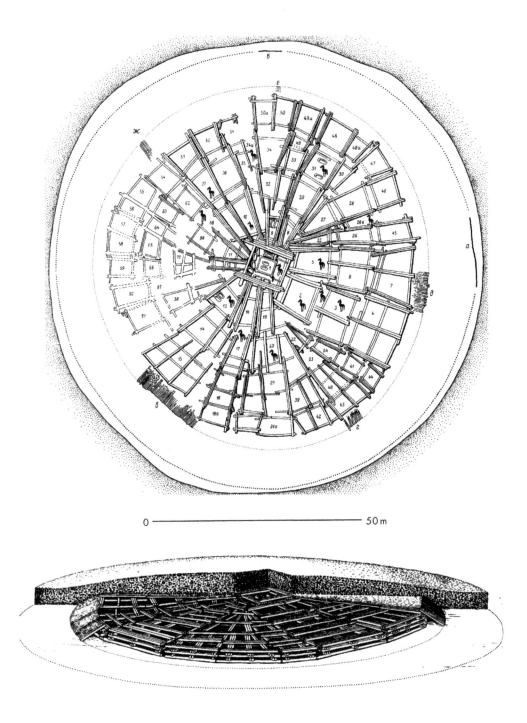

0 ——————————————— 50 m

4.13 Plan and section of the Arzhan 1 kurgan dating to the late ninth century. The grave pit in the centre was surrounded by a radially planned timber structure and the whole was covered by a thick layer of rubble.

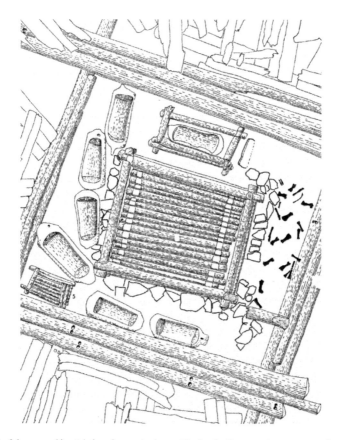

4.14 Detail of the central burial chamber at Arzhan 1. The log-built grave pit containing the king and his female partner was surrounded by burials of his retainers and his favourite horses.

4.15 The radial timber structure at Arzhan 1 was built of larch logs. It was well preserved at the time of excavation.

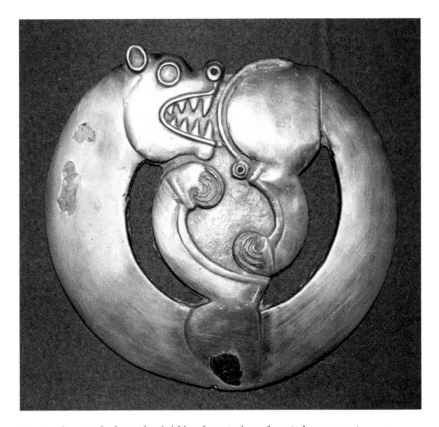

4.16 Bronze plaque in the form of curled feline from Arzhan 1 (late ninth century BC).

in groups of between fifteen and thirty; some were accompanied by human bodies, probably of the equerries who in life had looked after them. Other deposits included weapons and standards.

A careful study of the cultural attributes of the horse gear suggested that the horses had been brought in from surrounding territories, often from a considerable distance away, the implication being that the dead chieftain commanded the allegiance of people across a very large area. In other words he may well have been the leader of a warrior horde. The sheer size of the burial mound also reflects his coercive power. Some 6,000 tree trunks were needed to build the timber part of his monument requiring an estimated 9–10,000 person days of work. If the project had been spread over a month it would have involved 300 people to complete this aspect alone. In addition, the 2.5 metre high surrounding wall and the stone paved topping had also to be provided. Here, then, was buried a man of considerable status with coercive power.

The construction of the great mound was careful and deliberate. Some observers have suggested that it embodies a vision of the universe, with the plan of the timber structures representing the radiating rays of the sun. There were certainly differences in treatment between the eastern and western parts. To the east about 300 large rounded boulders had been arranged in a crescent shape, and more horses were found in the eastern sector of the mound than in the western part. Much has been made of the number of horse burials, with the suggestion that the actual numbers may have had a symbolic significance, each horse representing a day. It is difficult to validate such theories but we can at least be reasonably certain that many more levels of meaning were embedded in the great structure than are apparent to the modern observer.

And then there was the funeral feast, the detritus of which was deposited in 300 small stone enclosures arranged outside of the kurgan. In all, some 300 horses, together with cattle, sheep, and goats, were slaughtered, though it is not known whether this represents a single event or a succession of feasts spread over a period of time. To proclaim the activity for all to see the skins of many of the horses with their lower legs and heads still attached were set up on timber structures nearby as though the beasts were still alive.

There is one final detail to note. A deer stone, similar to those found across northern Mongolia, had been set up on the top of the mound. Only the bottom part survived depicting a belt from which hung a ring-headed knife and a whetstone with a frieze of animals below, including deer and pigs. Its presence is a reminder that the Arzhan community shared beliefs with their southern neighbours on the Mongolian steppe.

4.17 The lower part of a deer stone was found at Arzhan 1. It shows a belt from which hang a dagger and a whetstone. Below is a frieze of deer and pigs.

 99

The astonishing discovery of Arzhan 1, with its very close similarities to later Scythian burials on the Pontic steppe, immediately generated a lively debate centring on its date. Initial uncertainties have now been resolved through a systematic programme of radiocarbon dating showing that the kurgan was probably constructed in the late ninth century, thus preceding the earliest Scythian burials on the Pontic steppe by a century or so. The implications are considerable and we will return them again later (pp. 104–5).

Arzhan 2 was slightly smaller than Arzhan 1, being 80 metres in diameter and 2 metres high. The central area beneath the mound was found to be occupied by two square chambers of the kind that could have held graves. Both had been dug into by robbers sometime in the past, but the complete absence of anything that could have come from a disturbed burial such as fragments of bone or small items that had been missed was puzzling. One possible explanation, suggested by the excavator, is that these central grave pits had been constructed as a decoy to convince would-be robbers that someone had got there before them. This suggestion is to some extent supported by the discovery of an intact and exceptionally rich burial chamber placed well off centre. The chamber was rectangular, 5 m by 4.5 m, built of horizontally laid logs and lined internally with felt. On the floor were placed two bodies, a man and a woman, richly adorned with gold ornaments and gold appliqué work once attached to their clothes. In all, some 5,700 gold items were recovered. The man was accompanied by a dagger and two ring-handled knives, while nearby lay his bow in a sheath, a quiver of arrows, and a battleaxe. The woman carried a knife and a miniature gold cauldron. The amount of gold and precious stones, including turquoise, amber, garnet, and malachite, and the quality of the animal art into which the gold was worked leave little doubt of the exceptionally high status of the deceased and his partner.

The mound also covered other burials. About 10 m from the royal burial was a small timber chamber containing a wooden saddle and a set of elaborately decorated horse gear symbolic of a horse burial. Elsewhere within the mound fifteen human burials were found in stone-built cists. Most were in individual graves, but one grave contained two men and three women. All the women's graves were placed in the south-western half of the kurgan, while the men lay in the north-eastern part. This echoes the placing of the two bodies in the royal tomb. One young woman had been killed by several blows to the head using a sharp-pointed battleaxe. In the south-eastern part of the mound a large pit, 8 m by 3 m, was found containing fourteen horses placed with their legs folded beneath the bodies and their heads facing west, all provided with their harness. The pit had been dug after the mound had been finished, but the fact that the stone covering of the mound had been carefully restored above suggests that the horse burials represented a late stage in the burial ritual rather than

4.18 The kurgan of Arzhan 2 during excavation.

4.19 The undisturbed burial at Arzhan 2. The chief was accompanied by a female companion. Both were elaborately dressed, their clothes adorned with small gold attachments. Their regalia, including a gold decorated gorytos, was laid around them.

an isolated later incident. The material found in the Arzhan 2 mound is typologically later than that found in Arzhan 1. This is confirmed by dendrological and radiocarbon dating, which suggests that the burial took place towards the end of the seventh century.

The two burials, nearly two centuries apart in date, reflect the opulence of the community commanding the Uyuk Valley. The readiness of the elite to conspicuously consume in their burial rites their acquired wealth—gold and precious stones, items of high craftsmanship, and horses— reflects, in large part, the productivity of their immediate homeland. But it also implies that they had established authority over a much wider territory enabling them to call on distant resources. Rare raw materials such as turquoise, amber, and gold could be acquired through systems of exchange, but the great number of fine stallions decked out in their flamboyant gear ridden from far afield to Arzhan 1 to be sacrificed in honour of the deceased warlord speak of more than just trade. Here, surely, we are seeing something of the networks of social obligation now at work—people sending, or bringing, gifts of great symbolic value to the graveside to acknowledge their subservience to an overlord and his lineage.

While there is much that we will never know about the social dynamics of the nomadic communities of the Altai–Sayan region—the names of the tribes, the events which structured their lives, and the true extent of their mobility—the archaeological evidence allows certain broad deductions to be made. The improvement in the climate at the beginning of the first millennium, increasing the biomass of the valleys and plateaus, released a new energy in society that resulted in the rise of a warrior elite, recognizable in the archaeological record by their rich graves, but in real life most likely expressed in their ability to lead, to raid, and to enter into alliances with distant elites. This was a time of great mobility, with horsemanship becoming a dominant way of life. Weapons were now common: the bow and arrow for engagements at a distance and the vicious battleaxe and the short sword for close hand-to-hand fighting. Pervading it all was an animal art, deeply rooted in earlier Bronze Age traditions, manifest now in decorative attachments for clothes and horse harness, moulded extensions to the handles of knives and daggers, petroglyphs carried on the deer-stone markers, and tattoos on the human body. The flying stag, the perched argali ram, and the curled feline were everywhere to be seen.

By the end of the ninth century BC warrior lords, like the individual interred at Arzhan 1, were being buried in grand ceremonies involving large assemblies of people willing to invest their effort in the construction of the kurgan and thereafter to indulge in lavish feasting. The burial of a leader was a spectacle designed to display, for all to see, the might of the clan. The greater the consumption in labour and material resource, the greater its power. The burial ceremonies were occasions to restate alliances. But they were also times when aspiring leaders could proclaim intended expeditions and exploits to outshine the achievements of the deceased. It was in this way that ambition escalated and the horde was spurred on to greater mobility.

Meanwhile on the Pontic Steppe ...

We saw in the previous chapter how the Pontic, Caspian, and Kazakh steppe began to experience a more arid climate from the beginning of the eleventh century BC and how, in the region between the Don and the Danube, populations seem to have declined as communities began to concentrate in the well-watered river valleys, where cattle breeding and agriculture could be practised, leaving the open steppe for more sporadic seasonal pastoralism. Those communities living in the Pontic region in the eleventh and tenth centuries are referred to archaeologically as the Belozerka culture and are believed to have developed from the preceding Late Bronze Age cultures.

At the end of the tenth or early in the ninth century BC it is possible to recognize a distinct cultural change that heralds the beginning of the Chernogorovka culture, which dates to c.900–750 BC. This develops into the Novocherkassk culture, which probably lasts to the middle of the seventh century. The distinction between the two is based largely on changing styles of horse gear. Some archaeologists have argued that the two 'cultures' were broadly contemporary and that the stylistic differences in their artefact sets reflect differences in status or ethnicity, but recent work has suggested that they are broadly different phases in cultural development with only a slight chronological overlap. What all agree is that these archaeologically defined cultures are pre-Scythian, that is, they represent a significant development of the Pontic steppe communities before the arrival of the historically attested Scythians in the second half of the seventh century. As we have seen (above, pp. 30–1) the classical sources refer to those who inhabited the Pontic steppe before the arrival of the Scythians as Kimmerians. If we accept the generalization that the Chernogorovka and Novocherkassk cultures are the archaeological manifestation of the Kimmerians, two questions then arise: do the cultural changes which characterize the beginning of the Chernogorovka culture mark the influx of the Kimmerians and, if so, where did these people come from?

Archaeological evidence can seldom provide precise answers to questions of this kind but a careful analysis of material finds and of the behaviour patterns preserved in burials allows three distinct cultural threads to be distinguished. That there is a strong indigenous tradition rooted in the Belozerka culture need occasion no surprise. Pottery styles and burial traditions owe much to what had gone before. But superimposed upon this are two alien traditions, one coming from the Kuban culture of the Caucasus region, the other coming from much further to the east from the Altai–Sayan. The Kuban influence is largely restricted to the appearance of similar types of mace head and bimetallic daggers in the two regions and need imply no more than exchange between neighbours, but the impact of Altai–Sayan culture can hardly be explained in this way and almost certainly implies the influx of new people arriving in the ninth century. Among the new items of material culture introduced are distinctive daggers, horse gear (including bits with stirrup-shaped terminals), characteristic arrowheads, stelae carved in the manner of deer stones, and animal art. The simplest explanation for these new traditions is that bands of nomadic horsemen from eastern Kazakhstan or the Altai–Sayan region

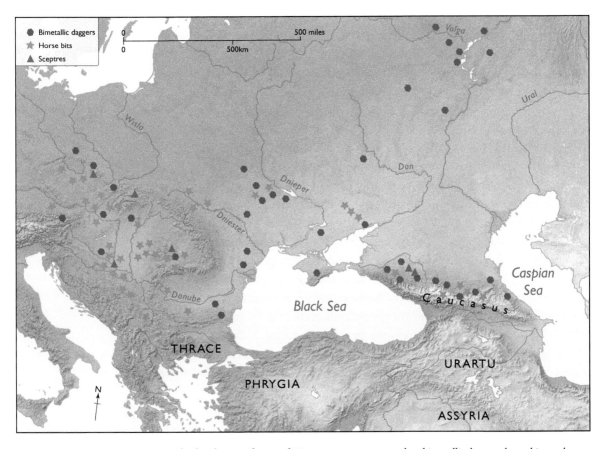

4.20 The distribution of items of Kimmerian equipment such as bimetallic daggers, horse bits, and sceptre tops show the extent of Kimmerian settlement and influence from the Kuban to central Europe.

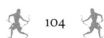

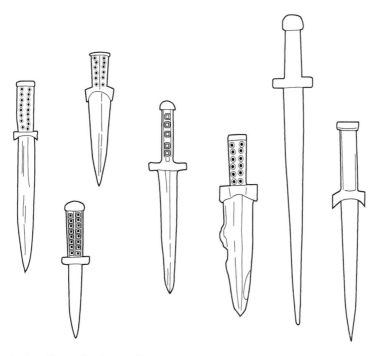

4.21 A selection of bimetallic daggers of Kimmerian type.

spread westwards across the steppe during the ninth and eighth centuries, some of them arriving on the Pontic steppe and establishing their authority over the local population. To what extent the incoming elites maintained their separate identity is unknown, but Herodotus' story of how, when later the Kimmerians came under pressure from Scythians moving into the Pontic region, there was discord between their kings and the common people, hints at a hierarchic divide perhaps based on ethnicity.

If this scenario is correct, it means that during the ninth and eighth century movements of warrior nomads from the mountain region of eastern Central Asia to the west took place episodically. The driving forces were, no doubt, varied: population growth, the lure of better pastures in the west, and the ambition of these aspiring to power would all have contributed. While the distances were not inconsiderable—some 3,000 km from the Altai to the Black Sea—to a practised horseman used to the steppe this could have been covered in a matter of a few months. The details of these early migrations will remain unknown but the reality is likely to have been complex, with some bands moving fast over long distances, others stopping on the way to establish themselves in favoured locations. Battles will have been fought, the winners

becoming the dominant elite and imposing the names of their lineages on the local populations. Those who became the Kimmerians on the Pontic steppe were probably just one of the warrior bands on the move. The next to arrive in the area were known to the Greeks as Scythians.

The Kimmerians in History

Herodotus provides a simple account of the Kimmerians at the time when they were attacked by incoming Scythians towards the end of the eighth century BC (above, pp. 30–1). His description, based on oral tradition more than two centuries old, offers three pieces of information. First, the Scythians crossed the Volga and took over a territory on the Pontic steppe once occupied by the Kimmerians. Second, uncertainty arose among Kimmerians about how to respond to the Scythians, the Royal tribe wishing to stay and fight, the rest of the people pressing to move on. It was resolved by a battle on the Dnieper at which the Royal tribe was annihilated. Third, some Kimmerians fled into Asia Minor, travelling along the shore of the Black Sea, and set up a base where the Greek city of Sinope was later to be refounded (*Hist.* iv. 11–12).

A complementary account can be pieced together from the contemporary Assyrian records covering the period between *c.*714 and *c.*625 during which one or more bands of Kimmerians were actively involved in the rapidly changing politics of Asia Minor. Herodotus says that they were not finally driven out until about 600 BC. During the century or so that they were in Asia Minor they were credited with destroying the Phrygian empire, attacking and eventually capturing the Lydian capital, Sardis (except for the citadel), and campaigning in Cilicia in the south. It is also possible that some Kimmerians were involved in raids on Israel described by the Old Testament prophets, Isaiah and Ezekiel.

Although it is likely that at least some of the Kimmerians active in Asia Minor arrived from the north, following the north and east coasts of the Black Sea as Herodotus says, it remained a possibility that other bands may have come via Thrace, along the western shores of the Black Sea and then crossing the Bosphorus or the Dardanelles. According to Strabo the Kimmerians had established alliances with the Thracian tribes, so an attack on Asia Minor from the west is not unlikely and could explain why the Kimmerians were particularly active on the Aegean coastal region where the Greek sources describe raids on coastal towns including Magnesia and Ephesus following their successes at Sardis.

Archaeological evidence for the presence of steppe nomads in Asia Minor is difficult to interpret. In the southern Caucasus and in Anatolia there are many finds of weapons of the type used by steppe nomads. Most numerous are bilobate and

trilobate socketed arrowheads but there are also short swords (*akinakes*), horse gear, and occasionally battleaxes and animal art. Some of these items occur in burials and some, particularly the arrowheads, are found in destruction layers in settlements like the Urartian fortress of Karmir Blur. It is, however, impossible to assign them specifically to Kimmerians or to Scythians. Indeed, the fact that some of these arrowheads occur in contexts as late as the fifth century show that these types had been adopted by the local communities. That said, there can be little doubt that much of the nomadic-style metalwork was introduced by raiders from the steppe between the late ninth and late seventh century BC. In Georgia, in the south Caucasus, ten burials containing nomad gear may well be the graves of steppe nomads. Four of them were buried with their horses.

One burial of particular interest was found at Imirlev in Amasya province. It was a kurgan grave in the form of a square-built chamber containing a single human burial accompanied by at least one horse, an iron *akinakes* (short sword), a bimetallic battleaxe, a bronze horse bit with stirrup-shaped ends, twenty-eight or more bilobate arrows, and a gold bracelet with animal-style decoration. Here, clearly, was the grave of a steppe raider, his equipment showing that he was broadly a contemporary with the Arzhan 1 chieftain dating to the late ninth century. The discovery shows that nomadic warriors were penetrating the region possibly as much as a century before the first mention of Kimmerians in the region in 714 BC.

Kimmerians in the West

The simple narrative offered by the Greek sources of Kimmerians who were living around the northern shores of the Black Sea being forced to leave their homeland by incoming Scythians offers a convenient model against which to compare the archaeological evidence. If Strabo is to be believed, Kimmerians were present in Thrace and were negotiating alliances with Thracian tribes. This has led archaeologists to write of a hybrid Thraco-Kimmerian culture and to link it with a widespread distribution of bimetallic daggers, horse gear, and other artefacts of eastern type which extends into the Great Hungarian Plain, along the middle Danube valley, and northwards into southern Poland. Some archaeologists have taken this to represent the westward migration of Kimmerians, either the ultimate extension of the initial spread from the Altai–Sayan in the ninth or eighth century or the population displaced from the Pontic region by the arrival of the Scythians in the late seventh century.

In the puszta—the steppe region of the Great Hungarian Plain lying within the eastern part of the Carpathian arc—a distinctive culture, named after the Hungarian site of Mezöcsát, has been recognized. It is known almost entirely from cemeter-

ies which concentrate in the valley of the Tisza River and its tributaries. Unlike the preceding Bronze Age communities who cremated their dead, the Mezöcsát people practised inhumation in small cemeteries, the bodies usually being laid out in a west–east orientation, accompanied by a large pot and a cup or bowl and joints of meat, usually mutton or beef. Other small items of personal equipment were sometimes included, but never weapons. The lack of settlements suggests that communities were mobile pastoral nomads relying largely on their flocks and herds, but the presence of quernstones in some graves shows that grain-growing was practised, though probably on a limited scale. The Mezöcsát group is of particular interest in that it marks a cultural break from what had gone before and could represent communities of horse-riding pastoralists coming from the east, either across the Carpathians or by way of the lower Danube valley. If so, that the earliest dates for the Mezöcsát group in Hungary are ninth–eighth century would suggest that the incomers were part of the initial spread from the Altai–Sayan rather than refugees driven west by the Scythians. That said, it may have taken several generations for people to move from the Pontic steppe to the Hungarian puszta, their culture being modified over that time. Some such explanation would account for the fact that the burial of weapons with the dead, normal in the east, was no longer practised west of the Carpathians.

Once established the Mezöcsát pastoralists seem to have played a significant role in the exchange systems which provided steppe horses and their harnesses, together with high-status equipment like daggers, for the Hallstatt elites of middle Europe. Exchanges could account for the distribution of eastern-style horse gear and bimetallic daggers extending west of the Danube where it flows through Hungary, dividing the steppe of the Great Hungarian Plain from the more varied landscapes of Transdanubia. In the west the high-quality steppe horses and the elite panoply accompanying them were absorbed into the local Hallstatt culture, with the horse gear being modified, where necessary, to meet local needs.

A good example of this cultural conflation is represented in a cremation burial found at Pécs-Jakabhegy in south-western Hungary. The burial in tumulus 1 was one of a number of cremations extending along a track leading to a hillfort. The deceased's ashes were buried with a Caucasian dagger and an iron spearhead and axe, both of Caucasian type, together with horse gear inspired by eastern examples but made locally. His iron knife, whetstone, and accompanying pottery were all in the local Hallstatt tradition. Here, then, we have a member of the indigenous Hallstatt elite whose mode of burial was entirely according to local traditions but whose weapon set came from the Caucasus. He probably rode a steppe breed of horse harnessed in the eastern manner. By accepting the style of eastern nomadic warriors, and by acquiring the appropriate equipment, he was demonstrating his exalted status to his peers.

The model, then, which seems to best fit the available archaeological data is to see the Mezöcsát culture as the westernmost outpost of steppe culture, the result of bands of pastoral nomads moving into the Great Hungarian Plain in the ninth and eighth century but maintaining their links with the east—a reality demonstrated by pottery imported from the valleys of the Bug, the Dniester, and the Dobrogea region of the lower Danube. It was probably from these areas that horses were acquired to be used for breeding and to provide stock for exchange. By trading horses with the west the nomads of the Great Hungarian Plain would have been able to access an array of commodities. It may have been in this way that they acquired their grain rather than growing it for themselves.

Kimmerians in the *Longue Durée*

The arrival of the nomadic horse riders on the Pontic steppe in the ninth–eighth century and their eventual penetration of the Great Hungarian Plain is part of an age-old story. It had happened before in the twenty-eighth century BC with the westerly movement of the Yamnaya culture (above, pp. 67–9) and it was soon to happen again in the seventh and sixth centuries when the Scythians from Central Asia burst into the Pontic steppe ousting the Kimmerians (if we are to accept the simple narrative provided by Herodotus). But it was not to end there. Shortly after came the Sarmatians, the Alans, and the Huns, to be followed eventually by the Mongols. In each case they moved west into the Carpathian Basin where the puszta of the Great Hungarian Plain represented the westernmost remnant of their familiar steppe; beyond lay the forests, mountains, and agricultural lands which offered little attraction to those whose lifestyle depended on the horse.

It is difficult to appreciate the complexities of these movements from the few historical scraps available, which can only be augmented by the mute archaeological evidence. Using names like Kimmerians and Scythians or the plethora of archaeological cultural names on offer tends to oversimplify the fluid situation created by nomadic mobility. How many people were on the move at any one time is impossible to say, nor is it possible to be sure how the different groups related to each other politically. The migration of nomadic peoples over great distances led to a breakdown in old tribal systems, while kinship relations weakened as more competitive social structures developed and the prowess of prominent individuals led to the forging of new alliances. The new elites that emerged, having established their authority over local populations, might have chosen to stay, leaving men of lesser status, and those displaced, to move on to search out new pastures. It was a time of restless mobility, a vigorous gusting east wind that sent ever-changing ripples across the swaying grasslands.

5

THE RISE OF THE PONTIC STEPPE SCYTHIANS

700–200 BC

THE arrival of the Kimmerians in the Pontic region in the ninth century heralded the beginning of a series of incursions from the steppes of Central Asia that were to characterize the first millennium BC. The story is complex, much more so than the archaeological sources and the limited historical record allow us to sketch out, as has already been noted, but the broad outline is clear enough. Next to arrive on the Pontic–Caspian steppe were the people the Greeks called Scythians, who began to arrive after the middle of the eighth century and gradually expanded their control to eventually dominate the region. By the end of the fifth century the Sauromatae from east of the Don had begun to move west, bringing about changes in Scythian culture until, at the beginning of the second century, the westward movement of the Sarmatians, who seem to have developed in the original homeland of the Sauromatae, brought the rule of the old Scythian/Sauromatians elites to an end. The division of the Scythian period into three, Early (or Archaic) (750–600), Middle (600–400), and Late (400–200), followed by the Sarmatian period, broadly contains the archaeological evidence.

Writing of the origin of the Scythians, Herodotus summarized two rambling mythologies, one told by the Scythians themselves and one by the Greeks living in the Black Sea region (below, pp. 266–7) before presenting a much simpler hypothesis: that the Scythians came from Central Asia where, having come into conflict with the Massagetae, they decided to move west, crossing the River Volga into the terri-

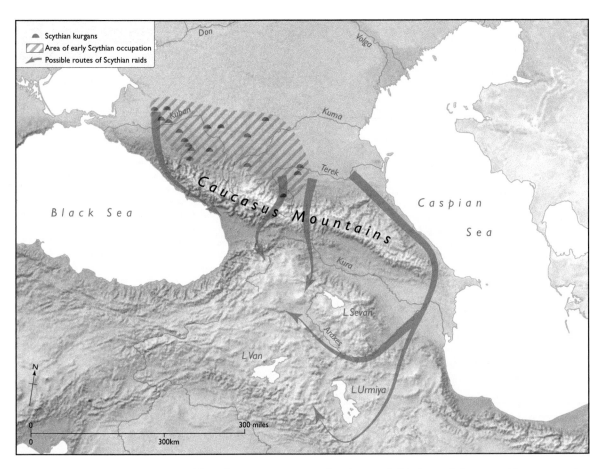

5.1 One of the earliest incoming groups of Scythians settled in the north Caucasus with a concentration in the valley of the River Kuban. From here warrior bands crossed the mountains in the late eighth and seventh centuries to become involved in the conflicts being fought out between the Kingdom of Urartu and the Assyrians.

tory which at the time was occupied by the Kimmerians. In this story, he said, 'I am more inclined to put faith than in any other'. An ultimate homeland in eastern Central Asia, possibly in eastern Kazakhstan or the Altai–Sayan region, has archaeological support. Not only are many elements characteristic of Scythian culture—aspects of burial rites and types of weaponry—to be found there, rooted in the Final Bronze Age Karasuk culture, but the animal art that pervades Scythian culture so clearly has its origins in the Mongolian–Siberian region. The simplest hypothesis, consistent with the available evidence, would be to see the Scythian migration to the west as part of a general flow of horse-riding nomads, of which the Kimmerians had formed

112

a pioneering element, originating in eastern Central Asia and following broadly the same route to the west a hundred and fifty years or so later.

For migrating nomads the west offered many opportunities. Across the Volga, to the south-west, lay the steppe of north Caucasus, in particular the lush valley of the Kuban River, giving way to the more wooded slopes of the Caucasus range. The grassland was good but command of the region also offered the opportunity of being able to mount raids to the south, through or around the mountains, to engage with the sedentary states of Asia Minor. For others crossing the Don there was the Pontic steppe stretching around the Black Sea as far as the Danube delta. Here was a familiar landscape, congenial to warrior pastoralists, made even more attractive both by the proximity of Greek colonies scattered along the Black Sea coast and by the forest steppe to the north inhabited by agro-pastoralists. By occupying the Pontic steppe the Scythian warlords had direct access to the two things they needed most to sustain their social hierarchy, grain from the forest steppe to supplement their diet and a supply of exotic luxury goods from the Greek world with which to display and manipulate status. It was not long before the Scythian elite began to extend their power to include much of the forest steppe while some of the more enterprising individuals pushed further west, through the Carpathians into Transylvania and the Great Hungarian Plain.

The North Caucasus and Asia Minor

Herodotus, looking back on the early Scythian period, offers a somewhat conflated narrative suggesting that when the Scythians swept in, some chose to occupy land previously settled by the Kimmerians while others, moving along the western shore of the Caspian Sea around the eastern end of the Caucasus, took up residence in the land of the Medes on the border of the Assyrian empire. From here they became involved in the political upheavals gripping the states of Asia Minor: 'Their insolence and oppression spread ruin on every side.' One Scythian force moved through the Levant and threatened Egypt but was bought off. Eventually, after 28 years, they were outwitted by the Medes and forced to return to their home north of the Caucasus.

Herodotus links the ousting of the Kimmerians and the march of the Scythians into Asia Minor in single narrative but in all probability the chronology was far more extended and there may have been little direct connection between the two events. The archaeological evidence suggests that Scythians were settling in the north Caucasus in the second half of the eighth century and it may have been several generations before they had begun to explore the prospects of Asia Minor. Limited raids with the warriors returning home in the winter may eventually have given way to more extended periods away from home until some war bands decided to stay and

make the most of the opportunities, serving as mercenaries or acting as freebooters as the occasion arose. There may have been many groups of Scythians seeking their fortunes in Asia Minor at any one time.

The Greek and Assyrian texts provide a broad chronology for the period. Scythians in Asia Minor are first mentioned in an Assyrian cuneiform tablet dating to the 670s and are referred to thereafter on several occasions until the 630s, when the cuneiform record comes to an end. According to Herodotus, Scythian power was broken by the duplicity of the Median king, Cyaxares (625–585 BC). When, exactly, this took place is not recorded, but Scythians were still active in Asia Minor as late as 612 BC serving as allies of the Medes and Babylonians at the sack of Nineveh. The long chronology is at odds with Herodotus' assertion that the Syrians were in Asia Minor for only 28 years before those who survived Cyaxares' treachery decided to return home. In all probability the story he tells is that of just one of the many groups of Scythians marauding through Asia Minor over a period of several generations.

The archaeological evidence from the north Caucasus, and in particular the valley of the Kuban River, shows that Scythians were present in some number at least from the second half of the seventh century. Rich burials at Kelermes and Krasnoye Znamya testify to the early presence of a wealthy elite. The region was comparatively restricted and as populations grew one way to relieve the inevitable social tensions that arose was by the lesser aristocrats leading their followers through the mountains in search of adventure and plunder in a febrile world where Assyrian power was beginning to crumble. The Scythians of the North Caucasus benefited in many ways from this involvement in Asia Minor. Many would have returned with spoil acquired as diplomatic gifts or as plunder, their status enhanced. The pair of gold cups found in one of the Kelermes kurgans probably reached the Kuban valley in this way, while the presence of horse gear comparable in style to that found in the kingdom of Urartu and in Assyria might suggest the acquisition of horses from the south. Similarly the appearance of jewellery decorated in granulation and filigree could reflect the arrival of southern women brought back as wives or concubines. In this context one might recall the story of the Scythian king Bartatua, who asked the Assyrian king, Asarhaddon, to provide him with one of his daughters as a wife. The context of the proposed deal is nicely defined by the question which Asarhaddon asked the oracle of the sun god Shamash, 'Will Bartatua, if he takes my daughter, speak words of true friendship, keep the oath of Asarhaddon, King of Assyria, and do all that is good for Asarhaddon, King of Assyria?' In other words, can you trust a Scythian? The oracle's answer is not recorded, nor do we know if Bartatua acquired his Assyrian bride.

The constant flow to the North Caucasus of luxury goods, people, and ideas from the conflict zone of Asia Minor throughout the seventh century greatly enriched the

repertoire of the craftsmen working for the Scythian aristocracy. Figures of animals in Near Eastern style mingle with nomadic beasts, while compositions incorporating the tree of life that enlivened the gold sheaths of the swords from Kelermes and from the Melgunov kurgan would not have been out of place in Urartu or Assyria. It remains a strong possibility that among the spoils returning to the north Caucasus were captive craftsmen highly valued for their skills.

That the return of Scythian freebooters from their adventures in Asia Minor was not always welcome is reflected in the story told by Herodotus about the force that had been away for 28 years.

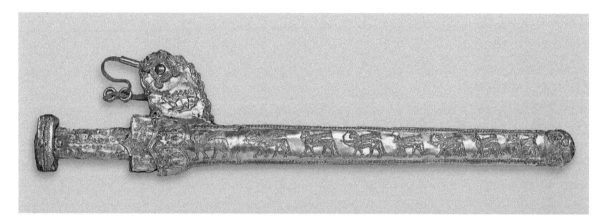

5.2a/b Iron sword with a gold handle in a gold sheath from the kurgan of Kelermes in the Kuban (seventh century). The scabbard is decorated with fabulous creatures (*detail*) similar to motifs current in the Kingdom of Urartu, south of the Caucasus, suggesting that it may have been made by Urartian craftsmen.

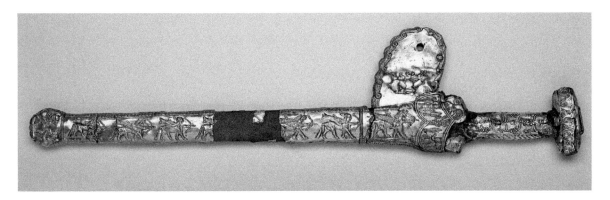

5.3a/b The sword and sheath from the Melgunov kurgan. The 'Tree of Life' depicted on the hilt with winged goddesses on either side (*detail*) may reflect the influence of Urartu.

On their return they found an army of no small size prepared to oppose their entrance. For the Scythian women, when they saw that time went on and their husbands did not come back, had intermarried with their slaves…. When therefore the children sprung from these slaves and the Scythian women grew to manhood and understood the circumstances of their birth they resolved to oppose the army which was returning from Media.

(*Hist.* iv. 1–3)

It is not difficult to understand the attitude of the younger generation when faced with a horde of raddled old veterans returning to upset their social order. But in the end it was the veterans who won the day.

West of the Don

The archaeological evidence shows that the initial influx of nomads coming from Central Asia in the late eighth and early seventh century took up residence in the north Caucasus. Some may have continued on into the great sweep of the Pontic steppe but at first their numbers were limited and it was not until the late seventh and early sixth century, partly as the result of new people coming from Central Asia and partly from groups moving westwards from the north Caucasus, that the steppe began to be occupied on any scale. Even then the actual numbers cannot have been great. Of the three thousand or so Scythian tombs found on the steppe only sixty are so far known to date to the seventh or sixth centuries.

The nomadic Scythians who reached the Pontic steppe found themselves to be in a highly favoured position. To the north lay the forest steppe, already well populated with farming communities, producing a range of desirable commodities including iron, charcoal, furs, honey, and slaves, as well as grain, while to the south, along the Black Sea coast were the Greek colonial establishments eager to obtain raw materials and manpower for themselves and for export to the motherland. The steppe nomads were able to articulate the exchanges between their neighbours and to begin the long process of integrating with them.

The forest steppe zone to the north was divided into a number of discrete territories by the great rivers that flowed across it towards the Black Sea. The different regions were occupied by different cultural groups with roots deep in the past. Those to the far north were tribes described by Herodotus as lying beyond the Scythians, but there were also forest steppe tribes with much closer links to the Scythians of the steppe. The relationship of this periphery to the steppe dwellers was complex and changed over time. At one level there was cultural interaction between the two spheres involving various systems of trade and exchange. This resulted in the forest

117

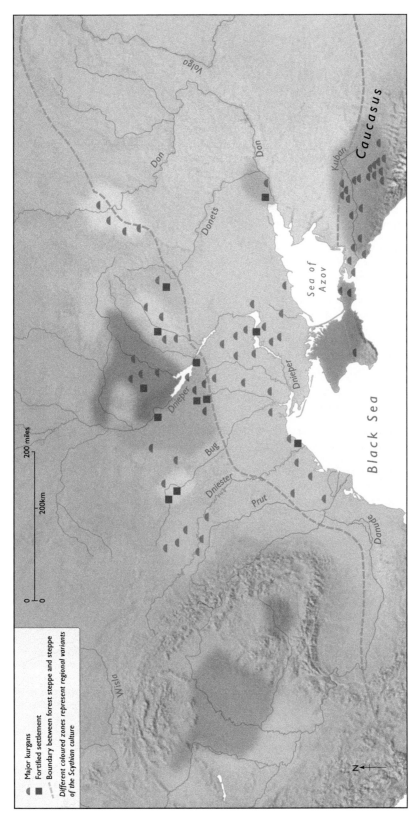

5.4 Within the broad zone of steppe and forest steppe extending from the Pontic region to the Carpathian Basin, across which Scythian culture spread, a number of culturally distinct regional groups can be identified (indicated by different colours on the map). The fortified settlements were centres of manufacturing and trade. They formed the central places of networks linking the disparate communities.

Major kurgans
Fortified settlement
Boundary between forest steppe and steppe

Different coloured zones represent regional variants of the Scythian culture

200 miles
200km

Volga

Don

Don

Donets

Dnieper

Dnieper

Bug

Dniester

Prut

Danube

Wisla

Kuban

Caucasus

Sea of Azov

Black Sea

N

steppe elites emulating Scythian styles of burial, but there were also military interventions. In the middle Dnieper region many forts were built by the indigenous population in the seventh and sixth centuries, which implies a period of social tension, but in the fifth century, after some had been violently destroyed, most were abandoned. A likely scenario is of a long period of conflict initiated by raiding warlords from the steppe attempting to establish authority in these distant regions. Pressures from without are likely to have exacerbated internal tensions. The intricacies of the situation are difficult to grasp from the archaeological evidence but it is reasonable to assume that over two centuries or so the forest steppe communities came increasingly under Scythian domination.

Standing back from the mass of archaeological detail it is possible to characterize the development of the Early and Middle Scythian periods (c.750–c.400 BC) in terms of the outside influences to which the Scythian communities were subjected. Throughout the seventh century the most important influences came from Asia Minor through the Scythians who had settled in the North Caucasus, but after about 600 BC the contacts had all but dried up and there is some evidence to suggest that people were moving away from the Kuban region to settle on the steppe west of the Don. The sixth century saw an intensification of interaction with the farming communities of the forest steppe to the north and west, the nomadic steppe Scythians now establishing their authority over the native populations. This was also the time when Scythian influences extended westwards through the Carpathian Mountains to the Great Hungarian Plain and beyond (below, pp. 150–6). Finally, towards the end of the sixth century, throughout the fifth, and reaching a peak in the fourth century, it was the Greek cities of the north Pontic coast that had the greatest cultural impact. Olbia at the mouth of the Dnieper river and Panticapaeum on the Crimean peninsula overlooking the Kerch Strait were the two main foci, the first feeding the demands of Scythian elites concentrated in the Dnieper valley, the second serving the Crimea and the Kuban regions.

The Middle period (c.600–400 BC) also saw considerable changes to Scythian society on the steppe as the nomads began to become more sedentary. More than one hundred settlements are known from this period along the River Dnieper, including large complex trading sites like Kamenskoe (below, pp. 129–31), and there is now ample evidence for crop growing, with some of the settlements producing considerable quantities of wheat and millet, probably consumed in the form of porridge, and also barley grown as animal feed. One of the reasons for this shift in lifestyle may have been a change in climate that led to a diminution in quality pastureland on the steppe, but the impact of growing links with the Greek world and the intensification of trade cannot have failed to have been factors in the changes now coming about.

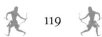

According to Pseudo-Hippocrates, towards the end of the fifth century or the beginning of the fourth Sauromatae from the Volga River region moved westwards across the Don into Scythian territory. In a slightly later text the particular group on the move were referred to as Syrmatai, which may be just a variant spelling. The infiltration of the Scythian Pontic steppe by Sauromatae can be recognized in the

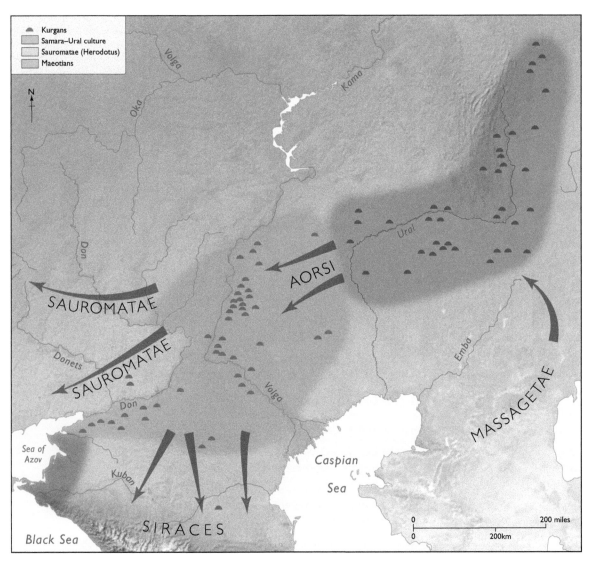

5.5 The Sauromatae, who occupied an extensive region east of the River Don, were nomads culturally similar to the Scythians of the Pontic steppe. From the fourth century BC there was a general movement to the west involving different tribal groups mentioned by name by classical writers.

 120

archaeological record and is taken to mark the beginning of the Late Scythian period, which was to last until the end of the third century BC. It was a time of social change resulting in the destruction of a number of Scythian settlements on the lower Dnieper. How many Sauromatae were involved in the incursions and over what period of time the movements took place is difficult to say but at the very least it is likely that the Royal Scythians were ousted from the Dnieper region and replaced by a new Saurmatian elite. A clear sign of the new order was the appearance of a novel style of burial. Kurgans were still being built, but it was now usual for the deceased to be laid in a catacomb dug from the side of the main shaft (below, pp. 299–300).

The remaining Scythian elite moved west. They probably retained control of the coastal strip west of the River Bug and established a new centre of power in the Dobruja south of the lower Danube. One of the last Scythian kings we hear about in this much reduced domain was the elderly Atheas, who was soundly beaten by Philip of Macedonia in 339 BC.

The nomadic incursion into Scythian territory disrupted the trading networks of the earlier period. Olbia was now cut off from the rich middle Dnieper region and began a slow decline while trade with the Bosporan cities continued to flourish. It was through these ports that fine Greek tableware and wine together with luxury goods from Thrace moved and it was here that the Greek craftsmen worked to produce sumptuous gold work to suit the demands of the new rulers.

In many ways the influx of Sauromatae did little to change the culture of the Pontic steppe. The number of incomers is likely to have been small and was probably confined to an elite with their immediate entourages, allowing the infrastructure of life to continue much as it had been before. It is for this reason that archaeologists choose to refer to the period of Sauromatian overlordship as Late Scythian.

Who were the Sauromatians?

'When one crosses the Don', writes Herodotus, 'one is no longer in Scythia: the first region on crossing is that of the Sauromatae' (*Hist.* iv. 21). They stretch, he says, from the upper reaches of Lake Maeotis (i.e. the Sea of Azov) northwards for a distance of 15 days' journey across a countryside completely bare of trees. This is the swathe of steppe which extends around the north-west side of the deserted wastes fringing the Caspian Sea and is crossed by the lower reaches of the Volga. Herodotus repeats a myth he had heard about the origin of the Sauromatae—that they were the descendants of fierce Amazon women from Cappadocia and a group of Scythian soldiers—to explain why they speak a version of the Scythian language and why women played a significant role in Sauromatian society.

> The women of the Sauromatae … frequently hunt on horseback with their husbands, sometimes even unaccompanied, in war taking the field, and wearing the same clothes as the men… . Their marriage law states that no girl shall wed until she has killed a man in battle. Sometimes it happens that a woman is unmarried in old age having never been able, in her whole lifetime, to meet this condition.
>
> (*Hist.* iv. 116–17)

The archaeological evidence bears out the prominent role of women. A number of rich female burials have been found with the body of the deceased being accompanied by the equipment of a warrior (below, pp. 218–19).

Herodotus, then, is clear that in spite of close similarities to the Scythians, the Sauromatae believed themselves to be a separate people. At the time when Darius made his ill-advised advance through Scythian territory in the late sixth century, the Sauromatae joined the anti-Persian confederacy conscious of the fact that Darius was fast approaching their territory.

There is a further problem of terminology which has to be faced. While Herodotus was clear that the people he had heard about living between the River Don and the Urals were called Sauromatae, later writers, from the fourth century BC onwards, refer to the inhabitants of this broad region as Sarmatian, and the Sarmatian tribes feature large during the following few centuries. It may simply be that the two names were interchangeable as their similarity might suggest. But there are other possibilities. It may be that the Sarmatians were a horde from the east who began to penetrate Sauromatian territory and then gained ascendency over them. Another possibility is that all the nomadic peoples stretching from the Urals to the Don were called Sarmatians and that the Sauromatae were one branch living on the Lower Volga who took their name from their leading family. The historical texts are no help and the archaeological data, while copious, are difficult to interpret. Here we will continue to use the term Sauromatian where it is not in conflict with the historical evidence.

The Sauromatae are known almost entirely from the many hundreds of graves that have been excavated. They demonstrate a degree of cultural similarity stretching from the River Don to the southern Urals, but within this area two discrete groups can be identified, one focused on the Lower Volga, the other in the Samara–Ural region. These differences are likely to reflect the Late Bronze Age substratum from which they emerged. The Lower Volga group developed from the Srubnaya culture, while the Samara–Ural group arose in the area of the Andronovo culture. What gave Sauromatian (or early Sarmatian) culture which developed from these disparate origins its appearance of unity was the impact of nomadic bands coming from the east who brought with them a more warlike culture predicated on elite bands of horse-riding warriors.

 122

The majority of the graves were comparatively modest. The bow and arrow was the most widely represented weapon set, although swords and daggers were not infrequent. Less common were spears, battleaxes, helmets, and scale armour. Horse gear was sometimes included and, less often, the horses themselves. Female burials were often accompanied by quernstones and some were provided with jewellery. The richer graves contained bronze mirrors, some of which can be identified as products of the workshops in Olbia. Herodotus' account of the warlike Sauromatian women is supported by the fact that about a fifth of the excavated female graves contained weapons and some were buried with their horses.

The cultural differences already apparent between the communities of the Lower Volga and those in the Samara–Ural region intensified in the fifth century with the appearance in the Samara–Ural region of a range of new equipment of eastern origin, from Central Asia and Siberia—items such as distinctive dagger types and flat bronze mirrors—and with the appearance of Siberian animal style decoration. While all this need imply little more than an increase in exchanges with the east, it is more likely to reflect the arrival of a fresh influx of nomadic migrants from Central Asia since new methods of burial were introduced at the same time. Bodies were now laid diagonally across the bottom of a deep grave shaft or were placed in a catacomb dug out of the side of the shaft. The appearance of all these new features (referred to as the Prokhorovka culture) is first identified in the region of Orsk and Orenburg, within the Samara–Ural group, from where they gradually spread westwards. By the end of the fourth century the new cultural elements had reached most of the Sauromatian region.

Taken together, the evidence is best interpreted as the spread of nomads from Central Asia infiltrating the old Sauromatian culture and contributing to the emergence of a new cultural complex which can now be referred to as Sarmatian. Who the incomers were is debatable but they are most likely to have been one of the branches of the Massagetae who occupied the region to the east of the Caspian Sea at the time when Herodotus was writing.

The Caspian steppe, between the southern end of the Urals and the River Don, served as a broad corridor for east–west movement and as a temporary holding ground for nomads moving in stages westwards from Central Asia. It was through this region that the ancestors of the Kimmerians and the Scythians had passed and now, towards the end of the fifth century, a fresh influx was creating tensions out of which new ethnic configurations were emerging, putting pressure on the existing population to relocate south and west away from the disrupting thrust. One of these groups, called the Siraces, moved south into the North Caucasian steppe in the fourth century, becoming involved in wars of succession fought between the contenders for the Bosporan kingdom. As neighbours they were able to benefit from the wealth of exotic goods made available through the ports of the Bosphorus, luxuries such as wine from Sinope and Greek tableware from Rhodes. Other displaced Sauromatians, as we have seen, moved westwards across the Don into the land of the Scythians; these may have been the Syrmatai (above, p. 120).

Greeks and Scythians

The establishment of Greek trading colonies along the Scythian shore of the Black Sea began towards the end of the seventh century as an enterprise driven largely by the Ionian city of Miletos (above, pp. 35–9). Since the principal aim of the early settlers was to develop trade with the natives, the locations of the port cities were carefully chosen to have a safe approach and good docking facilities and to command major routes into the hinterland along the major rivers. One of the earliest trading enclaves to be established was on the island (then perhaps a peninsula) of Berezan commanding the entrance to the wide inlet into which flowed the two great rivers, the Dnieper and the Bug. From its foundation in the mid seventh century and throughout the sixth century Berezan flourished but was gradually eclipsed by Olbia, sited further inland on the River Bug where the latter is still 6 km wide. One hundred kilometres or so to the west lay the mouth of the Dniester offering another ideal location and here, on a headland overlooking the estuary, the trading post of Tyras was founded.

A vital route node, but of a rather different kind, was the Strait of Kerch, known in antiquity as the Kimmerian Bosphorus—a fast-flowing stretch of water between the Kerch and Taman Peninsulas linking the Sea of Azov with the Black Sea. The particular attraction of the location was that it commanded access both to the River Don and also to the exceedingly rich reserves of fish that gorged themselves in the nutrient-rich waters of the Sea of Azov. The Strait of Kerch provided a magnet for Greek settlement. The most important city was Panticapaeum, founded in the seventh century. Others soon followed until there were about a dozen clustering within 50 km of the Strait. More Greek colonies were founded around the coasts of the Crimean Peninsula, but their success depended more on the agricultural produce of their *chora* than on the throughput of high volumes of trade goods.

The importance of the north Pontic colonies to the Greek world changed dramatically in the middle of the fifth century when the advance of the Persians into Egypt cut off the grain supplies upon which the Greek city-states had depended. Athens, now playing a leading role in Greek affairs, began to look to the Pontic region to increase its grain output. So vital were Pontic grain supplies to the well-being of Greece in general, and Athens in particular, that the Athenians decided to establish new, strongly defended colonies close to the old Greek cities: Nymphaeum near Panticapaeum, Ath-

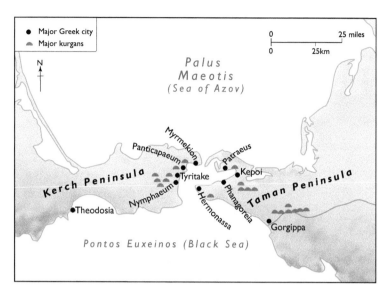

5.6 The Kimmerian Bosphorus joining the Black Sea and the Sea of Azov was a much-used seaway. On either side on the Kerch and Taman peninsulas Greek cities clustered and around them were many tombs of the Scythian elite.

enaeum near Theodosia, and Stratokleia near Phanagoreia. From now on the high-quality grain produced on the arable lands of the Kerch Peninsula was loaded onto convoys of ships and sent south to feed the citizens of Athens. Other exports such as fish, furs, and slaves were more widely distributed throughout the Aegean world.

The Bosporan Kingdom

In the early decades of the fifth century the towns of the Kimmerian Bosphorus, some thirty or so of them, banded together, with Panticapaeum as their leader, to form the Bosporan state the better to organize trade and to coordinate protection against the steppe nomads. In or about 438 BC leadership of the state was appropriated by one Spartocus, a member of an aristocratic family of Thracian origin resident in Pantica-paeum. Thus began the Bosporan kingdom which was to survive until the arrival of the Goths in the third century AD. Under successive rulers the kingdom flourished and expanded. By the end of the fourth century BC it included not only the whole of the Kerch and Taman Peninsulas but also a wide swathe of territory along the east side of the Sea of Azov as far north as the mouth of the Don, the homeland of the Maeotians.

The Bosporan kingdom was a cosmopolitan state comprising the descendants of the original Greek families, Hellenized Thracians, and the more recently arrived

 125

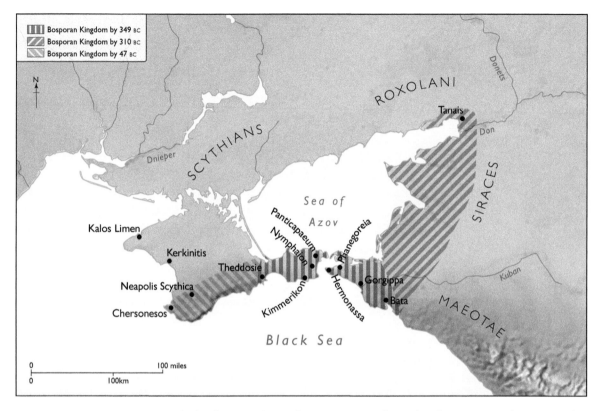

5.7 In the fourth century the Greek communities on the Kerch and Taman peninsulas came together in an alliance that became known as the Bosporan Kingdom. By the end of the first century BC it had expanded to include the east side of the Sea of Azov up to the mouth of the Don.

Greeks sent in by Athens. Intermarriage with the Scythians of the Crimea and the Pontic steppe and Sauromatians living to the east of the Don added to the ethnic mix. The eclectic culture of the kingdom is well illustrated by the wide variety of burial practices in use. Until the end of the fifth century Greek customs prevailed, but from the fourth century onwards some of the burials took on a distinctly Scythian appearance. Athens tried to maintain its hold on trade, sending no less a person than Pericles to negotiate, but by the end of the Peloponnesian War (431–404 BC) Athenian influence had all but disappeared and the Bosporan kingdom continued on its independent course, led by a succession of tyrants.

A significant advance in the kingdom's fortunes came with the appropriation of the east shore of the Sea of Azov and the mouth of the River Don by Parisades I (348–310 BC). The Don was at this stage still something of a frontier between the Scythians and Sauromatae (Sarmatians) and the estuary provided an ideal place for the Greeks to trade with both ethnic groups. Early evidence of Greek activity is provided by East Greek pottery of the late seventh century dredged from the river mouth. A little later a large fortified trading base was established at Elizavetovskoe in the delta. It covered some 40 hectares and contained within it a smaller fortified area where the native elite lived. The discovery of large quantities of Greek imports suggests that there may have been Greek merchants actually in residence. With the annexation of the area by the Bosporan kingdom at the end of the fourth century new opportunities for trading opened up and early in the third century Tanais, a trading port overlooking the estuary of the Don was founded. Strabo, writing at the beginning of the first century AD reports:

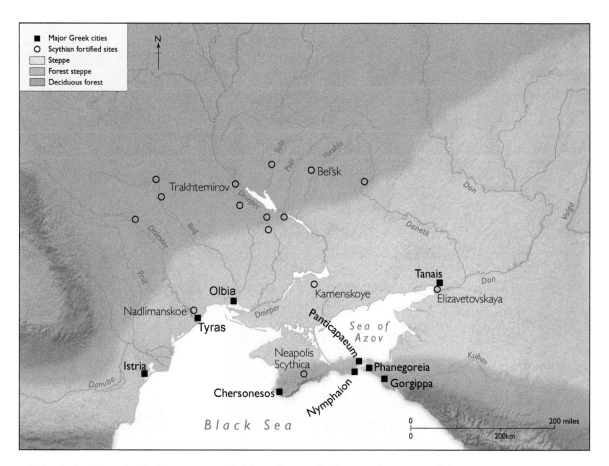

5.8 The Greek cities on the Black Sea coast provided the trading interface between the Aegean and the steppe worlds, but other trading and manufacturing centres developed inland, usually on river routes where regional exchanges could take place. Greek merchants may well have taken up residence in these enclaves.

It was the market of both the Asiatic and European nomads and those who navigate the sea from the Bosphorus. Some bring slaves and hides and such things that nomads have; others exchange wine and clothes and other items of civilized life.

(*Hist.* xi. 2–3)

For the Greek traders who resided here, huddled in their own quarter, this was the very end of the world. They were totally surrounded by nomads with only the sea behind them. It required a 300 km voyage back to Panticapaeum before they could once more enjoy the familiar comforts of civilization.

Coming Together in Times of Change

The Greek cities of the Pontic coast maintained their Hellenistic lifestyle but the population living and working within the walls was very mixed at all social levels. The cities attracted the Scythian elite and some of them, like the person buried at Kul'-Oba on the Kerch Peninsula, chose to be buried in Greek style in a stone-built tomb, while still retaining many aspects of their Scythian way of death. Herodotus tells the story of the Scythian king, Scylas, of mixed Greek and Scythian birth, who embraced city life in Olbia by wearing Greek clothes and building for himself a house 'set about with marble sphinxes and griffins'. He was careful, however, to keep his two lives strictly separate, being aware that his kinsmen would disapprove of his philo-Greek behaviour. He was right to be cautious. When the news got out that he had taken part in a Greek religious ceremony, he was hunted down and beheaded. 'Thus rigidly do Scythians maintain their own customs and thus severely do they punish those who adopt foreign habits.' The incident that Herodotus was describing probably took place in the early fifth century. By 300 BC, about the time that the Kul'-Oba prince was buried, attitudes had dramatically changed and a level of integration had become widely acceptable.

The Greek cities offered many attractions for the Scythian elite. They were, above all, the source of luxury goods used in both life and death to proclaim exalted status through conspicuous consumption. Wine and the vessels used to mix and to drink it were imported in quantity, finding their way eventually into the tombs of the rich. The cities were also places where skilled craftsmen were at work making exquisite items, usually in gold or electrum, to suit the Scythian market. The subtle combination of Greek and nomad art is one of the great achievements of the ancient world— but it was a well-kept secret. The masterpieces made in the north Pontic workshops were for the Scythian market, not for Mediterranean consumption, and they quickly disappeared into the tombs of the wealthy. It was not until the late eighteenth century AD that they began to reappear, to the delight of an astonished world.

Not all the Greek cities of the north Pontic region thrived. Already by the fifth century Olbia was beginning to decline while the cities of the Kimmerian Bosphorus became more prosperous, taking over much of its trade. With the incursion of the Sauromatians at the beginning of the fourth century Olbia suffered still further. It lost its markets on the middle Dnieper, thus reducing its sphere of influence to a limited coastal region between the estuaries of the Dnieper and Dniester. A further blow came from Macedonia. Already in 339 BC Philip II had confronted a Scythian army operating south of the Danube (above, pp. 55–7). Four years later Alexander crossed the river in pursuit of the Getae. All this disruption upset the trading networks upon which Olbia depended. Not long after, in 331 BC, one of Alexander's generals, Zopyrion, then serving as governor of Thrace, mounted a direct attack on the city. This was repelled by a defending force of Scythian-Sarmatians, but it was the beginning of the end of Olbia as tribes from the west, among them the Celts, began to move into the region. From now on the interaction of the Greek and Scythian worlds became firmly focused on the Bosporan kingdom.

Inland Markets and Royal Residences

Although settlements are known throughout the forest steppe zone, where they were characteristic of the sedentary lifestyle of the indigenous population, such sites played no part in the life of the early nomads on the open steppe. But with a more settled economy developing in some parts of the region from the sixth century and trade with the Greek cities intensifying, permanent settlements, sometimes of considerable size, began to appear. The best known are Elizavetovskaya at the mouth of the Don, Kamenskoe on the middle Dnieper, Trakhtemirov further upriver, Nadlimanskoe near the estuary of the Dniester, and Bel'sk on the River Vorskla, a tributary of the Dnieper.

The fortification (*gorodišče*) of Kamenskoe sits on the left bank of the Dnieper some 300 km upriver from the estuary. By making use of the natural defences provided by the river, its tributary the Konka, and the salt lake of Belozërka, and by constructing lengths of rampart and ditch between them, it was possible to create an enclosure of 12 square kilometres. The defended area was further divided into two parts, an 'acropolis' sited high above the river with its own defensive earthworks, and a much larger space within which were areas devoted to metalworking and an open tract possibly reserved for grazing flocks and herds.

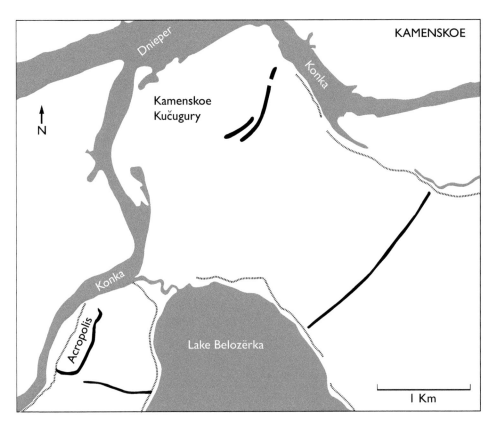

KAMENSKOE

Dnieper

Konka

Kamenskoe
Kučugury

N

Konka

Acropolis

Lake Belozërka

1 Km

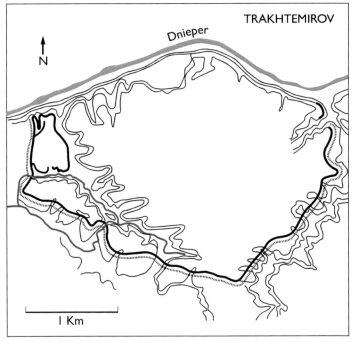

TRAKHTEMIROV

Dnieper

N

1 Km

5.9 (*Opposite*) The fortified manufacturing and trading centres of Kamenskoe and Trakhtemirov, both on the River Dnieper.

The rampart enclosing the acropolis was topped by a wall built of sun-dried mud bricks, similar to Greek construction, while the buildings within were based on stone foundations. An abundance of imported Greek Red-Figured pottery, wine amphorae, and an unusually high percentage of bones of game animals, reflecting the hunt, suggest that the acropolis may have been a royal stronghold. The clustering of a number of rich burials in the vicinity of Kamenskoe adds support to this view. Within the main outer enclosure some 900 hectares were given over to metal production on an industrial scale. Iron smelting and forging predominated, the iron ore being brought to the site from the rich deposits of Krivoi Rog 60 km away. All the processes were carried out here from the initial smelting to the forging of finished items, notably weapons, armour, and horse trappings. Other metals—copper, lead, and zinc—were also smelted and gold and silversmiths were at work. Such a massive industrial operation would have consumed huge quantities of timber, a commodity in ample supply along the nearby river valleys. Indeed, it may well have been the availability of timber that first encouraged metal works to the site.

Although the excavations at Kamenskoe were of limited extent and have not been published in detail, sufficient is known of this remarkable site to provide an insight into Scythian social organization on the steppe at the end of the fifth century. Here, at a dominant location on the river corridor, a Scythian ruler presided over a massive industrial enterprise. Some of the products manufactured would have been used by the elite themselves or would have been given to dependants as a reward for their loyalty. But some, perhaps ingots of iron and other metals, would have been transported downriver to Olbia and there traded for the fine pottery and the wine consumed in the princely acropolis. It was a lifestyle very different from that of the pioneers who had arrived on the steppe two centuries before.

The princely residences overseeing production and distribution at Kamenskoe, Elizavetovskaya, and Nadlimanskoe were all sited on route nodes commanding major river corridors, their locations being determined by commercial imperatives. Rather different were the fortified settlements of Crimea like that of Kermenchik, now modern Simferopol. It is comparatively small, occupying the edge of a plateau and dates from the end of the fourth century. In building style and decoration the settlement owes much to the Greek world, which is hardly surprising since it is less than 60 km from the Greek coastal cities of Chersonesos and Kerkinitis. The settlement is probably to be identified as Scythian Neapolis mentioned by Strabo as being the residence of Scythian kings. From the third century BC the number of fortified settle-

  131

ments increased on the Crimean peninsula as the Scythian elites moved away from the open steppe and began to embrace a Greek lifestyle with growing enthusiasm.

Far away from the direct influence of the Greek world, in the forest steppe, fortified settlements have a long ancestry pre-dating the arrival of the Scythians. Fairly typical of these settlements is the fortified site of Trakhtemirov overlooking the River Dnieper, about 100 km south of Kiev. It is a fortified plateau some 12 by 7 km (630 hectares) surrounded by rivers on three sides. At the eastern extremity was a fortified acropolis. The economy of the community was based on the raising of cattle and pigs and the growing of wheat, millet, barley, and legumes. Iron was extracted and a wide range of domestic crafts practised. The occupants were engaged in trade with

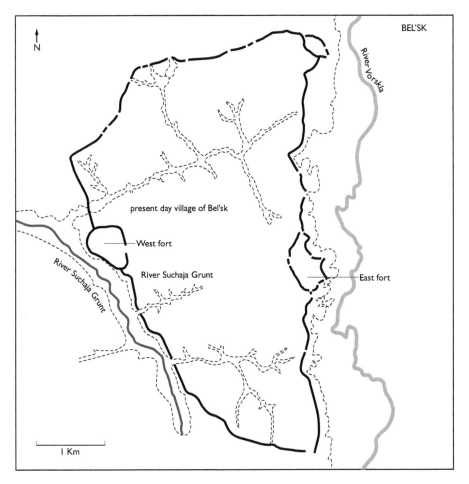

5.10 The fortified centre of Bel'sk.

 132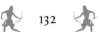

the outside world, offering forest products like livestock, leather, wax, and honey in return for steppe horses, Greek pottery, and wine from Ionia and Lesbos. The community thrived from the second half of the seventh century until about 500 BC, when the settlement was destroyed. It was probably typical of many of the fortified settlements of the forest steppe, remote from the world of the open steppe but productive of the commodities that enabled the steppe Scythians to build their trading networks with the Greeks.

One fortified settlement stands out by virtue of its enormous size—Bel'sk—sited on a plateau 60 m above the river Vorskla, one of the tributaries of the Dnieper. The enclosed area, roughly triangular in shape, is 4,000 hectares in extent, defended by ramparts 34 km in total length. Embedded within the defensive system are two separate forts, an east fort and a west fort, covering 62 and 72 hectares respectively. It

5.11 Bel'sk, the landscape today. Compare with 5.10. The fortifications can just be traced.

is a colossal construction. The earthworks of the east fort, for example, were 18 m wide and 7 m high, fronted by a ditch 6 m wide and deep. One estimate is that the defences alone would have taken eleven million person-days to complete. Occupation began on a limited scale in the first half of the seventh century, but the settlement was destroyed by fire before being reconstructed on a grander scale in the sixth century. It was at this time that the two forts were incorporated into a single, much larger system by the construction of the enclosing scarp-edge rampart. Thereafter the site continued in use into the third century.

Excavations within the great enclosure have identified areas of occupation associated with a range of productive activities. Iron was smelted on a large scale and horse gear, weapons (including trilobate arrowheads), and cauldrons were manufactured. Grain was collected for bulk storage and areas were set aside within the enclosure for pasturing animals. Taken together the evidence suggests that Bel'sk served as a market centre for a considerable hinterland. It produced manufactured goods and presided over the redistribution of iron, cereals, animal products, and perhaps slaves destined for the Greek market. Greek goods such as fine pottery and wine arrived from the south in the fifth and fourth centuries for consumption or for onward trading. Production, redistribution, and marketing on such a scale were likely to have been carried out under the authority of the Scythian royalty.

How such a system worked in practice we can only guess but there was probably a resident population of craftspeople present throughout, augmented at certain times during the year by an influx of people from the countryside bringing in surplus grain and livestock—perhaps as tithes for the king—which could be used in transregional trade. The larger meetings may have been occasions for feasting, for communal worship of the gods, and for negotiating social deals like marriage agreements. Such occasions would have attracted foreign traders, particularly from the Greek ports of the Pontic coast, entrepreneurs willing to make the 500 km journey in the interests of a quick profit. Some sense of the considerable size of the population dependent on the site can be appreciated by the many cemeteries in the immediate vicinity, some of them containing more than a thousand burials.

That a vast fortified market could arise in the forest steppe close to the edge of the steppe proper is something of a surprise. Already a place of some authority in the seventh century, its spectacular development did not take place until the sixth century, by which time trade with the Greek world was underway. It is possible, therefore, that it was the Greek consumer market in the Pontic region, eager for grain, slaves, furs, and other raw materials, that encouraged the spectacular growth of Bel'sk into what soon became an international market. Sited on the edge of the forest steppe, it was well placed to draw in surplus grain supplies and the many products of the forest as well as a good crop of slaves generated by local wars and augmented by organized slave raiding if the price was right. The growth of these forest steppe fortified markets in the sixth and fifth centuries BC is nicely paralleled in western Europe by the growth of *oppida* in the second and first century BC encouraged by the consumer demand of the Roman world.

Herodotus was well aware of great markets of this kind. In describing the Bundi, one of the tribes on the northern edge of the Scythian zone, he says:

> There is a city in their territory called Gelonus, which is surrounded with a lofty wall thirty furlongs each way built entirely of wood. All the houses in the place and all the temples are in the same material. Here are temples built in honour of the Greek gods and adorned after the Greek fashion with images, altars, and shrines all in wood. There is even a festival held every third year in honour of Bacchus at which the natives fall into a Bacchic fury. For the fact is that the Geloni were originally Greek who, being driven out of the trading centres along the coast, fled to the Budini and lived with them. They still speak a language half Greek, half Scythian.
>
> (*Hist.* iv. 108)

Gelonus, known to Herodotus through hearsay, was evidently a very large site, though not apparently as large as Bel'sk. The presence of Greeks, or people of Greek ancestry, implies that there were resident middlemen who helped articulate the trade. Herodotus' narrative also conjures up the image of the natives eagerly await-ing the arrival of the next consignment of wine—an occasion for celebration. Some archaeologists have argued that Bel'sk was Gelonus. It could be, but the number of trading centres of this kind scattered along the edge of the forest steppe makes posi-tive identification impossible.

The Presence of Kings

Implicit in the discussion so far has been the existence of a powerful elite dominating all aspects of Scythian life. That such people existed is amply demonstrated by many rich burials, usually marked by large mounds, found scattered across both the steppe and the forest steppe. Among the many thousands of Scythian burials known, about 3,000 have been subjected to some kind of excavation since the eighteenth century, though the standards of recovery and recording have varied considerably. Most had been dug into by tomb robbers in the distant past, but even so the quantity of infor-mation they have provided allows belief systems, social hierarchies, and changes in burial ritual to be considered in some detail. Our understanding of belief systems is also greatly enhanced by Herodotus' famous description of highly complex burial

rites afforded to Scythian kings (*Hist.* iv. 71–3). This theme will be discussed in detail in Chapter 11. Here the focus will be on the use of burials in establishing social hierarchies and the way in which the structure of the tombs changed over time.

The typical Scythian burial consisted of a pit dug into the ground to take the body and a mound (*kurgan*) piled over the top. The elaboration of the grave pit, the range of the grave offerings, and the size of the mound reflect the status of the deceased. The majority of the burials that have been excavated are comparatively simple. The common people had few grave goods but warriors could be provided with weapons, horse gear, and sometimes even a horse. The more elaborate and well-furnished tombs with larger kurgans belonged to the elite, though the distinction between kings and the aristocracy is not always clear.

The richest are usually indicated by the size of the kurgan which, by the fourth century, could vary from between 14 and 21 m in height; earlier kurgans of the seventh and sixth century are somewhat smaller. An examination of the great kurgan, 21 m high, heaped up over the burial at Chertomlÿk showed that it had been built of carefully stacked turves, the structure stabilized with rings of compacted mud which had set like concrete. The total volume of the mound, some 80,000 cubic metres, required about a million turves to be cut and carried to the burial site, amounting to about 75 hectares of grassland (below, p. 305). To add to its grandeur the structure was bounded by a stone wall and covered with stone slabs nearly to the top. This would have involved quarrying 8,000 cubic metres of stone and hauling it for distances of between 3 and 8 km. No one who looked in awe upon the kurgan of Chertomlÿk could have been in any doubt about the power wielded by the lineage of the deceased.

Another criterion for judging status is the number of humans and horses sacrificed to accompany the deceased. In the tombs regarded as royal, human sacrifices vary between three and eleven and the number of horses placed within the central burial, between four and sixteen. Other indications of high status are the use of gold in the harnesses of the horses and the general richness and range of the funerary equipment. Using these criteria, twenty-one burials have been identified as probably being royal, ten belonging to the seventh–sixth centuries, four to the fifth century, and seven to the fourth century.

The structure of the grave chambers changed over time. The earliest type of construction, beginning in the seventh century and continuing throughout the sixth and fifth centuries, was the large quadrangular grave pit dug deep into the subsoil with a wooden roof often covered with mats. This type was used in the royal tombs at Kelermes in the seventh century. In kurgan 1/V, much disturbed by looters, the chamber was divided up by posts with one area set aside for the king's body. Twelve horses

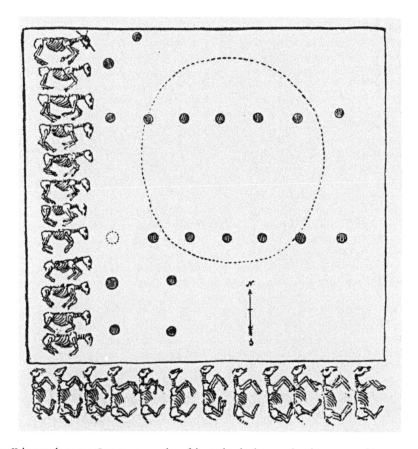

5.12 Kelermes, kurgan 1. Contemporary plan of the timber-built grave chamber excavated in 1904.

were lined up along one wall with another twelve outside the chamber. A different type of burial, constructed at the same time, involved building the superstructure of the tomb above the original ground level and subsequently covering it with the kurgan. Kostromskaya conforms to this type. It was built on an earlier burial mound. The burial chamber was constructed of four substantial corner posts with six smaller timbers along each of the sides forming the framework for wattle and daub walls. Above was a pyramidal arrangement of rafters supporting the roof. The main chamber had been extensively robbed but the robbers had missed the magnificent recumbent gold stag which may once have formed the central decoration of a shield or a gorytos. Outside the tomb chamber twenty-two horses had been buried, some with their horse gear. Other early shaft graves like those at Zhurovka and Elizavetovskaya

 137

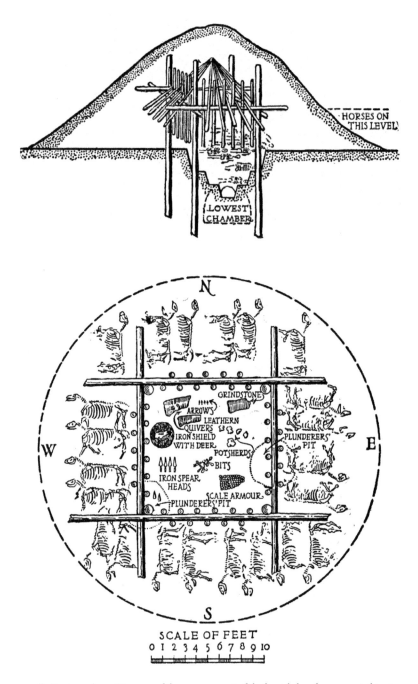

5.13a/b Kostromskaya. Diagram of the arrangement of the burial chamber excavated in 1897.

were provided with access ramps leading down to the grave chamber. In the latter, horses and the funerary vehicle they had drawn were laid out on the ramp. In Zhurovka it was only the horses.

In the fourth century BC a new style of construction was adopted for royal burials. This involved digging a vertical shaft with a short corridor opening from the bottom that led to one or more cave-like chambers. This catacomb-style of burial seems to have been introduced with the influx of a new elite from the Sauromatian region beginning in the fifth century (pp. 299–300). It quickly became the preferred mode of burial adopted by about 65 per cent of all Scythian burials of the period, including all the aristocratic and royal tombs.

The great kurgan of Chertomlÿk covered an elaborate burial of this kind. The entrance shaft, 11 m deep and widening towards its base, gave access to four chambers leading directly from it. The north-western chamber led to a larger sub-rectangular chamber with three niches opening out of its walls. This chamber had later been accessed by a tunnel dug by grave robbers, but a roof collapse put an end to their activities before they could reach the other chambers. It may well have been in this rectangular chamber that the royal burial had been placed. The king was accompanied by his entourage dispersed in the other chambers: a richly adorned woman, his queen or concubine; his cup-bearer laid close to the amphorae of wine lined up and arranged along the chamber wall together with a magnificent silver gilt vessel for mixing wine; two warriors of high rank; and one of lower status with a spear. To the west of the main burial complex were three separate grave pits roofed with logs, two containing four horses and one containing three. Two grooms were buried in separate graves nearby.

The kurgan of Tolstaya mogila at Ordžonikidze, excavated in 1971, shows variations on the catacomb type. Here there were two graves beneath the mound, a central grave and a side grave: each was reached by a deep, vertical entrance shaft. The central grave consisted of the access shaft out of which opened three tunnels, each leading to a catacomb. The burials had been robbed in antiquity by a gang digging a tunnel from the side of the mound to the main burial. The accuracy of the operation suggests that the perpetrators had a detailed knowledge of the position and depth of the burial. They may, indeed, have been present at the time of the interment and returned as soon as it was safe to do so. The side grave was undisturbed. From the bottom of the central shaft a series of catacombs opened out. Five burials were found, the principal internee being a richly equipped young woman with a two-year-old infant. Nearby was a young man provided with his bow and arrows, interpreted by the excavators as a protector or guard. At their feet was a young woman, probably a servant, while towards the entrance of the chamber was the spoke-wheeled wagon

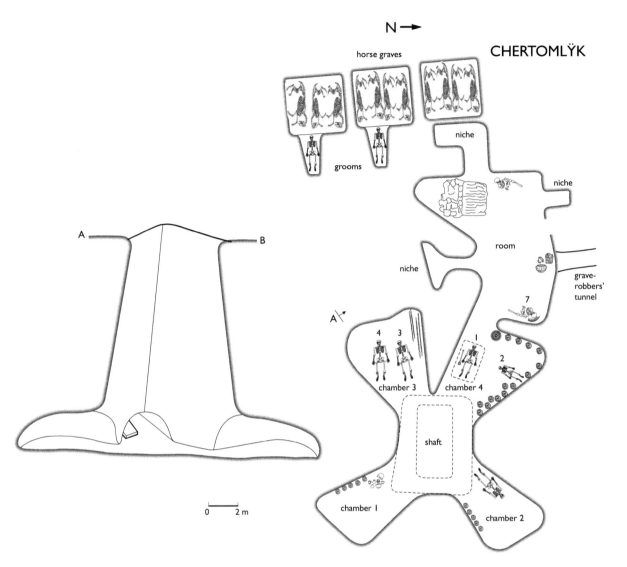

5.14 Chertomlÿk. The central grave chamber and the separate graves for horses.

which had probably been used in the funeral procession, together with the body of
the driver.

The movement of the Sauromatian elite into the land of the Scythians in the fourth
century brought with it not only the new style of catacomb burial but also a social
system which allowed women to hold the status of warriors. This is manifest in a
number of burials. The female who was buried at Kut in the lower Dnieper region

 140

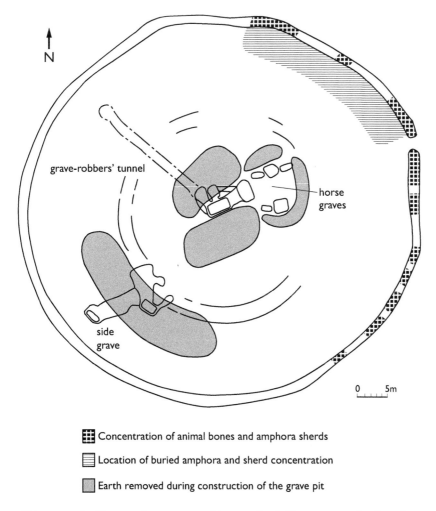

Concentration of animal bones and amphora sherds

Location of buried amphora and sherd concentration

Earth removed during construction of the grave pit

5.15 Tolstaya mogila. The general arrangement of the central and side graves extending from the access shafts.

was provided with a sword and a bow with a quiver of arrows as well as her mirror and jewellery, while another woman buried at Akkermen on the River Molochna had with her a bow and quiver of arrows, four spears, and a suit of scale armour, but she, too, did not forgo her jewellery and mirror. Grave goods also begin to reflect new influences from the East. The female buried at Nowosiólka was accompanied by a camel which at some point in its life must have made a long trek from Central Asia.

Proximity to the Greek cities of the Pontic coast encouraged the adoption of new methods of tomb construction, particularly after the beginning of the fourth century.

This first becomes apparent on the Crimean peninsula when the walls of the grave pits were faced with stone. In the case of the burials at Dort Oba the masonry extends above the edge of the shaft and is roofed with a dome-like stone vault. The rise of the Bosporan kingdom further encouraged the adoption of Greek and Thracian ideas. This is best shown by the famous tomb of Kul'-Oba on the Kerch Peninsula. Here the burial chamber was built of regularly cut stone blocks and has a corbelled stone roof. It was reached by a stone-built passageway (*dromos*). The body of the man for whom the tomb was built was placed in a painted wooden sarcophagus. His wife was laid on a couch at his side with the body of a male servant placed behind them. Even more remarkable is the Great Bliznitsa kurgan on the Taman Peninsula. Here a number of separate burial chambers had been set into the mound. Three of them were rectangular chambers with corbelled roofs and short entrance passages. In one of them a bust of the goddess Demeter had been painted in the centre of the vault. Three of the burials were of rich women, and all contained items which could be related to the

5.16 Contemporary illustration of the excavations in progress on the Great Bliznitsa kurgan in 1864.

5.17 The central chamber in the kurgan of Great Bliznitsa with a painting of Demeter in the middle of the vault. The structure of the vault and the painting betray strong Greek influence, probably the actual involvement of Greek craftsmen in the planning and construction.

Eleusinian cult then popular in Greece. It is tempting to see the great mound as the tomb of a family who were in thrall to the Eleusinian mysteries. In many respects the monument compares with the great mound at Vergina in Macedonia in which Philip II and other members of the royal dynasty were buried. It is a reminder that Macedonian and Thracian ideas and beliefs as well as Greek ones were part of the cultural mix which made up the Bosporan kingdom in the second half of the fourth century.

The distribution of the Scythian royal burials presents an interesting pattern. The earliest burials of the seventh and sixth centuries were concentrated in the Kuban region, with others scattered around the forest steppe, while in the fifth and fourth centuries there is a considerable concentration in the Dnieper valley within a radius

 143

of about 45 km from the series of rapids which prevent further upriver transportation. Six of the nine largest kurgans of the fifth century—the time when Herodotus was writing—lie within this radius and the pattern continues into the fourth century, when twelve of the sixteen largest kurgans are concentrated in the same area. This offers support to Herodotus' statement that 'the tombs of the kings are in the land of the Gerrhoi, the last point where the Borysthenes (Dnieper) is still navigable' (*Hist.* iv. 71). The more peripheral distribution of the seventh and sixth centuries may represent a different pattern of behaviour, the pioneering royalty preferring to use their spectacular burial mounds to define the boundaries of their territories.

Conflict and Change on the Pontic Steppe

The inexorable movement of nomadic hordes from the Caspian steppe westwards into the territory occupied by the Scythians intensified in the fifth century and by the fourth century classical writers give names to some of the newcomers. The Siraces move southwards into the north Caucasus, while the Syrmatai crossed the Don into Scythia proper (above, p.120). In all probability a gentle flow continued during the fourth and third centuries, but at the beginning of the second century everything changed as the tempo of immigration intensified. The historian Diodorus, writing in the first century BC but using earlier sources, says that the Sarmatians, having become much stronger, plundered large parts of Scythia and turned much of the country into a desert by exterminating the Scythian population (*Hist.* ii. 43). Even allowing for a degree of exaggeration this sounds like a significant upheaval which could explain the widespread disruptions seen in the archaeological record. It was at this time that the great inland trading bases were abandoned. The incoming Sarmatians belonged to the group called Roxolani, whose home, in the fourth century, was centred on the steppe to the east of the Volga (below, pp.319–24). They were soon to take over the Pontic steppe east of the Dnieper, leaving only the Crimean peninsula and part of the coastal region around the estuaries of the Dnieper and Bug as refuges for the remnant Scythian population.

To the west of the Dnieper the situation was somewhat confused. Sometime in the early third century Celtic war bands crossed the Carpathians and began to settle in the valleys of the Dniester and Pruth and around 230 BC Pompeius Trogus talks of the people living in this region as Bastarnae. While the Celtic presence can be recognized in the archaeological record, the actual immigrants were probably not numerous and it is better to regard the Bastarnae as a cosmopolitan mix of Celts, Getae, and

Scythians who were strong enough by the beginning of the second century BC to halt the advance of the Sarmatians roughly along the line of the Danube. So it was that by about 200 BC the Scythian world was at an end.

In Perspective

The Pontic–Caspian steppe was, in the first millennium BC, a remarkable melting pot of different peoples. Underlying it all was the culture of the indigenous population who, during the second millennium, had developed a pastoral lifestyle supported by grain growing wherever local conditions allowed. It was into this comparatively tranquil landscape that bands of nomadic horsemen rode, coming from the Central Asian steppe in waves: Kimmerians in the ninth century, Scythians in the seventh century, Sauromatae in the fifth century, and Roxolani in the second century. It would be tempting to think that this apparently neat periodicity had some underlying cause. Could it be, at least in part, the result of population pressures in the Central Asian steppe building up like a volcano and erupting from time to time? Demographic pressures certainly had something to do with it, but there were other factors at work as well. Cycles of climatic change may have had the effect of drawing people to the west. Nor should we forget that the ever-present interference by the sedentary states living to the south, with their pressing economic imperatives, was a persistent source of disruption. The military campaigns of Cyrus, Darius, Philip, and Alexander caused ripples but it was the power of consumerism that had the greatest lasting effect. By making exotic luxury goods available to the nomad elites to help them maintain and enhance their status, the civilized world was putting pressure on the steppe societies to supply ever increasing quantities of grain, furs, metals, and slaves in exchange. This demand impacted on the lifestyle of the nomads encouraging slave raiding, which had a destabilizing effect, and agriculture, which demanded sedentism. And so the creative tensions between steppe and state grew. The Scythian culture that emerged was an exuberant manifestation of the raw energy of the steppe people as they contended with the multiple pressures of life.

6

CROSSING THE CARPATHIANS

THE great arc of the Carpathian mountains created a natural barrier to the westerly advance of the Scythians into central Europe. Some groups had spread into the forest steppe zone along the River Dniester and the Prut, a tributary of the Danube, but for a while Scythian influence stopped at the eastern foothills of the mountains. To the south the Carpathian range (here known as the Transylvanian Alps) swings west to flank the lower Danube valley as far as the Iron Gates, where the river cuts through the mountains in a spectacular gorge. South of the river the Balkan range and the Stara Planina create a formidable southern boundary to the lower Danube valley.

There were several possible routes between the Pontic steppe and the west. The most obvious is the lower Danube valley itself. Once through the Iron Gates the Carpathian Basin opens up to vast areas of steppe, the Great Hungarian Plain and then the Little Hungarian Plain, together occupying the land east and north of the river as it makes its dramatic bends through the basin. Across the river, to the west, lay the more varied undulating landscape of Transdanubia, eventually giving way to the Alps. The Carpathians were not an impenetrable barrier. The Mureş River, a tributary of the Tisza, rising high in the mountains created a way through and there were other passes, though more difficult to navigate. Nor should we forget that the Dniester River, flanking the east side of the Carpathians, offered easy access to the North European Plain and the great river systems of the Bug, the Vistula, and the

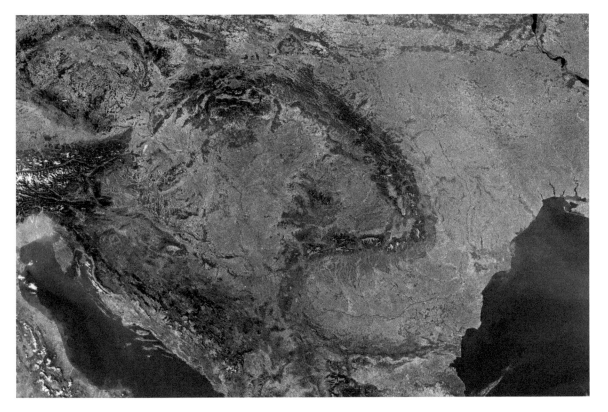

6.1 Satellite view of Eastern Europe showing clearly the great mountain ridge that separates the Carpathian Basin from the Lower Danube. Compare with 6.2.

Oder. Steppe nomads who were curious to explore the west had several routes to choose from.

Pre-Scythian Advances

The first major advance of steppe nomads into the Carpathian Basin began in about 2800 BC with the expansion and settlement of Yamnaya pastoralists moving along the Lower Danube valley to settle on the steppe of the Great Hungarian Plain (above, pp. 67–8). It was probably at about the same time that other steppe people moved along the northern route into the North European Plain adding their distinctive genes to the cultural mix. Current interpretations of recent studies of ancient DNA suggests that considerable numbers of immigrants may have been involved. Later, in the second millennium, many people from the steppe migrated to settle in the coastal region from the mouth of the Dniester to that of the Danube but there is no

148

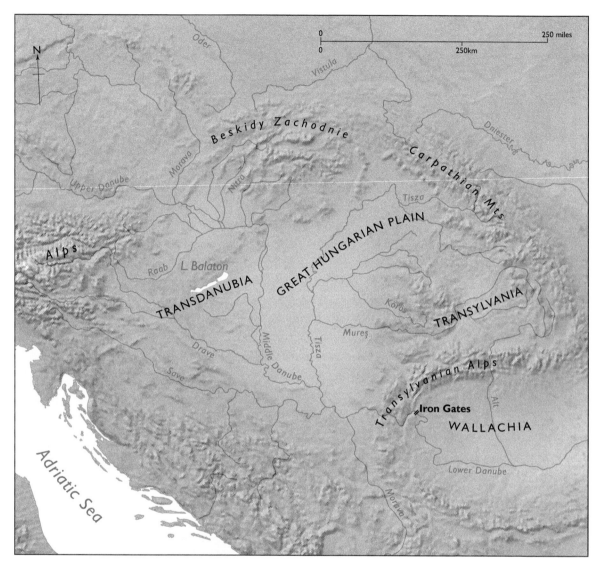

6.2 The great arc of the Carpathian Mountains separates the westernmost extension of the steppe, in the Great Hungarian Plain, from the Pontic steppe.

suggestion that they penetrated further. The next major influx came in the ninth and eight centuries with the movement of people, probably using the central passes through the Carpathians, to reach the Great Hungarian Plain, where they settled to create the Mezöcsát culture (above, pp. 107–9). These were people on the move at the same time as the historic Kimmerians, with whom they shared a broadly simi-

 149

lar material culture. The numbers of actual immigrants may not have been large but they made a considerable impact, introducing steppe horses and styles of riding to western Europe. Once established the Mezőcsát communities maintained links with the east, and it was the continuation of these systems of connectivity that encouraged new people, the Scythians, to migrate from the Pontic and forest steppe to settle within the Carpathian Basin.

Scythians in the West

The suggestion that people of Scythian culture made the journey from the Pontic region through the Carpathians to the west is based entirely on archaeological evidence; there are no historical sources to offer support. What the texts do report is that for a while the lower Danube and its estuary formed a southern boundary to Scythian expansion, but penetration into the Dobruja and, later, engagements with the increasingly powerful Thracian states to the south of the Danube eventually brought the Scythians into conflict with the expansionist ambitions of Philip of Macedon (below, pp. 55–7). For Scythians wishing to explore the west, the route through Thrace along the lower Danube and through the Iron Gates was not an option, but the well-established passes across the Carpathians were open to them.

Scythian involvement in the Carpathian Basin is manifest in the distribution of artefacts found in graves and as isolated finds. Most numerous are items of military equipment: arrows, quivers, short iron daggers, iron battleaxes, scale armour, and shields. Horse gear is also prolific. Other items include bronze mirrors, pole-top rattles, bronze kettles, gold ornaments, and dress attachments. In fact all the main attributes of Scythian material culture are found, and often in some quantity. For example, Scythian-type arrows are known from 120 different sites and the short iron daggers are recorded at thirty-five locations. Not all of the Scythian-style material necessarily came from the Pontic region. The horse gear, for example, was probably made locally but in Scythian style. On the other hand, some of the items were definitely imported. Many of the twenty-five known mirrors were probably made in the Greek workshops in Olbia. Nor can there be any doubt that the two spectacular repoussé gold animals, emblems adorning shields or gorytoi found at Zödhalompuszta and Tápiószentmárton in Hungary, were manufactured in the Pontic steppe. They were the trappings of a Scythian warrior elite.

In the face of so much Scythian-style material in the Carpathian Basis it is tempting to argue for an incursion of warriors in the sixth century establishing themselves in this westernmost enclave of the steppe. But alternative explanations must be considered. The presence of Scythian material could be explained as the result of trade

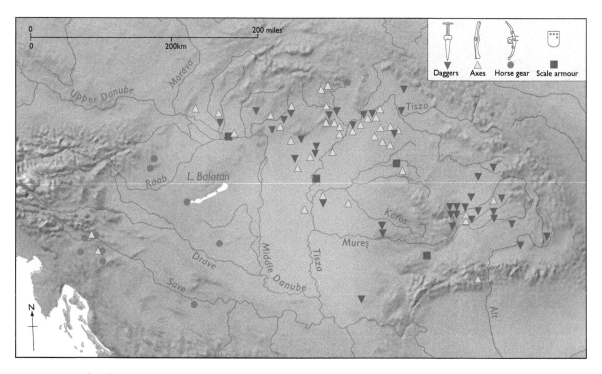

6.3 Quantities of Scythian and Scythian-style artefacts reached the Carpathian Basin. The distribution of daggers, battleaxes, bridle side-pieces, and scale armour show areas where Scythian influence was most concentrated.

and exchange or of periodic raids. Indeed, there is every probability that these two modes of engagement did form a persistent feature of life in the sixth and fifth centuries, but the sheer range and density of the material and its appearance in distinctive graves is strongly suggestive that migration and settlement played a significant part. We can be reasonably certain that there were intrusive bands of male warriors, but whether they brought families with them or settled among the indigenous population taking local wives is more difficult to say.

There are two particular concentrations of material that probably reflect Scythian settlement, one in Transylvania centring on the valley of the Mureş River, the other in the Great Hungarian Plain extending westwards into the Little Hungarian Plain.

The Transylvanian group is represented by several hundred burials, both inhumations and cremations, with the inhumations usually buried in simple catacomb graves. The grave goods include weapon sets and jewellery of Scythian type dating from the sixth and fifth centuries but many elements of the culture, such as pottery styles, are rooted in indigenous traditions and suggest a degree of interaction with

 151

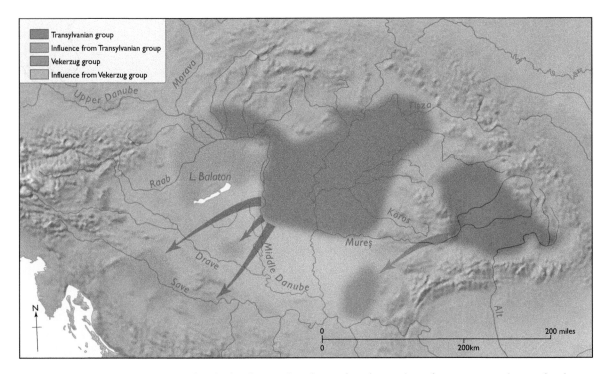

6.4 Based on the distribution of Scythian and Scythian-style artefacts two principal areas of settlement can be identified, each with its own distinctive assemblage of artefacts. Lesser concentrations of material indicate areas of influence emanating from the main settlement areas.

the local population. While the evidence could be explained in terms of indigenous elites acquiring exotic material by trade from the Pontic steppe to enhance their status, the sudden adoption of the catacomb-style graves points to immigration. Some commentators have suggested that those in the Transylvanian enclave were the Agathyrsae described by Herodotus as 'a race of men very luxurious and fond of wearing gold on their persons' (*Hist.* iv. 104). Although they acted independently of the Scythians at the time of the Persian invasions, this does not exclude them from having Scythian origins.

The second group, clearly recognizable from the archaeological data, occupied the steppeland of Hungary east of the Danube, which centred on the valley of the Tisza River and extended to the hillier region of north Hungary and south-west Slovakia. The group has been named the Vekerzug culture after a large cemetery site found at Szentes Vekerzug near Csongrád. Some writers suggest that they were the

152

6.5 Gold recumbent stag in Scythian style from Tápiószentmárton, Hungary. It may have ornamented a shield or a gorytos. The plaque is likely to have come from the Pontic steppe.

6.6 Gold stag in flight from Zöldhalompuszta, Hungary. It too is likely to have come from the Pontic steppe.

 153

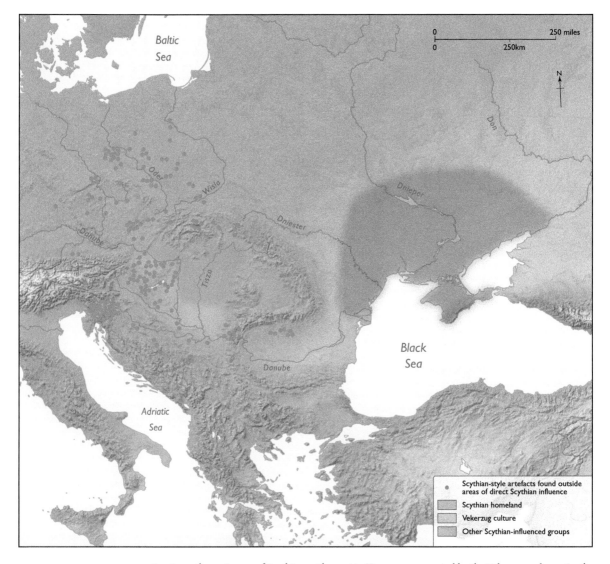

6.7 From the main area of Scythian settlement in Hungary represented by the Vekerzug culture, Scythian-style material, principally arrowheads, is seen to fan out across western and northern Europe. This may have been the result of exchange systems, raids, or both.

Sigynnae mentioned by Herodotus as a people who dwell beyond the Danube, dress like Medes, and use horse-drawn vehicles (*Hist.* iv. 9).

The Vekerzug culture is known largely from cemetery sites which display a variety of burial rites and have produced Scythian-style weapons and horse gear as well as locally produced material. One of the most elaborate burials, that of an elite warrior,

 154

was found at Ártánd in the Hajdu-Bihar region of Hungary. The grave goods included an iron battleaxe and spear, a shield, and a suit of iron scale armour together with a set of iron horse trappings and a number of personal ornaments. The deceased was also accompanied by two bronze vessels, a Greek hydria probably made in Sparta around 570 BC, and an early-sixth-century swing-handled pail common to the Hallstatt culture of western Central Europe. It is a remarkable collection showing that the dead man, or his lineage, was of sufficient status to be able to acquire luxury goods from far and wide. The swing-handled pail probably came from the Alpine region but most of the rest of the items were Scythian or Scythian-inspired. The horse gear, battleaxe, and spear could have been made in Hungary but the scale armour, a highly specialist product, is likely to have come from an armourer's workshop in the Pontic region. By what process the Greek hydria arrived is impossible to say. It could have come directly from Greece through the Balkans, but it is more likely that it was part of a consignment sent by sea to one of the north Pontic ports, there passing into the Scythian sphere and eventually travelling on west through the Carpathians and across Transylvania before ending up in the warrior's grave in the middle of the Hungarian pustza.

Another aspect of Vekerzug culture, which speaks of its close contact with the Pontic steppe, was the sacrifice of horses found at a number of cemeteries, including the type site of Szentes-Vekerzug. Horse sacrifice was a recurring feature, but the numbers involved were never large: individual burials seldom had more than one horse.

The Scythian-style artefacts and burial practices characteristic of the Vekerzug culture spread westwards into the Little Hungarian Plain and south-west Slovakia. This subgroup is named after the cemetery of Chotin near Komarno, where the usual range of Scythian-style weapons and horse gear are found together with the occasional horse killed to accompany the deceased.

Again we return to the question of how to interpret the archaeological evidence in terms of the movement of people. There can be no doubt that there were very close cultural links between the Vekerzug culture and the Pontic communities in the sixth and fifth centuries BC and it must remain a strong possibility that at least some of the leaders came from the steppe. The simplest model would be to imagine a pioneer force of Scythians riding westwards in the early sixth century through the Carpathian passes, some setting themselves up in Transylvania, while others rode on to appropriate pastures in the Hungarian pustza. In this they were following routes already opened up by horse riders from the steppe two or three centuries before. It is possible that the warrior buried at Ártánd with his full panoply of armour and his prized Greek hydria, was himself one of the pioneers. Once established, the pioneer nomads would have intermarried with the local population and maintained contact with their eastern homeland through the exchange of goods. From time to time they may also have hosted (or repelled) incoming bands of young warriors arriving from the Pontic region in search of excitement and quick rewards.

Relations with the West

Throughout the period from the ninth to the fifth centuries the Danube formed a cultural frontier between the nomadic-based communities of the Mezöcsát and Vekerzug cultures to the east and the Hallstatt culture of western Central Europe to the west. The Carpathian range discouraged contact between the nomads and the farming communities of the North European Plain.

The distribution of Scythian material, mainly arrows and horse gear, in the middle Danube valley, in Transdanubia, and right up to the flanks of the eastern Alps show that contact must have been maintained between the nomads and the Hallstatt world. The most likely mechanism would have been trade. What the nomadic communities had to offer were sturdy riding horses, larger and more robust than those native to Western Europe. These well-trained horses with their riding tackle would have been avidly sought by the Hallstatt elites. It may even be that from time to time they employed bands of horse-riding mercenaries—this could account for the large number of arrows found. In return for horses and services the nomads would probably have received grain as a welcome addition to their diet. Mutually beneficial exchanges of this kind would have encouraged a relatively peaceful symbiosis. Yet the temptation for the nomad bands to raid the sedentary Hallstatt farmers was ever present and sporadic raids could account for at least some of the scattered arrowheads found in Transdanubia.

One unusually dense concentration of Scythian-style artefacts stands out: it focuses on the upper valley of the Sava river in what is now Slovenia. The finds, predominantly military gear, including arrowheads, battleaxes, and spearheads together with horse trappings, are found in inhumation graves, which sometimes also contain horse skeletons. Superficially it looks as though these may have been the graves of warriors coming from out of the Great Hungarian Plain but other possibilities must be considered. The upper Sava region is crucially sited on an important route which provides access between the greater Danube river system and the head of the Adriatic linking directly to the Mediterranean. Already by the seventh century trading ties were developing across the 80 km or so that separates the two systems, and with the establishment of two trading colonies, Spina and Adria in the Po delta, trade intensified in the sixth and fifth centuries. The communities commanding the upper Sava valley will have benefited from this interaction particularly if, as seems likely, they were controlling the export of horses of steppe origin from the Hungarian puszta to the Mediterranean. The concentration of Scythian-style weaponry and horses in this upper Sava region could represent an influx of nomads but it could have resulted from the adoption of aspects of nomadic culture by the local elites controlling trade. A further possibility is that entrepreneurs from the Vekerzug culture set themselves up as middlemen in the exchange system and lived in harmony with the local population. At any event the horse traders of the Upper Sava would have found a ready market for their produce, both in the Mediterranean and among the Hallstatt communities of western Central Europe.

Scythian-style artefacts of military type—arrowheads, swords and daggers, battleaxes, and spearheads—are also found widely across the North European Plain in sixth- and fifth-century contexts, with particular concentrations in Silesia and Greater Poland. While some will have arrived from the Carpathian Basin through passes in the northern Carpathians such as the Moravian Gate, it is likely that the Scythian communities occupying the upper part of the Dniester valley were also involved since the headwaters of the Dniester are not far from the upper reaches of the Vistula, which offers easy access to the forest zone extending between the Carpathians and the Baltic.

Scythian trilobite arrowheads are not infrequently found in destruction layers in hillforts, and one was actually found embedded in a body lying in a destroyed fort gate. These have led some archaeologists to argue that they represent extensive Scythian raids which were instrumental in the weakening of the local Lusatian culture. But, as always, it may not have been this straightforward. While raiding is, indeed, a strong possibility, it could be that the Lusatian polities employed Scythian mercenary bands in their local conflicts or simply that they adopted Scythian war gear and horses acquired through trade. In the confusion of unrest many different interactions may have fuelled the aggression.

One find from the northern zone stands out as quite exceptional. It comes from Witaszkowo (originally Vettersfeld), near Lubsko, close to the western border of Poland, and comprises a collection of Scythian objects ploughed up by a farmer in 1882. Most impressive is a large gold repoussé decoration in the form of a scaly, blunt-nosed fish which once adorned a shield or gorytos. Other items include an iron dagger, a sword in a gold-covered sheath, a gold phalera from a horse harness, a whetstone in a gold surround, a massive gold bracelet, and a number of smaller items of gold, including earrings. All date to the late sixth or early fifth century and are the

6.8 Large gold fish in Scythian style found with other Scythian material at Witaszkowo, Poland (formally Vettersfeld). Whether a hoard or a burial, the assemblage would seem to suggest the presence of a member of the Scythian elite in the far west. The fish is 0.41 m long.

kind of assemblage that might have accompanied the burial of an aristocratic Scythian male and perhaps his female companion. At the time of the original discovery, however, shards of a large pot were found suggesting that the treasure may, instead, have been a hoard deposited in the pot either as an offering to the gods or for safekeeping. No human bones were found at the time of the original discovery nor were any recovered when the Berlin museum mounted an excavation in the following year.

The Witaszkowo find remains something of a puzzle. How is it that the assemblage of an elite Scythian warrior was buried so far from the Pontic steppe where many of the items had originated? It is tempting to believe that these trappings of aristocracy were carried by a Scythian warlord curious to explore the extremity of his world. Perhaps he was moved to dedicate his prize possessions to the gods or perhaps he was buried somewhere in the plain and his grave was robbed, the loot later being concealed in a pot. At the very least, this remarkable collection is a stark reminder of the mobility of the times.

A View from the West

The Danube in its middle reaches, flowing from north to south across the Carpathian Basin, marked an important cultural divide. To the east lay the horse-riding nomads whose ancestors come from the Pontic steppe while to the west were a kaleidoscope of farming communities sharing a broad heritage that archaeologists, for convenience, refer to as the Hallstatt culture.

Until about 800 BC the Hallstatt communities were bronze-using and most of them buried their dead in cremation cemeteries following deeply rooted traditions. But already in the ninth century significant changes were underway. Most interesting was the appearance in some of the cremation graves of the bits and side pieces of horse bridles made in bronze, hinting at the increasing importance of horse-riding. That this coincides with the first appearance of nomadic communities in the Great Hungarian Plain bringing with them fine long-legged horses from the steppe may be no coincidence. Extensive exchanges took place between the newcomers and the indigenous people in Transdanubia (above, pp. 107–9) and horses are likely to have featured large in these transactions. The new breed of horse, superior in appearance and performance to the native horse, fast became a symbol of elite status among the Hallstatt communities, and throughout the eight and seventh centuries evidence for horse-riding became widespread, even as far west as Britain. It has also been argued that the new type of slashing sword that developed at this time was used as a cavalry weapon, though without stirrups the wielding of such a sword on horseback would have been difficult.

During the eighth and seventh centuries a new type of funerary rite was adopted by the Hallstatt elite across a large expanse of territory stretching from the upper Rhine along much of the upper Danube valley and as far east as Bohemia. Burial was now by inhumation, the body being placed with its funerary cart in a wooden burial chamber set within a pit accompanied by the trappings of the two horses that pulled the cart and an additional riding horse. The burial was covered by a large mound, in some cases with a stone statue of the deceased placed on it. Many of these characteristics are closely similar to those adopted by steppe communities as early as the ninth century. While this could simply be coincidence, it is tempting to see in the new style of elite Hallstatt burial some influence from the east. It need not have been direct. Through the channels of connectivity created by trade, knowledge of the value systems of the eastern horsemen could quickly have spread to be taken up, in modified form, by other elites. Developing elites often adopt foreign, esoteric behaviours to distinguish themselves from lesser beings in their communities.

It is not surprising, therefore, to see the Hallstatt chiefs of western Central Europe adopting ideas emanating from the steppe, along with the new breed of horses now becoming available, even though they may never have encountered a steppe nomad face to face.

Then Came the Celts

By the middle of the fifth century there were major changes in western Central Europe as the Hallstatt culture gave way to new developments, known archaeologically as the La Tène culture. Centres of power shifted from the old Hallstatt core to the northern periphery, a zone spreading from Bohemia through the Moselle and the Marne region to the central Loire. It was here that new elites emerged. In the confusion caused by rapid social change the growing population became destabilized, creating waves of folk movement known from classical times as the Celtic migrations.

By the end of the fifth century Celtic groups were moving eastwards along the upper Danube and into Transdanubia, which formed a holding ground where incoming communities settled among the indigenous people. With population pressures building some Celtic groups moved on, settling in the southern part of the Carpathian Basin, in southern Hungary, and Serbia, while others moved into the Great Hungarian Plain from where some pushed eastwards into Transylvania. So it was that during the fourth century Celtic communities from western Central Europe began to settle in territories occupied by people of steppe origin. There is little evidence of overt conflict, the incomers at first keeping to the least occupied areas and later probably intermarrying with the resident population. The middle Danube region, then, was a zone where, in the late fifth and early fourth centuries, the Celtic immigrants were exposed to alien beliefs and practices and to a totally different art style emanating from the steppe. To what extent were these nomad values incorporated into the Celtic ethos?

To approach this question it has been conventional to consider Celtic art. In its developed form in the fourth to second centuries Celtic art was a flamboyant expression of a restless people willing to absorb ideas from far and wide and to meld them into highly original abstract creations. In the earliest pieces, like the pair of wine flagons from Basse-Yutz in the Moselle region, the disparate influences are still apparent. The form and some of the decoration is strikingly Etruscan while the more geometric motifs around the base hark back to Hallstatt ancestry, but the fierce wolf-like beast that provides the handle is quite different. There is something of the steppe about it

6.9 One of a pair of flagons found at Basse-Yutz, France. It dates to the early fourth century and is a masterpiece of Early Celtic art, no doubt made by local craftsmen influenced by the form of the Etruscan flagon, examples of which were being imported into Western Europe at this time. The style of the animal which forms the handle is strongly reminiscent of Scythian animal art. The use of scrolls on the fore-joints and ears is a Scythian characteristic.

in its predatory ferocity and the way in which the ears and shoulder joints are turned into spirals. The flagon dates from the early fourth century when the Celtic bands migrating eastwards made their first contact with the descendants of the steppe nomads living in the Carpathian Basin. These similarities were noted by early commentators but more recently the literature on Celtic art has tended to downplay the possibility of eastern inspiration in an attempt to give greater significance to Etruscan influence. Yet to an observer less enamoured with Mediterranean civilization the eastern contribution is unmistakable.

At a more homely level there is the pottery vessel from Lábatlan in Hungary, a vessel in the La Tène tradition but decorated with a scene of predation with two wolf-like creatures bringing low a deer. For all its crude simplicity it is a motif taken directly from the more sophisticated Scythian repertoire.

Another construct common to the Scythian and Celtic worlds are pairs of beasts—mirror images of each other—in close confrontation. This is a motif well represented in the wood carvings decorating harnesses from the Pazyryk. In the Celtic world 'dragon-pairs' were a favoured decoration for the top of sword scabbards and, while they do sometimes dissolve into palmette patterns of Mediterranean inspiration,

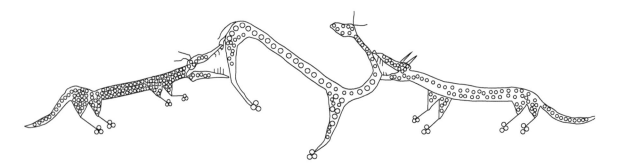

6.10 A scene decorating a pottery vessel from Lábatlan, Hungary. The vessel is of a type used by the immigrant Celts but the image of a deer being attacked by predators is highly reminiscent of Scythian art.

6.11 (*Opposite top*) Wooden pendant from Pazyryk, kurgan 1, showing two deer face to face, a common motif in Scythian art.

6.12 (*Opposite bottom*) Two facing deer carved from wood from a ritual shaft of the La Tène period at Fellbach-Schmiden, Germany.

6.13 Dragon pairs—two confronting beasts—were often used to decorate the tops of La Tène sword sheaths, particularly those in use in Hungary. This example is from Taliándörögd, Veszprém. It dates to about 300 BC.

6.14 Detail from a gold arm-ring found at Rodenbach, Germany. It is typical of the Early Style of Celtic art and dates to the fourth century BC. The central head is framed by two backward looking recumbent deer highly reminiscent of Scythian animal art.

the dominant contribution comes from the reflected beasts of the steppe. The same arrangement, though on a larger scale, is to be seen in the wooden carving of the late second century found in a ritual shaft at Fellbach-Schmiden in Germany.

The final comparison to be made is, perhaps, the most striking. From kurgan 1 at Tuekta in the Central Altai came a circular wooden carving, the frontal plate of a horse bridle. It depicts two griffins in the form of fantastic birds with predatory beaks and powerful wings, their manes resembling deer antlers. They perch on a central roundel ready to fly off and strike. At the other end of Eurasia another circular boss, slightly larger and made of bronze, was dredged from the Thames at Wandsworth in 1858. Here again are two bird-like beasts with fearsome beaks and great spreading wings tensely balanced on either side of a central roundel. The

6.15 Bronze shield boss dredged from the River Thames at Wandsworth (third or second century BC). Its design is composed of two fearsome birds with hooked beaks, their wings dissolving into typical Celtic tendrils.

Wandsworth boss is probably from the centre of a shield and the creatures dissolve into Celtic scrolls, but the iconography of the two pieces, found 6,000 km apart, could not be closer.

What we are seeing, in the few examples quoted here, is not a simple borrowing of artistic styles but a continuity of ideas expressed in similar ways across different cultures briefly interacting in the centre of Europe in the fourth and

6.16 Wooden disc from Tuekta kurgan 1 in the central Altai showing two griffins with powerful wings and predatory beaks grasping the central boss. This formed the forehead ornament of a horse's bridle. The iconography strongly echoes that of the Wandsworth shield boss.

third centuries. There was something in the nomadic belief systems, expressed through predatory beasts, which appealed to the Celts and was quickly assimilated into their being. Had the Altai horsemen and the owner of the Wandsworth shield ever confronted each other, it is tempting to believe that they would have recognized a shared thread of common belief.

7

SCYTHIANS IN
CENTRAL ASIA
700–200 BC

B ETWEEN the southern end of the Ural Mountains and the northern limit of
the desert, created when the Caspian Sea shrank to its present size, is a comparatively narrow corridor of steppe and forest steppe providing easy access
between the Pontic–Caspian steppe to the west and the great monotonous expanse
of the Kazakh steppe to the east. This is the divide between the European Scythians
and the Asian Scythians.

The Greeks had very little idea of what lay beyond this Ural corridor but the
Olbians traded at least this far and a few more entrepreneurial or more inquisitive
westerners were probably drawn to explore the unknown lands to the east. We have
already met Aristeas with his tales of one-eyed Arimaspi and griffins guarding gold.
Herodotus adds a few further details of other named peoples. There are the Argip-
paeans, who speak their own language but dress like the Scythians, and the Issedonians, who practise a kind of cannibalism, but he has little reliable evidence of their
exact location. Elsewhere he mentions the Massagetae, who occupy 'the vast plain
stretching out interminably before the eye' to the east of the Caspian Sea. They were,
he says, regarded by many to be Scythians. The Persians offer no more precise information. The people they confronted in the deserts and desert steppe of western Central Asia were called Sakā though they do distinguish between Sakā Tigrakhauda and
Sakā Haumavargā and Massagetae (above, pp. 39–42). Herodotus regarded the Sakā
as Scythian and the Persian sources used the two names interchangeably.

There is, then, no small degree of indecision and uncertainty over nomenclature. The simplest solution would be to regard all the nomads of Central Asia as belonging to a Scythian continuum divided into a number of individually named allegiance groups. The names of some are recorded in the Greek and Persian texts but others, like the groups recognized from the archaeological evidence in eastern Kazakhstan and the Altai Mountains, are anonymous. In what follows we will use Sakā for the people who confronted the Persians, reverting to Asian Scythians when other names fail.

Mountains, Deserts, and Steppe

The Kazakh steppe runs continuously across the centre of Eurasia from the southern extremity of the Urals to the confusion of mountains, fertile valleys, and upland plateaus created by the Altai and Sayan ranges. The steppe grades southwards through a zone of semi-desert steppe to a vast triangle of desert—the Muyunkum, Kyzylkum, and Karakum—within which lie the Caspian and Aral Sea (or what is left of it) and a number of lakes, of which Lake Balkhash is the largest. The desert is crossed by two great rivers flowing from the Pamir Mountains, the Amu Darya (Oxus) and the Syr Darya (Jaxartes). Bordering the desert on the south and south-east sides are discontinuous mountain ranges—the Kopet Dag, Zeravshan Talas Alata, Tian Shan, Dzhungar, and Turbayatai—forming an impressive but by no means impenetrable barrier before the Altai are reached.

The southern part of the desert zone, well provided with oases and including the valley of the Amu Darya, had been conquered by the Persians in the middle of the sixth century and brought within the Achaemenid empire to become the provinces of Bactria, Margiana, Sogdiana, and Chorasmia. Beyond, to the north and west, lay the territory of the Sakā—an uncompromising expanse of semi-desert eventually giving way to the more congenial steppe further north.

The Persians and the Sakā: A Symbiosis

The northern frontier of Achaemenid territory was not precisely delineated by a frontier fortification but along the line were a number of garrison towns of which the best known (from texts) is Cyropolis, said to have been founded by Cyrus the Great (559–530 BC). Although the site has not been positively identified, the most convincing possibility is modern Kurkath near the Syr Darya. Garrison towns such as this performed many functions. Above all, they were a reminder of the authority of the Persians, but they also served to articulate interactions between the nomads and the empire by providing frontier markets and places where natives could be recruited to serve in the

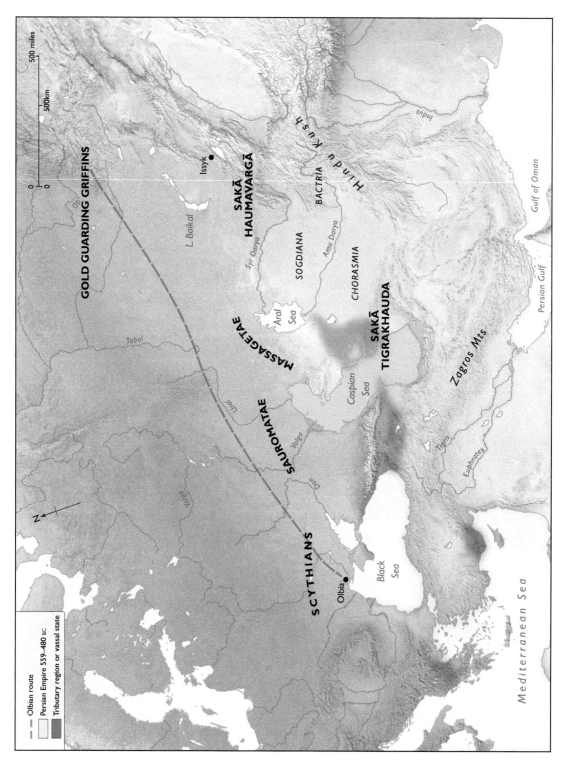

GOLD GUARDING GRIFFINS

L.Baikal

Issyk

SAKĀ
HAUMAVARGĀ

Syr Darya

SOGDIANA

Amu Darya

BACTRIA

Hindu Kush

Indus

MASSAGETAE

Aral
Sea

CHORASMIA

SAKĀ
TIGRAKHAUDA

Tobol

SAUROMATAE

Caspian
Sea

Zagros Mts.

Ob

Ural

Volga

Tigris

Persian Gulf

Gulf of Oman

Don

SCYTHIANS

Euphrates

Olbia

Black
Sea

N

Mediterranean Sea

500 miles

500km

- - - Olbian route
☐ Persian Empire 559–480 BC
▨ Tributary region or vassal state

7.1 The steppe zone between the Black Sea and the Altai–Sayan Mountains confronted the Persian Empire along a semi-desert frontier.

Achaemenid army. Attractive to the nomads would have been cereals and craft products such as textiles and pottery made in the Persian world. In return for these consumer durables they could trade surplus livestock and, of course, good riding horses.

At a higher level more exotic goods could change hands. The Sakā Tigrakhauda ambassadors depicted in the reliefs of the Apadāna in the Persian capital Persepolis were shown bringing gifts to the Persian king including a horse, riding cloaks and leggings, and gold torques. In return they could expect to receive high quality luxuries such as jewellery, horse gear, weapons, silver vessels, and fine textiles. Exotic goods of this kind would have been used by the Sakā elite, in gift exchanges, to establish and to reaffirm the social hierarchies within their own society. Indeed it could be argued that without access to a constant supply of luxury goods to fuel cycles of reciprocity the structure of war bands and retinues that characterized the nomadic system could not have been maintained. At many levels, then, nomads needed access to the commodities produced by sedentary states and therefore had a vested interest in ensuring regular supplies through stable markets.

Achaemenid luxury goods were distributed widely among the Asiatic Scythians and beyond. The Achaemenid vessels and jewellery, now in the Siberian collection of Peter the Great, were probably robbed from Sakā burials in the Kazakh steppe. Persian-inspired silver, silver gilt, and gold vessels, as well as jewellery and armour are found in burials in the southern Ural region dating to the fourth and third century BC and similar material

7.2 The sculptured relief on the Apadāna in the Persian capital of Persepolis, Iran, shows ambassadors from all parts of the world bringing gifts for the Persian king. The Sakā, distinguished by their pointed hats, bring gifts of gold neck rings, saddlecloths, and horses.

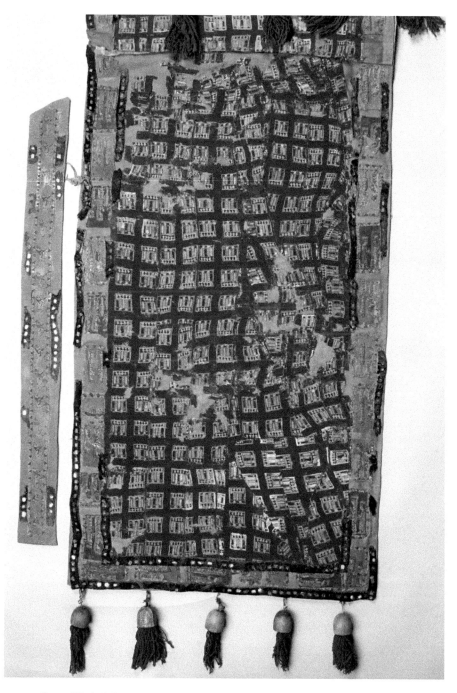

7.3 Woollen saddlecloth from Pazyryk, kurgan 5. The cloth was probably woven in Iran and may have reached Pazyryk as a diplomatic gift or through an extended trading network.

7.4 Carpet made from knotted woollen pile from Pazyryk, kurgan 5. It was probably made within the Persian Empire or at one of its border territories and reached the Altai through a process of gift exchange.

has come from Scythian burials of the north Pontic region. Even more dramatic are the Persian knotted pile carpet and the woollen saddlecloths from kurgan 5 in the cemetery at Pazyryk in the Altai. From the same tomb came seeds of coriander, totally foreign to the area. The relishes and the textiles probably originated in Bactria or Sogdiana. Silver belt plates and gold earrings from kurgan 2 also come from the Achaemenid world.

There can be little doubt that large quantities of exotic goods flowed northwards into the nomadic realm from the eastern satrapies during the Achaemenid rule, but these trading networks were not a new development. More than a century before the conquests of Cyrus lapis lazuli from Bactria was reaching the foothills of the Altai, there to be buried in a nomad grave at Shilikty in the early seventh century. But after the establishment of an organized frontier with the empire the volume of high value goods reaching the steppe from Persian workshops grew exponentially.

While some of this material will have arrived as the result of trade or as diplomatic gifts exchanged between elites, some will have been brought to the nomad home-land by Sakā warriors returning from successful raids or bearing rewards for mercenary service. Mounted Sakā warriors, armed as archers, were particularly valued by the Persians and there are many examples of them serving with the Achaemenid armies. They were present at the battles of Marathon (460) and Plataea (479) when the Persians confronted the Greeks. The leader of such a group, known as 'a benefactor of the king' would expect to be lavishly rewarded to the benefit of his followers. Such contingents were called *symmachoi* (allies) and they were very different from hired mercenaries. The historian Arrian, describing the battle of Gaugamela between Alexander and Darius in 331 BC, writes of the Persian line of battle:

> They were followed by the Sakā, a Scythian tribe belonging to the Scythians who dwell in Asia. They were not subject to Bessus [a Persian regional governor] but were in alliance with Darius. They were commanded by Manakes and were horse-bowmen.
>
> (*An.* iii. 8. 3)

The distinction between an ally, a hired mercenary, and a raider was not always clear-cut and one might easily morph into the other; allegiances could change and forces split into rival factions. Arrian gives an interesting example when writing of the confusing period in 329–328 BC when Alexander, in the final stages of destroying the Persian state, was campaigning in Sogdiana and Bactria. A group of Sakā had attacked the Macedonians and their king was forced to explain himself:

> Envoys arrived from the king of the Scythians, who were sent to apologize for what had been done and to say that it was not the act of the Scythian state but of certain men who set out for plunder in the way of freebooters.
>
> (*An.* iv. 5. 1)

175

7.5 Gold plaque in the form of a fabulous winged lion-griffin. One of the items from a hoard known as the Oxus treasure which was probably found at Takht-i Kuvad, Tajikistan. It is of Persian inspiration. Items like this introduced the symbolism of exotic mythological beasts into the Scythian repertoire.

In another incident a year later 3,000 Sakā horsemen joined the rebellion of the Bactrians and Sogdians against Alexander, but when the battle turned against them they decided to plunder the baggage of their allies and made off with their spoils into the steppe. Later, in 327, when news came that Alexander was intending to lead an expedition to India, Sakā detachments flocked to his cause unable to resist the lure of plunder.

The proximity of the thriving Achaemenid empire and the chaotic period which saw its demise created a variety of opportunities for contingents of Sakā horsemen to thrive. The rewards and the plunder generated by this involvement flowed back into their steppe homeland to be used in cycles of gift exchange, the exotic items much admired, until finally they were consigned to the earth as the burial goods of their last owner.

For more than 200 years the nomads had confronted the Persian empire receiving, through a myriad of social mechanisms, a wide variety of valuable craft goods feeding their senses with new images redolent with meanings. While they may not have fully understood the iconography of these items, they reminded them of the exotic elite world which they so valued. Thus new motifs began to enter the nomad repertoire—lotus flowers and palmettes, lions and fabulous beasts such as winged bulls and sphinxes. Some of these alien images were copied by nomad craftsmen from Achaemenid imports and skilfully incorporated into the native milieu, while in the frontier markets there will have been craft-workers, schooled in the Persian tradition, eager to provide luxury goods to satisfy the tastes of their nomad customers. It was a situation not dissimilar to that existing between the Scythians and the Greeks towns along the north Pontic coast.

Landscapes with People

The various classical texts that survive do scant justice to the great variety of people who occupied the 3,000 km of the Central Asian steppe and desert steppe stretching between the Urals and the Altai–Sayan mountains. To understand something of that variety we have to rely on archaeological evidence gained from the examples of many hundreds of graves which reflect an attitude to death. Comparable evidence of daily life gained from settlements is very limited, not least because the settlements of

nomads tend to be transient and hard to identify. Nor do they promise the spectacular results that have attracted excavators to the kurgans.

The considerable variation in landscapes across Central Asia led to the development of many different food-producing strategies to sustain the population. The great expanses of open steppe grassland crossed by rivers occupied much of the region but around the edges there was more variety to be had. The desert edge where the Amu Darya and Syr Darya once flowed into the Aral and Caspian seas was a deltaic area of rich soil encouraging more permanent settlement. Similarly, the Semirechye, or Seven Rivers, region of southern Kazakhstan offered an unusually rich environment where the rivers flowing from the Tian Shan Mountains into Lake Balkhash deposited rich alluvial fans along their courses. Very different were the gold-yielding Altai Mountains, with the upland grasslands and alpine meadows offering all-year-round pasture for flocks and herds. In such varying environments communities developed in different ways but they shared a social system in which aristocratic elites exercised power over extensive regions through their control of tight-knit units of armed cavalry and were able to set up alliances with similar elites, often across great distances. It was this ever-changing world glimpsed at a distance that the classical writers attempted to comprehend.

The Stags of Filippovka: Between East and West

The narrow corridor of steppe that lay between the desert around the north side of the Caspian and the southern end of the Ural Mountains was a favoured area. Not only was it good grassland, well-watered by major rivers like the River Ural and its tributaries, but those who commanded it controlled the flow of goods from east to west. This was the homeland of the Samara-Ural culture from which the Sarmatians were to emerge. Many kurgan cemeteries are known in the region, but most of the more impressive mounds have been dug into by grave robbers in the past.

One of the more rewarding of recent excavations was carried out between 1986 and 1990 near the village of Filippovka on the watershed between the River Ural and its tributary, the Ilek. The cemetery is composed of twenty-five kurgans spread in a sinuous line over about 5 km. The individual mounds varied considerably in size: kurgans 1, 3, and 4 were 6 to 7 m high and

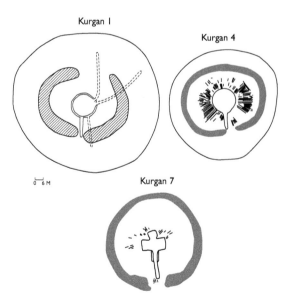

7.6 Plans of kurgans from the cemetery of Filippovka, Kazakhstan. Each had an entrance passage leading to the burial chamber.

 177

7.7 Wooden stag covered in gold foil found together with four others in the entrance passage of one of the kurgans at Filippovka (fourth century BC). The creation embodies concepts taken from Scythian animal art but also the art of the southern Caucasus.

were probably royal burials. The rest were significantly smaller, some barely half a metre in height. Most conform to a standard type. First a burial chamber was dug with a long sloping ramp leading down to it. The excavated earth was arranged to form a bank around the chamber but at some distance from it, leaving a gap for the entrance to the ramp. A tent-like structure of logs was set up to cover the burial chamber and ramp and was then sealed by thick layers of branches before the entire structure was covered with a mound of soil and turf. During this process rituals were performed and sacrifices made, often involving horses. In kurgan 3 twenty horses had been killed and buried with their tackle nearby. The intention of the builders was, clearly, to create a crypt that could be opened and added to until such time in the cycle when they considered the burial process to be complete. Then they sealed the entrance. The number of burials varied: seven were recorded in kurgan 3, while four of the others each contained five.

The grave goods consisted mostly of weapons for the men, with jewellery, toilet sets, and mirrors accompanying the women. Wooden vessels with attached gold plates decorated in animal style are recorded, together with wooden figures of deer covered with gold and silver foil. These figures resemble items found at Pazyryk, thus demonstrating links with the Altai region. Other objects of Achaemenid origin or inspiration were recorded including a quiver clasp, six bridle pieces, and several silver vessels belonging to a drinking set.

The Filippovka kurgans, with their provision for collective burial, are typical of a tradition found in Sauromatian/Sarmatian contexts in the southern Urals extending from the northern Don to the Trans-Ural region. It reflects a belief system that requires members of the same lineage to be buried together in a single family tomb. The Achaemenid goods and the stags made in the animal style of the Altai–Sayan are a reflection of the long-distance networks which bound the steppe nomads together.

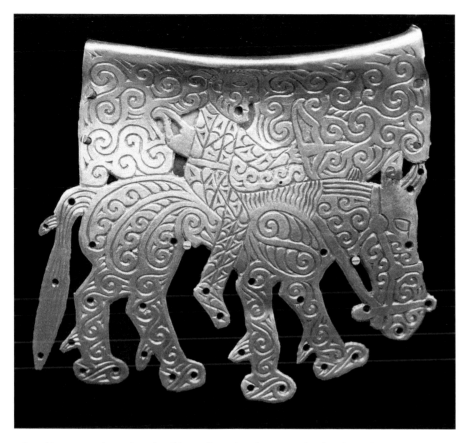

7.8 Gold mounting from a large bowl from Filippovka. The mounted archer shown here is stalking saiga antelope attached further around the rim of the vessel (fourth century BC).

Life on the Desert Edge

The two Central Asian rivers, the Amu Darya and Syr Darya, which flow towards the Aral Sea, have changed their courses over the centuries. Originally the Amu Darya flowed into Lake Sarakamysh (now dry), which was drained by another river, the Uzboy, taking the surplus water westwards to the Caspian Sea. The Syr Darya ended in the Aral Sea but its main channel has shifted its course many times. The changes have created two deltaic fans crossed by old river beds that are both fertile and comparatively well-watered. These favoured regions, settled by the Sakā, lay largely beyond the limit of the territory conquered by the Persians in the late sixth century.

 179

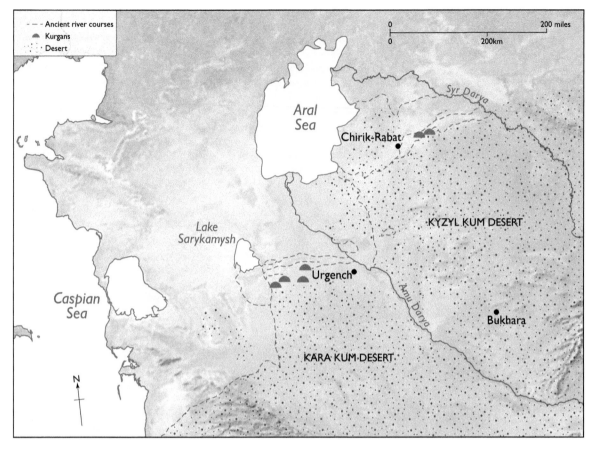

7.9 The northern edge of the Kyzylkum and Karakum deserts. The settlements of the Sakā favoured the deltaic regions.

In both deltaic regions the population depended on raising domestic animals and lived a semi-sedentary life. Several cemeteries have been excavated producing grave goods including swords, arrows, and horse gear of classic nomad type, together with gold buckles, bosses, and other attachments decorated in animal style, the most distinctive creatures being coiled felines, stags standing with hoofs together, and couchant saiga (steppe antelope). Most of the burials were modestly equipped and no examples that can be regarded as princely have yet been found.

In the Sarykamysh delta to the west of the Amu Darya the method of burial and certain characteristics of the skeletons suggest that the population was made up of two culturally distinct groups of people. One group were inhumed in shallow graves of restricted width; they were laid on their backs with their limbs extended. These people were buried without weapons and without items decorated in the animal style. A study of the skeletal remains, particularly skulls, suggests that the population may have originated in the southern Ural area. The second group were cremated or inhumed either as single burials or with several individuals buried together. In some cases the burials were placed in deep pits beneath kurgans and were accompanied by weapons, horse gear, and ornaments decorated in animal style. The morphology of their skulls compares with that of the population living in the eastern steppe and forest steppe region. The burials from the cemeteries in the Syr Darya delta all belong to this second group.

If one takes the data together, it would seem that these desert-edge communities were made up largely of people who came from the east, perhaps from the Altai–Sayan region, but that west of the Amu Darya they were intermixed with people of Volga–Ural origin. Some observers have related these differences to tribes mentioned by the classical sources, assuming the eastern group to be Sakā and suggesting that the western population were derived from the Massagetae. Given the paucity of the evidence it is probably safer to leave aside these attributions and regard the differences simply as reflecting the mobility of populations in the first millennium BC.

The Country of the Seven Rivers

The Semirech'ye region of southern Kazakhstan is a particularly favoured zone, benefiting from a varying topography. To the south lie the high Tian Shan Mountains, the melting snows from which feed the seven main rivers which flow northwards to meet the Ili River that carries the spring flood waters onwards to Lake Balkhash. The rivers have created fourteen large alluvial fans of deep rich soil above well-drained gravels. Not far to the south the land rises to the foothills and upland plateaus with mixed forest interspersed with meadow before the higher mountain slopes with their stands of conifers and alpine meadows are reached. From the semi-arid areas of the Ili valley, interspersed with marshland, to the mountain slopes is a mere 60 km. Thus a community choosing to settle on the alluvial fans would be able to exploit a wide range of different ecologies easily accessible within a day or two's journey from home. Crops could be grown on the fertile soil while the animals were enjoying the upland pastures, and when the harvests were in the animals could be brought down for the winter to feed off the stubble and fallow, at the same time providing the much needed manure.

Several first millennium BC settlements have been excavated on the Talgar fan, not far from the modern city of Almaty, providing clear evidence that millet, wheat, barley, and grapes were grown. Millet was more common at first but after about 400 BC

181

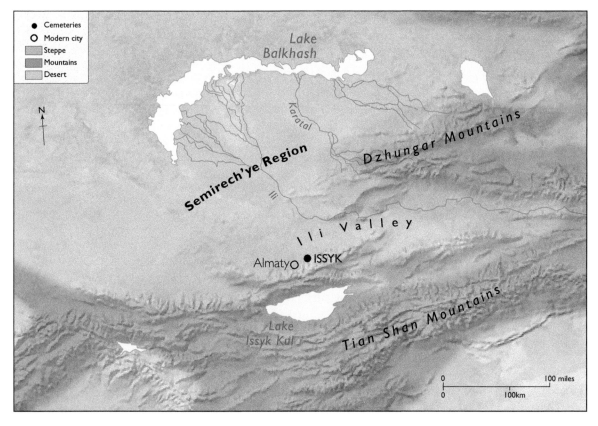

7.10 The Semirech'ye region of south-eastern Kazakhstan. The rivers flowing from the mountains created rich deltaic fans ideal for settlement and animal rearing.

wheat became the predominant crop as cereal growing intensified. Domesticated animals included sheep, goats, cattle, horses, camels, and dogs. Wild animals were hunted but made little significant contribution to the diet. The settlements for the most part were small hamlets or villages, but one reached the extent of 13 hectares. Kurgan cemeteries were interspersed with the settlements, usually grouped in clusters aligned along ancient stream beds. The kurgans were modest in size but elsewhere in Semirech'ye cemeteries containing more substantial kurgans have been found. At Besschatyr, on the north bank of the Ili, 130 km north-east of Almaty, a large ensemble of thirty-one kurgans has been identified with the largest measuring 106 m in diameter and 17 m in height. It was surrounded by ninety-four megaliths. Excavation showed that the graves, which dated from the fifth to the third century, had all been robbed.

Something of the grandeur of these aristocrats can be appreciated by a spectacular discovery made in 1970 at Issyk, 50 km east of Almaty. The cemetery at Issyk is large, comprising sixty-seven kurgans, but many of them had been plundered with their central graves dug out at some time in antiquity. A farmer ploughing over one of them spotted gold glistening in the furrow and reported his find. In the professional excavation that followed it was confirmed that the central grave had been robbed but the gold had come from a side chamber built of fir logs in which the body of a young man or woman aged 17 or 18 had been interred. The deceased wore a red leather tunic, tight trousers, and red boots covered with some 4,000 gold ornaments. Even more remarkable was his/her headdress. It was sharply pointed, 0.65 m high, and surmounted by a model ram. On the front of the base were fabulous animals carved out of wood and covered in gold leaf, while on the side and back were animals cut out of gold foil—snow leopards, ibexes, winged tigers, and birds, all placed in a landscape setting. The front was further enhanced with four miniature spears which appear to be growing out of a leafed calyx. It is altogether a stunning creation, no doubt redolent of meaning but now beyond recovery.

The body wore a belt decorated with gold animal figures from which hung a sword and a dagger, both in decorated sheaths. Around the neck was a gold neck ring with attached lions' heads. Two gold rings adorned the fingers. He/she also carried a whip bound in gold as a symbol of authority. Among the many other items buried with the body was a silver bowl with an inscription which remains undeciphered. This burial, we must remember, was in a secondary position in the kurgan. For this reason he/she is usually referred to as a prince (or princess). How magnificent had been the robbed central burial must remain a matter of speculation.

The relationship of the occupants of these rich graves to the farmers living in the villages is unclear but in all probability they were an aristocratic elite commanding dedicated bands of mobile followers with little or no direct contact with the sedentary farmers other than to demand their subservience and a tithe of their produce in return for protection.

The Frozen Tombs of the Altai

The Altai and Sayan Mountains lie within the steppe zone but their great height has created a varied vegetation. The southern slopes exposed to the sun tend to retain their steppe flora while the north-facing slopes are wooded. The upland plateaus and valleys with their rich subalpine meadows provide an ideal environment for stock rearing all year round. Another great advantage of the region is that the high winds

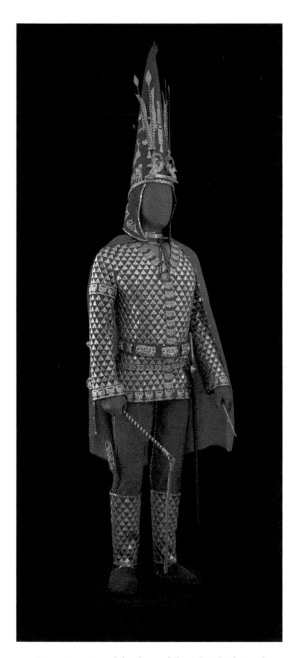

7.11 Reconstruction of the dress of the Sakā chieftain whose burial was found at Issyk in southern Kazakhstan. The reconstruction is faithfully based on detailed archaeological evidence (fourth–third century BC).

blow the snow off the steppe-covered mountain slopes making the winter grass easily accessible for the herds of horses and other animals that can be turned loose in winter to fend for themselves. Winters are long with comparatively short dry, cool summers, but high mid-day temperatures and the ample presence of running water ensures that the meadows are luxuriant. Harsh and extreme though the weather may at times be, for a community basing its livelihood on pastoralism the Altai–Sayan valleys had a lot to offer.

Horses were the most important of the animals, with sheep coming second. Other beasts reared in lesser numbers were goats, cattle, and yaks. Hunting does not seem to have been significant for augmenting the food supply but leopard, steppe cat, squirrel, sable, otter, and ermine were caught for their fur. Deer, elk, mountain goat, boars, and saiga antelope—depicted with great understanding in the animal art of the region—may have been hunted for their meat and hides. Certainly deer hair was used as stuffing for saddles and cushions. Swans, geese, and black grouse, all featuring in the art, may also have been trapped or shot to add variety to the diet. No grain was found in the excavation at Pazyryk and there is no other evidence of agriculture even though wheat would ripen in parts of the central Altai where the climate was milder. The Altai herders, then, depended on the domesticated animals for their food: the milk, cheese, butter, koumiss (fermented mare's milk) of the daily diet supplemented by meat, mainly mutton, produced on special occasions. Fruits, berries, shoots, and fungi collected in the woodlands also would have added a welcome supplement.

The discovery and excavation of the frozen tombs is one of the great stories of archaeology (above, pp. 16–20). It was in 1865 that Wilhelm Radlov, then a school teacher at Barnaul, dug into two large kurgans in the High Altai, one at Berel, the other at Katanda, discovering organic

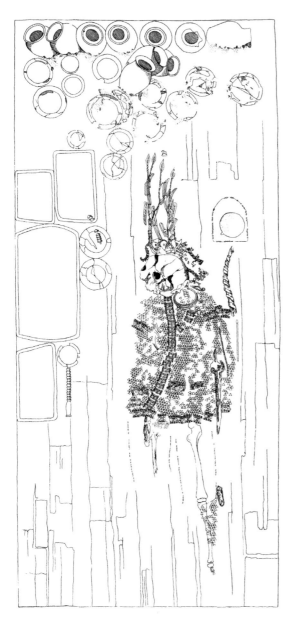

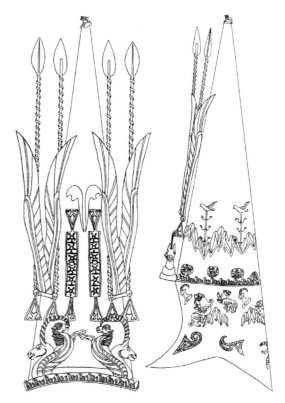

7.12 (*Left*) Plan of the grave chamber in the Issyk kurgan. The deceased, elaborately clothed and wearing a complex headdress, was provided with two swords, a whip, and a mirror. To the right were placed four wooden trays and several ladles, while at the head end of the burial chamber a number of bronze, silver, and ceramic vessels were stacked.

7.13 (*Above*) Reconstruction of the headdress from the Issyk kurgan. It was decorated with carved wooden animals covered with gold sheet and gold foil attachments in the form of leaves or wings.

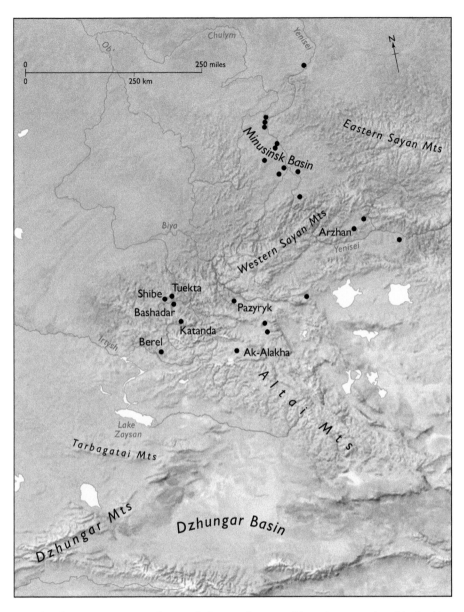

7.14 The Altai–Sayan Mountains showing the location for some of the major cemeteries of the Scythian period.

materials preserved in the frozen ground. It was not until 1927 that another kurgan was dug at Shibe. By this time archaeologists were already exploring sites in the Pazyryk region under the direction of Sergei Rudenko and in 1929 the first of the Pazyryk kurgans was thoroughly excavated. The team returned in 1947–9 to excavate four more. In subsequent years graves at Bashadar and Tuekta were examined and more recently, in 1998, teams have returned to Berel on the west flank of the Altai to excavate more of the kurgans, using an array of modern techniques to recover and conserve the delicate grave goods preserved in the tombs. Another spectacular find, that of a rich female burial, was made in 1993, at Ak-Alakha on the Ukok plateau further to the south, close to the border between Russia and China. Taken together the frozen tombs offer a unique insight into the rich and colourful life of the mountain pastoralists, adding much to the discussion of Scythian life explored in subsequent chapters.

The kurgans in the Pazyryk cemetery were all built in much the same way. The first stage involved the digging of a large rectangular grave pit varying in depth from 4 to 7 m and within the pit the burial chamber was constructed of larch logs. Sometimes these were complex structures with double walls and roofs. The chamber contained a coffin hollowed out from a tree trunk to take the mummified body of the deceased, who was often accompanied by a female partner. A wide range of grave goods were stacked in the chamber beside the coffin—everything needed for a comfortable existence in the afterlife—vessels holding food and drink, small tables, carpets, wall hangings, cushions, musical instruments such as harps and drums, and personal items,

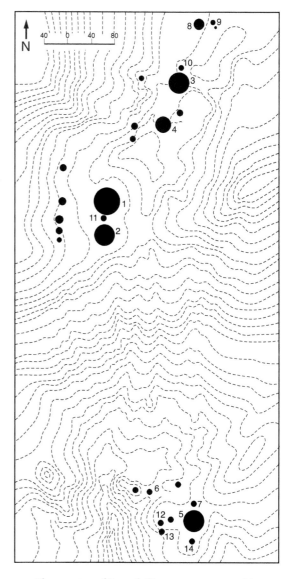

7.15 The cemetery of Pazyryk. Kurgan 1 was excavated in 1929 and kurgans 2–8 were excavated between 1947 and 1949.

including weapons. In some tombs horses, decked out in ceremonial gear, were killed and placed on the floor of the grave pit outside the tomb chamber and in kurgan 5 dismantled parts of a carriage were packed next to the horses. Once the grave goods were all in place the burial chamber was covered with birch bark and twigs and then

 187

7.16 Kurgan 5 at Pazyryk as it now appears long after excavation and reconstruction.

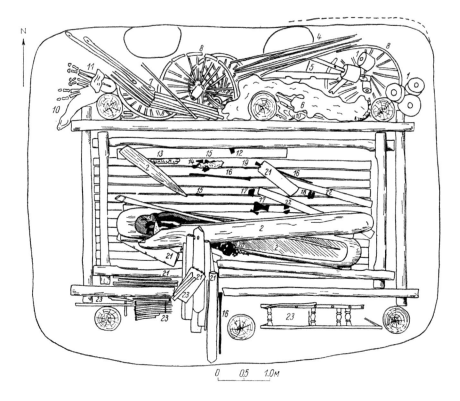

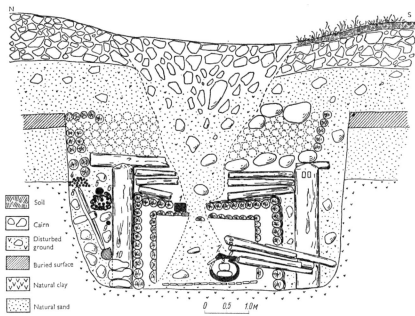

7.17a/b Kurgan 5 at Pazyryk. The burial chamber was built of horizontally laid logs. Between it and the sides of the grave pit a range of equipment, including a dismantled spoke-wheeled vehicle and four horses, was packed. The whole was sealed by several layers of horizontally laid logs, above which the kurgan mound was piled. The pit dug by robbers is clearly to be seen.

by several layers of larch logs which would have made it difficult for grave robbers to get through to the chamber. The earth removed when the pit had been dug was then piled up over the graves and was covered by a thick layer of large stones creating a burial mound. At Pazyryk the largest is 5 m high and 60 m in diameter. The cemetery contained six kurgans more than 15 m in diameter and a number of much smaller ones that tend to cluster around the larger mounds.

The remarkable preservation of the buried remains is due largely to the loose rubble piled up to form the kurgans. This facilitated a free flow of air, and as the temperature dropped, warm air from the grave pit rose to be replaced by inflowing cold air. This lowered the temperature sufficient to freeze what water remained, thus preventing the organic materials from rotting. As the winter progressed the ground froze to the depth of many metres. In spring the frozen ground began to thaw out but the kurgan mound provided a protective blanket ensuring that the ground beneath it remained well below freezing point. In these icy conditions, without oxygen, the organic material remained intact preserved as if in a deep freeze. So it is that the wood, herbs, leather, fur, and fabrics, together with human bodies, packed with vegetation after embalming and with skin tattooed, remained for the astonished archaeologists to recover.

There has been much debate concerning the dates of the Pazyryk burials. It was originally thought that they spread from the fifth to third centuries but a series of recent radiocarbon data has provided a more precise date range. Kurgan 2, which is generally regarded as the earliest, has been dated to the first decade of the third century while kurgan 5, thought to be the latest, dates to the third quarter of the third century. These dates are independently supported by dendrochronology which suggests that the timbers for kurgan 5 were cut about 50 years after those used in kurgan 2.

The cemetery of Berel lies on the western edge of the Altai on a terrace of the River Bukhtarma, a tributary of the Irtysh. The excavation of kurgan 1 by Radlov in 1865 showed that permafrost conditions had preserved organic materials but lack of conservation expertise meant that little survived after the graves had been opened. A new programme of work, beginning in 1998, has examined twenty-four kurgans, mostly dating to the Iron Age, showing them to have been of the same general struc-

7.18 (*Opposite top*) Diagrammatic representation of kurgan 10 at Berel, Kazakhstan.

7.19 (*Opposite bottom*) Kurgan 10 at Berel during excavation showing the state of the burial before the pit was refilled. The timber grave chamber and the bodies of the ten horses buried next to it were covered with sheets of birch bark. The roughly circular hole cut by the grave robbers can be seen in the centre.

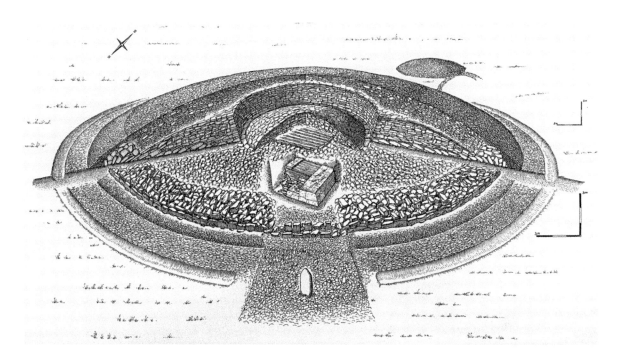

 191

7.20 Reconstruction of how the burials in kurgan 10 at Berel would have looked before the last covering of birch bark sheets was placed over the bodies of the dead horses.

ture as those excavated at Pazyryk, with timber-built burial chambers set in pits beneath mounds of loosely packed stone rubble. In some cases (kurgans 10 and 11) the burial chambers were built of thick, carefully trimmed planks slotted together, while in the case of kurgan 36 stone slabs had been used to build the walls. Where horses accompanied the dead they were always placed within the northern part of the grave pit but outside the burial chamber. Numbers vary from one to seventeen. Where many were included in a single grave they were buried in layers separated by sheets of birch bark. In all, more than eighty horses have been found, all stallions. In most cases the horses were equipped with their full ceremonial tack. The burial chambers had all been robbed in antiquity but the artefacts remaining are closely comparable to those found at Pazyryk, including different kinds of animals carved

7.21 Kurgan 9 at Berel seen here towards the end of the excavation, showing the timber burial chamber and the bodies of the horses laid against it in the burial pit.

from wood and covered in gold foil for use as harness decoration and a range of leather work and textiles.

The Ukok plateau lies high in the Altai range on the border between Russia and China about 150 km west of Berel. It is a remote place suffering harsh winters mitigated only by the fact that the strong winds constantly sweep the snow from the upland pastures making it possible for animals to browse all year round. In 1993, at Ak-Alakha, a kurgan closely similar to others found in the Altai, was excavated exposing a burial chamber built of larch logs laid horizontally. The walls inside were decorated with cut-outs of leather depicting deer. The burial, placed in a coffin made

193

from the trunk of a larch tree, was of a young woman aged between 20 and 30 years. She had been tattooed on one arm with a deer motif and wore a yellow silk blouse, a red-and-white striped woollen skirt, white felt leggings, and a tall headdress made of wood covered with felt to which were attached wooden carvings of felines covered with gold foil. The grave goods buried with her included two small wooden tables with offerings of horse meat and mutton, a wooden vessel containing a milk-based substance, and a horn cup holding a drink of another kind. Coriander seeds were found in a stone dish and cannabis had been placed in a container close to her body. She was also provided with a mirror. Her six horses, saddled and bridled, were buried within the grave pit outside the timber burial chamber.

The Ak-Alakha female was evidently a person of some status in society. She may have been a member of an aristocratic family—a princess as she is now popularly known—but it is equally possible that she was a priestess with shamanistic powers. No matter which, it is interesting to see that in the nomadic society of the Altai women could gain exalted status in their own right and were not always attendant on men.

The Ak-Alakha woman and the people buried in the Berel cemetery clearly belonged to the same culture as did those interred at Pazyryk, even though the cemeteries are hundreds of kilometres apart and separated by mountain ranges. What this shows is that the people of the Altai, far from being remote from each other and isolated in their own valleys, maintained contact across very considerable distances. How this was achieved we can only speculate but it must in some way reflect the mobility of the elites constantly moving through networks built on alliances, exchanging gifts, sharing ideas and beliefs, negotiating marriages, and, of course, feasting. In all probability the death of a revered leader would have provided the occasion for the disparate bands to come together to reaffirm alliances through storytelling, reminding those gathered of the exploits and valour of the ancestors. At such times it would have been the structures and ritual of burial displayed before them that provided the outward and visible sign of their cultural unity.

The organic remains preserved in the frozen tombs are a vivid reminder of the craft skills of nomads reliant largely on the raw materials immediately to hand—leather, wool, fur, and wood. Tough leather provided the essential horse gear but finer cuts were chosen to provide the silhouettes of animals used in appliqué work and for clothing. Wool had many uses. Sheep's wool pounded together created felt of various qualities for use in a wide range of domestic situations. Larger sheets were made into covers for wagons or into temporary dwellings, like the Mongolian gers, while smaller, finer pieces were fashioned into clothing or used as the base of flat polychrome appliqué figures made for decoration like the swans found in kurgan 5 at

Pazyryk. Wool was also spun and woven to create serges of different qualities, textiles with long pile, with whole or cut loops, that could be used as carpets and much finer plaited-weave or lace-weave fabrics, like the delicate patterned lace used to make the pigtail cover found in kurgan 2 at Pazyryk. The fibres of Siberian hemp (*kendyr*) were also woven and made into shirts.

The skill of the woodworker was everywhere to be seen, especially in the intricate relief or three-dimensional carvings of animals, often covered with gold foil, and painted bright red, used to decorate harnesses. Small items of furniture were also made, like the circular table with detachable legs carved in the form of rampant lions found in kurgan 2 at Pazyryk. The advantage of such a piece was that it was small, comparatively light, and could easily be taken apart and packed when the community was preparing to move. In nomadic society there was little place for larger items. That said, the coffin from the Bashadar cemetery shows what could be achieved. More than 3 m long and half a metre wide, its surface was intricately carved with eleven animals—snarling tigers, mountain rams, elks, and boars—all vigorously interacting, in a composition displaying great skill in the use of space, not unlike the famous tattoos on the arms of the man buried in kurgan 2 at Pazyryk.

Most members of the community would have been involved in making items for everyday life in the spare time between caring for the flocks and herds and preparing food. The more skilled craft workers created products that could have been used in gift exchange with neighbours. For more distant exchanges, fine horses and raw materials such as gold, leather, and furs were the currency. These would have been exchanged for the exotic luxury goods sought by the elite. What is remarkable about the people of the Altai is their ability to acquire items of value from great distances away. We have already referred to the carpet and saddle cloth made in Persia that found their way to Pazyryk (pp. 170–5). Other items came from India and from China. India provided two cotton shirts and a tin bronze mirror with a handle made of ox horn, while from China came silk fabrics, items of lacquer work, a large mirror, and a bronze helmet. It is also possible that the tall narrow wagon with spoked wheels found in kurgan 5 at Pazyryk was made in China. It is closely similar to a contemporary example found in the deposits associated with the burial of the First Emperor at Xian.

By what route and through what complex exchange mechanisms these exotics reached the Altai we will never know. One possibility is that they were simply trade goods transported along the caravan routes around the Taklamakan Desert (occupying much of the Xinjiang province of modern China) and used in local dealings, but it may be no coincidence that the Chinese goods first appeared in the Altai in the third century BC at about the time when cavalry was being rapidly developed in

China during the Zhao period. Perhaps the need for constant supplies of high quality horses encouraged the development of long-distance exchange networks, linking the Altai directly to China. It was the beginning of a complex series of interactions that were to have widespread effects on the region in the second and first centuries (below, pp. 316–17).

Further East: Into the Sayan Mountains

The complex folds of the Sayan Mountains and the winding course of the Yenisei River provided many favourable environments for nomad pastoralists and, as we have argued above in Chapter 4, this may have been the region in which Scytho-Siberian culture had its origin. In the Minusinsk Basin, one of the most densely occupied micro zones, the roots of nomadic culture can be traced back to the Late Bronze Age and throughout the first millennium BC the continuous and largely uninterrupted development of the Tagar culture can be followed in the rich archaeological record.

In the Saragash phase of the Tagar culture, dating from the sixth to the third centuries BC, burials tended to become larger and more elaborate with a greater emphasis on hierarchical differences. Like those in the Altai the deceased were placed in rectangular burial pits, lined and roofed with logs, but the kurgans covering them, occasionally reaching 20 m in height, were constructed within a square enclosure defined by stone slabs. The grave pits usually contained multiple burials and examples are known containing up to 200 individuals interred over a period of time using a special entrance. One of the more impressive burials of this period was the kurgan of Bolshoi Salbykskii in the Salbyk valley. It was 11 m high with the enclosing wall constructed of massive stone slabs 6 m high and weighing up to 50 tons each. The expenditure of labour was colossal. The central burial pit, 5 m square, had been robbed but originally contained seven bodies. A few scraps of gold and a bronze knife are all that survived of what may have been a sumptuous burial.

The Tagar burials differ in some respects from those of the Altai and evidently reflect a distinct regional tradition which had developed over the centuries in the relative isolation of the Minusinsk Basin. Further into the mountains, following the valley of the Yenisei to where its tributary, the Uruk, joins the main flow, is the high plateau upon which the famous cemetery of Arzhan is situated. The cemetery consists of several hundred kurgans, some of them arranged in rows. The two that have been excavated, Arzhan 1 dating to the end of the ninth century, and Arzhan 2, constructed in the middle of the seventh century (above, pp. 95–103), were extremely rich and must have belonged to elite members of an influential nomadic group. How long the cemetery continued in use is unknown.

The Arzhan community is the easternmost of the nomadic group who shared in and contributed to Scytho-Siberian culture. That a people in so remote a region could remain part of a cultural continuum covering such an enormous area is a reflection of the remarkable mobility that lay at the heart of the nomadic social system. It was a mobility rooted in the transhumance of everyday existence but it was more than that: it was a restlessness of spirit that, when the occasion arose, encouraged communities to uproot themselves and move on in search of better pastures, always to the west, displacing others and pushing them before. For much of the time the flow would have been gentle but there were episodes of more intense movement causing great dislocations that the Greek world came to hear about and to vaguely record. Forlorn tombs rooted in the land belie the nomadic compulsion always to be on the move.

8

BODIES CLOTHED
IN SKINS

DIFFERENT observers see different things. This is particularly true of Herodotus and the anonymous writer usually referred to as Pseudo-Hipprocrates, whose text *On Airs, Water, and Places* was found among the medical works of the Hippocratic school. Both were observing the Scythians in the second half of the fifth century but their interests were very different. Herodotus was concerned to provide a background for his great historical narrative, while Pseudo-Hippocrates was interested in showing how environment and lifestyle impacted on the health and well-being of steppe nomads. The first probably gathered his data from the relative comfort of the Greek colony of Olbia while the second gives the impression of having travelled more widely, making his observations in the open steppe. Herodotus is interested in men's deeds; Pseudo-Hippocrates has far more concern for the people themselves and it is to him we must first turn for a glimpse of the Scythians.

He begins with landscape, describing the level treeless steppe well-watered by wide rivers. But it is harsh place to live: 'the winds from the north always blow, congealed by snow, ice, and much water … a thick fog covers the plains during the day … so that winter may be said to be ever-present: if they have summer it is only for a few days and the heat is never strong'. Living in such a monotonous climate, eating the same food, and wearing the same clothing the year long the nomads all look much alike, not least since the men have no facial hair. 'Nor do they make any laborious excursions, for neither body nor mind is capable of enduring fatigue when the changes of the seasons are not great. For these reasons their shapes are gross and fleshy' (*On Airs, Waters, and Places*, 19). In the words of Greek medicine the cold, damp environment affects the humours of the body leading to 'softness and moistness'.

But Pseudo-Hippocrates is sufficient of an empirical scientist to realize that lifestyle also has a direct effect on physical wellbeing:

> The Scythians … are called nomads because they have no houses but live in wagons. The smallest have four wheels, others have six wheels. They are covered over with felt and are constructed like houses, sometimes in two compartments and sometimes in three, which are proof against rain, snow, and wind. The wagons are drawn by two or by three yoke of hornless oxen…. Now in these wagons live the women, while the men ride on horseback followed by their sheep, cattle, and horses. They remain in the same place just as long as there is sufficient fodder for their animals: when it gives out they move on.
>
> (*On Airs, Waters, and Places*, 18)

It is because of this kind of existence, he says, that they grow up fat and flabby. They sit about too much. 'The young males, until they are old enough to ride, spend most of their time sitting in the wagons and they walk very little since they are so often changing their place of residence. The girls get amazingly flabby and pudgy.' And being out in the open air, 'the cold causes their skin to be burnt and reddened'. He might have added that a predominantly milk- and meat-based diet would have been one of the contributing causes of weight gain.

He also comments on the low level of fertility among the Scythians: 'people of such a constitution cannot be prolific'. Obesity, he argues, reduces sexual desire among both men and women, and men showed a tendency to impotence caused, he believed, by horse-riding. Another effect of constantly being in the saddle was varicose veins 'because their feet are always hanging down from their mounts. This is followed by lameness and, in severe cases, those affected drag their hips.' To treat this, the Scythians cut the vein behind the ears—an act which Pseudo-Hippocrates thought contributed to impotence. He has more to say on this subject as we will see later (below, pp. 219–20).

Altogether it is not a particularly flattering picture. The dumpy, bow-legged Scythians unable to grow facial hair and too exhausted for procreation. But how true is it? The writer is stressing characteristics which enable him to distinguish between the urban Greek and the barbarian nomads. This is what any classical observer would do to distance self from 'other', but there is clearly a scientific mind at work, carefully noting differences and attempting to explain them in terms of the science of the times. A sedentary lifestyle does lead to obesity and excessive horse-riding in tight trousers does cause the testes to overheat, leading to a reduced sperm count. This much we can accept, but lack of facial hair is belied by iconographic representations of Scythians with their healthy beards, unless, that is, the observer was referring to a specifically Mongoloid band or tribes like those living in the Altai who preferred to shave. Nor is the generalization about squatness supported by the archaeological evidence. In some elite burials men are often over 1.80 m in height, but this is a factor of status and the lower classes are consistently shorter, averaging 1.64 m. Pseudo-Hippocrates may not have been enamoured with the nomads he encountered and may have exaggerated a little but the picture he conjures up is probably not far from the truth.

Recent scientific analysis of Scythian inhumations has thrown new light on the health of the nomad. Four of the skeletons from the southern Siberian cemetery of Aymyrlyg had bony lesions caused by gastrointestinal infections resulting from bovine tuberculosis. Given the diet of the nomads the disease may well have been widespread. Cancers are also attested. The elite male from the Arzhan 2 kurgan died at the age of 40–50 from prostate cancer after months of being bedridden, while the 30-year-old woman from Ak-Alakha suffered from terminal breast cancer and died not long after a serious fall from a horse. Evidence of bed sores suggests that she, too, had become bedridden. In her last years she relieved her considerable pain by inhaling hemp, traces of which were found in her hair. Had Pseudo-Hippocrates known of all this it would have confirmed his low opinion of the nomadic lifestyle.

Dress and Display

There are many depictions of Scythians on items of precious metal made in the north Pontic workshops. Two are particularly informative: the gold-plated silver bowl from Gaymanova mogila and the gold beaker from Kul'-Oba, both dating to the second half of the fourth century. The bowl (Gallery, no. 3) depicts six men in various sitting or reclining positions, apparently in an easy social context, while the beaker (Gallery, no. 1) shows seven men kneeling or sitting on the ground engaged in activities which would seem to suggest two separate scenes, one before and one after a battle. Twelve of the thirteen figures have shoulder-length hair and long beards, in one case the hair being held off the face with a bandana. The figures on the Kul'-Oba beaker wear long-sleeved thigh-length tunics, tightly belted and cut somewhat longer at the back than the front, over close-fitting trousers with soft calf-length boots bound at the ankle. Three of the figures wear tall pointed hats coming down to the shoulders and covering the ears. It is not clear what material the clothes were made of but in all probability it was thick felt or soft leather lined with felt or fur. The trousers were heavily decorated with what appears to be embroidery. The tunics and hats were

8.1 The gold beaker from Kul'-Oba was decorated with a zone showing seven Scythian males engaged in a range of activities. The depiction of the figures provides much detail of hairstyle, clothing, and weaponry (see Gallery, no. 1).

also enlivened by bands of embroidered decoration. It was clothing well designed for a rider, comfortable on a horse, warm and windproof. The style conforms well to Ovid's description of Scythians he encountered at Tomis near the mouth of the Danube: 'they wear skins and stitched trousers as protection from the cold and the only part of the body one sees is the face'.

The figures on the Gaymanova mogila bowl are similarly dressed but since they are inside they are without hats. The only significant difference is that their tunics are longer and fringed, with the long pointed flaps extending to mid-calf length. Such elaboration might be indicative of higher status. Riders shown on the gold neck ring from Kul'-Oba are dressed like the warriors on the Kul'-Oba beaker, as are the horse trainers depicted around the top of the Chertomlÿk amphora, but in both of these cases the trousers were baggy.

8.2 Silver vessel from the tomb of Gaymanova mogila. The figures are picked out in gold. The two scenes, showing elite males in discourse, provide details of clothing and weapons (see Gallery, no. 3).

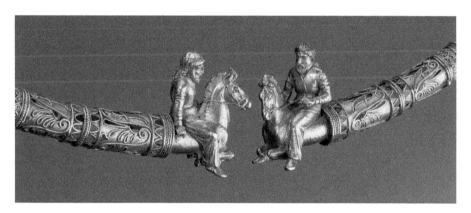

8.3 The gold torc from the tomb of Kul'-Oba was made from twisted wire. Its cast terminals are in the form of Scythian riders confronting each other.

The dress of the Central Asian Scythians seems to have been broadly similar to that of those living on the Pontic steppe. The famous relief at Bisitun of the Sakā king, Skuka, being brought before Darius, shows him with a thigh-length belted tunic, trousers, and a pointed hat, in this case with the neck flap turned up. This dress is similar to that of the Sakā ambassadors depicted on the reliefs of the Apadāna in Persepolis. The prince (or princess) from the Issyk kurgan in Kazakhstan wore the same style of clothing, the only difference being that the tunic was shorter and the boots, tunic, and hat were elaborately decorated with gold appliqué.

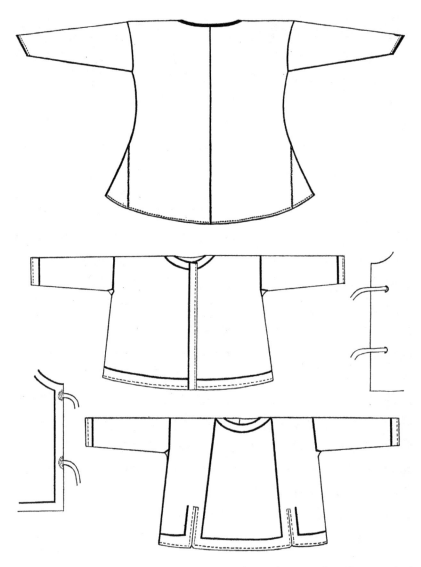

8.4 The clothing of the deceased buried in the cemetery of Pazyryk is generally well preserved. Above: shirt from kurgan 2 woven from hemp and kendyr fibres. Below: caftan from kurgan 3 made from a double thickness of thin white felt.

But it is the frozen tombs of the Altai, where organic materials are well preserved, that provide the most vivid and detailed insight into nomad dress. Men wore shirts of woven hemp or kendyr fibres, stitched with fine red woollen braid. Over the shirts they wore longer tunics, well-tailored and covered with appliqué designs in cut-out leather and gold. One of the tunics was made simply of leather, another of leather lined with sable, while a third was made of a double thickness of fine white felt. Surprisingly trousers are only rarely found but footwear is well represented. The man in kurgan 2 at Pazyryk wore short stocking boots of felt with a leather sole sewn on. The top was edged with a band of dark red felt ornamented with blue, green, and white felt arranged to create plant and animal motifs. Hats found in kurgans 2 and 3 were tall and made of felt with flaps extending down over the neck and ears and tied under the chin. One was decorated with pieces of thin leather. Overall the Altai male clothing from the frozen tombs was much like that depicted on the metal vessels from the Pontic region, but what it shows in brilliant detail is the variety of materials used, especially the importance of felt, and the love of bright, contrasting colour.

Another great advantage of the frozen tombs is that they preserve the remains of female clothing virtually unknown in the Pontic iconography. The female from kurgan 2 at Pazyryk wore a caftan with tight sleeves made from squirrel fur, with the fur inwards. The lower border was edged with bands of black colt's hair, otter fur, and another fur dyed blue, while the outer surface of the garment and the sleeves were sewn over with large stitches of sinew thread or covered with bands of cut-out leather patterns dyed dark red. She was also provided with two pairs of boots. One was made from dark red leather entirely covered with ornaments made from cut-out leather covered with gold foil and stitching of sinew covered in tin foil. The second pair was knee-length, made from brown leather, and had the sole decorated with diamonds made up of pyrite crystals edged with thread wrapped in tinfoil which would have been displayed when the woman was sitting cross-legged or with legs outstretched.

The female buried in the frozen tomb at Ak-Alakha was also brightly dressed. She wore a yellow silk shirt, a red-and-white striped woollen skirt and thigh-length white

8.5 Stockings from kurgan 2 at Pazyryk. Made from thin white felt trimmed around the top with applied strips of white felt embroidered with coloured thread to create different forms of palmette patterns.

 205

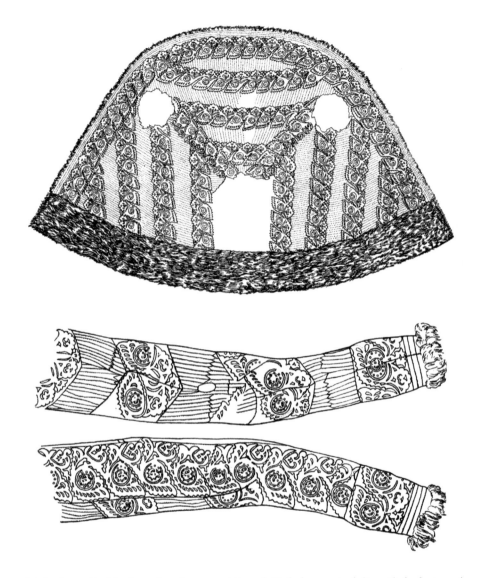

8.6a/b Cape with tight sleeves from kurgan 2 at Pazyryk. Made from squirrel skin with the fur inward. The outer surface is ornamented with leather cut-out patterns dyed dark red. The lower edge is trimmed with a band of black colt's fur with a border of another fur dyed blue.

8.7 (*Opposite*) Woman's shoe from kurgan 2 at Pazyryk. Made from leather with fur upper sewn together with red thread. Decorated with appliqué work of fine red leather and sinew covered in strips of tin foil to imitate beadwork. The sole is made of leather wrapped with red cloth decorated with diamond shapes made of strips of rolled red leather inset with pyrite crystals. They were clearly meant to be seen.

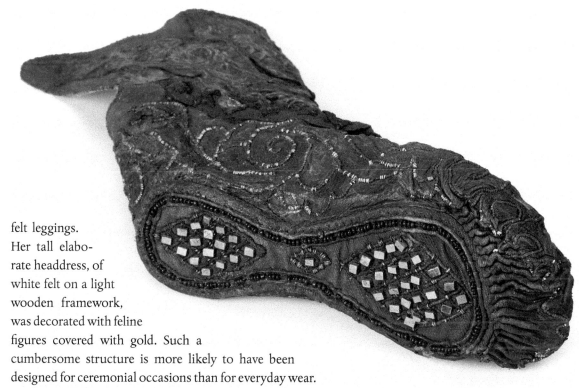

felt leggings.
Her tall elabo-
rate headdress, of
white felt on a light
wooden framework,
was decorated with feline
figures covered with gold. Such a
cumbersome structure is more likely to have been
designed for ceremonial occasions than for everyday wear.

While the images of Scythians on the metal vessels found in the kurgans
of the Pontic steppe give a fair impression of the warm, close-fitting clothing of the
horseman, the clothing from the frozen tombs of the Altai provide an incomparable
vision of the sheer exuberance of nomad dress, the love of bright, contrasting colours
and of intricate decoration formed by stitching, embroidery, and the attachment of
leather cut-outs. It also shows the varied materials in use: leather of differing qualities, a range of furs, and, above all, the ubiquitous felt made from beating wool fibres
together. In the intricate decoration of their clothes both sexes carried with them a
constant reminder of the traditional craft skills of the community, the styles of decoration perpetuating the beliefs and values of their ancestors.

The frozen tombs have yielded several examples of body tattooing, including
the male and female from both kurgans 2 and 5 at Pazyryk and the female from Ak-
Alakha. The best preserved is the male from kurgan 2. His arms, shoulders, and legs
were covered with energetic renderings of animals which extend onto his chest and
back. The animals on his arms—deer, an onager, and a fanged carnivore—are mostly
drawn with their hind quarters twisted round. The tattooed decoration on his right
leg was dominated by a fish that extended between the knee and the ankle. The female

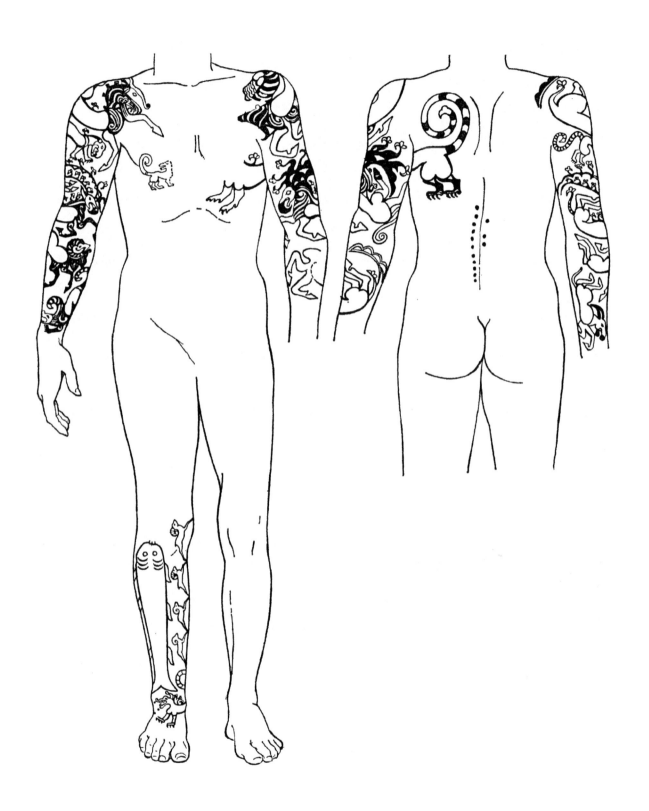

8.8 The body of the man buried beneath kurgan 2 at Pazyryk was heavily tattooed (*opposite*). The inset (*right*) shows two of the images of twisted animal motifs adorning one of his arms.

from Ak-Alakha had animal tattoos on one of her shoulders and on her wrist and thumb (above, pp. 193–4). The tattooing of both sexes was presumably a mark of status. What beliefs lay behind the choice and arrangement of the motifs is difficult to say. It may be that they were believed to be protective but they could have proclaimed the ancestry of the individual, applied perhaps during the rites of passage that marked the beginnings of adulthood. Tattooing was probably quite widespread among the nomads. The first-century writer, Pomponius Mela, commenting on the Agathyrsi, says that they 'draw over the face and body … drawing which even washing cannot remove' and when Pliny, writing at about the same time, observes that the Sarmatians 'paint their bodies', he is probably referring to tattooing.

It seems that scarring was also practised by some groups of Scythians. Pseudo-Hippocrates refers to them 'cauterizing their shoulders, arms, hands, chests, thighs, and loins for no other purpose than to avoid weakness and flabbiness and to become energetic'. Although the writer is keen to suggest a medical reason for this deliberate scarring, it may simply have been a coming of age ritual. Herodotus also mentions ritual mutilation during funerary ceremonies when the mourners slit their ears, cut their hands, and thrust arrows through their left hand. Such activities will have left visible scars as a sign that the correct rites had been observed.

Clean in Body and Mind

Most societies feel the need to clean the body from time to time and this must have been all the more necessary for nomads after weeks or months of riding wearing tight-fitting clothing of leather and felt. Herodotus offers the alarming observation that 'they never by any chance wash their bodies with water' but he goes on to describe two practices concerned with personal hygiene. The first is an act of purification following the burial ceremony:

> First they well soap and wash their heads; then, in order to cleanse their bodies they do as follows: they make a booth by fixing in the ground three sticks inclined inwards towards one another, and stretching around them woollen felt, which they arrange so as to fit as close as possible: inside the tent a bowl is placed on the ground into which they put a number of red-hot stones and then add some hemp seed … it gives out such a vapour as no Grecian vapour-bath can exceed; the Scyths delighted, shout for joy, and this vapour serves them instead of a water bath.
>
> (Hist. iv. 73–5)

Getting high on the cannabis is clearly one of the attractions of the procedure. The description seems to imply that people went into the tent and that steam was involved. If so, in the hot smoky atmosphere they would have sweated profusely, which would have cleaned the pores, the smoke fumigating their hair and beards. On some occasions they may have gone in naked and by throwing water on the heated stone may have created the steamy atmosphere of a sauna bath. Saunas, sometimes quite simple structures, are found widely among contemporary people across Europe.

It is, however, possible that Herodotus was making a false comparison between the Greek vapour bath and a quite different Scythian ritual. Evidence for inhalation comes from kurgan 2 at Pazyryk where two sets of gear were found, each consisting of a bundle of six long poles designed to form the framework of a tent, one of felt, the other of leather. Each was associated with a small cast-bronze vessel filled with burnt stones among which were found charred hemp seeds. Both vessels were provided with handles, the handles of one being wrapped with birch bark for insulation so that it could be taken out, without burning the hands, for reheating over a fire. While these finds are clear evidence that inhalation was practised, the scale of the equipment is such that it would have been quite impossible to get even one body into the tent. Its only use would have been to allow a person to put his head under the covering to inhale. This does not, of course, exclude the possibility that there were also larger structures allowing one or more people to enter to enjoy the invigorating atmosphere. In such a case comparison with the Greek vapour bath may have been appropriate.

Sauna baths, with or without the benefit of cannabis inhalation, may well have been the preserve of men. For the women Herodotus describes a different process. They make a paste by pounding cypress, cedar, and frankincense wood with water in a stone mortar and use it to cover their faces and their whole bodies. 'A sweet odour is thereby imparted to them and when they take off the paste the next day their skin is clean and glossy' (*Hist.* iv. 75). After trekking for days across the steppe, cooped up together in claustrophobic covered wagons, such a cleansing process would have been to everyone's benefit.

Attention to personal appearance is amply demonstrated by the fine clothes worn by both males and females. The women buried in the Pazyryk cemetery had pierced ears, though not all were wearing earrings. They also styled their hair into long plaits, sometimes bulked up with horsehair, sometimes twisted with felt braids, and sometimes tied at the end with ribbons of white felt. These rigid plaits were arranged to stand up vertically from the top of the head. To aid them in preparing these creations they used mirrors and fine-toothed combs made of horn. Combs of this kind would probably have been used by both sexes to provide some relief from nits and lice which must have been a constant irritation.

The Comforts of the Home

The classic picture of the Scythians as wandering nomads travelling on horseback accompanied by their covered wagons derives largely from the Hippocratic text quoted above (p. 200) supported by Herodotus, who writes of 'people who have built neither cities nor walls, who take their dwellings with them … whose homes are their wagons' (*Hist.* iv. 46). For much of the open steppe this kind of mobility would probably have been the norm during the summer months with communities moving every few days to find new pastures for the animals, but in the winter more permanent bases were likely to have been established in the river valleys. The wagons that carried the household goods, the women, the aged, and the young are known from a few clay models which suggest that the upper part was built of hoops of light wood covered with fabric, probably felt. A single family would have needed several such vehicles to carry everything and everyone. When a stop was made the wagon would have provided some shelter but it is likely that other shelters were carried, like wigwam-style tents or more elaborate structures like

8.9 Clay model of a wagon with solid wheels and covered to protect the people and goods carried in them.

211

8.10 Petroglyph from Boyer in the Yenisei valley showing a row of circular structures with domed roofs similar to the felt-covered gers or yurts traditionally used on the steppe. Probably dating to the Tagar period or perhaps later.

the yurts (or gers), used today in many areas of the steppe. The Mongolian ger with its lattice walls, light wooden roof poles, and fabric covering, when disassembled takes up little space and is easily stowed. It can be put up by two or three people in an hour and provides ample space for a family. In those areas of the steppe where mobility could be restricted to only a few moves within the year larger structures like the gers would have been practicable, offering the great advantage of a communal space suitable for ordered family life.

In the Altai–Sayan Mountains where the lush upland grasslands could provide pasture for longer periods of time, it is likely that more permanent houses were built of larch logs similar to the structures of the burial chambers found in the tombs. With walls of horizontally laid timbers and roofs waterproofed with large sheets of birch bark, made pliable by boiling, such structures could have been made warm and

 212

weatherproof. If the tombs can be seen as houses for the dead copying the houses of the living, then they give some idea of the comforts of the domestic house. Floors were covered by thick layers of felt and walls were hung with embroidered fabrics or carpets. One of the patterned wall hangings found in tomb 5 at Pazyryk measured 4.5 by 6.5 m. Fittings of this kind could easily be taken down and packed on those occasions when the community needed to move on.

The Pazyryk burials also give a detailed insight into the equipment of the nomad household. The principal item of furniture was the four-legged table, which could be taken apart for packing. The tabletop, hollow and with a rim around the edge, was really a large plate on which the communal food could be heaped. Nearby was a large pottery jug for koumiss—fermented mares' milk. There were no chairs. People either sat on the ground or on blocks of wood, waisted in the middle and sometimes covered with elaborately decorated leatherwork. Cast bronze cauldrons were used for cooking and vessels of wood or earthenware served as plates. For lighting, oil lamps were carved from sandstone. The other essential item of nomad life was the ubiquitous bag made of leather or fur, which could vary in size and shape from pouches and purses to large saddle bags. A mobile community needed the means of packing up all its smaller possessions from time to time.

8.11 Table (*right*), or more correctly, large tray with legs, from kurgan 2 at Pazyryk. The turned legs are detachable. *Below*: table leg in the form of a predator also from kurgan 2.

8.12 Bronze cauldron with four handles from the Semirech'ye region, south-east Kazakhstan.

If the model wagons accurately represent the vehicles in use, then the average wagon was substantially built with solid wooden wheels, either four or six according to Pseudo-Hippocrates. The text also says that they were pulled by two or three yokes of oxen. These tough, resilient structures were efficiently designed to carry heavy loads on long journeys across the rough steppe. A quite different style of vehicle was found in kurgan 5 at Pazyryk. It was a light, elegant carriage built of birch, sprung on four spoked wheels each 1.6 m in diameter. The four horses that had pulled the carriage were buried with it. One pair was harnessed to the pole using a primitive horse collar, while the second outside pair hauled on traces. The quality of the vehicle and

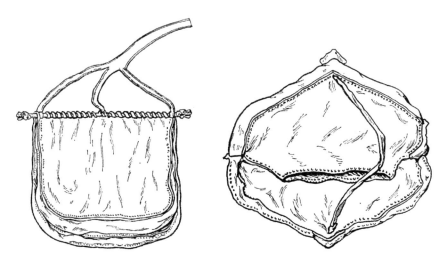

8.13 Leather bag from kurgan 2 at Pazyryk.

8.14 Cart with spoked wheels from kurgan 5 at Pazyryk. The vehicle was built so that it could easily be dismantled to be transported across rugged ground. It was not well suited to the Altai environment and may have been used only for ceremonial purposes.

  215

its delicacy of construction imply that it was for ceremonial use. It is closely similar to contemporary Chinese examples and may have been of Chinese origin, arriving in the Altai Mountains perhaps as a diplomatic gift. Such a contraption would have been suitable for making grand gestures to enhance the status of its owner but would have been of little use for hauling the family possessions from one pasture to another. Indeed, the fact that it could easily be dismantled meant that it could, itself, become part of the baggage when the family moved on.

The idea of packing up the family home and having to move several times a year may seem arduous but this is how half the population of Mongolia lives today. It takes less than a day to dismantle the ger and to pack it and all the other belongings into a small lorry—the modern equivalent of the ox-drawn covered wagon—before the trek to the new pasture begins.

Social Structure

To generalize about social structure based on the few scraps of evidence that survive is dangerous, not least since there must have been considerable variation from one part of the Scythian world to another. It is unlikely, for example, that the same social rules applied to communities living in the Altai as to those existing on the Pontic steppe. While Herodotus says that those whom he calls the 'Royal Scyths' adopted a form of hereditary succession to appoint their leaders, the archaeological evidence from Pazyryk suggests that this may not have been so in the eastern mountains, where the elite all seem to have been exceptionally tall, implying that physical prowess may have been a factor in the selection of a leader. At best, using the literary sources we can create a generalized picture for the Pontic region but one must remember that it may be biased by the behaviour of the leading tribe, the Royal Scyths, best known to the classical world. Those who lived in the forest steppe and cultivated grain may have lived by different social rules, while the Sakā of Central Asia and the Altai dwellers may have been different again.

That said, the classical sources give a picture of the social hierarchy of the Pontic steppe entirely consistent with the burial evidence. The Scyths seem to have been ruled simultaneously by three kings of different status, the chief king having the largest kingdom. Succession was hereditary. Under the kings many different classes were recognized, nomarchs (land owners) and other ranks called 'noble' and 'distinguished'. Then came the class of skilled men such as sceptre bearers, spear bearers, and soothsayers. Below them were the ordinary people and at the bottom of the social scale, the slaves. Not much is heard of the slaves but Herodotus offers a rather confused account of the practice of blinding those slaves who were involved in the task of milking the mares and making the staple fermented mares' milk, koumiss. No reason is given but there may have been some kind of superstitious belief involved.

The story that Herodotus tells about the unfortunate Scythian king, Skyles (*Hist.* iv. 78–80), gives an insight into kingship. Skyles' father, Ariapeithes, was the king-in-chief of the Scythians in the mid fifth century. Arapeithes had three wives, a Greek from Istria who was Skyles' mother, the daughter of the Thracian king, Teres, and a Scythian woman, Opoea. When Ariapeithes died, Skyles acceded to the kingship, being given his stepmother, Opoea, as a bride. He had two half-brothers, Oricus, son of Opoea, and Ocamasades, son of the Thracian princes. Skyles' pro-Greek behaviour was unacceptable to his followers and he was deposed in favour of Ocamasades. He fled but was hunted down on the borders of Thrace by his half-brother and beheaded. The story offers a number of interesting reflections of Scythian kingship. Polygyny seems normally to have been practised, with the wives chosen to strengthen political alliances, in this case with the Thracian royal house and the Greek urban elite. Kingship was evidently hereditary, though not always without contest, while the practice of the new king acquiring one or more of his father's wives was, at least in theory, a mechanism designed to enhance social stability.

Ariapeithes' wives appear to have survived his death. This may imply that it was not customary for the wives of kings to be killed to accompany their dead husbands into the other world. The females found in the rich tombs of the Pontic steppe may, therefore, have been concubines as, indeed, Herodotus implies, strangled along with the king's cupbearer, cook, groom, messenger, and personal servant to provide for his needs in the afterlife.

Another practice, which helped to bind society, was blood brotherhood—the creation of a sacred and unbreakable bond between two warriors. This was done by two men drinking together from the same vessel a mixture of wine and their own blood into which their swords, spears, arrows, and axes had first been dipped. The drink was made even more potent by formulaic incantations said over it. The drinking ceremony is faithfully depicted on a gold plaque found in the kurgan of Kul'-Oba showing the two men nose to nose sharing the same drinking horn. It is tempting to think that the pairs of warriors shown on the gold beaker from the same tomb may also have been blood brothers.

Public approval was another way in which behaviour was manipulated. Herodotus describes how, once a year, the governor of each province, called a meeting at which a bowl of wine was presented. Every man who had slain an enemy was allowed to drink, while those who had slain many were rewarded with an extra cup. The men with no tally of a dead foe 'sit aloof in disgrace'. Such a procedure would have been a powerful incentive to embrace warfare with enthusiasm.

8.15 Plaque of gold from the tomb of Kul'-Oba depicting two Scythian men drinking from the same drinking horn. It is likely that they were engaged in the ritual joining them as blood brothers.

Gender Fluidity

Both Herodotus and the writer of the Hippocratic text *On Airs, Waters, and Places* were aware that gender among the Scythians was a more fluid concept than they were used to and both comment extensively on the fact. We have already referred to warlike women (above, pp. 121–2). Pseudo-Hippocrates is explicit:

 218

> In Europe there is a Scythian race called Sauromatae... . Their women ride on horseback, use the bow and throw the javelin from their horse, and fight with their enemies as long as they remain virgins; and they do not lay aside their virginity until they kill three of their enemies nor have any connection with men until they perform the sacrifice according to the law. Whoever takes to herself a husband, gives up riding on horseback unless she is obliged to by the necessity of a general expedition.
>
> (*On Airs, Waters, and Places*, 17)

He goes on to explain that when the girls are young their mothers cauterized their right breast to stop it from developing; 'all the strength and fullness are driven to the right shoulder and arm', giving the young warrior enhanced strength as an archer.

Herodotus calls these women Amazons (*a-mazos* in Greek, 'without a breast') but says that in the Scythian language they are known as *oiorpata* ('man-slayers'). He provides them with a fanciful origin myth to explain how they eventually reached the territory of the Sauromatae, going on to say, 'and have continued to today to practise their ancient customs, frequently hunting on horseback with their husbands, sometimes even on their own; in war taking the field; and even dressing like men' (*Hist.* iv. 116). He confirms the point made in the Hippocratic text that no girl is allowed to marry until she has killed a man in battle. If we take these two texts at face value, it does seem that women among the Sauromatae may have been allowed or encouraged to adopt male gender roles. Herodotus' passing remark, that some died unmarried at an advanced age, hints that not all women were prepared to revert to female gender roles in later life.

The general validity of these accounts is, at least to a degree, supported by the archaeological evidence. In the territory of the Sauromatae one fifth of the excavated warrior burials dating from the fifth to fourth century are females, while in Scythian territory more than forty female warrior burials are known. At Chertomlÿk, where fifty warrior graves have been found, at least four are anatomically female. That females were able to serve as warriors is not in doubt. Herodotus' observation that among one of the more distant of the nomadic people, the Issedonians, men and women shared equal power may be a further hint that not all nomadic societies were male dominated. Nor should we forget that the Sakā were at one time led against the Persians by a warrior queen, Tomyris.

Pseudo-Hippocrates has an interesting comment to make on male sexuality:

> There are many eunuchs among the Scythians who perform female work and speak like women. Such persons are called *Andrieis* (effeminates). The Scythians attribute the cause of their impotence to god, and venerate and worship such persons, everyone dreading that a similar fate might befall himself.
>
> (*On Airs, Waters, and Places*, 22)

 219

This usually happened, he said, after the men had found themselves to be impotent. Accepting the condition as the will of the gods 'they put on female attire, reproach themselves for effeminacy, play the part of women, and perform the same work as women do'. Noting that gender transfer was more prevalent among the rich, who habitually rode horses, Pseudo-Hippocrates puts the cause of impotence down to the evils of horse-riding, of which he evidently disapproves (see p. 200), 'because they always wore trousers and spend most of their time on horseback, unable to fondle themselves, and from cold and fatigue they forget their sexual desires'.

Herodotus was aware of the effeminate males among the Scythians. He calls them *Enarees* and says that they were punished by the deities with the 'female sickness'. They were adept at divination, using a special method taught to them by Venus, which involves taking a piece of the inner bark of the linden tree and splitting it into three, twining and untwining the strips around their fingers while they prophesy (*Hist.* iv. 67). Herodotus, always keen to offer a plausible explanation, says that the Scythians who plundered the temple of Venus in Ascalon were punished with the female sickness by the goddess—a punishment passed down the generations (*Hist.* i. 100). Both Herodotus and Pseudo-Hippocrates, then, agree that the desire of some Scythian males to take on the female role was induced by the gods and that such people had supernatural powers enabling them to become diviners and shamans. Transgender behaviour was a characteristic of shamanism in various parts of the world in the recent past.

Work and Play

The life of pastoral nomads was controlled by the needs of their animals, needs which varied with the seasons and with the constraints of the territories over which they ranged. It was a life of movement demanding interminable hours in the saddle or cooped up in the cramped space of the covered wagons, waiting for the relief of making camp. But even in these sedentary interludes the animals had to be guarded and moved from pasture to pasture, requiring that men spent long periods away from home.

The composition of the flocks and herds varied from region to region. Horses, sheep, and cattle were the favoured beasts but goats are known and yaks have been identified in the Altai. For many of the Scythian communities, horses were their principal concern. Nomad communities living on the steppe in recent times ran herds of about a thousand beasts, half comprising breeding mares, half foals and geldings together with a few stallions, some fifteen to twenty. The management of so large a herd required skill simply to keep it together and on the move. A variety of horses could be present in any herd. At Pazyryk most numerous were the tough herd animals, not too far removed from the wild Przewalski's horse, but there were also thoroughbreds, perhaps acquired from outside the region by exchange. Horses suitable for cavalry use and riding horses for everyday use can also be distinguished. Details of hoof growth show that the more valued beasts were penned during the winter and provided with special feed while the herd horses were left out to look after themselves.

Work horses needed special training and this is nowhere better illustrated than in the frieze of the silver-gilt amphorae found in the kurgan of Chertomlÿk (Gallery, no. 10), where the man/horse relationship is brilliantly depicted with wild horses, manes untrimmed, being caught with lassos, while the trained horses, with short-trimmed manes, are given more specialist training, the saddled beast being hobbled to restrict its movement.

8.16 Frieze of figures applied to the shoulder of the bronze vessel from Chertomlÿk (see Gallery, no. 10) showing various stages in the training of horses.

The large herds of non-working horses served two purposes. They had a recognized value and could be used in barter, the size of the herd serving as an indication of the status of the owning family. The second use was to provide food for the community, milk on a daily basis and meat on those occasions when a feast was called for. Mare milking is not an easy task. Herodotus describes one method. They 'thrust tubes made of bone, not unlike our musical pipes, up the vulva of the mare and then blow into the tubes with their mouths, some milking while others blow' (*Hist.* iv. 2). Modern mare-milkers in Mongolia and Kyrgyzstan use a less intrusive method by taking foals to the mares to encourage them to lactate. Milking in this manner is sometimes done six times a day. The milk would then have been put into large vessels and left to ferment to make koumiss. The benefit of this process is that it converts the lactose content into lactic acid, ethanol, and carbon dioxide, creating a slightly effervescent mildly alcoholic drink that can safely be taken by those with lactose intolerance. It is easy to digest and has medical benefits.

Flocks of sheep were also important. The gold pectoral from Tolstaya mogila (Gallery, no. 9) shows a boy milking a ewe while in another part of the scene two men stretch out a fleece. Sheep were also a prime source of meat. Most of the deceased buried at Pazyryk were provided with an ample quantity of mutton to sustain them on the journey to the other world. An analysis of the sheep bones found at Pazyryk showed the beasts to have been of agile build, some at least being of the much desired fat-tailed variety. Two types of wool were identified, coarse wool for felt making and much finer wool for other tasks like embroidery. Clearly the sheep, rather like the horses, were carefully selected to provide a varied range of end products.

The Tolstaya mogila pectoral also depicts goats and cattle with comparatively short horns. Both animals would have been widely herded but not necessarily in large numbers in all regions. Cattle have the need to drink large volumes of water at least twice a day and on the open steppe away from the river valleys this would not have been possible. In favoured areas, however, cattle might well have predominated. The milk of cattle, sheep, and goats was made into cheese, the different kinds of milk often being mixed. Cheese was an extremely efficient way to store food through the winters. The quantity found in the Pazyryk tombs is an indication of its importance to the community.

8.17a/b (*Opposite*) Rural scenes of animal husbandry displayed on the gold pectoral from the tomb of Tolstaya mogila (see Gallery, no. 9).

222

A text, preserved in the Hippocratic corpus, gives details of the process of separation used by the Scythians to make curd and cheese.

> For they pour the milk into wooden vessels and agitate it. And as it is agitated it foams and separates. The fat, which they call butter (*bouturon*), separates to the surface, as it is light, but the heavy solids separate to the bottom and they set it aside and dry it. When it has become firm and dry they call it 'hippake'. The whey of the milk lies in the middle.
>
> (*Diseases* iv. 51)

The process of agitation, presumably carried out by slaves, was extremely labour-intensive. In recent times the Kalmyks spend three hours on a single separation.

In spite of the demands of a nomadic life, there would have been time for leisure. One has only to glance at the stunning array of home crafts recovered from the Altai tombs to appreciate the amount of time spent (presumably by women) on tasks designed to brighten life through the use of colour and form. It is estimated that to make the famous pile carpet from Pazyryk kurgan 5 with its one and a quarter million knots would have taken an experienced worker, working every day, a year and a half to complete. Although the carpet is Persian in style it could have been made by Sakā living within the Persian Empire.

One of the leisure activities enjoyed by horsemen (and among some tribes horse-women as well) was hunting, and in particular hunting the hare using a short spear. Just such a sport is depicted on two gold plaques from the Kul'-Oba kurgan. We have already encountered the amusing story of the confrontation between the army of Darius and the Scythians during the Persian campaign of 513/512 (above, pp. 42–4). The two forces were drawn up facing each other when 'it chanced that a hare started up between them … and set to running. All the Scythians who saw it immediately rushed off in pursuit with great confusion and loud cries and shouts' (*Hist.* iv. 134). It is not clear from the context that Herodotus fully appreciated what delight Scythians took in the wild excitement of the hunt. Hunting was widespread, motivated largely by the sport it provided. Spirited representations of wolf, roebuck, and hare in the Pazyryk tombs leave little doubt that they were the prize, while the discovery of the fur of leopard, steppe cat, squirrel, sable, otter, and ermine give an idea of the other animals caught in the chase whose skins could be put to good use.

8.18 (*Opposite top*) Gold plaque of a Scythian horseman from the tomb of Kul'-Oba. The rider is probably hunting a small animal. The figure has been cut out of a rectangular plaque.

8.19 (*Opposite bottom*) Gold plaque from Kul'-Oba showing a rider about to spear a hare.

8.20 Man playing a musical instrument like a lyre. This is one of the figures depicted on a gold, repoussé-decorated diadem from the kurgan of Sachnovka (see Gallery, no. 8).

In more mellow moments the Scythians enjoyed music. An embossed headband from the kurgan at Sachnovka (Gallery, no. 8) shows a bearded man playing a lyre. Pan pipes made from bird bones were found in kurgan 5 at Skatovka in the lower Volga region and references are made to flutes crafted from eagle bone by some of the Scythian's northern neighbours. The Pazyryk tombs also have details to add. In kurgan 2 a remarkable harp-like stringed instrument was recovered and several of the tombs also contained drums made from two halves of an ox horn stitched down one edge with a membrane stretched over one end. Music would no doubt have accompanied rituals and ceremonies but it is tempting to imagine the tired horseman settling down with his kin to enjoy an evening of singing and dancing. But it was not to all tastes. One Scythian king is claimed to have said that he preferred the neighing of his horse to the strumming of music.

8.21 Stringed musical instrument from kurgan 2 at Pazyryk. The resonator is made from a single hollowed-out piece of wood. The middle part of the body was covered by a wooden sounding board, while sounding membranes were stretched over the open part of the body. There were at least four strings, suggesting that the instrument may have been a kind of harp.

The Scythian love of undiluted wine has been described above (p. 54). The topos of the drunken Scythian was well known in the Greek world. The phrase 'get ourselves as drunk as Scythians', used by the sixth century poet Anacreon, would have brought a knowing smile to the faces of his Greek audience. The archaeological evidence supports the large-scale consumption of Greek wine by the Scythians of the Pontic steppe. Amphorae are found in some numbers accompanying burials of the elite and are often found with wine-drinking gear of the kind that would be expected in any upper-class Greek household. Amphorae are also found at the large inland trading sites. There can be little doubt that wine drinking was avidly taken up by those able to obtain supplies. But further away from the Black Sea interface, in Central Asia and beyond, nomads would have had to rely on koumiss with its significantly lower alcohol content. The drunken Scythian, then, was most likely a product of contact with the classical world—yet another example of the debilitating effect which interaction with supposedly developed societies could have.

9

BENDING THE BOW

ONE of the characteristics of all human societies is innate aggression resulting from the desire of individuals to protect themselves and their own. It
is hardwired into our genetic make-up. If uncontrolled, it prevents communities living and working together and it is for this reason that societies devise
rules and procedures to contain and to control these potentially destructive instincts.
Steered into competitiveness, aggression can become creative. It can drive the individual to greater feats of personal achievement and it can foster team spirit bonding
a community, or a sect of that community, closely together in common enterprise.

For horse-riding nomads on the steppe, hunting was just such an activity. The ease
with which the Scythian riders, confronting the army of Darius, were distracted by
a fleeting hare is revealing. Hunting expeditions across the open steppe were perfect
outlets for pent-up energy focusing the aggression and competitive desire on a single,
harmless (at least for humans) objective. It also honed the skills of the rider. The game
of *buzkashi*, played extensively across Central Asia, which involves large numbers of
riders vying to take command of the dead body of an animal, usually a goat, is simply
a more stylized version of the hunt. The horse-racing events, wrestling matches, and
hunting with golden eagles, characteristic of the sports of modern Mongolia, have a
deep ancestry in the practices that steppe societies have evolved to provide a harmless outlet for ever-present aggression.

But warfare is endemic in human society and can break out when communities come under strain, imposed by factors like population growth or climatic change which upset the holding capacity of the land, causing social stress. At such times raids on neighbours, to acquire their livestock or simply to appropriate their pastures, provides some relief. The raid, which builds upon the skills and camaraderie of the hunt and competitive sport, can soon escalate into more confrontational hostilities. These episodes of warfare create the conditions in which war leaders emerge, new hierarchies form, and clans reformulate their identity. Once the imminent threat has been dealt with, status gained by military prowess is not easy to suppress. The band, gathered around a successful military leader, will look for further adventures and the anticipation of action will draw in new members. The crucial moment of change comes when a cohort of fighters is able to detach itself for long periods from the productive base of the community and become a fully fledged predatory horde, leaving the young, the old, and the women to look after the animals and the home base during the summer months while they are away.

There are many different factors which excite aggressive behaviour. Ecological stress is certainly one but, so too, is its antithesis, climate amelioration. In times of lush growth brought about by warmer, damper weather the life of the nomadic pastoralists becomes easier. Energies once bound up in caring for the livestock can now be invested in further, more extensive raiding leading to the discovery of new fertile pastures beyond the traditional grazing grounds. This, in turn, encourages mobility on an increasing scale. These dynamics are prone to escalation. It was processes such as these that initiated the successive waves of nomadic movement that flowed westwards from the Altai–Sayan region and the eastern Kazakh steppe in the ninth and eighth centuries BC.

The sparse archaeological evidence does not allow us to model the subtleties of these movements. At one level warrior hoards may have spearheaded migrations with their dependants and livestock following in their wake. But there are many other scenarios. Young men, eager to gain fame through adventure, may have gone off on raids with the intention of eventually returning home. Such a group, caught up in the turmoil in Asia Minor, were away 28 years, if Herodotus is to be believed. Other cohorts may simply have left for good, intent on taking land, flocks, and wives when chance allowed. Mobility ruled the day and the mobile hoard was all-powerful.

Learning from the Other

The fighting methods of nomads in the steppe environment focused around the rapid cavalry attack using simple weapons, principally the bow, while protecting their bodies with a shield of wood or leather. But from the seventh century contact with Persians in Central Asia introduced the nomads to quite different forms of warfare involving more organized and heavily armed troops, including infantry detachments as well as cavalry. Later, in Asia Minor, Scythian bands fought with or against Urartians, Medes, Assyrians, and even confronted Egyptians, and on the Pontic steppe they came into direct, but largely non-confrontational, contact with Greeks. In the late sixth century they were again fighting Persians and in the fourth century they were engaged in struggles with Thracians and Macedonians. From friends and foes alike they learned much, adopting new types of weapons and armour, though usually modifying them to suit themselves, and changing fighting tactics wherever appropriate. They may have come to appreciate the benefit of scale armour from the Persians, while helmets and greaves were borrowed directly from the Greeks. Against the forces of Darius they were able to field infantry in addition to their fearsome cavalry.

The Scythians living around the Black Sea and the Sakā, facing the Persian empire in Central Asia, were very differently attired to their contemporaries in the Altai Mountains and yet the ethos of the Scythian horde, men (and sometimes women) at one with their horses, armed with the same basic weapon sets, was to be found the length and breadth of the steppe.

Mobility

The horse was an essential part of the steppe nomad's life and not to have fought from horseback would have been unthinkable to an aspiring warrior. The burials at Pazyryk all included horses killed to accompany the dead person to the grave. Numbers varied, some graves containing as many as fourteen. The majority were steppe ponies not far removed from the wild breed, but usually there was at least one thoroughbred averaging 15 hands high comparable to the 'blood sweating' horses of Ferghana so much in demand by the Chinese emperors. Mostly they were bays and chestnuts. The scientist who studied the Pazyryk horse remains suggested that the deliberate choice of these colours was because the breeders believed coloured horses, especially those with white fetlocks, to have weaker hooves. Given that the beasts were not shod, the quality of the hoof was a prime concern. All the riding horses found in the elite tombs of Pazyryk and elsewhere in the Altai–Sayan were geldings. The preference among the Scythians for geldings as opposed to mares or stallions is also confirmed by the first century BC writer, Strabo (*Geog.* vii. 4. 8) and continues today among the Kazakhs.

The age of the riding horses buried with the Pazyryk elite varied. There were usually one or two young beasts of less than three and a half years, several in the middle age range, and some older animals more than fifteen years old. The range suggests that the deceased was being accompanied by his horses in daily use, young horses in training, and veterans kept for sentimental reasons.

The actual horse remains from Pazyryk and the depiction of horses on metal items from the Pontic kurgans show that it was customary to trim the manes short on beasts in active use, presumably to remove any impediment to the rapid action of the mounted archer. The distinction between horses with trimmed and flowing manes on the Chertomlÿk amphora is intended to show animals in different stages of training. The beasts being ridden, depicted on the gold neck ring from Kul'-Oba and the gold comb from Solokha, all, appropriately, have well-cropped manes. The horse remains from Pazyryk show that, here at least, the tails of the beasts were either plaited or were knotted at half length. The carpet found in kurgan 5 at Pazyryk, probably made in Persia, depicts a procession of riders mounted or leading their horses. All have elaborately knotted tails and cropped manes but in this case they are self-evidently stallions. The Chertomlÿk amphora shows a trainer apparently encouraging a horse to kneel—an interesting detail which hints that horses were taught to do this to facilitate mounting, much as camels are made to kneel by desert nomads today. This would certainly make mounting a less testing and more elegant process, especially for a heavily armed and overweight rider.

Although some of the depictions of riding scenes on Pontic metalwork (like the Solokha comb) imply that some riders may have ridden bareback, there is ample evidence for saddles, which seem to have been a seventh-century Scythian invention. A simple and unadorned version, attached by girth strap and breast strap, is carried by the horse shown being hobbled on the Chertomlÿk amphora. The horses on the Pazyryk carpet are all saddled and are wearing elaborately decorated saddle cloths. Even more spectacular are the actual saddles and saddle clothes recovered from the Pazyryk tombs. Although there was much variety in the detail of saddle construction, the basic forms were similar. They consisted of two felt cushions, stuffed with stag's hair, mounted on felt sweatbands. In some examples the cushions were attached to wooden saddle frames placed back and front. The saddles were kept in place by a girth strip, a breastband, and a tail strap. All elements of the saddle were richly decorated with wool, appliqué leather, and felt, and with wooden carvings covered in gold foil. They were highly coloured in red, yellow, dark blue, black, and white.

9.1a/b Two scenes from the Chertomlÿk amphora showing the hobbling of a horse (*top*) and a horse being trained to kneel or to lie down (*bottom*) (see Gallery, no. 10).

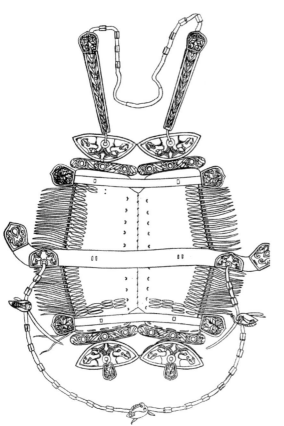

9.2 (*Left*) Saddle from kurgan 5 at Pazyryk drawn out to show the arrangement of the various elements.

9.3 (*Below*) Saddle from kurgan 5 in its original form. Made from leather, wood, plucked deer hair, and sinew. The sweat-cloth attached to the underside was of felt, while the cover is made from leather, woollen textile, and fur with lacquer, silk, and gold decoration.

9.4 Saddle cover from kurgan 1 at Pazyryk made from felt, leather, fur, and hair, with some gold decoration. Its main polychrome decoration is composed of two scenes of predation showing an eagle-like griffin attacking a mountain goat.

Beneath the saddles were saddlecloths (*shabracks*) extending from below the saddle on each side, adding further elaboration and colour to the ensemble. They were usually made of felt but one was of Chinese silk. The parts obscured by the saddle were usually plain but the exposed lengths hanging below were invariably highly decorated with appliqué work and with tassels along the bottom edges.

Nor was any effort spared to make the bridles striking and brilliant. The halter-like structure was composed of nose, cheek, and head straps attached to the metal, bone, or wood S-shaped cheek pieces of the two-linked bits, the whole thing secured in place by a single buckle on the left-hand side. In the centre of the forehead was a metal plate attached to the bridle by a leather thong. The bridles were usually highly decorated with wooden attachments carved in the form of animal heads and sometimes covered in gold foil. Some of the horses wore elaborately carved head pieces. Only the more durable part of the bridle survives in the kurgans of the Pontic–Caspian region but the general form of the arrangement seems to have been much the same throughout the steppe. Plainer and more functional forms of bridle, which may have been preferred in battle, are clearly depicted on the horse dominating the Solokha comb and on two of the horses on the Chertomlÿk amphora.

9.5 Bridle from kurgan 1 at Pazyryk made from leather, wood, and bronze.

A Pazyryk horse complete with saddlecloth, saddle, and bridle to a modern eye seems garish and encumbered to the point of hindering the animal's ease of movement. The contrast with the functional gear worn by the riding horses depicted on the Pontic metalwork is, indeed, striking. It could be argued that such remarkable finery was created specifically for the rituals associated with burial but many of the items show evidence of extensive use. A likely explanation, therefore, is that the elaborate ensemble was designed for parade and for use on ceremonial occasions rather than for everyday life or the rigours of warfare. When visiting a Mongolian ger today it is not at all unusual to find the owner's highly ornate saddle displayed prominently in pride of place for guests to admire. It is there as a clear and immediate indication of his status and prestige. The saddle for daily use is kept well out of sight.

9.6 Bridle from kurgan 5 at Pazyryk made from leather and wood.

9.7 Detail of the gold comb from the tomb of Solokha (see Gallery, no. 5) showing a Scythian bridle in use.

9.8 Reconstruction of three horses wearing saddles and bridles representing successive stages in the development of horse gear in the Altai based on excavated evidence. *Top*: Bashadar, kurgan 2; *middle*: Pazyryk, kurgan 1; *bottom*: Pazyryk, kurgan 3.

Attack

The weapon for which the Scythians were famous throughout the ancient world was the bow and arrow. Since the bows were fired from horseback they were short, seldom more than 0.8 m in length, the strength of the shot relying on the compression of the composite structure rather than upon its length. While bows are frequently included in scenes depicted on gold items from the Pontic steppe, little remains of them among the grave finds, but what survives is sufficient to show that they were composite structures of wood and sinew glued together and strung with animal

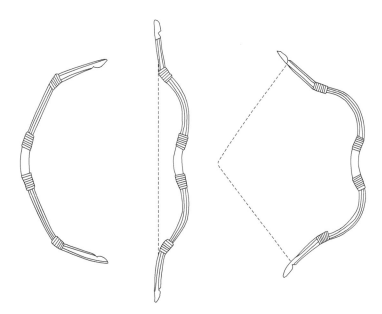

9.9 The Scythian bow was made from strips of wood and bone glued together. When strung, an act requiring skill and strength, it was under much tension, imparting great power to the arrow.

sinew. Ammianus Marcellinus describes them thus: 'While the bows of all peoples are made of flexible branches, Scythian bows resemble the crescent moon with both ends curved inwards.' He was, in fact, describing the unstrung bow. To string it required the two ends to be bent back on themselves. This was done by hooking one leg over the middle of the bow to force it forward and bracing one end (with string attached) on the thigh of the other leg so that the loose end of the string could be hooked over the other end of the tensely retracted bow. The action is captured with great clarity in one of the scenes on the Kul'-Oba gold beaker. Stringing a bow required strength and dexterity. Even greater strength was needed to draw the string against the compressed forces locked into the shaft.

The range of such a bow was considerable. A Greek grave monument found at Olbia records that Anaxagoras, son of Dimagoras, shot an arrow over a distance of 282 *orgyiai*. This converts to more than half a kilometre—a staggering achievement by any standards. Used in open warfare a volley of arrows fired at about ten a minute by rapidly advancing cavalry would have had a devastating effect upon a densely grouped enemy. The other tactic, used to great effect, was for the horde to ride away from the enemy, drawing them in hot pursuit and then to turn their bodies around to the left side and fire arrows into the advancing enemy. The tactic was made famous by the

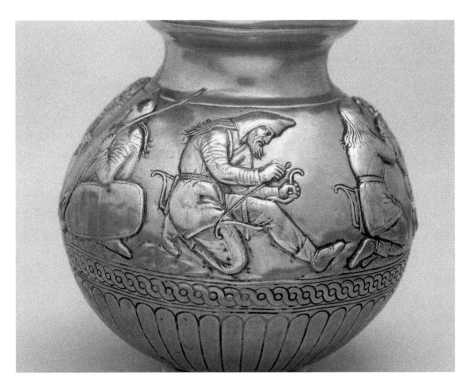

9.10 Detail from the Kul'-Oba gold beaker (see Gallery, no. 1). The Scythian warrior, characteristically dressed, is stringing a recurved bow. Since he is already wearing his own bow in its gorytos on his left side, he may be giving a demonstration of how it should be done.

9.11 Scythian arrowheads were commonly cast from bronze. The point was formed into two or three blades. Some had a hooked spike at the base making them difficult and damaging to pull out after they had become embedded. This group, dating to the seventh century BC, came from kurgan 29 at Kelermes.

Parthians—the Parthian shot—but it may well have been developed first by the Scythians.

Arrows were short, usually made of birch wood or reeds and tipped with points made of bronze or iron, or occasionally of bone. They were fletched with birds' feathers. Shafts found in the Pazyryk graves were painted black and red in elaborate designs representing feathers or snakes, perhaps magically to enhance their flight and bite. The metal heads were made in varying forms, one of the most characteristic being of trilobate section. Some were provided with long backward-curving barbs, making them difficult to pull from a shield in the height of battle and very damaging to tear out of a wound. Scythians were also known for poisoning their arrows. Aristotle provides a do-it-yourself account of the technique:

9.12 Gold plaque from Kul'-Oba depicting Scythian archers in action.

They say that they make the Scythian poison, which they smear on their arrows, out of snakes. The Scythians look out for those that have just borne young and taking them put them to rot for several days. When they consider them to be completely decomposed they pour human blood into a small vessel and put it in a dung hill and cover it up. When this has decomposed they mix the part which floats on the watery liquid blood with the juice of the snake and so make a deadly poison.

(Aristotle, *On Marvellous Things Heard*, 141)

Ovid was also familiar with Scythians from the time of his exile in Tomis. He describes Scythian arrow heads with barbs smeared with poison 'which carry a double death'. The poison, he says is 'yellow with viper's gall'. The topos of Scythian poison was well known throughout the classical world. It would have greatly enhanced the fear of conflict with an enemy so effectively equipped.

As has already been mentioned, to carry the bow and a quiver of arrows conveniently on horseback the Scythians developed a special case known to the Greeks as a gorytos, which was slung on the belt on the left-hand side of the body. It was big enough to contain at least two thirds of the bow with the quiver section of sufficient size

9.13 Coin showing a mounted archer in action. His gorytos is slung on his left side. The inscription, ATAIAS, suggests that the figure may have been the Scythian king Ateas, who was killed in battle against Phillip of Macedon in 339 BC.

 241

to hold an average of 70–100 arrows. The gorytoi were made of leather. Early examples have been found with the quiver section covered by an embossed gold plate. Later, in the fourth century BC, it became conventional to cover the front of the entire case with elaborately worked gold facings made in the Greek workshops on the Pontic shore. The decorative scenes chosen to embellish them tended to be drawn from classical mythology but one, from the burial at Solokha, depicts five Scythians engaged in hand-to-hand combat (Gallery, no. 7). Other items of metalwork from the Pontic kurgans provide images of the gorytoi in daily life. One of the figures on the Chertomlÿk amphora carries a large leather gorytos, capable of covering the entire bow, slung from his belt on his left side (Gallery, no. 10). Two of the sitting figures on the bowl from Gaymanova mogila have gorytoi partially cut away so that the arrows can be easily accessed (Gallery, no. 3). Two of the warriors on the Kul'-Oba beaker also have their gorytoi clearly in view, hanging from their belts (Gallery, no. 1). The copious iconography is a reminder that the Scythian was seldom parted from his bow, even in repose.

The plethora of bows and arrows recorded on the Pontic steppe contrasts with the paucity of finds in the Pazyryk tombs. No trace of any bows was recovered and arrows were represented only by arrowheads from kurgan 2 and painted arrow shafts from kurgan 3. It could be that archery featured less in the Altai than in the Pontic region. Alternatively, the absence could reflect local burial practice, bows and arrows being considered to be an inappropriate accompaniment for a burial. That said, the rider

9.14 The gold casing of a gorytos from the burial of Chertomlÿk depicting mythological scenes. The gorytoi of the elite were usually chosen for elaborate embellishment to display the person's status.

9.15 (*Right*) The silver bowl, with figures covered in gold sheet, from Gaymanova mogila depicts two scenes each of pairs of men in conversation (see Gallery, no. 3). The individual shown here wears his gorytos on his left side, his left hand resting on his arrows. In his right hand is a whip. Another gorytos containing a strung bow is by his right knee.

9.16 (*Below*) The gold beaker from Kul'Oba (see Gallery, no. 1). In this scene both men hold short spears. One has his shield, probably of leather, by his side. The other wears his gorytos on his left side with the end of the bow just showing.

depicted on the felt wall hanging from kurgan 5 carries his gorytos with him as he approaches a goddess.

Beside the bow Scythian warriors were usually equipped with a variety of spears and lances, and with swords and daggers. Among the former, short spears less than 2 m long were common. They could be thrown at the commencement of an engagement or used for thrusting in close fighting much as the mounted warrior depicted on the Solokha comb is about to do (Gallery, no. 5). Short spears were also used for hunting. Some

examples are considerably longer, sometimes more than 3 m in length. These are more properly classed as lances and were used in combat between mounted warriors. Spearheads, usually made of iron, were leaf shaped with central midribs and could vary in length between 0.3 and 0.7 m. Javelins with triangular tanged points on a long shank are also known. Efficient in penetration, the barbs made them difficult to extract. A warrior who had raised his shield in defence and had caught a javelin or two in it would have been more inclined to discard it, leaving himself unprotected, than to attempt to remove them, with their cumbersome long shafts, in the heat of battle.

Swords and daggers come in many shapes and sizes and complex typologies have been drawn up to contain the variations. Swords were usually double edged, around 0.7 m long, while daggers averaged about 0.4 m. The principal change in sword types over time lay in their shape. Swords pre-dating the fifth century were generally parallel sided while after this date the blades were often tapered to the point; single-edged varieties are also known. Scabbards were made of wood and leather with a projection at the top to accommodate a thong for attachment to the belt, usually on the right side. Those belonging to the elite were faced with embossed gold plates, a tradition which began in the sixth century with the scabbards from Kelermes and Melgunov, and continued into the fourth century with the even more elaborately decorated scabbard facings from Belozerka and Kul'-Oba.

9.17 Gold plaque found with the Oxus treasure. The figure wears his akinakes (short sword) on his right hand side with its chape at the lower end tied around his leg to keep the sheath in position to facilitate the drawing of the sword.

Swords, or at least the longer versions, could have been used from horseback but the shorter swords and daggers were normally used in hand-to-hand fighting after dismounting. Such engagements are well depicted on the gorytos and comb from the Solokha burial (Gallery, nos. 5 and 7).

Other weapons designed for hand-to-hand fighting were battleaxes and maces. One of the young warriors shown on the Solokha gorytos is wielding a battleaxe: a long shaft with the cutting blade mounted at right angles. Battleaxes often accom-

 244

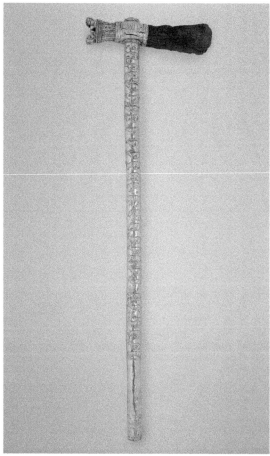

9.18 Iron battleaxe from Kelermes, its butt end and haft encased in a highly decorated gold sheet. Such a fine object, while perfectly effective, was probably largely ceremonial.

pany burials. One of the most highly decorated examples, that found in the Kelermes kurgan, has its shaft and part of the blade covered in repoussé-decorated gold sheeting. Physical evidence of the effectiveness of the battleaxe is present in a number of burials. The most dramatic is the warrior buried in kurgan 2 at Pazyryk who had been killed by axe blows to the head before being scalped.

Highly decorated battleaxes like the fine example found at Kelermes, while being useful weapons, were also emblems of status. So, too, were the maces that are sometimes found. The heavy bronze head of the mace accompanying the Solokha burial with its six projecting lobes could have done a great deal of damage if swung at the head of an enemy.

 245

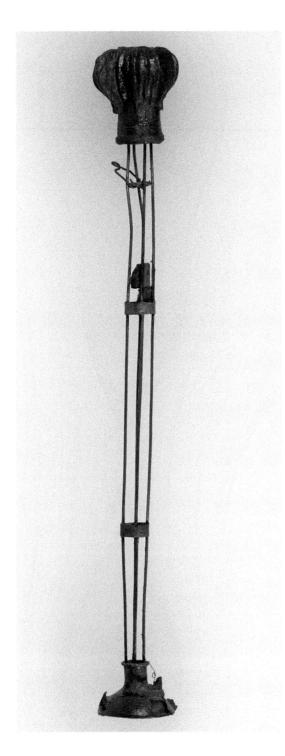

Finally, among weapons of aggression, must also be listed whips. As has been mentioned earlier (pp. 115–17), Herodotus tells the rather enigmatic story of the return of a band of Scythian warriors to their home after 28 years in Asia Minor. In their absence the womenfolk had married their slaves and the children of these matches were now determined to prevent the warriors' return.

> Many battles were fought but with no advantage to the Scythians until finally one of them addressed the remainder, 'What are we doing? We are fighting our slaves, diminishing our own number when we fall and that of those who are our property when we kill them. Take my advice—lay spear and bow aside and let each man fetch his horsewhip and confront them.'
>
> (*Hist.* iv. 3)

It turned out to be an effective strategy. Herodotus' interpretation of the story was that the sight of the whip reminded the slaves of their servile status. It may be that tradition simply recorded the use of whips on this occasion and Herodotus felt the need to offer some explanation of why they were successful. No explanation is really necessary: the whip, in skilled hands, is a lethal weapon and was widely used for hunting and fighting in the Pontic region until comparatively recent times. The German traveller, J. G. Kohl, visiting the region in the early nineteenth century, writes that when people have run out of bullets and arrows and have broken their lances they resort to the whip (*nagaicas*): 'it is not actions with pistol or sabre that determine the victor but whip combat'. Remains of whips are found in a number of elite burials and one of the reclining warriors depicted

9.19 The bronze head and pommel of a mace accompanying the burial at Solokha. The projecting lobes on the heavy bronze head would have made it a formidable weapon.

on the Gaymanova mogila bowl ominously holds a whip in his right hand (Gallery, no. 3).

Protecting the Body

With so many lethal weapons to hand, protecting the body with shields and body armour was an imperative.

The essential characteristic of a shield used in horseback fighting is that it must be light and easily manoeuvrable but tough enough to prevent, or at least in inhibit, penetration. The most effective way to meet both requirements is with wood and leather. A thin wooden board faced with robust leather is ideal, the leather providing a resilient surface dulling the slash of the sword. Shields of this kind were widespread. The warrior buried at Kul'-Oba in the fourth century was provided with just such a shield, thought to have been emblazoned with a great gold stag 0.3 m in length. Similar emblematic gold animals are known from sixth-century graves at Kelermes and Kostromskaya and are found as far west as the Great Hungarian Plain at Zoldhalomputza and Tápiószent-márton, though it has recently been argued that they may have been embellishments for gorytoi. The sub-rectangular shield carried by one of the seated warriors shown on the Kul'-Oba vessel also appears to be of leather stitched to an outer wooden frame, strengthened with a bar across the centre (Gallery, no. 1).

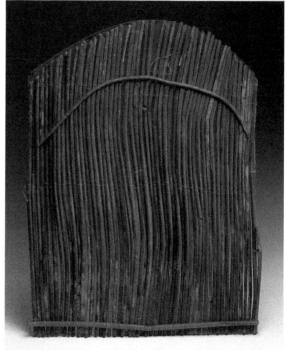

9.20 (Top) Small shield from kurgan 1 at Pazyryk, made from rounded sticks of wood threaded through slits in a sheet of leather to hold them in place in a way that formed a pattern. Shields were usually attached to the right side of the saddle.

9.21 (Bottom) Small shield from kurgan 3 at Pazyryk made of rounded sticks attached to a leather base. Transverse sticks were added to give rigidity.

247

Another type of construction was to use round wooden sticks bound together. Shields of this kind were found in four of the Pazyryk kurgans representing two basic types, small rectangular shields 0.28 by 0.36 m and larger shields with a convex upper edges 0.5 by 0.7 m. In both types the carefully whittled wooden sticks were threaded through slits in a thin leather sheet in such a way as to create a geometric pattern. A broad leather loop on the inside provided a handhold. A round shield of similar construction, with a concave top, is shown in action on the Solokha comb (Gallery, no. 5). The other shield shown on the comb gives the impression of being made from interwoven wattles but an alternative, and perhaps more likely, interpretation is that it was intended to depict a shield faced with iron scales. Shields of this kind have been found at a number of sites. The one from Volkovtsi was covered with strips of iron sewn together onto the wooden backing with wire, the whole being edged with leather. A unique shield from kurgan 3 at Khutor Popovka was made of wood faced with thick plates of bone. In all these cases an acceptable balance between lightness and resilience was achieved.

9.22 Scale armour from kurgan 401 at Zhurovka in the Dnieper region. The scales are of forged iron sewn, through holes in their upper edge, to a leather backing. The scales overlap in such a way that the stitching is well covered and three thicknesses of metal were created.

To directly protect the body the Scythians used scale armour girdles and corselets as well as metal helmets and greaves. The girdles—wide bands of leather faced with plates of bronze and iron and worn around the waist—were more common in the earlier period but were later largely replaced by corselets. The effectiveness of metal waist girdles may have been first noted by the Scythians active in the south Caucasus, where such items were in common use among the local Urartian elite. Corselets varied considerably in style but were essentially short-sleeved shirts covered in metal scales sewn on in rows that overlapped in such a way that the body was protected by several thicknesses of metal. In the early period only the shoulders or the chest were covered, but by the fifth and fourth centuries it was more normal for the armour to cover the entire upper part of the body. The warrior buried in kurgan 3 at Staikin Verkh, in northern Ukraine, had scale armour covering arms and legs as well as his torso, while the warrior from Novorozanovka, in addition to his armoured corselet, wore armoured leggings and a leather cap with cheek pieces and a neck guard covered with iron scales. Armour of such intricacy would have been costly to make and thus out of reach of all but the elite.

Helmets were also popular among those who could afford them. The earliest, known as Kuban helmets and dating to the sixth century, were heavy affairs made of cast bronze. They fitted tightly to the head covering the forehead to the eyebrow line, with cheekpieces to protect the face, and additional neck protection. It is usually assumed that this style of helmet came from, or at least derived its inspiration from, Asia Minor, but there are striking parallels with helmets in use in China from the Shang dynasty and later, and direct influence from eastern Asia, perhaps via Mongolia and southern Siberia, remains a possibility. From the fifth century head protection based on scale-covered leather hoods became more common while Greek helmets of Corinthian, Attic, and Chalcidian type were now becoming available. Some sixty are known from Scythian burials. At the same time, metal greaves of Greek style were adopted, though they were sometimes modified to

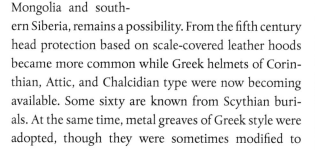

9.23 (*Top*) Helmet with cheekpieces covered with iron scales from kurgan 2 at Novofedorivka in the Khersonska region.

9.24 (*Bottom*) Cast bronze helmet from kurgan 2 at Kelermes. Helmets of this kind have been found in other burials in the Kuban region but the type probably came from northern China.

9.25 Reconstruction of a heavily armed Scythian warrior based on armour and weapons found in 1982 in kurgan 2 at Hladkivshchyna in the Cherkesta region of Ukraine (fifth to fourth century BC).

make them more comfortable for horse riders. The mounted warrior depicted on the Solokha comb wears greaves over his trousers and is also wearing a Corinthian helmet (Gallery, no. 5). Actual armour found in the tomb included a Greek helmet that had been modified and a pair of greaves cut off at the knee so as not to impede the grip of the rider.

If one stands back from the wealth of detail, it is abundantly clear that the Scythians living in the Pontic region were both eclectic and inventive in creating weapons and armour appropriate to their lifestyle. Those in more remote regions like the Altai seem to have lacked the inspiration or the need to invest much effort in manufacturing these war-driven embellishments, though the violent death of the man in kurgan 2 at Pazyryk is a reminder that aggression was ever present.

Evidence from the Graves

The many thousands of Scythian graves that have been excavated provide a wealth of evidence about weapons and armour—far too much to review here. But one example – the kurgan at Solokha, 20 km south of Nikopol — can be chosen to illustrate the richness of the data and variations within.

Solokha is the source of the famous battle scene comb and of a number of items mentioned in the descriptions of weapons outlined above but here we will consider the equipment in context. Solokha was a huge mound 18 m high containing two elite burial complexes. The one in the centre had been plundered in antiquity but the second, set to one side, was found undisturbed when Russian archaeologists began their work in 1913. It consisted of a deep shaft with a long corridor linking to the main burial chamber out of which opened three recesses. The largest contained the principal burial. The buried person was wearing a Greek manufactured gold torc around his neck and was surrounded by his personal equipment. On his right-hand side lay his ceremonial sword in a wooden scabbard covered with elaborate repoussé-decorated gold sheeting with a second sword placed next to it. To the left beyond the swords was a small side chamber created to contain a gold *phiale* (vessel) and a gorytos sheathed in gold and silver decorated with battle scenes. It originally contained the bow, of which nothing now survives, and 180 arrows recognizable by their bronze points. Close to his right arm was the mace with a six-lobed head. Nearby were six silver vessels, the famous battle scene comb, a bronze helmet, Greek in origin but modified to suit the wearer's needs, and a pair of Greek bronze greaves with the tops cut off.

At the entrance to the chamber containing his body a fourth set of equipment was laid out: a short-sleeved tunic covered with iron scales, two spears, a sword, and a number of arrows. Close by, along the north wall of the chamber, was the skeleton

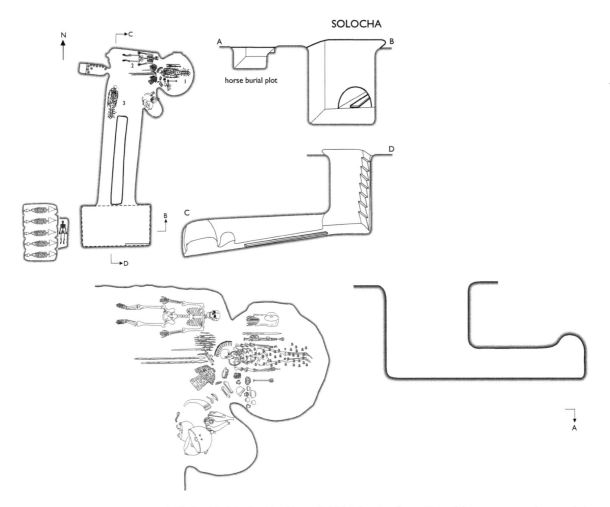

9.26 The burial of the Scythian king at Solokha showing the position of the gorytos, swords, mace, helmet, greaves, and scale armour. The second burial, accompanied by spears, sword, and arrows, was probably of the king's armour-bearer.

of another man who appears to have been wearing scale armour. He may have been the armour-bearer of the warrior king. To complete the picture, to the south side of the royal burial was a small recess containing the funerary feasting equipment. There were three cauldrons with an iron flesh hook and a bronze ladle. The burial assemblage also included a bronze basin, a *rhyton* (drinking horn) with silver rim, and ten Greek amphorae, once containing oil and wine. Not far away was the body of the cup-bearer.

The burial is remarkable for the huge range of evidence it provides that reflects on different aspects of Scythian life. What is of particular interest to the present discussion is that the warrior-king was closely surrounded by his most valuable ceremonial weapons, while his set of more functional equipment, his iron-plated corselet, spears, and spare arrows, seem to have been in the care of his armour-bearer. This is a reminder of the importance that such retainers must have had, not only in ceremonial life but on the battlefield. Such a man would have provided support for his master if in need, rather like the squire serving the knight in medieval Europe.

Images of Conflict

The Greek craftsmen, working in the towns along the north Pontic coast, were sufficiently familiar with the world of the nomad to be able to create images, usually in fine gold work, of Scythians engaged in conflict. The veracity of the detail depicted is confirmed by the close similarity between the weapon sets illustrated and the physical remains found in contemporary graves. That the Scythian patrons would have been reluctant to accept inaccurate representation of their dress, equipment, and behaviour gives an added level of reassurance that these scenes fairly reflect life on the steppe. Among a considerable corpus of material available, three items stand out: the Kul'-Oba cup, and the comb and gorytos from Solokha. All three include scenes which offer a narrative of action, albeit sometimes fleeting, which might be intended to recall an actual event.

The Kul'-Oba cup (Gallery, no. 1), with its four separate scenes, is open to various interpretations, the simplest being that the first pair represent preparation for battle while the second pair show the aftermath of the conflict. The first scene depicts two armed, but seated, figures engaged in an intense conversation, followed by the image of a single figure, part kneeling, stringing a bow. That he already has a strung bow in the gorytos hanging at his left side might suggest that he is doing it for someone else or to demonstrate how it should be done. The third scene shows two kneeling men, one exploring with his finger the inside of the mouth of the other who is evidently in discomfort, while the final composition shows one man bandaging the leg of the other. The general message seems to be comradeship expressed through discussion and advice, practical aid in preparation and in diagnosis, and caring. In the first two scenes weapons and armour are prominent. In the second pair of scenes, while the gorytos is present, it is incidental to the main action. The possibility that the sequence may represent the same characters presented in comic book style can be ruled out

9.27 The gilded silver facing plate from the gorytos found in the Solocha burial. Though brittle and broken, it shows a battle scene between young (unbearded) Scythian warriors and older Scythians (with beards), perhaps illustrating the story told by Herodotus of the attempted repulsion of warriors returning after a long absence.

since the artist has been at pains to distinguish them as different individuals by their clothing, especially by the decoration of their trousers. A storyteller, armed with the beaker, would have been able to use it as a visual aid, either to tell of an event and of individuals who had taken part or to use it as a moral guide for young men approaching battle for the first time.

The Solokha comb is altogether different (Gallery, no. 5). Here are three men at a tense moment in battle. In the centre is a heavily armed warrior on horseback wielding a short spear confronting another man on foot with a short sword/dagger ready for action. Between them is an expiring horse bleeding profusely from a neck wound—presumably the mount of the man now forced to fight on foot. Behind the mounted warrior, advancing in his support, is a simply dressed foot soldier with shield and short sword/dagger poised. The two principal adversaries, both wearing armour, though of different kinds, are presumably members of the elite, while the bare-headed foot soldier—an undistinguished participant—could be the armour-bearer of the mounted warrior.

It is a strong possibility that this scene represents a crucial moment in an actual conflict, the specifically drawn clothing of the two adversaries providing the observer with clues to their identity. The fact that the mounted warrior is shown wearing armour very similar to that of the warrior king with whom the comb was buried in the Solokha kurgan raises the tempting possibility that the comb records a memorable triumph in the dead man's life.

The Solokha kurgan produced a second battle scene, this time on the gilded silver plate covering the gorytos (Gallery, no. 7). It shows a battle in action between young, unbearded warriors and older, bearded men. The engagement on the left is between a young man on foot, wearing a gorytos and wielding a long-handled battleaxe against a bearded horseman about to counter with a spear thrust as his horse rears up. In the group on the right a bearded warrior has just dismounted from his wounded horse and has been grabbed by the hair by a young man fighting on foot who is about to slash with his long sword. The older man is trying to free his hair with one hand while drawing his sword with the other. Meanwhile another young man approaches from behind holding a round shield for protection with spear raised ready to strike. It is a dramatic piece which vividly brings out the brutality of close combat. The question again is: is this brief moment intended to represent a real engagement? The clear distinction between the young and the old suggests that it is. One possibility is that it depicts the battle between the Scythians returning from their long campaign in Asia Minor and the sons of the wives they had left behind, the story so vividly told by Herodotus. A very similar battle scene is depicted on a gold helmet from Perederiyeva mogila (Gallery, no. 6).

The three vignettes described here have much to offer to our understanding of Scythian conflict but above all they give a stark vision of the destructive brutality of war. Few would have escaped such engagements unscathed.

Strategy and Tactics

While the scenes of engagement so brilliantly depicted by the goldsmiths provide an insight into individuals in action, evidence of the Scythian army in the field and the conduct of war are more difficult to gather. We know of many engagements recorded by various Greek writers. In the seventh century bands of Scythians were active in Asia Minor and the Near East, fighting either for themselves or with the armies of Near Eastern states. Later, in 529 a force of Massagetae led by Queen Tomyris successfully won a major engagement against the Persian army whose leader, Cyrus, was killed in action somewhere in Central Asia, but the nomad army was eventually brought to heel by his successor Darius. Then came the long defensive action fought by Scythians and their allies against the advance of Darius and his army in 513–512 who were setting out from the lower reaches of the Danube eastwards across the Pontic steppe. Later, with the Persians no longer a threat, Scythian warlords turned their aggressive attention to the Thracians and, in doing so, inevitably came up against the Macedonians, who were advancing through Thrace at the time. This culminated in 339 in a battle where the Scythian king Ateas was killed and Philip II sustained a serious leg injury. Nine years later the Macedonians attempted to follow up this advantage when Alexander sent his general, Zopyrion, with a force of 30,000 men, against the city of Olbia. The Scythians rallied to the side of Olbia and the Macedonians were soundly defeated. The final recorded engagement came in 310–309, when Scythians became involved in the contest between the heirs of Paerisades for control of the Bosporan kingdom.

With so many conflicts recorded by contemporary historians, it is surprising that so little can be deduced about Scythian warcraft and the way in which, over the span of four centuries, it is likely to have evolved to suit the particular enemy confronted. What is abundantly clear, however, is that throughout, the cavalry horde formed the backbone of the army. The early incursions into the Near East were by men fresh from the steppe—these were elite horsemen led by war leaders whose strength lay in the speed and ferocity of the advance. As the Old Testament prophet, Jeremiah, tells his fearful audience,'they shall hold the bow and the spear: They are cruel and shall not show mercy; their voices shall roar like the sea, and they shall ride upon horses, everyone put in array' (Jer. 6:23). The cavalry onslaught, with the riders firing volleys of arrows at their opponents as they advanced, would have characterized the Scythian attack. Once the forces were engaged the spear, sword, and battleaxe came into their own.

The long account which Herodotus gives of the Persian advance through the Pontic steppe in 513–512 gives a number of insights into Scythian organization. The army was divided into three parts based on tribal allegiance, each led by a king, Idanthyrsus, Scopasis, and Taxacis, with Idanthyrsus serving as supreme leader. As the action proceeded the armies led by Scopasis and Taxacis worked as one, strengthened by forces provided by neighbouring tribes. The essence of the arrangement was its flexibility and the speed with which the troops could respond to the developing situation.

Realizing at the outset that the Scythian force was unlikely to succeed in open battle with the Persians, the Scythian leaders decided on a scorched earth policy, 'driving off their herds, blocking up all the wells and springs as they retreated, leaving the whole countryside bare of forage' (*Hist.* iv. 120). They endeavoured to stay one day's distance from the enemy, falling back as the other advanced: it proved to be an effective strategy, drawing the Persians further and further from their escape route across the Danube. One interesting detail, which Herodotus mentions in passing, is that the Scythian army was followed by their baggage wagons in which their women and children lived, and by their herds of cattle. While having the advantage of keeping the comforts of home and an assured food supply close to hand, the practice had its dangers since a sudden Persian advance could have driven the Scythian force back on its own baggage train. In Celtic warfare, too, the baggage train sometimes followed the army and when battle commenced the women had a grandstand view from on top of the wagons. There is no evidence, however, that the Scythians followed the Celts in regarding the battle as a spectator sport.

When, eventually, they decided to begin to confront the Persians, they adopted guerrilla tactics, making lightning raids on the Persian camp when the troops were eating. 'In these attacks the Scythian riders always put to flight the cavalry of the enemy [which], when routed, fell back on their infantry' (*Hist.* iv. 128). This achieved, the Scythian horsemen withdrew before the Persian infantry could reassemble. Night raids were also effective.

Drawn further and further into the interior and now constantly harried, the Persian army was becoming demoralized. It was at this stage, so Herodotus believed, that the Scythians decided to confront Darius in open battle, 'drawing out in battle array horse and foot'. This is the first time that Scythian infantry are mentioned. If the statement is correct the infantry are most likely to have been allies recruited from among the tribes of the forest steppe. It was at this crucial moment, so the famous story goes, that the Scythians were distracted by a hare. While the anecdote is feasible a more prosaic interpretation is that the amassing of the Scythian force was a feint designed to further demoralize the Persian army. If so, it was successful and Darius decided to withdraw.

The Persian expedition has gained prominence because Herodotus chose to describe it at length and in such loving detail. For the Persians it was little more than an exploratory foray into a foreign land. For the Scythians it was an exercise in restraint and an opportunity to learn about the workings of a well-schooled state army. The episode, however, has the advantage of throwing at least a little light on Scythian military organization and strategy at the end of the sixth century.

By the middle of the fourth century prolonged contact with the Greek world had led to changes in fighting methods. Greek armour was available for those who could afford it and knowledge of the exploits of the Greek armies might have encouraged at least some degree of emulation. There is, however, little to be learned from the engagements with the Macedonian army in Thrace and in the approaches to Olbia.

The death of the Bosporan king, Paerisades in 310 BC created a rivalry between his three sons, Eumelus, Satyrus, and Prytanis. The story is told by the Greek historian, Diodorus Siculus (*Hist.* xx. 22). The eldest, Satyrus, succeeded his father but his right to rule was contested by Eumelus. To support his claim Eumelus sought the help of the Thataeans, who lived in the valley of the Kuban River, and the Siraces, a Sarmatian tribe. Together they were able to supply him with a force of 22,000 cavalry and 20,000 infantry. Satyrus set out to confront his brother. Crossing the Thates River he set up camp, surrounding it with the wagons which had brought his supplies. In front, facing the enemy, he arranged his army, 'taking his place in the centre of the phalanx as was the Scythian custom'. His force was composed of 2,000 Greek mercenaries and an equal number of Thracians. All the rest were Scythians, 20,000 infantry and about 10,000 cavalry. Satyrus initiated the action by leading a cavalry charge against the Siraces, occupying the centre of the enemy line, and after a hard fought battle, routed them. Meanwhile Eumelus was gaining against the Greeks and Thracians on the right flank, so Satyrus turned into the battle 'and for the second time becoming the author of victory, he routed the entire army of the enemy'.

In the battle of the Thatis River the army of Satyrus was overwhelmingly Scythian and he acted as a Scythian commander should by leading the cavalry charge from the centre. But the Scythian force was now predominantly infantry, by a factor of 2:1. This could be because the troops were raised from sedentary Scythians living within the Bosporan kingdom, but it might reflect the changing shape of the Scythian fighting force under the impact of creeping Hellenization. The main action of the heavily mounted and armed Scythian elite against a comparable force of Sarmatians (the Siraces) broke the enemy's centre but it was their ability to quickly reassemble and join the fighting on the flank that won the battle. This was Scythian cavalry at its most effective.

In the Service of Others

There was always the potential for wandering hordes of horsemen to be employed as specialist troops by others engaged in conflicts. And so it may have been from time to time with the Scythians, but evidence is sparse. The armies which roamed Asia Minor and the Near East in the seventh century certainly formed alliances with some of the local states. The story of the offer made by the Scythian war leader, Bartatua, to marry a daughter of the Assyrian king indicates a willingness to consider offering mutual support, but there is a significant difference between this kind of arrangement of equals and simply providing military service as mercenaries. That there were bands of Scythians who were prepared to seek employment in the courts of kings is, however, made clear in a story which Herodotus tells (*Hist.* i.75) of just such a band which had taken refuge in Media where the king, Cyaxares, 'recognizing them as suppliants ... began treating them with kindness'. He put them to work teaching the Scythian language to the sons of the elite and training them in archery. They also spent time hunting, bringing home the game for the royal court. When one day they returned empty-handed the king insulted them and they responded by killing one of the boys in their charge and serving him up on the king's table. Satisfied that they had repaid the insult the Scythians rode off to place themselves as suppliants under the protection of the king of Lydia. The story is interesting in showing that bands of Scythians with specialist skills could find service and protection in the courts of Near Eastern monarchs. It is quite likely that there were many such groups enjoying a comfortable existence in the political turmoil of the seventh century.

During the Persian wars of the early fifth century Scythian troops were used by the Persians in their attack on the Greek homeland. When Xerxes landed on the Greek coast in 480 BC with a force estimated to be about 200,000, only about 10,000 were elite Persian troops. The rest were recruited from neighbouring tribes. Among the list of participants mentioned by Herodotus were Scythians.

> The Sacae [Sakā] or Scyths were clad in trousers and had on their heads tall stiff caps rising to a point. They carried the bow of their country and the short sword as well as the battleaxe. They were really Amyrgian Scythians but the Persians called them Sacae since that is the name they call all Scythians.
>
> (*Hist.* vii. 64)

Herodotus is telling us that they were Scythians recruited from Central Asia bordering on the Persian Empire. He goes on to say that they and the neighbouring Bactrians, who were also archers, were under one command. The Sacae are again mentioned among the troops commanded by the Persian, Mardonius, at the battle of Plataea in 479 BC.

It remains a possibility that the Greeks at this time were also employing Scythian mercenaries likely to have been recruited from the north Pontic region. The evidence is slight. The orator Andocides describes how, after the battle of Salamis in 490 BC, the Athenians fortified the Piraeus and built the North Wall. They also 'equipped 300 cavalry and bought 300 Scythians'. Aeschines, describing the same events, adds that the Scythians were archers. Thereafter, Scythian archers were regularly used to police Athens (above, pp. 52–4).

In the fourth century the Bosporan kingdom, in origin a Greek inspired construct, regularly depended on armies recruited from the local nomadic tribes. As we have seen, in the dispute that arose following the death of Paerisades in 310 BC Scythians and Sarmatians constituted a major part of the opposing armies. This was the time when Sarmatians were beginning to move against the Scythians, so by employing natural opponents the contestants for the kingdom were manipulating regional antagonisms for their own benefit. It is, however, unclear from the description of the event whether the tribal fighters were hired mercenaries or were allied troops, but by now the distinction was, anyway, fast disappearing.

Celebrating Victory

At the end of a military engagement there would be celebrations closely bound up with religious observances. The description which Herodotus gives of Scythian practices following the battle is intended to shock his readers and to emphasize the difference between the barbarians and the civilized Greek (*Hist.* iv. 64–6).

First, the Scythian must drink the blood of the first man he kills. Behind this lies the belief that blood represents the essence of the person and by drinking it the victor gains power over the dispatched enemy. The drinking of the blood of the two men mixed with wine to seal the bond of blood brother (above, pp. 217–18) embodies the same notion, that blood is potent. The next imperative was to cut off the heads of the slain enemies. At one level this is a simple form of accountancy since the number of heads brought in by the triumphant warrior enabled the king to calculate what portion of the spoils of war was due to him. Heads of enemies were also a sign of prowess and as such needed to be displayed. But rather than carrying around a clutch of bulky heads it was easier simply to retain the scalp. Here Herodotus evidently relishes the detail:

> In order to strip the skull of its covering he makes a cut around the head above the ears and, holding on to the scalp, he shakes the skull out. Then he scrapes the scalp clean

9.28 Detail from a gold ornamented headdress found in the kurgan at Kurdžips in the northern Caucasus. The warrior on the right holds the head of an enemy.

with an ox rib, and softening it by rubbing it between the hands he then uses it as a kind of napkin.

(*Hist.* iv. 64)

The male buried in kurgan 2 at Pazyryk had been scalped. An incision had been made across the forehead from ear to ear and the scalp had been torn back to the neck just as Herodotus describes. He goes on to say that the Scythian is proud of the scalps he has acquired and hangs them from his bridle rein to display his valour and success in battle. He also made cloaks by sewing scalps together. It is tempting to see this as a procedure adopted by the more successful warrior whose bridle reins could no longer provide the required display space.

Headhunting is also depicted from time to time. A belt from Tli in the Caucasus shows a mounted warrior returning from battle with a whip in one hand and his bow and quiver of arrows to his left side. From the bridle of his horse hangs what is evidently a severed head. In another representation on a gold plaque from a headdress found in a kurgan at Kurdžips a warrior is shown carrying an over-large head, rather unceremoniously by the hair, holding it well away from his body.

Herodotus notes other, more extreme behaviour related to the display of prowess. Some, he says, 'flay the right arms of their dead enemies and make the skin which is stripped off, with the nails still attached to it, into a covering for the quivers'. He compares the quality of human skin favourably to that of other animals. Others, he says, flay the entire body and carry the skin about with them stretched on a frame. Beyond self-promotion, embedded in these practices is the belief that by owning the scalp or skin of an enemy one exercises control over him, thus preventing the spirit from doing damage.

The skull of a particularly detested enemy, such as a relative killed in a feud, might be turned into a drinking cup. 'Having sawn off the part below the eyebrows and cleaned out the inside, they cover the outside with leather.' A rich man would also line the inside with gold. On the occasions when the cup was being handed round to prestigious visitors stories would have been told of the exploits which led to its creation. Here the intention seems to have been to insult the memory of the deceased and induce the visitors to share in the insult. The veracity of Herodotus' description of skull cups is shown by the discovery of a workshop specializing in skull cup production in the fortified settlement of Bel'sk. In 529, when the Sakā queen, Tomyris, defeated the Persian leader, Cyrus, in battle, it is said that she took his head as a trophy. The thought that the skull of the great conqueror could have ended up as a drinking cup at Sakā feasts must have been hard for the Persian royal household to contemplate.

The post-battle behaviours which Herodotus describes, involving the manipulation of the physical remains of the dead enemy, served two deep-seated needs in warrior society: it was a means of controlling spirits of the enemy and a way for the warrior to display his valour. But the record had to be affirmed and, as has been mentioned above, this was done in the public forum held once a year at which those who had killed an enemy had the right to drink wine from a communal bowl, while those who had not killed had to sit in shame for all to see. There could hardly be a more effective way to incentivize a society whose survival lay in maintaining its predatory ethos.

There was nothing exceptional about the attitudes and beliefs of the Scythians. Their contemporaries in western Europe, the Celts and the Germans, and the tribes on the northern borders of China, behaved in much the same way and head-hunting was still practised in some parts of the world in recent times. The same logic, control over enemies, prevailed: it was simply one of the many outward and visible signs of innate aggression ritualized into warfare.

In fighting against, and fighting with, the armies of the Assyrians, Medes, and Persians, in their contacts with the Greek world around the north shore of the Black Sea, and in their campaigns against the sedentary communities of the forest steppe, the Scythian warlords had ample opportunity to observe other modes of warfare and to assimilate what they found to be of interest. Perhaps the most obvious change was the introduction of infantry, but this need have been little more than a formalization of the ragged groups of the poor who followed the horsemen eager to pick up what benefits they could.

Raiding and warfare were a way of life, an extension of the hunt which all enjoyed. At one end of the steppe, near the Sea of Azov, 30,000 Scythians, cavalry and infantry, could fight alongside Greeks and Thracians in the army of the Bosporan king while at the same time in the Altai mountains a man could be felled by the battleaxe of his opponent and lose his scalp before his relatives were able to retrieve his body for a decent burial. Men involved in both engagements would have fully understood each other's motivation and values.

10

OF GODS, BELIEFS, AND ART

T HE intricately tattooed torso and limbs of the slaughtered warrior buried in kurgan 2 at Pazyryk immediately draw us into the wonder and energy of the designs. The images are far from our experience and difficult for us to begin to understand, yet they embody values and beliefs familiar to the man and his contemporaries, packed with messages intelligible to his contemporaries. Similarly the gold stag from Kostromskaya, with its antlers flowing across its body and legs neatly tucked beneath would have been redolent with meaning to the warrior on whose shield or gorytos it was emblazoned.

It is difficult for us now to arrive at an understanding of the religious beliefs and practices of a non-literate people like the Scythians because, except in their imagery, they have nowhere left a record of what they believed. Some attitudes to the 'other world' are implicit in their burial practices revealed through excavations—these will be considered later in Chapter 11—but to try to understand the Scythian world view and to see how it impacted on human behaviour we are forced to rely largely on what the few classical sources have chosen to communicate. At best they offer entertaining anecdotes, usually unexplained, invariably incomplete, and filtered through the values of the observer. That said, the insights provided by Herodotus and a few lesser sources are invaluable, and when seen in the context of the belief systems of the wider Indo-Iranian world, it is possible to begin to comprehend something of the Scythian world view. However, given the ethereal nature of the evidence, and the ingenuity of the scholarly mind, there is much scope for speculation. What is offered here is a minimalist, though hopefully coherent, analysis; other interpretations are available.

The Origin Myth

Most societies create origin myths to explain the world and to distinguish themselves from others. But myths, by their very nature and through constant retelling, evolve into many versions. Herodotus records two variants of the Scythian myth (*Hist.* iv. 4–10). The first, which he says was told by the Scythians themselves, begins when the countryside was a desert. Into this was born Targitaos, whose mother was the daughter of the River Borysthenes and whose father was the god Zeus. Targitaos sired three sons, Leipoxais, Arpoxais, and Colaxais, each of whom ruled a different part of the kingdom. One day four gold objects fell from the sky, a plough, a yoke, a battleaxe, and a drinking cup. Each brother in turn tried to pick them up. When Leipoxais approached, the objects burst into flames. They did so again when Arpoxais made an attempt, but when Colaxais walked towards them the flames were extinguished and he was able to take charge of the sacred gold. Accepting this as a sign from the gods, the other brothers agreed that Colaxais should become high king, king of the Royal Scythians, while they would lead different branches of the Scythian race. The story neatly explains why, thereafter, the Scythians were ruled by three kings, one of whom served as the prime leader.

The second myth was the one favoured by the Greeks who lived on the Black Sea coast. It begins with Hercules leading the cows of Geryon into the desert that was to become Scythia. One night, while he was asleep, the mares that had pulled his chariot were stolen by the mistress of the country, a cave-dwelling creature, human female above the waist 'while all below was like a snake'. Asked to return the animals she agreed, subject to Hercules sleeping with her which, needing his horses back, he felt compelled to do. The result of the union was three sons, Agathyrsus, Gelonus, and Scythes. When Hercules was about to depart the land, the snake-tailed female asked what to do with the boys when they were grown to manhood. Hercules replied that they should each be asked to string a bow and put on a girdle in the correct way, which he described to her. When, eventually the young men were put to the test, only the youngest son, Scythes, was able to complete the task correctly. From him were descended the Scythian kings.

Three other versions of the origin myth are recorded. Valerius Flaccus tells a story similar to Herodotus' first tale in which the father of the Scythians, Colaxais, was born of Zeus and Hera, a semi-bestial water nymph living in the springs of Tibisis. Diodorus Siculus has a similar story of Zeus and a viper-limbed woman giving birth to Scythes. In the version recorded in the *Tabula Albana*, it was Hercules who fathered sons from Echidna (viper), the daughter of the river god, Araxes. The boys were Agathyrsus and Scythes. These three later accounts echo the two sources known to Herodotus, and may indeed have been taken either directly or indirectly from the *Histories*: the differences are hardly significant.

The two traditions have in common the union between a god and a female, half woman, half snake, who is a daughter of a river god or who lives in a cave. In both cases she is a chthonic deity belonging to the earth. A number of sons are born—three in both of Herodotus' versions—and one becomes the king, or over-king, of Scythia. The only significant difference between the stories is who is the father, Zeus or Hercules? The version told by the Pontic Greeks, giving Hercules as the father, reflects their desire to link the Scythian origin story to Greek mythology in a way that supported the notion that the Scythians were a much younger nation than the Greeks. Even so, the Scythian Hercules differs from the Greek hero in that he is a god and rides in a chariot. It is conceivable that he has been conflated with Targitaos named in Herodotus' first story, a being intermediate between Zeus and the father of the Scythians, Colaxais/Scythes. In other words the origin myth, which Herodotus specifically stated to be the one told by the Scythians themselves, is most likely the original, while the others are modified and simplified versions suited to a Greek audience.

As we have seen, the original myth, which accounts for the division of Scythia into three kingdoms with the king of the Royal Scyths serving as high king, accords with the hierarchy of leadership seen, for example, at the time of the Persian campaign led by Darius. It was the king of the Royal Scythians who guarded the sacred gold and each year made sacrifices in its honour (below, p. 270).

The Scythian Gods

Herodotus (*Hist.* iv. 58) says that all Scythians worship a pantheon of seven deities. These he names, giving their Greek equivalents. It is clear from his presentation that three ranks are to be recognized. In the first rank is Tabiti (Hestia). In the second are Papaeus (Zeus) and Api (Gaia), while the third contains Goetosyrus (Apollo), Argimpasa (Aphrodite Ourania), and two gods equivalent to the Greek Hercules and Ares. Their Scythian names are not given but as we have suggested above, it is possible that Scythian Hercules is Targitaos.

The structure of the Scythian pantheon is similar to that found elsewhere in the Indo-Iranian tradition. At the head is Tabiti, the flaming one, goddess of heat, fire, and the hearth. The flaming objects falling from the sky come from her realm and they are kept in trust by the king. She, in turn, is guardian of the king and of his

 267

hearth. Thus the bond between them is strong and the king may be seen as an intermediary between the goddess and the people. The royal hearth is an especially sacred place and swearing an oath by it is an act of great solemnity: a false oath can affect the king's health (*Hist.* iv. 68). Since Tabiti is really the abstract notion of fire, rather than a personified deity, there are no physical representations of her. The concept of fire as the primeval substance upon which the universe is based is deeply embedded in the Indo-Iranian belief systems and plays a prominent role in Zoroastrian religion, the roots of which can be traced back into the Early Bronze Age in Central Asia.

The second rank of deities includes Papaeus (Zeus) and Api (Gaia), who are the father and mother of the universe. They are binary opposites: Papaeus, the sky/father, Api, the earth (or water)/mother. Earth/water gives life, fertilizing, nourishing, and healing all living things. In the Indo-Iranian tradition the union of sky and earth gave rise to the other gods.

The four deities of the third rank have specific characteristics. The Scythian Hercules, if identified with Targitaos, is the progenitor of the Scythian kings. Scythian Ares is the god of war, who is venerated in the form of an ancient sword (below, p. 269). Goetosyrus (Apollo) is more enigmatic, but may be associated with the sun. The fourth deity, Argimpasa (Aphrodite Ourania), is an altogether more complex conception. She is probably cognate with the Iranian Arti, a goddess of material abundance—a characteristic which would have encouraged Herodotus to equate her to Aphrodite. She is a patron of fertility, having power over sovereignty and the priestly force, and was served by an hereditary priesthood, the Enarees.

In addition to the pantheon of seven deities worshipped by all the Scythian tribes, there were other gods venerated in different regions. Herodotus specifically mentions that the Royal Scythians worshipped Thagimasadas. In relating him to the Greek god Poseidon, Herodotus was specifically thinking of Poseidon's power as a tamer of horses rather than any direct association with the sea.

The Scythian pantheon, then, reflects a vision of the structure of the universe. At the head is the primeval fire, the basic essence from which everything was created. Then followed the sky/father and earth/mother who together, or separately, were responsible for the birth of the gods. Since the world was conceived to have four sides regulating the universe, so four custodian deities were needed in this third range. Between this heavenly realm and the chthonic zone beneath the earth existed the world of people.

There will always be obscurities and inconsistencies in cosmologies that have evolved over time. So it is with the Scythians. One problem is the identity of the woman/snake, often presented as the daughter of a river god, who consorted with Papaeus (Zeus). Some commentators see her as Api (Gaia). But the daughter of a mere

 268

river god can hardly have a status equivalent to the great earth mother. Others have argued, more reasonably, that she is more likely to be Argimpasa. Another question is whether Targitaos can be regarded as cognate with Scythian Hercules. While there is a certain logic to the suggestion, Targitaos sits uncomfortably as one of the four deities of the third range. These are matters unlikely ever to be resolved. Where gods are concerned there is always ambivalence and confusion.

Another issue, which is sometimes debated, is whether there is some symbolic significance in Targitaos having three sons. Could they represent the three zones of the cosmos or the three levels into which society was divided—warriors, priests, and agriculturalists? But this is asking too much of the sparse evidence. What we are dealing with in the origin myth is a broad cosmology shared across much of the Indo-Iranian world onto which are grafted scraps of local folk memory moulded into a satisfying and memorable narrative. Such creative confusion does not benefit from too rigid an analysis.

Relating to the Gods

Belief in the gods takes with it the need for humans to develop systems to help the two worlds to communicate. Herodotus is clear that the Scythians have no images, altars, or temples except structures devoted to the worship of Ares. He was contrasting the Scythians to the well-furnished, monumentalized religion of the Greek world. At this level of comparison he was right—a nomadic people are hardly likely to have created large building complexes adorned with statues, but this does not mean that they had no sacred locations offering structure to the landscape through which they moved. Indeed, he specifically describes the places where Ares was worshipped. They were fixed locations at which sacrifices to the god took place and they existed in every district, at the seat of government:

> It is a pile of brushwood made of a great quantity of bundles, in length three furlongs, in height somewhat less, having a square platform at the top. Three sides are precipitous, while the fourth slopes so that men may walk up it. Each year a hundred and fifty wagonloads of brushwood are added to the pile, which sinks continually by reason of the rain. An ancient iron sword is planted on the very top of the mound and serves as an image of Ares. Yearly sacrifices of cattle and horses are made to it.
>
> (*Hist.* iv. 62)

Leaving aside the measurements, which are clearly exaggerated, it is a credible description of a high place. Its annual renewal, by bringing in more brushwood,

 269

would have been necessary to maintain the structure as Herodotus says, but it would also have symbolized a recommitment, creating an awareness of the continuity of worship at this place. The deeply stratified nature of the monument would have been a reminder of the great ancestry of the community. What symbolism lay behind the four-square nature of the platform and the standing sword is debatable but one suggestion is that the square mirrored the cosmological concept of a four-sided universe while the sword served an *axis mundi* uniting the world of the gods to that of humans.

Since these open air altars to Scythian Ares occurred in every region, the annual ceremonies would have been a reaffirmation of tribal identity. The question then arises as to where the annual ceremony focused on the four sacred golden objects which had fallen from the sky was held. Since it was presided over by the king of the Royal Scyths it could have been at his hearth, wherever that was on the appointed day. But it is more likely that he travelled to a fixed location known to everyone. A hint of this is provided by Herodotus in his description of a special place called Exampaeus (holy ways) situated between the Dnieper and the southern Bug (*Hist.* iv. 81). Here, he says, stands a vast bronze bowl. It was 'six fingers breadth in thickness' and could 'hold with ease six hundred amphorae' (24,000 litres). Herodotus visited the place and asked the natives about its origin. He was told that in the distant past king Ariantas, wanting to know the number of his subjects, ordered everyone to bring him one arrowhead and it was from the vast heap that had accumulated that the great bowl was made. A plausible explanation is that the great cauldron located at 'holy ways' was conceived to be the centre of the world. The story of the arrowheads could embody the understanding that all Scythians had ownership of it. Such a place would have been especially holy, the proper location for the annual ceremony of the sacred golden objects.

Herodotus explains that at the annual feast one man was chosen to look after the gold; 'if he should fall asleep in the open air, the Scythians say he is certain to die within the year. His pay therefore is as much land as he can ride around on horseback in a day' (*Hist.* iv. 7). This is a difficult passage to interpret but it would seem to suggest that a man was chosen annually for the task of guardian. He was given high status but was sacrificed before the next year's celebration. One interpretation would be to suppose that the guardian was a surrogate for the king and that his death and the appointment of a successor represent the death and rebirth of the king. It was a moment of renewal in harmony with the annual cycle of the sun.

Where the concept of focusing religious observation around a great cauldron originated is unknown, but such vessels existed in the south Caucasus during the Urartian period and it may well have been from here that the Scythians appropriated the belief. One of the largest of the surviving cauldrons was found in a seventh-century context at the Karmir Blur fortress. It is about 1.8 m in diameter and 1.5 m high and has the capacity of 1,000 litres, no match for the monster reported by Herodotus.

At religious ceremonies cattle and horses were sacrificed to the gods using a ritual that was widely practised among the Scythians (*Hist.* iv. 60–1). A rope is tied around the front legs of the animal and the person making the sacrifice stands behind and pulls the rope making the beast fall forward. As he does this he invokes the particular god to whom the sacrifice is dedicated. He then 'puts a rope around the animal's neck and, inserting a small stick, twists it and so strangles him'. The animal is then cut up, the pieces put into a cauldron and boiled, the bones having been extracted and added to the fire beneath the cauldron. When the meat is cooked, the person initiating the sacrifice makes an offering to the god by throwing some of the cooked meat and entrails onto the ground. For those who had no cauldron the paunch of the animal could be used as a container. Herodotus implies that the fire was lit from the raw bones but this could hardly be since bones will not easily burn without other fuel. The probable explanation is that the bones were being added to an existing fire so that they could be consumed according to the approved ritual.

In sacrifices dedicated to the Scythian Ares cattle and horses were slaughtered in great numbers (*Hist.* iv. 62). In addition, when prisoners of war had been taken, one out of every hundred was sacrificed. First of all a libation of wine was poured over the heads of those chosen before their throats were cut over a vessel placed to catch the blood. The vessel was then carried to the top of the platform and the blood poured over the sword. Meanwhile, below, by the side of the mound, 'the right hands and arms of the slaughtered prisoners were cut off and thrown high into the air'. When this activity was over, 'those who had offered the sacrifice depart leaving the hands and arms where they had chanced to have fallen with the bodies separate'. That prisoners taken in battle should be sacrificed to the god of war would have been considered entirely appropriate.

The open-air altars to Ares, which Herodotus says existed in each province, may well have been the locations where annually those who had slain one or more enemies in battle were acknowledged by being allowed to drink from a communal bowl of wine before the assembled company (above, p. 262). Whether this performance was carried out on the same occasion as the annual sacrifices is not clear.

The Intermediaries

Most societies have a class of specialists, broadly characterized as priests, who mediate between humans and the gods. In the pan-Scythian ceremonies involving the

sacred gold objects it seems to have been the king of the Royal Scyths who took on the role, becoming for the occasions a priest king. In the Indo-Iranian tradition the king had charisma (*farnah-*) which materialized in the form of gold, the royal metal. Thus in controlling the sacred golden objects the king was displaying the outward and visible signs of his extraordinary powers. In the rituals surrounding the worship of Scythian Ares no intermediaries are mentioned, the implication being that the animals offered in sacrifice were dispatched and prepared by those making the offering. Who dealt with the human sacrifices is not specified.

That there was, however, a distinct priesthood practising among the Scythians is mentioned by several sources. They were called Enarees, androgynous transvestites drawn from prominent families and were therefore probably an hereditary priesthood. Little is known about their activities except that they had a method of prophesying that involved taking a piece of the inner bark of a lime tree, splitting it into three strips, and twining the strips between the fingers. It was a skill, they claimed, that was taught them by Aphrodite, implying a close relationship with the goddess Argimpasa (Aphrodite Ourania). Herodotus, always looking for tidy explanations, implicitly links the observation and the origin of their 'female sickness' to the curse put on a band of Scythians by the goddess Aphrodite Ourania when they plundered her sanctuary at Ascalon during their rampage through the Levant. The more sober author, Pseudo-Hippocrates, put their altered sexual state down to too much horse riding (above, pp. 219–20). The supposed link between the priests at Ascalon and the Enarees may be little more than a rationalization based on the observation that both priesthoods were strongly transgender. It is simpler to see the Enarees as shamans born of a deep-rooted steppe tradition in which transgender behaviour was the norm for such people and was believed to endow those who displayed it with great power.

Herodotus also mentions that in Scythia there were many who could foretell the future. Their favoured method was to place a bundle of willow sticks on the ground. By untying the bundle and laying out the individual sticks they were moved to make a prophecy. If the king fell sick these soothsayers were called in and asked to identify who it was who had caused the king's illness, the belief being that royal malaise was caused by someone swearing a false oath by the king's hearth. If, when a suspect was identified, he claimed his innocence, six more soothsayers were consulted. If they upheld the charge the first group decapitated the suspect and shared out his goods. If, however, the second group acquitted him, another group was brought in to adjudicate and so on. If the greater number decided that the man was innocent, then those who first accused him were put to death by being crammed into a wagon filled with brushwood and set alight. No son of theirs was allowed to survive. Prophesying for a Scythian king could be a precarious occupation.

The magic practised by those able to communicate with the supernatural world through interpreting bark and sticks would have impressed the onlookers. It was in the interests of all priesthoods that they should present themselves as different from ordinary mortals. This was done through dress, behaviour, and secret ritual. The Ena-rees, with their effeminate behaviour and transvestism, were distinctly 'other' and we may suppose that other intermediaries like shamans behaved and dressed in ways that distanced them from ordinary people. They would also have adopted equipment and regalia to enhance performance. The bark and the bundles of sticks belong to this category but there must have been much else besides. Headdresses such as the antlers worn by Siberian shamans in the recent past are likely to have been favoured by some and it is not impossible that grandly adorned horses, like the one with a headdress

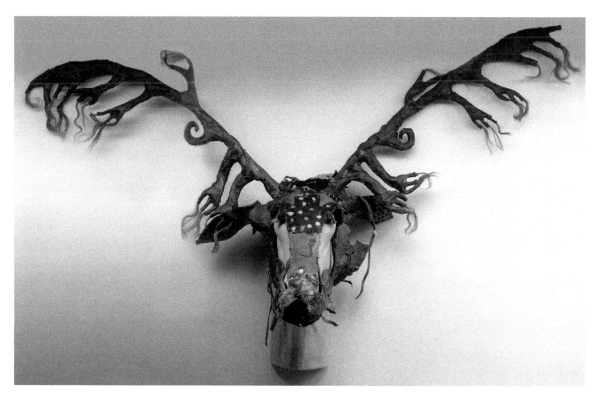

10.1 Elaborate headdress worn by one of the horses buried in kurgan 1 at Pazyryk. Such elaborate con-fections, transforming the horse into a stag, were probably worn only on ceremonial occasions and may have been associated with shamanistic rituals.

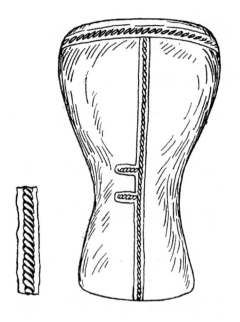

10.2 (*Left*) Drum made from two plates of ox horn sewn together. The membrane covering the upper end was also stitched in place. From kurgan 2 at Pazyryk. The drum may have been used in religious ceremonies.

10.3 (*Below*) Long staffs with bronze rattles at the end were common among the steppe nomads. They are likely to have been of ceremonial use and carried by a shaman. This example is from a burial at Makhoshevskaya in the Kuban region.

10.4 (*Opposite top*) Ceremonial pole top from the Dnepropetrovska region of Ukraine.

10.5 (*Opposite bottom*) Highly elaborate ceremonial pole top from Lysa Hora in the Dnepropetrovska region of Ukraine.

resembling antlers found in kurgan 1 at Pazyryk, were decked out in this way by the shaman conducting the burial ceremony. Another accompaniment to shamanic rituals was drums. Drums were found in three of the Pazyryk tombs but there is no proof that they were used for rituals rather than simply as musical instruments.

Widely occurring across the steppe from Mongolia to the Great Hungarian Plain are ornate pole tops, sometimes incorporating rattles and often crowned with animals. The earliest, dating to the eighth century, coming from Tuva and the Minusinsk Basin, incorporate the stag or ibex standing feet together as if balancing on a rocky eminence. Later examples are often more elaborate. One example, from the fourth century BC Alexandropol kurgan, depicts a female goddess, hands on hips. Another from the same kurgan shows a winged griffin in a frame from which hang two bells, while a third splits into three branches upon each of which perches a hunched, predatory bird holding a bell in its beak. Staffs, capped in this way, were symbols of authority and were probably carried by priests, the rattling noise or tinkling of the bells calling the audience to attend to the rites about to be performed. The sound itself was unsettling and the sight of the predatory birds in the flickering lamplight looking as if they were about to swoop would have unnerved the superstitious. It is upon such artifice that priests build their power.

Images of the Deities

The deities of the upper ranges of the pantheon, Tabiti, Papaeus, and Api, do not seem to have been anthropo- morphized, or at least no certain depictions of them are known, but persistent in Scythian iconography from the seventh century onwards are images of a goddess displaying a variety of characteristics but all probably representing different aspects of Argimpasa (Aphrodite Ourania). The images can be divided into four groups. Most closely related to the mythological foremother of the Scythians is the Anguiped goddess displayed as half woman but with snake legs, sometimes with distinct serpents' heads, sometimes morphing into tendrils. The general form in which she is presented is reminis- cent of the tree of life (*ficus mundi*), a basic notion shared throughout the Indo-Iranian region. She is often shown as clutching tendrils of vegetation and sometimes with legs splayed in a birth-giving position. Occasionally she is associated with severed heads implying a relationship with human sacrifice. In her second form the goddess is shown with raised hands in a position of prayer and is frequently flanked by animals. In this incarnation she is the Mistress of the Beasts (*Potnia theron*) but is still very close to the tendril-legged goddess. The different depic- tions are stressing different aspects of the same deity. She presides over plants and animals, displaying her control of the natural world, while at the same time her fecundity ensures the well-being of the human race. She is the idealized mother of the Scythian tribes.

In the third manifestation she appears as a winged figure. The earliest examples of this are on the rhyton and silver-gilt mirror from the Kelermes kurgan dating

10.6 Gold bridle decoration, covering the front of the horses' faces, from the kurgan of Tsimbalka. It depicts a goddess whose lower body resolves itself into serpent heads. She grasps the horns of the upper pair of serpents.

10.7 Gold plaque of a winged goddess from an unknown location in Ukraine.

to the late seventh century. The mirror is divided equally into eight segments with a large rosette in the centre, the arrangement probably reflecting a concept of the world or universe. In one of the panels the winged goddess stands holding a panther in each hand while the other seven panels display animals, creatures half man and half beast, and fantastic demons. The symbolism is clear: the goddess in this composition is also the Mistress of the Beasts. While the representation has close similarities to depictions of Artemis, Aphrodite is also often associated with animals and is sometimes referred to as winged. In all probability, therefore, the winged deity on the Kelermes mirror is a manifestation of Argimpasa.

10.8 Gilded silver mirror from kurgan 4 at Kelermes. It shows a winged goddess presiding over the world of beasts.

The fourth style of representation presents the goddess sitting and facing a man, sometimes shown on horseback. One of the clearest versions of this appears on the rhyton from Merdzhany dating to the fourth century. The goddess sits facing the viewer, holding a spherical vessel. To her right there is a seven-branched tree of life while to the left is a horse's head mounted on a pole. A bearded rider hold-

 278

10.9 Part of a gold rhyton (drinking horn) from Merdzhany in the Krasnodar region. The seated goddess, holding a beaker, is flanked on one side by the Tree of Life and on the other by a horse skull on a pole. She is approached by a suitor mounted on his horse. Similar scenes, known from elsewhere in the Scythian world, may represent the union of the goddess and a hero warrior.

ing a rhyton approaches from the left. Some writers interpret this as a marriage scene between the goddess and a local god or hero. Support for this comes from a fourth-century relief from the Trekbratniy kurgan which shows a woman sitting in a carriage pulled by four horses. She is approached by a young man on horseback waving a gorytos. Between the two is another gorytos hung on a pole. This seems to be a representation of an unusually efficient marriage custom described by Herodotus as common among the Massagetae: 'when a Massagetes desires a woman, he hangs his gorytos before her wagon and has intercourse with her without hindrance' (*Hist.* i. 216).

 279

10.10 Detail from a felt wall hanging from kurgan 5 at Pazyryk. The scene is comparable to that shown in fig. 10.9. Here the seated goddess grasps the Tree of Life on her left-hand side. Her elegant suitor, wearing his gorytos, approaches from the front. The horse is carefully groomed with a cropped mane and a plaited tail.

Another particularly vivid depiction of the seated goddess and approaching rider motif is to be found on the felt wall hanging from kurgan 5 at Pazyryk. Here the seated goddess—a stern-looking lady with a substantial headdress adding to her grandeur—holds the tree of life at her left side and faces the rider. The horseman who approaches her, though smaller, has a trim elegance matched by that of his horse.

In most of the representations of the seated goddess and the approaching male suitor, the goddess is the dominant figure with the male her subordinate. She is probably a manifestation of Argimpasa, the foremother of the Scythians, while he is not a mythological figure but a mortal who through communion with her becomes a hero-god.

A seated goddess is also depicted in the lower register of a gold plate found in the Karagodeuashkh kurgan dating from the fourth–third century. The plate once adorned the headgear of a female buried in the tomb. In this instance the goddess is flanked by two young men, one offering a rhyton, the other a globular vessel, while two female figures, their hair covered, stand in the background. The most likely

10.11 Gold diadem from kurgan 2 at Sachnovka in the Cherkaska region. The central scene shows a seated goddess holding a mirror in one hand and a vessel in the other. Before her is a kneeling man, presumably a suitor, holding a drinking horn and a staff. He wears a gorytos (see Gallery, no. 8).

10.12 Stele from the kurgan at Trekhbratniy. It shows a woman, perhaps a goddess, being carried in a four-horse vehicle. She is approached by a rider. Close by is a pole or tree upon which a gorytos is hanging. The imagery reflects a marriage ritual recorded by Herodotus in which the gorytos is a symbol of the man's claim to the woman.

10.13 Gold plaque once adorning a tall headdress, from Karago-deuashkh. It displays elite women, presumably deities, and their attendants.

interpretation is that the two young men are holy twins (like the Dioskouroi) while the females were probably mythological attendants. In Indo-European mythology the divine twins were companions of the mother goddess. The cult of the Dioskouroi was well established in the Greek cities on the Black Sea coast and here we see it merged with the cult of Argimpasa, though what subtleties the scene is meant to convey are beyond recovery. It is possible that the two young men were conflated with the sons of the Scythian Hercules and that the monstrous female was Argimpasa, in which case they represent the mythological founders of the Scythian tribes, but this is pure speculation.

While Herodotus was right to say the Scythians had no statues of the deities, small-scale images of their goddesses abound, usually crafted into gold and silver work. There is much variation in the way in which they were depicted but that variation underscores the breadth and power of the deity: she was the foremother of the Scythians, the progenitor of the founding heroes upon whom she bestowed regal authority. She was the Mistress of the Beasts and controller of the Tree of Life. For the ordinary Scythians roaming the wild steppe it would have been reassuring to have such a powerful and benign protector.

The Meaning of Scythian Animal Art

The very large number of decorated items made by the steppe nomads over the period 900–200 BC embody the visual expression of myths, beliefs, and events that featured large in their folk consciousness. The motifs they chose to display on their dress and on that of the horses, in their homes, and tattooed on their bodies were part of their identity. These images proclaimed shared values; they protected them, and, we can suppose, they pleased them. But it was seldom, if ever, art for art's sake. Even the painted decoration on such disposable items as arrow shafts is likely to have had meaning, ensuring that the arrow sped true to its prey and struck with a viper's sting.

For much of their long history the Scythians and related nomads were in contact with other peoples and learned from them: from the Persians, from the warring polities in the Near East, and from the Greeks. Even people remote from direct contact with neighbouring states could not escape outside influence. The communities of the Altai lived with ornate items from Persia, India, and China alongside their homegrown folk art. Outside influences can be recognized taking hold over time but the nomad tradition remained strong, allowing in only those alien expressions that sat comfortably with their central beliefs and values. Even when foreign craftsmen were at work serving the Scythian elite, as in the case of the Greek masters living around the Black Sea, the items produced conformed closely to Scythian demands, reflecting the nomad way of life and their understanding of the world.

Scythian art has its origins in the art of the early nomads of the Karasuk and Tagar periods in the Minusinsk Basin in southern Siberia, which itself has deep roots in the rock carved animal art of a larger region, including modern Mongolia and eastern Kazakhstan. The recurring motifs were wild animals that lived in the mountainous regions and the forest steppe, the most commonly chosen being stags, felines, and birds. The deer is depicted as a noble beast often in repose with legs tucked beneath its body. Conceptually it may have symbolized the source of life. The felines, often coiled upon themselves, and the birds of prey with sharp beaks are predators in competition for the deer. Thus all three interact, creating an interlocking cycle of tension. For pastoralists husbanding the flocks and herds in the mountains and forests, deer and of the other herbivores—the elk, the moose, and the ram—would have been familiar sights and scenes of predation would not have been uncommon. Life's struggle was ever present: it was the very essence of being and it is no surprise that it became a central theme in Scythian art. How the struggle was conceptualized to fit into a world view of the supernatural we can only guess at but the deer, or its herbivore substitutes, may have been conceived of as the Tree of Life sustaining a world always in tension. In the hands of a shaman it was powerful imagery through which to contain people's fears and superstitions and it pervaded their lives.

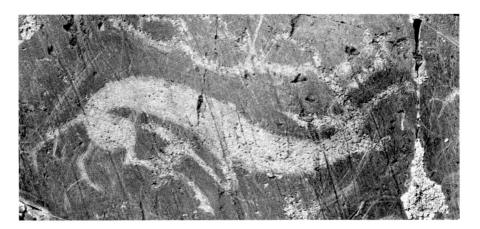

10.14 Petroglyph of a recumbent stag from Tsagaan Salaa, Mongolia, dating to c.900 BC.

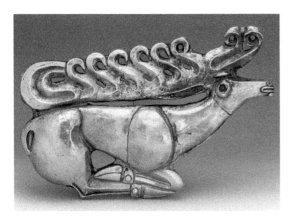

The recumbent deer as well as felines and, less often, birds are frequently found on early first millennium BC rock engravings—the deer in particular persisting largely unchanged through to the fourth century and later. Compare, for example, the rock carving of the deer at Tsagaan Salaa in Mongolia with the deer emblem used a central motif on Scythian arrows, the noble stag from Kostromskaya in the Kuban dating to the seventh century, the soulful creation from Tápiószentmárton in Hungary probably a century later, and the more stylized representation from Kul'-Oba in the Crimea made in the fourth century. This image in its various guises persists over a considerable area for more than half a millennium. The coiled feline wound back upon itself is another recurring image. One of the earliest representations came from Arzhan 1 in southern Siberia and must be of the ninth century. A closely comparable example from somewhere on the steppe is in the collection of Peter the Great, while an openwork plaque of the same

10.15 (*Above left*) Gold recumbent stag from Kostromskaya, Kuban region (sixth century BC).

10.16 (*Left*) Gold recumbent stag from Kul'-Oba (fourth century BC).

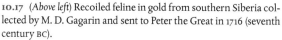

10.17 (*Above left*) Recoiled feline in gold from southern Siberia collected by M. D. Gagarin and sent to Peter the Great in 1716 (seventh century BC).

10.18 (*Above right*) Recoiled feline in cast bronze from near Simferopol, Crimea (sixth century BC).

10.19 (*Right*) Gold plaque from the Seven Brothers kurgan. A scene of predation with an eagle attacking a lamb.

basic form, though not so obviously feline, was found at Kulakovsky in the Crimea and may date from the sixth century.

In the early period the animals, predators and prey, were usually depicted singly and with the simple lines and planes of the woodcarver, reminding us that they originated as wooden ornaments, sometimes covered with gold foil or painted, for attachment to horse harnesses and other background materials. From the beginning of the fifth century there are changes brought about by contact with the Persian and Greek worlds. Greater texture is added to the animals in a desire to make them more realistic and the animals are now shown in juxtaposition, usually in mortal conflict. Under Hellenistic influ-

10.20 Detail from the gold pectoral from Tolstaya mogila. Two winged griffins attack a horse. This is part of a zone of figures representing scenes of predation (see Gallery, no. 9).

ence the animals change: the snow leopard-like feline morphs into a lion, while the raptor bird becomes a winged griffin. Even the stag, a great, majestic beast, becomes a docile deer or sometimes a horse or a ram. Yet for all the changes the central theme remains, the fight to the death between predator and prey. The sophisticated Scythian aristocracy living around the Black Sea coasts from the fifth century were immersed in images of it. The ferocity of the conflict is brilliantly displayed on a series of gold plaques from the Seven Brothers kurgan in the Kuban showing deer and rams impassively, almost stoically, waiting while lions and other winged beasts begin to devour them. In one even more spirited scene, comprising the lower register of the gold pectoral from Tolstaya mogila dating to the second half of the fourth century (Gallery, no. 9), lions and cheetahs attack stags and pigs, while in the centre two huge winged griffins have descended on a horse and are beginning to tear it to pieces. The violence and sheer horror of the carnage contrasts dramatically with the upper register, a bucolic scene celebrating the symbiosis between humans and their domesticated animals. It is difficult to resist the suggestion that the designer was setting out to counterpoint the harmony of the world of humans with the conflict of the supernatural world, though perhaps there was a more subtle message implied—

10.21 Gold finial from the kurgan at Bratoliubivskyi in the Khersonska region. A leopard, possibly a snow leopard, attacks a fallen stag.

the equivalence of humans and the predators in their relationships to the productive power of the earth. That said, the animal predator was the enemy of humans as is clearly displayed in the hunting scene on the gilded silver bowl from the Solokha kurgan showing humans and beasts in mortal conflict.

It is the dominance of the prey–predator image in the Scythian world that impresses. It was everywhere to be seen. Even in the remoteness of the Altai Mountains, away from the influence of the Greek and Persian worlds, it pervaded life, on the saddle covers from kurgans 1 and 2 at Pazyryk, on a leather flask, and even tattooed

10.22 Leather cut-outs from saddle covers showing scenes of predation. From Pazyryk. *Upper and middle: from kurgan 2; lower: from kurgan 1.*

on the body of the man buried in kurgan 2. There can be no doubt that the constant battle for life ramified into every corner of nomad existence.

A World View

Communities in the past needed origin myths to give them a sense of self and a right to existence, a pantheon of gods to offer moral support at times of adversity, and a class of interpreters to manage the communication between mortals and the deities. There is, as we have seen, ample evidence of all three among the Scythians and, although there are gaps and uncertainties, a system of beliefs and behaviours can be constructed. Yet it is difficult to get beyond mere description and into the minds of the Scythian as he or she navigated through the world. What is clear, however, is that reminders of the gods were always present in the symbols with which the individual was surrounded. The meaning of these would have been readily understood, giving reassurance: the world of the ancestors and the world of the present flowed on as ever before. Even in the face of powerful empires and states with their own alien belief systems, the traditional beliefs and values of the nomad remained largely unchanged. Earth–water generating the Tree of Life sustained the world but there was always a struggle with the predatory forces. The best that could be hoped for was that a balance could be maintained. Crucial in this was the annual propitiation of the god of war with animal sacrifices and the blood of enemies, and the dedication of the sacred gold objects to Tabiti, the eternal fire, by the high king, his symbolic death through a substitute ensuring the annual rebirth of the land and its continued productive vitality.

11

THE WAY OF DEATH

URING the human life cycle, people have to face episodes of significant change: birth, the coming of age, marriage, and death. Each represents a span of time—a liminal period—ending when the person involved passes from one state to another. Since liminal periods are perceived to be times of danger, when unknown forces are unleashed, societies construct systems—rites of passage—to contain their fears and emotions and to give reassurance by enacting familiar rituals. If the rites are carried out according to the rules, it is believed that the well-being of the individual and of society are ensured.

For most communities death, when a person is perceived to move out of the world of the living into oblivion or some other existence, is the most traumatic change that has to be contained through ritual. Death is seen as a process. It begins with physical death when the spirit leaves the body and ends when the body is put finally to rest. Many societies believe that during this period the spirit hovers near the body observing and even taking part in human affairs. It is easily alienated but can be placated by the proper rituals. At the burial of the body the spirit passes into the realm of the living dead. If the burial procedures are correctly followed the spirit will be content and will no longer interfere with the living world, but a discontented spirit will continue to cause trouble.

These deep-seated beliefs are translated in different ways by different societies. Usually the body is prepared and put on display. It is during this time that rites are performed. In modern Western societies these can include mourning, candlelit vigils,

signing books of condolence, partying (the Irish Wake), and processions. The process of exposure may be very short or it may be long drawn out: its function is to demonstrate to those concerned that the individual is really dead. This is particularly important in the case of royalty, where matters of succession need to be settled quickly and suspicions allayed. The period between death and burial is also a time for individuals to display their ties of loyalty to the family of the deceased and, through offerings, to demonstrate publicly the esteem in which the dead person (and therefore his or her lineage) is held. In other words it is a reaffirmation of the social hierarchy. If sufficient evidence exists to allow the process to be reconstructed in all its complexity, rites of passage associated with death can be highly informative about the nature of a society.

Scythian Sources

Evidence for Scythian burial practices is unusually rich. As we have seen, since the beginning of the eighteenth century the burial mounds of the elite have attracted attention, first of treasure hunters and later of antiquarians and archaeologists. It is estimated that about five thousand Scythian burials have now been excavated under some kind of archaeological control, providing an exceptionally large sample upon which to base detailed analyses. In the majority of the cases the organic component of the ensemble has disintegrated, but in the frozen tombs of the Altai Mountains much of it has survived, providing details of material culture seldom available in burials from the open steppe. Since the skin and flesh of the deceased also survives in the permafrost conditions, the methods used to prepare the body can also be studied in some detail.

The rich array of archaeological evidence is augmented by Herodotus' long and intriguing description of Scythian royal funerals (*Hist.* iv. 71–2), which appears to be based on a report provided by a very well informed correspondent, probably a Scythian with first-hand knowledge of the procedures. The space devoted to the account reflects Herodotus' deep interest in the matter and his realization, as an astute historian, that rituals of death are highly revealing about the values of the living.

A recent detailed study, comparing Herodotus' text with the reality of the burials revealed in excavation, confirms the accuracy of the account. Herodotus was writing in the middle of the fifth century at a time when royal burial practices were undergoing change. While his informant described the traditional method, which involved placing the body at the bottom of a large quadrangular pit in a chamber roofed over with timbers covered with mats, other styles of burial were being employed at the time incorporating wooden and stone chambers built on the surface of the ground. His decision to describe only the long established type, which comprised about 70 per cent of all burials of the seventh to fifth centuries, suggests a degree of conservatism. Another backward-looking observation was the statement that gold cups were buried with the kings but never vessels of bronze or silver. The lavish use of gold vessels is, indeed, well attested and may be linked to the belief that the charisma of the king was associated with gold (above, p. 270), but the only tomb in which golden vessels alone were buried is Kelermes; in all the others silver and bronze items were also present. Either the informant was intent on stressing the old ways or Herodotus had heard the story from another, less accurate source and had decided to insert it into his main narrative.

In addition to giving a stage by stage account of royal burial rituals Herodotus offers a briefer description of the burial of people of lesser status:

> When anyone dies his nearest kin lay him on a wagon and cart him around to all his friends in succession. Each receives them in turn and entertains them with a feast at which the dead man is served with a portion of all that is set before the others. This is done for forty days at the end of which the burial takes place.

> (*Hist.* iv. 73)

After the burial the participants purify themselves by inhaling cannabis.

This brief account, shorn of all the trappings afforded to high-status individuals, gives the essence of the rite-of-passage. For a period of forty days following death, the spirit is believed to remain close to the body, and the body has to be honoured as though alive by friends and family. Only when the liminal period is over can the deceased be buried, after which those involved can purify themselves from the contamination of death and return to the real world. A period of forty days or thereabouts for the interval between death and burial seems to have been widely adopted among other Indo-Iranian people.

The Burial Ground of the Kings

Herodotus gives two pieces of information about where the kings were buried: first that the burials took place in the land of the Gerrhoi at the highest point that the river Dnieper can be navigated and second that they were buried in the most distant region of all the tribes under Scythian rule. There is an apparent contradiction here and much scholarly effort has been invested in trying to find a compromise. The simplest explanation, however, is that two different traditions were used, both correct but representing different periods of time. The first tradition implies that Gerrhos was the region below the fast rapids on the Dnieper, 75 km upstream from the river's mouth. It is in this region, within a radius of 45 km from the rapids, that six of the

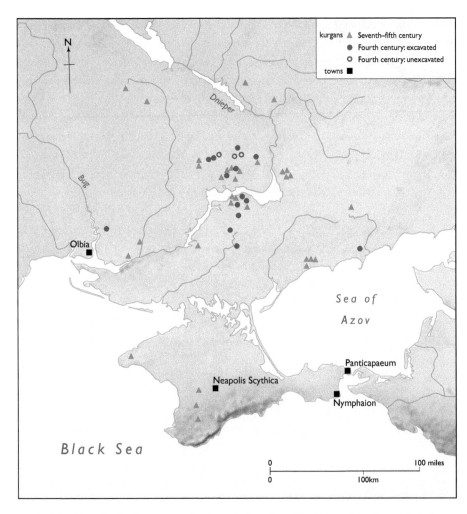

kurgans ▲ Seventh–fifth century
● Fourth century: excavated
○ Fourth century: unexcavated
towns ■

II.I Rich burials in the Pontic steppe tend to cluster in the valley of the Dnieper River immediately down-stream from the rapids which prevent upriver progress. This may be the land of the Gerrhoi referred to by Herodotus as being the burial place of the Scythian kings.

nine largest fifth-century tombs (excluding those of the Kerch Peninsula) and twelve of the sixteen richest fourth-century burials are to be found. In other words, by far the greatest number of fifth- and fourth-century tombs were concentrated in this one restricted area. At the time that Herodotus was writing it had already attracted a significant concentration of very rich interments and was to remain the focus for kingly burials for more than a century afterwards. The second statement implies that the burial grounds of the kings lay on the periphery of the Scythian domain. While this is clearly not so from the fifth century onwards, in the seventh and sixth century the elite burials were found towards the edge of the steppe, in the Kuban region in the south-east and in the forest steppe region crossed by the Dnieper to the north-west. Herodotus clearly had access to information about two traditions, one representing the contemporary situation, the other echoing a much earlier more dispersed pattern: he simply conflated them.

The definition of a royal burial is not altogether straightforward but there is broad agreement that the deciding factors are the height and volume of the burial mound, the number of humans and horses killed to accompany the deceased, the use of gold in horse harnesses, and the general opulence of the funerary equipment. It is a matter of degree and the criteria can vary from one time to another. Of the known fourth-century tombs it can be argued that eight were certainly, or probably, royal including Solokha, Alexandropol, and Chertomlÿk. Heights vary from 14 to 21 m, while the number of retainers buried with the dead king range between three and eleven and horse burials between four and sixteen. There is much gold present and some of the horse harnesses have gold attachments. But the strict application of these criteria excludes a number of other rich burials including Kul'-Oba and Tolstaya mogila which might be thought to qualify for royal status. The difficulty of distinguishing between royal and aristocratic burials can be explained in part by remembering that the Scythians had more than one king at any one time, one of higher status than others. But there is another confusing factor. The relationship between the height of the mound and the status of the deceased also varied over time. The mounds of the seventh- and sixth-century royal burials in the Kuban and forest steppe were significantly lower than those constructed in the fourth century. Given these variables the distinction between royal and non-royal is likely to remain somewhat ill-defined.

Preparing the Body

On the death of a king, says Herodotus, they dig a large quadrangular grave pit and they prepare the body for its procession. These are two separate actions since the grave pit is dug in the land of the Gerrhoi while the body is presumably prepared wherever it was that the king had died:

> They take up the corpse—the body is covered with wax, the stomach is ripped open and cleaned out and the cavity is filled with chopped galingale, incense, celery seed, and anise and sewn up again.
>
> (*Hist.* iv. 71)

The careful preparation of the body was a wise precaution given that the funeral party had to be in close proximity to the corpse for the next forty days. Removing the contents of the stomach and intestines was an obvious first step and the use of strong-smelling herbs as a packing material helped to hide the smell of putrefaction. It is not unlikely that the blood was drained at the same time and it may be that honey or salt was used as a preservative. The coating of the body in wax was to prevent flies from laying eggs in the skin, which would have hatched into maggots.

Further details of the process can be deduced from the well-preserved bodies excavated at Pazyryk. There is no direct evidence to show that these bodies were carried around the country in procession but that they were buried only at the beginning of summer or in the autumn implies that some at least had been exposed, and possibly displayed, for many months. This necessitated the careful preparation of the corpses. In the case of the elite burials in kurgans 2 and 5 the brains had been removed as well as the intestines. The skull of the male in kurgan 2 had been filled with horsehair, pine needles, and larch cones. Muscle tissue had also been removed through long slits and the bodies made up with packing materials. The breast and neck of the female in kurgan 2 were filled with horsehair to preserve the body shape. In addition to this, various smaller slits were made in the skin so that a preservative, perhaps salt, could be introduced. In most cases the incisions were then sewn up with sinew or horsehair. Traces of other preservatives have been found. The body of the woman from kurgan 2 at Pazyryk had been doused with a preparation containing shellac and beeswax, while her male companion had been treated with a mixture of oil and wax. This rather extreme form of preparation would have been desirable if the bodies were to be kept for many months before burial. The removal of muscles and brains, however, raises the possibility that ritual cannibalism may have been practised (below, pp. 308–9).

The preparation of bodies for exposure among the communities of the Altai was not necessarily determined by a desire to parade them between the different tribes. Indeed the remoteness and relative isolation of the region may have militated against this. Some societies recorded in recent times consider that the proximity of the bodies of important individuals enhanced the fertility of crops and animals. If such a belief existed in the Altai then it would explain why it was that burial took place only at prescribed times, at the beginning of summer or in the autumn—significant times in the lifecycle of the flocks and herds. There may, however, have been a more practical reason for delaying burial since in the winter and early spring the ground would have been frozen and impossible to dig.

The Processions

In the Pontic steppe the royal body was put on a wagon and taken from tribe to tribe.

> When they receive the corpse [they] do the same as the Royal Scythians. They cut off a part of their ears, crop the hair close, cut around their arms, slash their foreheads and noses, and pierce their left hands with arrows. Then they carry the king's body on the wagon to another of the tribes which they rule and those to whom they have come before follow them. When they have carried the corpse between all the tribes under their authority they are in the land of the Gerrhoi.
>
> (*Hist.* iv. 71)

This is probably an abbreviated account of the full mourning ceremony that would have included much feasting, which Herodotus elsewhere described as being a Scythian practice.

Displays of grief are not uncommon in mourning ceremonies and there are records of similar performances among later Central Asian communities. Ritual mutilation is a public demonstration of the depth of personal grief occasioned by the loss and this in turn is a measure of the attachment which the mourner felt for the deceased. Put another way, self-mutilation is an expression of one's commitment to a set of values, in this case embodying kingship, and to the lineage of the deceased. It is a public affirmation of loyalty. That said, the suspicion that the interfering spirit of the newly departed was closely watching the proceedings would have been an encouragement to show enthusiasm in the demonstration of grief.

Intriguing evidence that may relate to mourning practices comes from the filling of the entrance shaft for the northern grave at Chertomlÿk. Here, among the debris of feasting archaeologists found six phalange bones from human fingers, representing at least three or four different people. Two of the phalanges showed cut marks. The implication is that the removal of a finger or part of a finger may have featured in the performances of self-mutilation. Since fingers are in limited supply, that such as extreme act could have been contemplated, implies the expectation (or at least the hope) that the new king would have a long life.

Feasting also played an important part of the mourning rituals and, as Herodotus notes, each community visited would have been expected to make provision for such an occasion, with the dead person taking part. The value of such events was that they enabled the hosts to demonstrate their loyalty. Communal eating and drinking also reaffirmed the bonds between people and the recounting of stories about the exploits of ancestors, which no doubt accompanied such occasions, helped to remind the participants of their common heritage.

In some societies the viewing of the body provided the occasion for gifts to be made either to the deceased or to his or her family. There is no direct record that this was the case among the Pontic Scythians, but a system in which so much wealth was consigned to the ground with the king's body is an act of conspicuous consumption which would have required reciprocity benefiting the lineage of the deceased. Thus by showing not only the king's body but also the opulence of the material goods accompanying him to the grave, the lineage was displaying power through their readiness to destroy their wealth. It was incumbent on the hosts receiving the burial party to make a compensatory statement by offering gifts. In some societies items donated on these occasions accompanied the deceased to the grave. There is no clear evidence that this was the case with the Pontic steppe Scythians but the king buried in Arzhan 1, in southern Siberia, was provided with a large number of horses which, judging from their bridles, came from many different regions. It is quite likely that these were gifts either collected during the procession or brought to the graveside by supplicants arriving from afar.

Preparing the Grave

Herodotus tells us only of one kind of grave, a large quadrangular pit dug in the ground. This was, indeed, the type of grave preferred from the seventh to the fifth century in the Pontic steppe region. There are many examples of such chambers. One group, found at Zhurovka on the right bank of the Dnieper not far from Kiev, demonstrates something of the range of construction techniques in use. The shafts had large vertical oak timbers set in the corners and sometimes in the middle of the sides. Behind these the walls of the pits were lined with horizontal boards or posts set upright, embedded in the ground. The roofs were either made of horizontal tim-

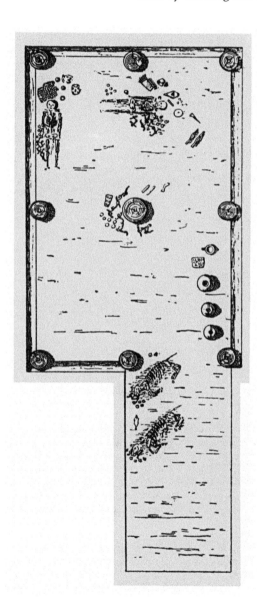

11.2 The timber-built burial chamber of kurgan 400 at Zhurovka excavated 1903–4 showing the entrance ramp where the horses pulling the funerary vehicle were buried.

 298

11.3 (*Right*) Kurgan 2 from the Seven Brothers cemetery excavated 1875–8. The excavation plan shows the burial chamber of the deceased separated from that in which his horses were buried.

11.4 (*Bottom right*) Kurgan 3 at Rjadovye is typical of the catacomb structure of burial in which a shaft is first sunk and from the bottom tunnels are dug, opening out into chambers for the burials.

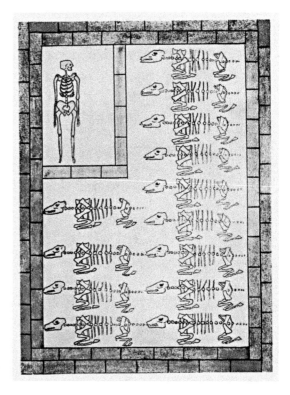

bers or of sloping beams meeting at an apex. Sometimes there were internal timber supports. The chambers were entered by means of sloping ramps which were sometimes timber lined and partly roofed. But there was much variety in construction. In the case of the Seven Brothers burials in the Kuban some chambers were lined with stone walls which had been plastered inside, with roofs of horizontal logs; others were built of mud bricks with vaulted roofs of the same material. Beyond the confines of the Pontic steppe, across Kazakhstan and to the Altai–Sayan, the timber-lined rectangular chamber is the norm, though they are usually quite modest in size compared with the elaborate constructions of the Pontic region. Other types of construction are also recorded. In some cases the chambers were built on the ground surface rather than set within a pit.

From the fourth century onwards a rather different style was adopted, probably as the result of Sauromatian influences. It consisted of an access shaft with an entrance passage leading from the bottom to a burial chamber or chambers hollowed out of the bedrock. The shaft is a consistent element but there is much variety in the number and arrangement of the chambers. Once the burials and the grave goods had been laid out, the shaft was filled and the mound built over it. If, for any reason, access was required again a new shaft had to be dug and a tunnel driven from it to the original grave. In some cases new shafts were later dug towards the edge of the mound to allow new burial chambers to be constructed. This catacomb style of grave became popular in the fourth century and was universally adopted for

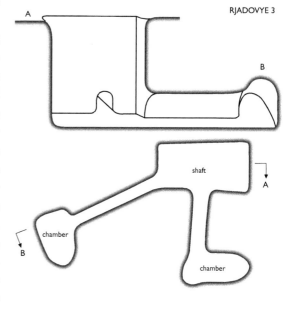

RJADOVYE 3

299

royal burials on the Pontic steppe. It required more skill and time to create but had the advantage of offering unrestricted space for laying out the various aspects of the burial array in different compartments.

Consigned to the Earth

When the procession at last reached the grave pit the body was consigned to the earth. Herodotus provides the details:

> Having laid out the corpse in the tomb on a mattress and planted spears on both sides of the body, beams are stretched across above it to form a roof, which is covered over with mats. In the space around the king's body they bury one of his concubines after strangling her and his cup-bearer, carver, equerry, attendant messenger, horses, the pick of everything else, and golden bowls (they are neither silver nor bronze). Having done this they heap up a great barrow....

(Hist. iv. 71)

There can be no doubt about the intention of the burial: it was to provide the king with all the comforts he would expect to have on hand in the afterlife, the hope being that he would be sufficiently content to remain in his new domain and not interfere in the world of the living.

Herodotus' brief description can be augmented by the rich archaeological evidence. The bodies were often laid on some kind of bedding, particularly in the seventh and sixth centuries, but by the fourth century, with the influence of the Greek colonies growing, sarcophagi came increasingly into use. Spears are prominent, often placed close to the king, and the bodies of female companions and retainers are regularly found, particularly in the fourth-century burials. The burial practices associated with the king's horses were a little more complex. In the earlier period the slaughtered horses were often divided into two groups, one placed in the grave pit, the other just outside. In Kelermes 1 there were twelve horses in each group, while at Kostromskaya all twenty-two horses were laid around the outside of the timber burial chamber. Although the tradition continued on the Pontic steppe, by the fourth century it was more usual for the horses to be placed in separate burial pits towards the periphery of the mound. In the case of Chertomlÿk there were three separate pits providing space for a total of eleven horses.

Across the north Pontic region variations in behaviour can be discerned. In the North Caucasus horse skeletons are found in most of the graves of the seventh to fifth centuries, but even among the richest burials of the forest steppe zone they are rare: instead, the horses are represented by their harnesses—as many as twenty sets

11.5 Kurgan 4 at Pazyryk. The log coffins for the male and female burials were placed on the floor of the log-built burial chamber.

in the richest graves. Horse burials are also unknown in this period in the steppe zone but from the fifth century they become common. Clearly, in the early centuries the different tribes under Scythian authority had different attitudes to the provision of horses for the dead.

The tradition of burying the king's horses close to the burial chamber goes back to the ninth century in the Altai–Sayan region. In the royal burial of Arzhan 1 six horses were placed in the pit up against the wall of the burial chamber within which the king and his female companion lay. At Pazyryk horses accompanied all elite burials. In the case of kurgan 5 nine horses were stacked with other items outside the burial chamber in the narrow space between it and the edge of the pit. In the other graves within the cemetery the number of horses varied. The elite burials in the cemetery of Berel at the western flank of the Altai adopted similar arrangements. Here, in kurgan 11, thirteen horses in full ceremonial regalia were placed in the burial pit to one side of the timber burial chamber. Even the poorer graves, like kurgan 36, had a single horse. The evidence from Pazyryk and Berel shows that the traditional way of placing the deceased's horses in the grave pit, while already underway in the ninth century, was still being practised in the fourth and third centuries. It was only in the elite burials on the Pontic steppe that separate grave pits for horses were being introduced.

Leaving aside the detail, it is clear that the burial of the dead person's riding horse or horses close to the body, a practice deeply rooted in the late Bronze Age of the Altai–Sayan region, had spread westwards across the steppe to the North Caucasus by the seventh century. This belief system soon reached to the forest steppe zone but was interpreted in a different way. It was not until the fifth century that it became the norm across the whole of the Pontic region.

The burial of a female beside or close to a male was a practice widespread both in time and space. In the Arzhan 1 kurgan the king and his female companion were placed side by side in wooden coffins within the same burial chamber. A similar pairing, though without coffins, occurred in the slightly later Arzhan 2 burial. Paired burials are also known at Pazyryk and Berel, though in the case of kurgan 11 at Berel the excavators argue that the female was a later addition.

In the Pontic zone the provision of a female companion for the king is known from the seventh century, but the practice was unevenly distributed. In the early centuries, from the seventh to the fifth centuries, it is evident in the North Caucasus, the Crimea, and the forest steppe zone, but not in the open steppe. Only in the fourth century does it become normal practice for the steppe elite to be so accompanied. Scythian kings had several wives but the chosen companion may have been selected from a wider range of available females: to be strangled at the burial ceremony may not have appealed to the more ambitious wives, though some may have regarded it as a privilege. We have no indication of how the choice was made.

The other retainers buried with the king were chosen for their specialist skills. This is borne out by the royal burials of the fourth century that contained between three and eleven ancillary burials. Chertomlÿk provides a very clear example. Here the main grave complex contained the body of the king and his female companion, evidently a person of high rank; three warriors, two well equipped; a cup-bearer surrounded by amphorae; and two equerries in separate graves close to the pits containing the horses.

The burial at Tolstaya mogila at Ordžonikidze tells a more complex story. Here the king or aristocrat had been buried in a central grave, with his horses in separate pits nearby. Not long after a side grave was dug to bury a much younger woman, richly equipped. Next to her was a child of about two, equally provided with rich grave goods. By her head lay a warrior equipped with bow and arrow, while at her feet a young female had been placed close to a niche in the tomb wall containing kitchen equipment and food. Towards the entrance pit was the body of another male not far from the remains of the funerary cart, placed on the floor of the entrance pit. It is tempting to identify her three attendants as a protector, a maidservant, and a driver. What is particularly interesting about the tomb is that the body of the child had been

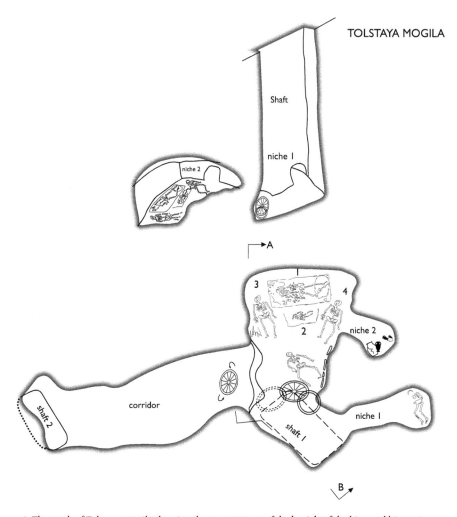

TOLSTAYA MOGILA

11.6 The tomb of Tolstaya mogila showing the arrangement of the burials of the king and his retainers.

placed in the chamber some time after the original burial. Since the entrance shaft had been filled, this required the digging of a new shaft and tunnel to provide access to the original chamber. The sequence of burials can best be interpreted by supposing that the king had died first and was buried in the centre of the mound with his horses nearby. Not long after a related female, perhaps a wife, died and was buried in a newly dug chamber; later the two year old was buried next to her. If the child was hers, which seems probable, then she may have died in childbirth or soon after. The sequence at Tolstaya mogila is a reminder that there could be much variation behind the simple narrative recounted by Herodotus.

11.7 The corpse of the female from kurgan 5 at Pazyryk. After her entrails and some muscle tissue had been removed the body was sewn up.

As already mentioned, the procession which preceded the interment involved transporting the corpse on a wagon from tribe to tribe and finally to the grave. The funerary wagons are sometimes found incorporated in the burial. In the case of Tolstaya mogila the wagon that had carried the female to her grave was dismantled and lowered down the shaft to be placed at the bottom. At the Elizavetinskaya kurgan, where the burial pit was reached by a ramp leading down from the surface, the six-wheeled wagon was dismantled and laid on the floor of the ramp together with the bodies of the six horses that had drawn it. Whether or not there is any symbolism to be read into this it is difficult to say. It may be that the dismantling of the wagons and the placement of the parts, in both cases close to the entrance to the burial chamber, was to deter the departed from attempting to leave the grave. Once the wagon had been dealt with the grave ramps or shafts could be filled in and work could begin on building the great mound.

Raising the Mound

'They all heap up a great barrow', says Herodotus, 'seeking to make it as great as possible.' Here is another example of conspicuous consumption since the mound was intended to stand forever as a dramatic reminder of the ability of the king's line-

11.8 The Elizavetinskaya kurgan excavated in 1914. The six-wheeled hearse and the bodies of the six horses which pulled it were buried in the entrance passage. Other horses and retainers were buried outside the main burial chamber.

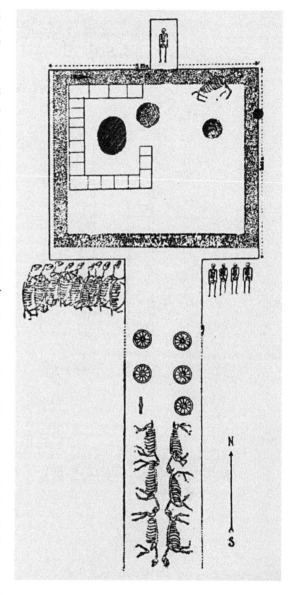

age to require large numbers of the followers to invest their otherwise productive effort in monument building. The greater the monument, the greater the human energy embedded in it. Although the prime function of mound-building was to display coercive power, it had other benefits. The process of construction, which involved the organization of large numbers of people working to a common end over a considerable period of time, was an act of bonding. It was a major event that would have remained vivid in the minds of those who had taken part and for generations the great mound would have served as a time mark in the folk memory of the people, one redolent of their social cohesion. Other, more practical advantages would have been to deter the activities of grave robbers and, perhaps, to give some assurance that the spirit of the dead king would find it difficult to return to the world of the living.

The material for building the mounds was not derived from deep surrounding ditches or nearby quarries but came largely from turves cut from the surrounding grassland. The recent, careful, excavation of the barrow mound at Chertomlÿk allowed the individual turves from which the structure had been built to be identified and it was estimated that since the volume of the mound was about 80,000 cubic m it would have required more time than a million individual turves to complete. To build Tolstaya mogila, which was significantly smaller at 15,000 cubic m, about 100,000 square m of grass-land must have been stripped of turf, soil analysis showing that some of it must have come from at least 4 km away. Since the black earth—the natural soil of much of the steppe—was at least a metre thick and could easily have been quarried from nearby, to build the mounds largely of turf requiring transport over considerable distances was an unnecessary labour. It must have been done for purely symbolic reasons, with the mound perceived to be encapsulating the pasture land of the dead king.

 305

Although Herodotus makes no specific mention of it, the completion of the mound will have been a time of celebration and most probably of feasting. Impressive evidence for feasting was found in the ditch surrounding Tolstaya mogila. Just over half of the ditch was excavated, producing the bones of thirty-five horses, fourteen wild boar, and two stags. If the unexcavated length of ditch had produced equivalent quantities the total amount of meat available would have been about 13,000 kilos, enough to glut 340 people for a week or 2,400 people for a single night. Large quantities of sherds of wine amphorae were also found, showing that it must, indeed, have been a festive occasion. There is no absolute certainty that the feast was a single event, but if it was not, the individual acts of feasting could have been spread over only a short period.

The source of the meat has interesting implications. The large number of horses is only to be expected since the domesticated herds would have been the normal source of protein, but the inclusion of stags and wild boar means that the feast is likely to have been preceded by hunting expeditions. It is a reminder that physical recreation in the form of hunting and games often accompanied funerary celebrations.

The final stage is likely to have been purifications, which Herodotus described in detail, beginning with the washing of the head and ending with the inhalation of the fumes of hemp seeds burning on red-hot stones in the confined space of a felt tent (above, p. 46).

A Year Later

Perhaps the most intriguing part of Herodotus' account is devoted to what happens when the burial party returned to the mound a year later:

> They take the most suitable of the rest of the attendants . . . they strangle fifty of them and fifty of the finest horses and, having removed their entrails, clean them and fill them with chaff and sew them up. Then they attach half of a wheel, turned upside down, to two posts and the other half to another pair and they set up many of these in this way, and then, driving thick stakes lengthwise through the horses' bodies to their neck, they set them on the wheels so that the wheel in front supports the horse's shoulder and the wheel behind props up the belly near the hindquarters and the legs on each side hang down freely. Each horse is provided with a bit bridle which is drawn out in front of the horse and attached to a peg. They mount each of the fifty strangled youths on the horses, mounting them in this way: they drive an upright stake through the body along the spine to the neck, and fix the end of this stake projecting from below the body into a hole made in the other stake that passes through the horse. Having set up the fifty riders thus in a circle around the tomb they leave.

(Hist. iv. 72)

In relishing the detail, offering sufficient instruction for the process to be replicated, Herodotus betrays his evident fascination with the subject. The re-excavation of Chertomlÿk in the 1970s provided what may reasonably be interpreted as evidence of the practice. Several areas were cleared outside the wall that revetted the base of the mound, exposing concentrations of horse bones, roughly equidistant from each other, associated with harness fittings and human bones. They lay on the original ground surface, no attempt having been made to bury them. Where gender could be distinguished the remains were of males. These death riders (*Totenreiter*), as they were called by the archaeologists, must have been a frightening sight to anyone who approached, the more so as they began to slump and lurch in their decay, gradually disintegrating into piles of whitening bones amid the rags and tatters of rotting clothes and rusting armour.

A simple explanation of the practice would be to suppose that the riders were the entourage of the deceased king provided for his protection in the afterlife. Their dramatic presence would also have deterred would-be tomb robbers. But why the interval of a year before they were installed? The answer might lie in a belief that the king still retained some earthly powers after his death and it was not until the transition period was over that the final act of closure could take place. The concept of a transitional year seems also to be embedded in the practice described above (p. 270) of appointing a substitute king to guard the sacred golden objects, after which he was killed. But how all this may have fitted together, if indeed it did, in a coherent belief system must remain speculative.

Ways of Death across the Steppe

It needs to be remembered that Herodotus' famous description of Scythian burial rituals refers specifically to those who lived in the Pontic region. Elsewhere across the vast expanse of steppe one might expect there to have been some variation. Yet what stands out are the broad similarities of practice through space and time: interment in a specially constructed chamber; the provision of a female partner for the male; the slaughter and burial of his horse(s) placed close to the burial chamber; the accompaniment of prize possessions and food for the afterlife; and the monumentalizing of the grave with a mound. In some regions a stone statue, perhaps representing the deceased, was erected on top of the mound while in other regions it is possible that wooden markers were erected.

Another similarity in practice, in both the Pontic region and the Altai, was the preparation of the body for a period of exposure, either for the long procession, as described by Herodotus, or until it was deemed to be a propitious time for burial,

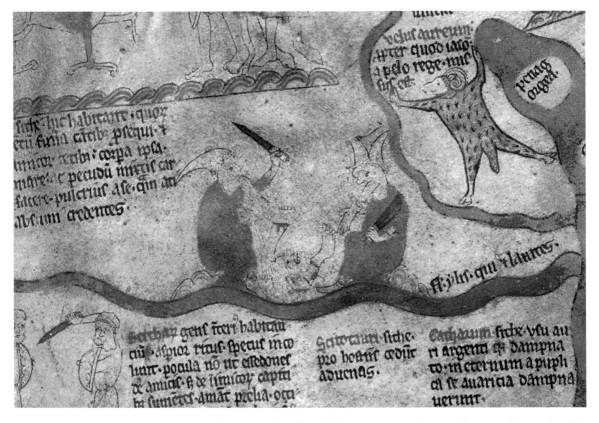

11.9 Herodotus' description of ritual cannibalism among the Issedones was known to the compiler of the Mappa Mundi (*c.* AD 1300) now preserved in Hereford Cathedral. Two Scythians are shown cutting up and eating the bodies of their dead parents.

as in the case among the Altai communities. This seasonal pattern may have been conditioned by the transhumance cycle. Exposing the body, for whatever reasons, required the removal of the entrails to slow down the processes of decay, but the removal of the brains and muscles as well at Pazyryk might seem a little excessive. As has been suggested above (p. 296), it could, however, be that they were eaten. In two passages, referring to the Issedonians and Massagetae, Herodotus describes just such a procedure. Of the Issedonians he says:

> When a man's father dies, all the near relatives bring sheep to the son's house, which are sacrificed and their flesh cut in pieces while at the same time the dead body is similarly treated. The two sorts of flesh are mixed together and served up as a banquet.

(*Hist.* iv. 26)

 308

The Massagetae had a more extreme custom:

> When a man grows very old all his family come together
> and offer him up in sacrifice at the same time offering some
> cattle. After the sacrifice they boil the flesh and feast on
> it. Those who end their life in this way are considered the
> happiest. If a man dies of disease they do not eat him but
> bury him in the ground, bewailing his ill-fortune that he did
> not live to be sacrificed.
>
> (*Hist.* ix. 216)

The essence of both stories, that the flesh of revered old
people was eaten by the family in a ritual meal, need
occasion no surprise. It was a way in which the family
could share the ancestral life force. The drinking of each
other's blood in a ceremony of bonding between blood
brothers (above, p. 217) embodies some elements of the
same concepts.

The complex and varied practices surrounding death
reflect deep-seated beliefs about the nature of life and its
continuous flow. The death of important men and women
provided the opportunity for society to reaffirm its values
and to ensure its continuity.

There can be little doubt that for the Scythians the
graves of their ancestors were of huge influence reflecting
their very being and providing an ever-present reminder
of the long and continuous history of the people. The
point is nicely made in the speech reportedly given by the
Scythian king, Idanthyrsus, to the Persians.

> We Scythians have neither towns nor cultivated land
> which might make us, through fear that they might be
> taken or destroyed, to hurry to engage you in battle. If,
> however, you want, quickly, to come to blows with us,
> look, these are our ancestors' tombs. Find them and
> attempt to interfere with them; then you will see whether
> or not we will fight with you. Until you do this, you can
> be sure we will not face you in battle—unless it pleases us.
>
> (*Hist.* iv. 127)

11.10 Granite stele from Plavni in the Odeska region. The figure's right hand is on the pommel of his short sword, which
is slung from his belt. His left hand holds a drinking horn. His
gorytos is attached to his belt on the left side of his body. Stelae
of this kind were placed on the summits of kurgans and were
probably intended to represent the person buried beneath. They
are in the tradition of the Late Bronze Age deer stones.

ΤΡΥΦΩΝ
ΑΝΔΡΟΜΕΝΟΥ ΑΝ
ΘΗΣ

12

SCYTHIANS IN THE
LONGUE DURÉE

THE wide expanse of steppe flowing through Eurasia, with its grey-green horizons receding in the distance and its shimmer as the wind rustles the grass, challenges everyone to be on the move. Like the sea, it is a world where nothing can stay still and, like the sea, it sweeps everything onward. For millennia people have progressed through the steppe, sometimes in repeating patterns of transhumance and sometimes with astonishing speed, crossing huge distances to seek out new pastures.

The Scythians occupy only one small part of the grand narrative. Before them, in the third and second millennia BC, antecedent movements can be detected in the archaeological record. Early in the third millennium nomadic pastoralists living in the Pontic–Caspian steppe, known as the Yamnaya culture, had begun to expand westwards along the lower Danube valley and into the Great Hungarian Plain and some archaeologists have argued that there was another expansion eastwards across 1,500 km of steppe to the edge of the Altai–Sayan mountains at about this time, introducing new techniques of metal-working to the region. The scale of these movements, recognizable in the scattered detritus of the archaeological record, is difficult to judge but it may have been comparatively modest.

It was sometime at the beginning of the first millennium BC that flows began of people from the east, from the area that is now eastern Kazakhstan, southern Siberia, and Mongolia—movements that were to continue in waves over more than two thousand years. Climate is likely to have been a prime mover, exacerbated by popula-

 311

tion growth, and driven by the innate desire of humans to be acquisitive. One important factor was that the western reaches of the steppe were moister and warmer than
the east due to the effects of weather patterns flowing in from the Atlantic: the further
west one ventured, the more congenial was the environment for a pastoral way of life.
This created what has become known as the steppe gradient and was no doubt one of
the reasons why the flow of people to the west increased. But what probably sparked
the westward migration from the Altai–Sayan to the Pontic steppe beginning in the
ninth century was the improvement of weather conditions in the home region, free-
ing people from the daily rigours of pastoralism practised in a harsh environment—a
freedom that gave rein to raiding and territorial expansion. This in turn encouraged
the emergence of war leaders demanding allegiance, and it was but a short step to
the development of predatory hordes willing to range widely in pursuit of reputation
and reward. Put another way, improved climatic conditions relieved the constraints
which had kept the natural aggressive instincts of people under control and so the
predatory nomad horseman was born.

　　This book has explored the story of the nomadic societies from the ninth century
BC, when the earliest movements to the west began, until the second century BC,
when new forces emerging in the east brought pressure to bear on the inhabitants
of Central Asia, thereby creating a further spate of westerly migrations. The earliest
predatory nomads to impinge upon the Pontic–Caspian steppe between the ninth and
seventh centuries BC brought with them a culture closely similar to that which had
developed in the Altai–Sayan region. While it is likely that the flow of incomers was
spread, perhaps continuously, over these two centuries, such documentary evidence
as there is identifies two separate peoples: first the Kimmerians, then the Scythians.
The archaeological record, however, shows that there was little significant difference
in their material culture that cannot otherwise be ascribed to gradual change or to the
influence of the indigenous folk culture on that of the incomers.

　　By the seventh century a degree of stability had emerged across the Pontic–Caspian
steppe and Central Asia creating what many archaeologists refer to as a Scythian–
Siberian culture (or cultural continuum). The classical sources name a number of
individual tribes within this vast area, emphasizing their individual peculiarities, so
far as they were known, but both Herodotus and the Persians failed to see significant ethnic differences between the Scythians of the Pontic steppe and the Sakā who
occupied much of Central Asia.

　　Over time the intrusive nomadic groups underwent acculturation, both as the
result of intermixing with indigenous people and through reciprocal exchanges with
the sedentary state societies with whom they came into contact. This was particularly true of the Scythians on the Pontic steppe, who on their northern border met

with settled agricultural communities over whom they established some degree of ascendancy and on their southern border confronted vigorous Greek trading enclaves. As a result we can see significant changes in the Scythian lifestyle, with some communities developing as agriculturalists, the better to benefit from the growing market for grain in the Greek world. Elite life also changed with the adoption of Greek feasting behaviours and the acceptance of the luxury goods created by craftsmen working in the Greek Black Sea cities, particularly Panticapaeum. In art, representations of humans became increasingly common and even the depiction of predatory beasts began to take on a more Mediterranean guise. The powerful animal art of the steppe was fast being diluted. Similar cultural borrowings were evident in Central Asia, where the Sakā adopted stylistic preferences from the neighbouring Persians and even the communities of the remote Altai were not immune from cultural influences emanating from India, Persia, and China, though their vigorous nomad culture continued to flourish.

By the beginning of the fourth century BC the traditional Scythian regions west of the river Don were beginning to come under pressure from their neighbours, the Sauromatae, and there is some evidence of conflict. What this actually involved in terms of population movement it is difficult to say, but it need mean little more than a Sauromatian elite taking over power on the Pontic steppe, forcing the old Scythian elites to move westward into the Danube delta region and into the Crimean Peninsula. The scene was now set for the dramatic changes that were to characterize the next six centuries.

Power Struggles in the Far East

Early in the second century BC the growing power of the Han dynasty in China began to destabilize the various nomadic tribes that lay on its northern border. The most powerful were the Xiongnu of the Gobi region. Between them and the Gansu corridor—the narrow zone which offered the easiest routes between the plains of China and the caravan trails around the Taklamakan Desert—were two indigenous peoples, the Yuezhi and the Wusun. Facing the rising power of the Xiongnu, both tribes were forced to migrate, there being no option but to move westwards. The first to migrate, between 176 and 160 BC, were the Yuezhi, their flight taking them along the northern side of the Taklamakan Desert and through the Tian Shan to the prolific grasslands around the lake Issyk Kul, an area at the time occupied by the Sakā. This inevitably had knock-on effects throughout Central Asia.

Hot on the heels of the Yuezhi came the Wusun, who, about 140 BC, forced them out of the Ili valley and took over the land for themselves. The Yuezhi then moved

 313

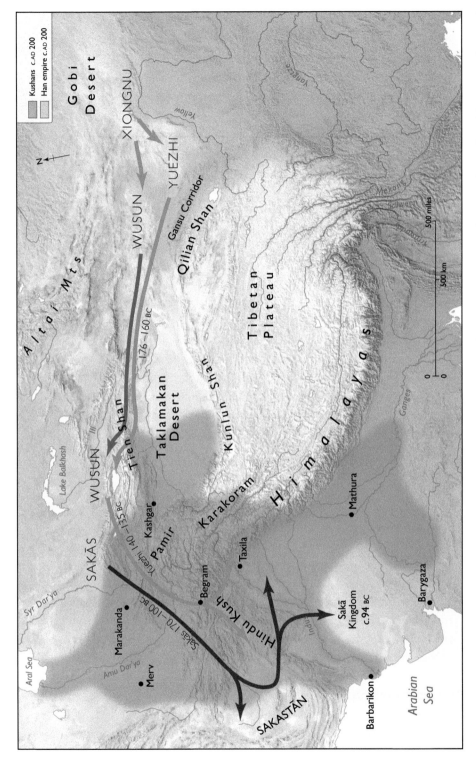

12.1 Conflict between the Han and the nomadic Xiongnu on their northern border destabilized other nomadic groups in the region, the Yuezhi and the Wusun, who moved westwards into Central Asia, driving some groups of Sakā to move into India and Iran. One branch of the Yuezhi created the Kushan empire.

around the western edge of the Pamir, arriving in Bactria, where they settled in about 135 BC. At this time the Yuezhi were composed of five tribes with different names. The king of one of these, the Kushan, became the acknowledged leader and began a process of expansion that by the beginning of the third century AD had created a vast Kushan empire extending from the Indus and upper Ganges valleys to the Aral Sea and from Parthia to the border of China.

The arrival of the Yuezhi and the Wusun in territory long occupied by the nomad Sakā caused widespread disruption, driving many Sakā southwards into western Bactria and through the Hindu Kush. Some chose to settle in southern Afghanistan and western Pakistan, expanding into southern Iran and establishing themselves in an area which became known as Sakāstan (now Sistan). Others moved into India and during the period 110–80 BC set up kingdoms to the east of the lower Indus valley and further north in Gandhara. By the first century AD, when the *Periplus of the Erythraean Sea* was being compiled, the Sakā-dominated region extended to the shores of the Arabian Sea, with its major entrepôt at Minnagara, modern Karachi.

The folk movements were complex and spread over a long period of time. Inevitably the interactions between the nomad invaders and indigenous population varied from region to region but something of the violence of the early stages of the exodus can be seen at Ai Khanum, a city founded by the Greeks in the upper valley of the Amu Darya, which, about 145 BC, was completely destroyed by the Sakā advance. But once the disparate nomad bands had found lands to control, they began to settle and to adopt aspects of the native culture, though the raiding of neighbouring territories lasted well into the first century AD.

In spite of the acculturation that must have gone on, enclaves of Sakā still adhered to their old ways of life. One is represented by a small cemetery found at Tillya Tepe in the north-west of Afghanistan, dating to the end of the first century AD. Here the central grave of a male was surrounded by the graves of six richly adorned females, probably his wives. Some of their jewellery was, as might be expected, of Graeco-Bactrian origin but other pieces were made in the style of the nomadic art of the steppe. The love of gold, the use of inset turquoise, and motifs of fabulous beasts are all characteristics strongly reminiscent of Sakā burials in the Kazakh steppe. Here, in this remote region a nomad community was still maintaining the culture of their ancestors who had been driven from their homeland two hundred years earlier.

The movement of the Yuezhi and the Wusun into Central Asia in the second century BC marked the beginning of a succession of movements from the east that were eventually to culminate in the advance of the Mongols early in the thirteenth century.

The turmoil created by the Yuezhi and Wusun had hardly subsided when a new confederacy of horsemen, the Huns, arrived in Central Asia. Their ultimate origin is

 315

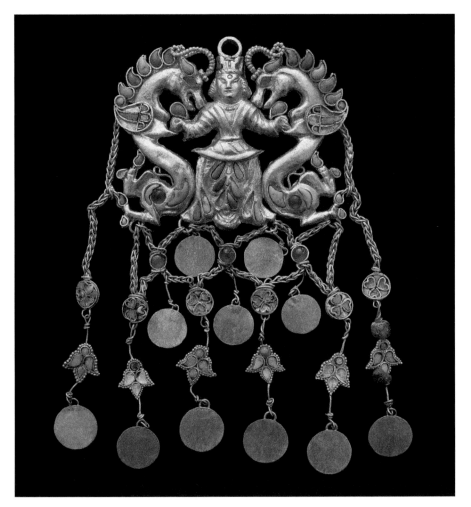

12.2 Gold pendant, known as the Dragon Master, inset with turquoise. From the tomb of Tillya Tepe in northern Afghanistan (first century AD). The style reflects the strong influence of steppe art at the time of the Kushan empire.

obscure and still much in debate, but that their racial type was predominantly Mongoloid suggests that they came from the east. Some writers have argued that they were a branch of the Xiongnu driven to migrate to the west by the advance of the Han Chinese, which began in 133 BC. The argument is based on the similarity in the names of both, which may have derived from the same root, and certain aspects of a shared material culture. Coming from the east they seem to have carved out a territory north of the Tian Shan, possibly extending from southern Siberia and Dzungaria to eastern Kazakhstan, and there over the years developed a unified leadership

and a distinctive culture. Sometime in the period 174 to 160 BC the Huns advanced westwards, defeating the Massagetae who were living in the region of the Syr Daria delta and the neighbouring Sakā, forcing them to abandon the Kazakh and Central Asian steppe and to move westwards. By the end of the first century AD, the Roman historian Tacitus records the presence of *Hunnoi* living in the vicinity of the Caspian Sea. The gradual build-up of Huns in the region was a long drawn-out process, and it was not until AD 370 that they began their sudden and spectacular advance westwards into Europe, driving the remaining Sakā/Sarmatian nomads before them.

Standing back from the broad swathe of history, while the detail is often obscure, the broad rhythms of life are clear enough. Central Asia was something of a holding ground. It received pulses of people coming from the east displacing the resident population and driving them to the south and to the west in a kind of domino effect. It was in this way that the horse-riding nomads first began to arrive on the Pontic steppe—people the classical writers called Kimmerians and Scythians. Thereafter the westerly flow continued steadily until the sudden incursion of the Yuezhi and Wusun in the second century BC drove the Sakā south into Afghanistan and India and westwards into the Pontic region. It was at this time that the Huns moved into the Kazakh steppe. Thereafter there seems to have been a period of relative calm until the end of the fourth century AD, when the Huns began their relentless sweep into Europe displacing the descendants of the Sakā/Sarmatians, driving them literally to the ends of the earth.

The Sarmatians in all their Variety

We saw in Chapter 5 how nomadic people broadly categorized as Sarmatians, but called by some writers Sauromatae, began to cross the river Don and oust the Scythian elite, driving them into the Crimea and into the region of the Danube delta. The first stages of this process began early in the fourth century BC. The westward flow of population probably continued on a gentle scale until the beginning of the second century BC when the migrations intensified, exacerbated by the pressure of new people arriving in Central Asia from the east—the Yuezhi, the Wusun, and the Huns. The period which this initiated, lasting from the early second century BC to the late first century AD, is referred to as the Middle Sarmatian period. A number of different Sarmatian peoples are mentioned in the surviving texts, the most prominent being the Aorsi, Siraces, Roxolani, Iazyges, and Alani, but all shared a broadly similar culture. They were bands of nomadic horsemen, intent on establishing their authority over new territories. While large-scale movements of populations were involved and people were displaced, it is likely that much of the indigenous population remained

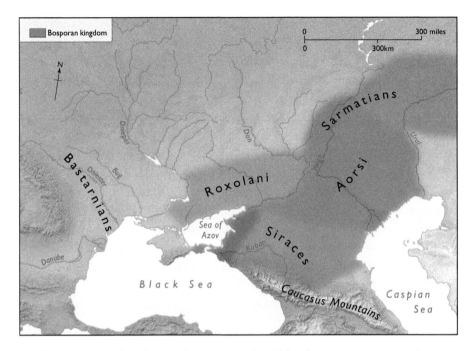

12.3 The Pontic steppe from the second century BC to the mid fourth century AD saw successive movements of Sarmatian bands to the west. But further movement was, for a while, halted by the Bastarnae, who may have been of mixed Celtic and German ancestry.

to merge with the newcomers, further mixing the gene pool and the culture. Thus, although a tribal name may have remained the same over several centuries, the culture of the tribe may have changed significantly. The one constant was that the elite males worked together as bands of predatory horsemen.

The dominant group to emerge in the early second century BC, centred on the lower Volga but extending from the Don to the Urals, were the Aorsi. They seem to have moved into the region from the central Kazakh steppe, ousting or absorbing the local population. Their neighbours to the south were the Siraki, who lived to the east of the Sea of Azov. The Aorsi, who are mentioned in Chinese sources in the late second century BC, are described as a formidable power able to field a force of 100,000 archers. The annals indicate that they extended from the Aral to the Caspian Sea, the original homeland of the tribe who had by now begun to move west to the Volga. Strabo, writing at the beginning of the first century AD, adds to the geographic uncertainty by referring to the Upper Aorsi, who occupied the region of the southern Urals from where they commanded the major trade routes to the south. In all probability the tribal name was applied to a confederacy of nomads extending over an extensive

territory from the Don to the Aral Sea. They were neighbours of the fractious Bosporan kingdom and during a dynastic dispute in 64–63 BC were able to offer the support of 200,000 horsemen to one of the contenders. Later, after Rome had taken over control of the kingdom, the Aorsi became their allies.

During the Early Sarmatian period, before the arrival of the Aorsi on the lower Volga, the region was occupied by the Roxolani, while the area between the Don and the Dnieper was the preserve of the Iazyges: both were closely related Sarmatian peoples. The westward migration of the Aorsi early in the second century BC forced the Roxolani to move westwards across the Volga and the Don to take control of the Pontic steppe. This in turn drove out the Iazyges, who carved out a new territory for themselves in the lower Dniester steppe bordered by the Bastarnae to the north and north-west and the Getae in the Dobruja to the south.

The Roxolani, now dominant on the Pontic steppe, were described as 'wagon dwellers' by Strabo. He writes of their transhumant lifestyle, dependent on their flocks and herds, moving from winter camps along the shore of the Sea of Azov, where in their leisure time they hunted deer and wild boar, to the inland steppe pastures, where they turned their attention to wild asses and roe deer. But in spite of this bucolic lifestyle they were a force to be reckoned with. The Scythians who had fled to the Crimea were under their control and towards the end of the second century BC, allying themselves with the Crimean Scythians, they attacked the Bosporan kingdom with 50,000 lightly armed cavalry. They were defeated but, undeterred, a few years later, in 107 BC, they joined Mithridates in his attack on the kingdom.

By the middle of the first century BC the geopolitics of the region were changing fast. The Aorsi, now coming under pressure from the Alans, crossed the Don forcing the Roxolani to move westwards across the Dnieper into the territory of the Iazyges flanking the Black Sea between the Dnieper and the Danube delta. Some Roxolani moved further west to the Carpathians, while others travelled northwards to the region of Kiev, but the main thrust of the advance took them into the plain of Wallachia flanked by the Carpathian Mountains on the north, where lay the stronghold of the powerful Dacians, and the Danube to the south, which at this time was the frontier of the Roman empire. The displaced Iazyges meanwhile, having come into conflict with the Romans on a number of occasions, managed to cross the Carpathians to reach the Great Hungarian Plain, where they settled soon after AD 20.

Sarmatians versus the Roman Empire

Throughout the first century AD the Roman frontier ran along the river Danube, creating a major obstacle against further Sarmatian advances to the south and west.

On two occasions, in AD 6 and AD 16, Iazyges had mounted raids across the Danube into Roman territory but to no effect, a failure which persuaded them to move on to the Great Hungarian Plain. By AD 62 the Roxolani had replaced the Iazyges on the plain of Wallachia and in the winter of AD 69 they mounted a major raid on the Roman province of Moesia, destroying a Roman legion before they were defeated and driven back. Another raid in AD 85–6, this time in conjunction with the Dacians, caused havoc in the province, during which time the Roman governor was killed. In retaliation a Roman force was sent into Dacia but was virtually annihilated. Two years later, in AD 89, another Roman army was sent into Dacia and was sufficiently

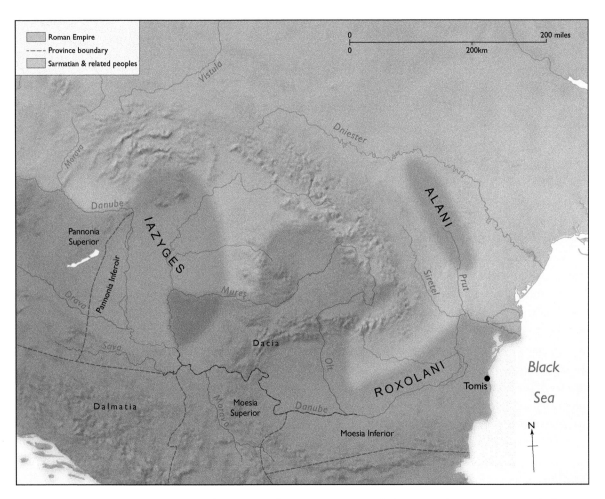

12.4 Groups of Sarmatians—the Roxolani, Iazyges, and Alans—moved west into Europe in the first century AD establishing themselves in close proximity to the frontiers of the Roman Empire.

 320

successful to force the Dacians to sue for peace. But it was an uneasy peace and the new emperor Trajan, who came to power in AD 98, decided that the only solution was for Dacia to be conquered and brought within the empire. It took two hard fought campaigns, in AD 101–2 and AD 106–7, to accomplish this. During this time the Roxolani fought on the Dacian side and at Trajan's triumph in AD 107 captive Roxolani were paraded alongside Dacians. A detachment of heavily armed Roxalanian cavalry is depicted in flight on Trajan's Column, the victory monument erected in the Roman forum. Roman citizens now for the first time had a clear image of the Sarmatian barbarians.

12.5 To celebrate Trajan's victories over the Dacians a celebratory column was erected in the Forum at Rome. It recorded episodes from the conflict. One scene shows heavily armoured Sarmatian cavalry, most likely Roxolani, fleeing from Roman cavalry.

As the new province of Dacia developed the Roxolani living on the Wallachian plain were given an annual payment but were required to stay well clear of Roman frontiers. The withdrawal of the subsidy in AD 117 led to a rebellion but this was quickly put down by the Romans and the subsidy reinstated. As a result of the new agreement the king of the Roxolani became a Roman vassal.

While these events were unfolding in the lower Danube valley the Iazyges were establishing themselves in the Great Hungarian Plain on the east bank of the Danube facing across the river to the Roman province of Pannonia. Although there was a degree of mixing with the indigenous population, the Iazyges managed to maintain their distinctive culture at least into the third century AD. To the Romans this was Sarmatia. Until AD 160 relations between the Romans and the Sarmatians Iazyges were generally good. The Iazyges provided auxiliary cavalry for the Roman army and fought as allies of Rome against the Dacians except for the brief period AD 117–19 when they attacked the Roman province of Dacia from the west while the Roxolani advanced from the south. Peace was soon restored but the incident was a reminder to Rome that the Sarmatians remained an ever-present threat.

In the second half of the second century AD a Germanic tribe, the Marcomanni, threatened Rome's northern frontier, initiating two long periods of warfare, the Marcomannic Wars of AD 166–72 and 177–80. During the first war the Sarmatians crossed the Danube and attacked the province of Pannonia, only to be severely beaten by Marcus Aurelius who assumed the honorific title 'Sarmaticus' for his achievements. As a result of their defeat the Iazyges were required to live well clear of the Danube frontier and to provide 8,000 cavalrymen to serve as auxiliaries in the Roman army. Of these 5,500 were sent to Britain to be dispersed in units of 500 among the forts in the north and west of the country. There is evidence of their presence at Chesters on Hadrian's Wall, at Ribchester, and at the legionary base of Chester, where the grave of an unnamed Sarmatian horseman was marked by a tombstone. He stares forlornly at his unfamiliar surroundings, 1,800 km from his home.

Relationships between the Romans and the Iazyges remained uneasy. A major campaign was fought between AD 236 and 238. In AD 248–50 the Iazyges raided Dacia and four years later they were involved in attacks on Pannonia. A generation later, in AD 271, the province of Dacia was finally abandoned by the Romans and left to the Visigoths. Thereafter the Iazyges continued to raid Pannonia, the most far-reaching attack, in AD 282–3, spurring a punitive and long drawn-out Roman response. A civil war which broke out among the Iazyges in the early fourth century for a while deflected attention from the rich pickings still to be had in Pannonia but

by the mid-
dle of the century
raids began again, last-
ing to the end of the century, when
the arrival of the Huns in the Great
Hungarian Plain in AD 430 brought
Sarmatian power to an end.

That the Sarmatian Iazyges were able
to maintain their identity for more than
four hundred years is remarkable, but
the steppe land of Hungary was a familiar environment that suited their mobile
lifestyle while the presence of the Roman
province of Pannonia just across the Danube
provided opportunities for both trade and

12.6 Funerary monument from the Roman fortress of Chester, England, showing a Sarmatian auxiliary
clad in scale armour. He may be one of the 5,500 Sarmatians who were sent to Britain in the late second
century AD.

unending lucrative raids. They were ideally located to sustain themselves in the way that predatory horsemen had forever done.

The Alans: The Last Spectacular Thrust

The origin of the Alans, like that of other nomadic hordes, is obscure but there is some evidence to suggest that they emerged from the confederacy of the Aorsi. That, at least, is what the Chinese annals imply when the say that the Aorsi were renamed Al'lan'ai. The likelihood is that the Alani originated as a power group among the Aorsi somewhere on the steppe north of the Caspian Sea, their rise forcing the rest of the Aorsi to migrate across the Don. In ad 68 the presence of Alans near the Sea

12.7 Funerary monument of marble from the Bosporan city of Tanais at the mouth of the Don. It was set up to commemorate Triphon, who, as a member of the Sarmatian elite, probably served in the army of the Bosporan kings.

of Azov led the inhabitants of Tanais to strengthen their city's defences. By this time they had already established control over much of the steppe east of the Dnieper and southwards to the Kuban, from where they mounted a series of attacks on Parthia, probably following the western coast of the Caspian Sea. Later, in the early second century ad, they raided Roman territory in eastern Asia Minor, this time following the route along the eastern coast of the Black Sea.

At the beginning of the third century AD a massive and sustained incursion of Goths coming from the Baltic region into the Ukraine changed the rhythm of life, blocking the westerly flow of nomads and keeping the Alans to the territory centred on the Don/Dnieper region. All this time the power of the Huns was building on their eastern flank. In about AD 360 the Huns suddenly burst out, surging across the Volga and the Don, and within fifteen years they had devastated the kingdom of the Ostrogoths. Some of the Alans joined the Huns, some moved southwards into the Caucasus, others fled west into Europe. One group, joining the fleeing Goths, were allowed, by the emperor Valens, to cross the Danube to settle within the Roman Empire, but conflict ensued culminating in the battle of Adrianople in AD 378 in which the Roman emperor was killed.

Many of those who fled westward took the route around the northern side of the Carpathians into the North European Plain, where they came into contact with Germanic tribes who were now beginning to amass for what was to be their final onslaught against the Roman Empire. The beginning of the end came in AD 401 when Alans and Vandals crossed the Danube and drove deep into the heart of the empire. A few years later, in AD 406, Alans, in company with Vandals and Suevi, crossed the frozen Rhine near Mainz and began a devastating, two-year-long rampage through Gaul before crossing the Pyrenees and settling in western Iberia. Ten years later, in AD 418, they were ousted by the Visigoths, working to the orders of the Roman emperor, but found a temporary home in Galicia in the north-west corner of the Iberian peninsula, where they merged as one people with the Vandals. When, in AD 429, the Vandals crossed into Africa and forced their way along the North African coast towards Carthage the remnant of the Alans were with them, but after the vicissitudes of the long trudge across Europe from their homeland on the Pontic steppe it is unlikely that the grandsons and great-grandsons of those who had fled from the Huns sixty years before would have carried much of their steppe culture with them. The expulsion of the Alans from their homeland marks the end of the Indo-European-speaking nomads of the steppe. Other horsemen were to follow but they were ethnically different—Turkic and Mongolian, speaking quite different languages. Like those who

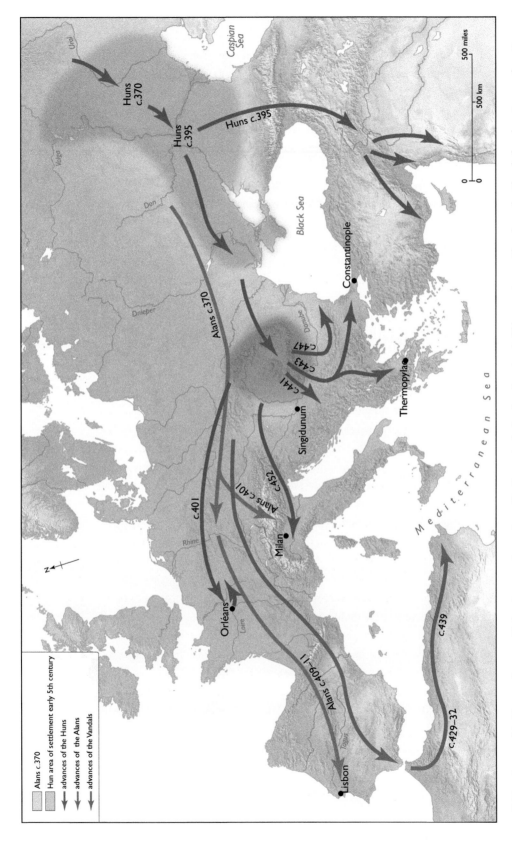

12.8 The advance of the Huns to the west added to the turmoil experienced by Europe in the late fourth and early fifth centuries AD. They drove the Alans before them into northern Europe, where they joined with migrating German tribes to sweep through the western Roman provinces, some of them eventually joining the Vandals on their conquest of North Africa.

came before them, their inexorable progress to the west was facilitated, indeed determined, by the timeless flow of the steppe.

The Alans who fled to the Caucasus fared better. Settling first in the comparative isolation of the foothills and then extending deep into the central Caucasian highlands, they were still known as Alans as late as the thirteenth century. When William of Rubruck passed this way en route to the court of Chinggis Khan he noted that the Alans were good at making weapons—an appropriate accolade to their Sarmatian heritage. Their descendants, the Ossetians, who live now in the Caucasian highlands, speak a language in which echoes of Scytho-Sarmatian may still be heard.

GALLERY OF OBJECTS

I N this Gallery ten objects have been chosen for individual consideration. All come from the excavations of elite burials on the Pontic steppe and all date to the fourth century BC. What gives them a particular relevance is that each one is decorated with scenes that illuminate Scythian life. We have had cause to refer to them a number of times in the preceding pages when dealing with themes such as personal appearance, clothing, weapons, and warfare. But by focusing on aspects of detail, as we have done, there is a danger that the integrity of the item will be lost sight of. It is for this reason that selected objects are presented here in their entirety.

But can the depictions be taken as true representations of Scythians and Scythian life? All were probably made by highly skilled Greek craftsmen working in one of the Greek colonies on the northern Black Sea coast, most likely Panticapaeum on the Kerch peninsula of the Crimea. The forms, the decorative motifs, and the technological skills employed are clearly Greek. But these items were made specifically for the top echelons of the Scythian elite and it was they who would have dictated what was pictorially acceptable: depictions of significant events in Scythian history, mythologies, and social interactions embodying the value systems of their nomadic ancestry. Had the scenes not been true to Scythian culture the items would surely not have been accepted. Yet there is still the lingering suspicion that they may slyly nod to the Greek caricature of the Scythians—barbarians with straggly hair and long beards, wearing pointed hoods, baggy embroidered trousers, and long belted coats. It is tempting to wonder whether the Greek goldsmiths, in the interests of accuracy, used props—perhaps manikins dressed in Scythian clothes and a set of Scythian weapons. We will never know. It may not have been necessary. By the fourth century the interaction between Greeks and Scythians was profound. Scythians were present, probably in some number in the principal Greek colonies, and it is highly likely that Greek traders and even Greek craftsmen travelled extensively through Scythian territory and were resident for periods of time at the great inland markets. These interactions provided ample opportunity for the two cultures to learn of each other's ways. While it is possible that the Scythians depicted on these objects may have been a little stylized, that the patrons accepted them gives us some reassurance that what we are seeing is a fair representation of the way in which the Scythian elites saw themselves.

The objects chosen here are housed in the two great collections of Scythian artefacts, the State Hermitage Museum, St Petersburg and the Kiev Museum of Historical Treasures.

1 The Kul'-Oba gold beaker

(State Hermitage Museum, St Petersburg)

The tomb of Kul'-Oba, near Kerch, was discovered accidentally in 1850 and excavated by Paul Du Brux. The famous gold beaker may have been held in the hands of one of the deceased. Second half of the fourth century BC.

The vessel is 130 mm in height. It is bulbous with a tall narrow neck and a cupped lip; the foot ring was added later. The body is divided into an upper and a lower register by a narrow band of guilloche decoration set just below the maximum diameter. The lower zone is decorated with long narrow petals growing from a flower head centred on the bottom of the vessel. The upper scene shows seven Scythians, bearded and long haired, arranged in four separate scenes.

 332

1. Two men converse face to face. One, wearing a headband, sits on a low hillock. He holds a spear; his gorytos slung on his left side is just visible behind him. The man facing him kneels on the ground holding a spear, his arm resting on his shield.

2. A single figure partially kneeling to string his bow. His own bow can just be seen in the gorytos that he is wearing on his left side.

3. Two men kneeling facing each other. One man steadies the head of his partner whilst examining his teeth or mouth with a finger. Both men wear gorytoi on their left-hand sides.

4. Two men sitting, one bandaging the leg of the other. Both are equipped with gorytoi.

There has been much debate about the meaning of the scene. At its simplest it could be illustrating aspects of companionship. Another view is that the first two scenes may depict preparation for battle, with the second two showing aspects of its aftermath. A more adventurous hypothesis is that the scene illuminates the Scythian origin myth (above, pp. 266–7) with Scythes successfully stringing the bow while his two brothers, Agathyrsus and Gelonus, are treated for injuries suffered in their unsuccessful attempts to perform the task. This interpretation would require the first pair of figures to be identified as Hercules (with head bowed) explaining the tasks he wanted his sons to perform. This is not entirely satisfactory since the myth requires him to give his instructions to the mother of his children, which is evidently not the case. Clearly there is much scope here for inventive imagination.

Beside the interpretation of the scene there is a great deal to be learned from the depictions of tonsorial styles, dress, and weaponry (above, pp. 238–51). The depictions of the hoods, thigh-length belted coats, trousers, and soft leather ankle boots are well drawn, showing much of the dress to have been elaborately decorated.

 333

2 Chastye Kurgany beaker

(State Heritage Museum, St Petersburg)

Forty-one burial mounds, sometimes known as the Frequent Barrows, lie on the right bank of the Don not far from the city of Voronezh. The beaker was discovered in kurgan 3 excavated in 1911 by S. E. Zverev. It was found next to the body of the principal occupant of the tomb. Fourth century BC.

The beaker, 105 mm in height, is made of silver with gilding used to enhance the figures. The vessel has a bulbous body with a tall narrow neck and out-curved lip.

The body is divided into two registers by a narrow ovolo band set just below the widest part of its girth; the lower part is decorated with narrow, closely spaced petals arising from a rosette centred on the base. The upper register depicts six male Scythians arranged in pairs, all deep in conversation.

1. A seated longhaired and bearded Scythian, resting his right arm on his battleaxe, talks to another bearded individual, who also sits, holding a whip.
2. A clean-shaven young man sits with one leg crossed over the other leaning on his battleaxe whilst listening to an older bearded man, who offers him a bow.
3. A bearded man holding a rod in his right hand stretches out his left hand to his partner. This second man, who is also bearded, is kneeling holding two spears in one hand and a shield in the other.

Interpretation is difficult. Whilst the scenes could simply represent male comradeship, it is more likely that they were intended to represent events from Scythian history or mythology familiar to contemporary viewers.

The individual depictions provide detailed evidence of the physical appearance of Scythian males and their clothing. A full range of weaponry is shown: spears, shields, battleaxes, and whips, while each man wears his gorytos.

The beaker is similar in form and decoration to the Kul'-Oba beaker. Vessels of this kind are depicted in scenes of Scythians rituals involving female deities, suggesting that they may have been cult objects.

335

3 Gaymonova mogila cup
(Kiev Museum of Historical Treasures)

From the kurgan of Gaymonova mogila, near the village of Balki in the Zaporizhzhya Oblast, excavated in 1969 by V. I. Bidzilya. Late fourth century BC.

The drinking cup, 92 mm in height, is made of silver with the figures gilded.

The cup has two lug handles. It is decorated in two registers separated by a horizontal band of ovoli set beneath its widest girth. The lower register is ornamented

 336

with closely spaced, narrow petals. The upper register depicts male members of the elite engaged in feasting. It is divided into two scenes.

In the less well-preserved scene two bearded figures, seated facing each other, are engaged in lively conversation. They are both dressed in decorated trousers and wear long belted coats with fringes at the bottom. Both have gorytoi slung from their belts; one holds a beaker. They are approached on both sides by subservient beings on their knees (fitting conveniently below the lug handles). The man on the viewer's right appears to touch his head in obeisance (though could it be that he banged his head on the handle?). The unbearded man on the right blows up a goat skin cushion presumably to provide his master with greater comfort.

The other pair of figures, on the better preserved side of the vessel, both bearded with long hair, recline towards each other. Both hold what could be a mace in one hand resting its end on one knee. The right-hand figure leans his right arm over his shield, his hand resting on what appears to be a whip. The hilt of his long sword, lying prominently on the ground, is within easy reach. The other man's left hand is at ease but sufficiently close to the quiver of his gorytos for quick action if necessary. A second gorytos is perched close to his right knee against what may be another whip. Both men wear elaborately decorated, belted coats with long fringes at the bottom.

All the men exude an air of authority, which is enhanced in one case by the subservient courtiers and in the other by the prominent display of weapons and symbols of authority. There can be little doubt that these were men of power and the scenes may be intended to represent historic meetings.

337

4   Solokha cup

(State Hermitage Museum, St Petersburg)

Found in a side chamber of the Solokha burial sited on the left bank of the Dnieper during the excavations by N. I. Veselovsky in 1913. Early fourth century BC.

The cup, 121 mm in height, is made of silver with the figures and other elements of the decoration highlighted with gilding. The cup has a simple rim, a foot ring, and two lug handles. The body is divided into two zones of unequal size by a band of guilloche set below its maximum diameter. Just below the rim is a two-strand garland of vine leaves. The lower zone is decorated with closely spaced elongated petals. The upper zone depicts four separate scenes.

1. Two unbearded young horsemen accompanied by their hunting dogs confront an angry lion, one with his hunting spear, the other with a bow and arrow. The lion has caught and broken a spear in his mouth.
2. A similar scene on the opposite side of the cup shows two young horsemen, one armed with a bow, the other with a spear, cornering a horned lioness.
3. Beneath one of the lug handles two lions face each other.
4. Beneath the other handle are two confronting dogs. The upper sides of the handles are each decorated with a pair of ram's heads.

The scenes are clearly mythological and probably depict the exploits of Scythian heroes defeating predatory powers. One suggestion is that they symbolize the battle between the world of the living and the world of the dead. Another possibility is that it illustrates the rite of passage when young men reaching puberty are required to face savage odds.

In addition to reminding us of the importance of the hunt in Scythian life, the scenes contain much detail of clothing, weapons, and horse gear.

5 Solokha comb

(State Hermitage Museum, St Petersburg)

Found in the main chamber of the Solokha tomb close to the principal burial during the excavations of N. I. Veselovsky in 1913. Early fourth century BC.

The comb, cast from gold, is 126 mm in height overall. The comb proper, with 19 tines, is topped by five crouching lions which together form the base. The comb depicts a lively battle scene involving combatants. The central figure on horseback confronts an adversary who approaches on foot, his horse having just been fatally injured. Another man on foot advances in support of the mounted warrior. The dress and armour are depicted in great detail. All three men wear loose embroidered trousers possibly with appliqué gold attachments but otherwise they are differently dressed and equipped. The foot soldier wears a Scythian-style belted long coat and carries a shield and a short sword with his gorytos attached to his left side. The mounted warrior is heavily armoured, wearing a tunic of mail, metal greaves, and a metal helmet, the latter two being both of Greek type. He carries his shield on his left arm and holds a short spear in his right hand. His gorytos hangs on his left side. He

appears to be riding bareback. The dismounted warrior is also heavily armed, wearing a metal helmet, body armour, and a short Greek-style skirt. He carried his shield on his left arm and holds a short sword in his right hand as he advances. His scabbard is attached to his belt on the left side. His dying horse has no saddle.

The scene clearly represents the crucial stage of a battle. Two high-status warriors have just clashed and one has been unmounted, his injured horse writhing in agony. He approaches his enemy, who is supported by a fighter of lower rank, probably a retainer. It is a tense moment; the onlooker's attention is fully engaged, anxious to know what will happen. In all probability the piece illustrates a significant event in Scythian history. The fact that the principal occupant of the Solokha grave, whose comb this is, was accompanied by greaves, a Greek helmet, and iron scale armour, just like the rider, suggests that the scene may illustrate an incident in his life. One writer has argued that the occupant may be King Octamasades.

The comb is valuable for the information it provides about armour and weapons, particularly the acceptance of Greek body armour among the Scythian elite. It also shows an interesting variety of shield types, reminding us of the possibility that the form and decoration of the shield may have proclaimed status or lineage.

6 Perederiieva mogila helmet
(Kiev Museum of Historical Treasures)

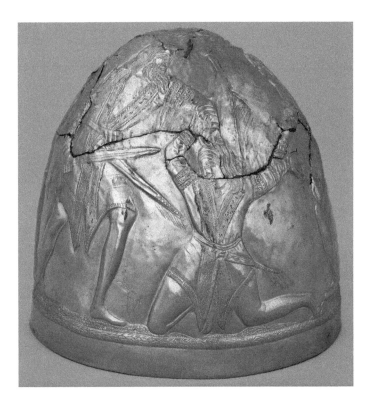

From kurgan 2 at Perederiieva mogila near the village of Zrubne, Donests'ka Oblast. Excavated by A. O. Moruzhenko in 1988. Fourth century BC.

Bell-shaped helmet in gold, 182 mm in height, showing scenes of warrior engagement set in an open landscape indicated by plants growing from the basal ground level. There are six figures arranged in two groups of three. Both scenes shows a youth (unbearded) brought to his knees while another youth protects him from a bearded aggressor. On the top of the helmet is a double rosette surrounded by a rope pattern. At the base is a floral band.

1. The kneeling youth unsheathes his sword as he turns to his companion, who holds his rectangular shield high to protect him whilst aiming his spear at the attacker. His gorytos hangs at his left-hand side. The older man grabs the shield with his left hand, threatening the kneeling figure with his sword. He wears an enigmatic looped coil over his shoulder and across his chest which may represent a whip.

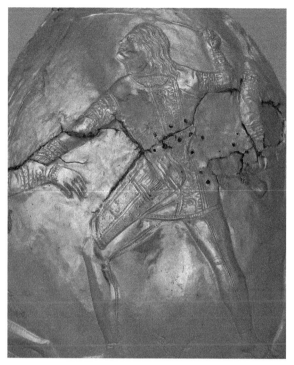

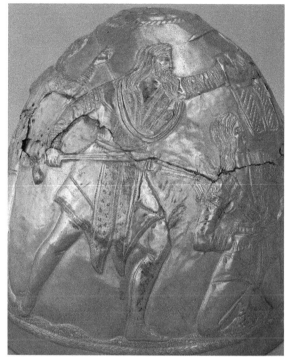

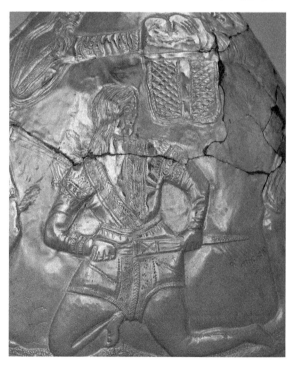

2. The young man in kneeling position is grasped by the hair by the older man, who has his sword unsheathed, ready for the kill. Meanwhile the second young man grasps his companion's arm, aiming his spear at the older man. He wears a gorytos on his left side.

All the figures wear tight fitting trousers with side seams but without other decoration. They also wear elaborately decorated thigh-length belted coats with fur facings.

What these remarkable scenes are intended to depict is difficult to say other than it was probably an event in Scythian folk memory or mythology. One possibility is that it was the confrontation, described by Herodotus, that arose when old, hardened warriors who had been campaigning in Asia Minor eventually returned home and were attacked by the children of the wives and slaves they had left behind.

7   Solokha gorytos
(State Hermitage Museum, St Petersburg)

From the main chamber of the kurgan of Solokha close to the principal burial. Excavated by N. J. Vesebusky in 1913. Early fourth century BC.

This silver plate, now much decayed, covered the original gorytos of leather. The figures have been highlighted with gilding. The ornamentation is divided into three scenes: a central panel depicting a battle scene, an upper band showing a griffin and a lion attacking a stag, and a separate plate covering the rectangular projection from the upper part of the gorytos, showing a volute pattern below a panel displaying two monsters.

The battle scene shows the interaction of two riders and three warriors on foot, but is divided into two separate engagements. On the left is a young (unbearded) warrior, naked to the waist with gorytos strapped to his left side, attacking a bearded horseman with his battleaxe while protecting himself with a shield held in his left hand. The bearded rider on his rearing horse attempts to spear the young man. To the right three men engage. In the centre is a bearded man who has just dismounted from his wounded horse. A young man to the left grasps him by the hair, his sword ready to strike. The older man struggles to free himself while drawing his sword in defence. Meanwhile, another young man behind him, holding a shield in one hand, prepares to spear the older man.

It is a lively scene full of activity and expectations, not at all unlike that depicted on the Perederiiva mogila helmet with its interaction between old and young warriors. It may be that it was intended to illustrate the same incident, whether historical or mythical.

8   Sachnovka diadem

(Kiev Museum of Historical Treasures)

Found in kurgan 2 near the village of Sachnovka in Cherkaska Oblast. Excavated by V. le Heze in 1901. Second half of the fourth century BC.

Embossed gold plate curved to form the lower part of a diadem, 98 mm in height and 365 mm in overall length. The upper edge and sides of the plate are perforated for attachment.

The scene is composed of ten figures. In the centre is a seated female with an attendant standing next to her. She wears a dress, with some kind of neck ornament, and a tall flat-topped hat. In her right hand she holds a cup and in her left a mirror, both to the left-hand side of her body as if showing them to a bearded man, who kneels

facing her. His hands are outstretched towards her and he wears a gorytos on his left side denoting his warrior status. Behind the bearded warrior is a bearded man playing a lyre; he is also kneeling. Then follow two beardless men relating to each other but facing front. Both are kneeling, but one only on one knee. He holds a beaker aloft in his left hand while in his right he holds a rhyton which the other man is filling from a fluted ewer. Between them, on the

ground, is a large basin containing three beakers with a ladle nearby. Behind the seated woman (to the viewer's left) the standing male attendant holds a drinking horn aloft in his left hand. Behind him are two kneeling men facing each other. Both hold on to a single rhyton from which they drink. One of the men wears a gorytos. Next is another pair of kneeling men. One, who holds a short sword in his left hand, grasps the hair of the other, who is evidently a captive wearing a loin cloth. In front of the captive's chest is what appears to be a ram's head. All the men, other than the prisoner, wear typical Scythian dress of trousers, thigh-length belted coats, and leather hats.

The scene as an entity defies interpretation, unless it is simply intended to illustrate different aspects of Scythian life. The seated female is evidently a goddess who seems to be being approached by a hero warrior as a suitor, a composition known elsewhere in the Scythian repertoire (above, pp. 278–80). Her male attendant and the musicians, who are encouraging the warrior in his quest, are part of the same engagement. The two comrades sharing a single rhyton may be enacting the blood-brotherhood ritual (p. 217), while the two men engaged in pouring drinks may simply represent convivial comradeship. This leaves only the scene of the captor and his victim, which is unusual in Scythian iconography. Implicit in it is the suspicion that the captive is about to be beheaded as an act of sacrifice.

If the entire compilation is meant to be read as one, the simplest explanation is that it displays the sacred marriage between the goddess and a hero with the attendant jollifications; all Scythian life is there.

9 Tolstaya mogila pectoral
(Kiev Museum of Historical Treasures)

From the kurgan of Tolstaya mogila near Ordzhonikidze, Dnipropetrovs'ka Oblast. Excavated in 1971 by B. N. Mozolevski. Second half of the fourth century BC.

The gold pectoral is 306 mm at its widest. It is formed of three concentric registers framed by four hollow, twisted tubes of gold of increasing thickness, the outermost being the thickest. At each end the tubes are brought together by a collar attached by hinges to terminal plates, each ending in a lion's head.

The lower register is composed of animals worked in the round. In the centre are three similar groups each showing a horse being brought down by two griffins. Beyond, to the viewer's left, a leopard and lion attack a boar. This is matched on the right by a leopard and a lion attacking a stag. Following these scenes of predation, on both sides in the narrowing spaces available a hound chases a hare, while beyond two grasshoppers confront each other.

The middle register is backed by a gold plate to which is attached stylized vegetation, worked in the round or in high relief, presenting a central acanthus plant from which emerge coiled tendrils sprouting flowers, some of which retain their original blue enamel inlay. Five birds enjoy the luxurious growth.

The third (top) register presents a scene of pastoral tranquillity with men and domestic animals living in harmony. The figures are all worked in the round. The centre piece is of two bearded men examining a fleece; both have laid aside their gorytoi. On either side are a horse and its foal and a cow and its calf. On the viewer's left the scene is followed by a boy milking a ewe. This is matched on the other side with a boy holding a vessel guarding his sheep. Then follow, on either side, a goat with its young and finally a bird.

Although evidently of Greek workmanship, the piece was created for a Scythian patron incorporating scenes of Scythian rural life and images of predation which inhabit the Scythian nether world. The simplest interpretation is that the animated compositions represent two worlds, the harmonious world of life and the chaotic world of death, the two separated by the Tree of Life.

10 The Chertomlÿk amphora

(State Hermitage Museum, St Petersburg)

Found in the north-west chamber of the burial beneath the kurgan of Chertomlÿk, north-west of Nikopol in Dnipropetrovs'ka Oblast. Excavated in 1862–3 by I. E. Zabelin. Fourth century BC.

A silver wine amphora, 700 mm high, with a maximum diameter of 390 mm. The mouth is fitted with a strainer to catch detritus as the wine is poured in. There are three openings at the bottom, also fitted with strainers, through which the wine could be allowed to flow into drinking vessels. One is shaped like a horse's head, the other two as a lion's. Each was stopped by a bung attached by a chain.

Below the shoulder the body of the vessel is decorated with an energetic floral design in relief incorporating pairs of birds. The particular interest of the piece, however, lies in the decoration around the shoulder of the vessel, which shows Scythian men attempting to control horses. The scene is composed of figures separately cast in relief and soldered to the vessel. They are gilded to make them stand out. The

centre of the composition shows a spirited horse, lassoed by three men, while another stands aside supervising the activity. On either side of the central action are bridled horses (one with a saddle) being attended by the minders, one of whom is hobbling the animal, while the other is encouraging his creature to kneel or to lie down. Next, on either side, is a man bracing himself to restrain a horse he has just lassoed, while beyond each is a quietly grazing horse, the two completing the circular arrangement back to back.

The men have long hair; some are bearded and some clean shaven. They all wear baggy trousers and thigh-length belted coats. Two wear a gorytos on their left-hand side. Some of the horses are shown with cropped manes whilst others have long manes, possibly to distinguish between trained and wild beasts.

The intention of the design seems to have been to illustrate the training of horses rather than to tell a particular narrative.

TIMELINE

	Peninsular Europe	Pontic Steppe
800		Predatory nomads arrive from the Altai–Sayan (Kimmerians)
		New bands of nomads (Scythians) arrive and drive out Kimmerians
	Some Kimmerians move into Thrace and the Great Hungarian Plain	
700		
		Early kurgans at Kelermes and Ulski Aul
		Scythian control of Pontic steppe underway
	Scythian bands move into Transylvania and the Great Hungarian Plain	
600	592 Scythian philosopher Anacharsis in Athens	
		513–512 Darius campaigns across the Pontic steppe. Scythian opposition led by High King Idanthyrsus
	510 Scythian envoys meet king of Sparta	
500	490–479 Persians attack Greece.	480 Creation of the kingdom of the Bosporus
	– Scythian mercenaries fight on Persian side	c.450 Herodotus in Olbia
		438 Spartocus takes leadership of Bosporan state.
	431–404 Peloponnesian War	– Sauromatae cross Volga into Scythian territory
400		Parisades (r. 348–310) incorporates eastern shore of Azov into Bosporan Kingdom
		339 Battle in Thrace between Macedonian and Scythians. King Ateas killed.
		331 Zopyrion besieges Olbia
		319–310 Scythians involved in Bosporan succession
300		c.300 Kul'-Oba burial
		c.230 Celts appear on Pontic steppe
200		Roxolani attack Bosporan kingdom and are defeated
		107 Roxolani join Mithridates in attack on Bosporan kingdom
100		

Asia Minor	Central Asia	Altai–Sayan	China
		Arzhan 1	
714 Kimmerians on northern frontier of Urartu			
707 Kimmerians defeat Rusā			
c.676 Scythian king Battuta seeks to marry Esarhaddon's daughter. Esarhaddon kills Scythian ally Ishpakai			
677 Kimmerians destroy Phrygia and under King Dugdamme attacks Lydia, Sardis (652), and the Greek cities of Ionia		Arzhan 2	
– Scythian king Madyes fights Medes and Assyrians and reaches borders of Egypt			
612 Scythians present at sack of Nineveh			
– Median king Cyaxares (625–585) kills Scythian elite at feast			
590–585 War between Medes and Lydians. Scythians side with Medes.			
	530 Cyrus moves against Massagetae led by Queen Tomyris but is beaten and killed.		
	520–519 Darius campaigns against the Sakā whose king, Skuka, is captured.		
336–321 Alexander conquers	Persian Empire		
		300–240 Pazyryk	
	176/160 Yuezhi and Wusun oust Sakā from Issyk Kul region and drive them south into Iran. Huns advance on Massagetae		133 Advance of Han against the Xiongnu
	110–80 Sakā settle in India		

SCYTHIAN KINGS
AND DYNASTIES

Scythian Kings

Scythian kings are mentioned in various historical sources, most particularly in Herodotus' *Histories*. The following list and the suggested dates was presented by A. Y. Alekseyev in his paper 'Scythian Kings and "Royal" Burial Mounds of the Fifth and Fourth Centuries BC', in D. Braund (ed.), *Scythians and Greeks* (Exeter, 2004), 39–55. The author makes a strong case for Oricus being buried in the kurgan of Solokha (burial 1) around 410 BC, with his brother Octamasades being buried in the same mound (burial 2) between 390 and 380. He also argues that Anonymous 2 was the first king buried in Chertomlÿk. The correlation of known kings to other royal burials is more difficult.

Dynasties

First dynasty

Ishpakai	*c.675*
Bartatua	*c.675–672*
Madycs, son of Bartatua	*c.650–600*

Second dynasty (Herodotus, *Hist.* iv. 76)

Spargapeithes	seventh century
Lycus, son of Spargapeithes	seventh–sixth century
Gnurus, son of Lycus	first half of sixth century
Saulius, son of Gnurus, brother of Anacharsis	mid sixth century
Taxcais	
Scopasis	last third of sixth century

Third dynasty (Herodotus, *Hist.* iv. 78)

? Argotus	*c.510–490*
Ariapeithes	*c.490–460*
Scyles, son of Ariapeithes	*c.460–440*
Octamasades, son of Ariapeithes	*c.460/440–c.390/380*
Oricus, son of Ariapeithes	second half of fifth century

Individual rulers

Ateas	*c.360–339*
Anonymous 1	*c.339–?*
Anonymous 2	– d. 328
Anonymous 3, brother of Anonymous 2	*c.329–*
Agarus	d. after 309

FURTHER READING

IN this section we offer some suggestions of further reading for those who want to follow up the themes presented in the chapters above. The arrangement is by chapter but is prefaced by a brief introduction to the relevant classical texts and by a listing of the most useful general accounts, many of them catalogues of international exhibitions which, in addition to illustrations and descriptions of objects, all contain helpful introductory accounts written by specialists.

I have suggested English language texts where they are available. There are comparatively few general accounts, rather more museum catalogues, and many more specialized articles published in monographs and journals. These are supplemented with publications in French and German and also a selection of publications in Russian, chosen either because they are basic sources, like excavation reports, or because they cover subjects not well represented in western European language publications. Titles are given first in Russian followed by an English translation in parentheses. It would have been possible to include many more references to Russian language publications but these works are difficult to find in Britain except in a few specialist university libraries, and even then we are not well served. A reader who wants to know something of the range of Russian literature available will find that many of the works cited here have full bibliographies.

For many readers one of the attractions of the Scythians is the brilliant art which they made for themselves and which was produced for them by Greek craftsmen. The various catalogues listed under *General Works* below provide excellent photographs of all the major items and we have included as many as possible in this volume. Consulting a good catalogue is an ideal way to gather first impressions of the Scythians and their remarkable way of life.

Classical Texts

In the fifth century BC a number of Greek writers were busy gathering information about the Scythians to include in their various works. Among the earliest was Hekataios of Miletos (*c*.550–467 BC), whose book, *Journey around the Earth*, no longer survives but was used as a source by later writers. One of them, Hellanikos of Lesbos (491–405 BC) devoted a section to *Skythika* in his book *Barbarita Nomina*. This, too, is no longer extant but was used by the later writer Strabo (64 BC–AD 21) in his *Geography*, in Book xi. 4 and probably in vii. 3–4. A near contemporary of Hellanikos was the writer of the tract *On Airs, Waters, and Places*, which is included in the Hippocratic Corpus. It was compiled by an unnamed author whose style suggests that he came from Knidos (see G. E. R. Lloyd (ed.), *Hippocratic Writings* (Harmondsworth, 1978)). Pseudo-Hippocrates, as he is generally known, wrote as though he had first-hand knowledge of the Scythians and their land, and his chapters 17–22 provide many valuable insights. The intricacies of the transmission of these early sources and their relationships is carefully assessed in J. R. Gardiner-Garden, *Herodotos' Contemporaries on Skythian Geography and Ethnography* (Bloomington, Ind., 1987).

The most comprehensive, though slightly later, source is *Histories* written by Herodotus of Halicarnassus (*c*.484–*c*.424). In Book i. 103–6 he deals briefly with the movement of the Scythians into Asia Minor, but it is the famous Book iv that provides the most detailed account of Scythian culture and history, full of intriguing detail and anecdotes. Many scholars believe Herodotus gathered his Scythian material first-hand during time spent in the Greek city of Olbia and he may even have made trips out onto the steppe. There are, however, those who argue that he never set foot in Scythia and instead constructed his topos of the Scythians from second-hand scraps moulded to give a generalized view of 'the barbarian other'. These views have been widely debated. Some of the relevant sources are given in the further reading for Chapter 2 (below, pp. 363–6). Other Greek writers mention the Scythians from time to time, among them Anacreon, Demosthenes, Aristophanes, Xenophon, and Aristotle. Where these are referred to in this book full references will be given. Roman writers were largely dependent on earlier Greek sources, but original observations were recorded by the poet Ovid, who, exiled in the Black Sea town of Tomis, took a rather dystopian view of the local people in his *Tristia* and *Epistulae ex Ponto*.

General Works

Surprisingly little has been written on the Scythians for a general audience over the last sixty years. T. Talbot Rice, *The Scythians* (2nd edn., London, 1958) offers a clear, if

somewhat dated, overview while the companion volume by T. Sulimirski, *The Sarmatians* (London, 1970) provides a detailed account of later developments on the Pontic/Caspian steppe. More recent works include: R. Rolle, *The World of the Scythians* (London, 1989), translated from the German version published in 1980; E. V. Cernenko, *The Scythians 700–300 BC* (London, 1983), focusing on arms and armour; and two comprehensive general books, H. Parzinger, *Die Skythen* (3rd edn., Munich, 2009) and I. Lebedynsky, *Les Scythes: les Scythes d'Europe et la période Scythe dans les steppes d'Eurasie, VIIIe–IIIe siècles av. J.-C.* (2nd edn., Paris, 2010). A far more detailed work, edited by J. Davis-Kimball, V. A. Bashilov, and L. T. Yablonsky, is *Nomads of the Eurasian Steppes in the Early Iron Age* (Berkeley, 1995). It presents a huge wealth of archaeological material in summary form brought together by a team of experts.

While general books are few, exhibition catalogues abound, presenting not only illustrations and descriptions of spectacular objects from Scythian burials but essays which provide context for the material culture. One of the most comprehensive, with an excellent introductory chapter and brilliant illustrations, is A. Alexeyev, *The Gold of the Scythian Kings in the Hermitage Collection* (St Petersburg, 2012). Others include: M. I. Artamonov, *Treasures from Scythian Tombs in the Hermitage Museum, Leningrad* (London, 1969); Metropolitan Museum of Art, *From the Lands of the Scythians: Ancient Treasures from the Museums of the U.S.S.R., 3000 B.C.–100 B.C.* (New York, 1975); British Museum, *Frozen Tombs: The Culture and Art of the Ancient Tribes of Siberia* (London, 1978); E. D. Reeder (ed.), *Scythian Gold: Treasures from Ancient Ukraine* (New York, 1999); J. Aruz et al. (eds.), *The Golden Deer of Eurasia: Scythian and Sarmatian Treasures from the Russian Steppes* (New York, 2000); S. Stark et al. (eds.), *Nomads and Networks: The Ancient Art and Culture of Kazakhstan* (Princeton, 2012); and St J. Simpson and S. Pankova (eds.), *Scythians: Warriors of Ancient Siberia* (London, 2017).

Chapter 1 Discovering the Scythians

The towering figure of Peter the Great (1672–1725) dominates the story of the early years of the discovery of the Scythians and their culture. The many facets of this fascinating man, modernizer, expansionist, explorer, and collector are considered in numerous books dedicated to his life, among the most comprehensive being P. Bushkovitch, *Peter the Great: The Struggle for Power, 1671–1725* (Cambridge, 2001) and E. Donnert, *Peter der Grosse: Der Veränderer Russlands* (Göttingen, 1987). For a briefer account, L. Hughes, *Peter the Great: A Biography* (New Haven and London, 2002) can be recommended.

The story of Peter's brief visit to Oxford is given in A. MacGregor, 'The Tsar in England: Peter the Great's Visit to London in 1698', *Seventeenth Century*, 19/1 (2004),

116–47. The creation of the Hermitage is described in some detail by G. Norman in *The Hermitage: The Biography of a Great Museum* (London, 1997). Of the early explorers in Siberia, P. K. Frolov's contribution is examined in N. Savel'ev, *Petr Koz'mich Frolov* (in Russian) (Novosibirsk, 1951) while that of D. G. Messerschmidt and G. F. Müller is given extended treatment in chapters 3 and 4 of H. F. Vermeulen, *Before Boas: The Genesis of Ethnography and Ethnology in the German Enlightenment* (Lincoln, Nebr., 2015). For a brief biography of V. Radlov see J. P. Laut, 'Radloff, Friedrich Wilhelm', in *Neue Deutsche Biographie*, 21 (2003) 96–7.

From the time of Catherine the Great (1729–1796), when the borders of Russia expanded to the Black Sea, Scythian material has poured into museums at an increasing rate, largely from the exploration of kurgans on the Pontic steppe. Brief overviews of these discoveries are given in P. P. Tolochko and S. V. Polin, 'Burial Mounds of the Scythian Aristocracy in the Northern Black Sea Areas', in E. D. Reeder (ed.), *Scythian Gold: Treasures from Ancient Ukraine* (New York, 1999), 83–91 and St J. Simpson and S. V. Pankova, 'Introduction', in St J. Simpson and S. Pankova, *Scythians: Warriors of Ancient Siberia* (London, 2017), 10–15. A more extended treatment of some of the kurgans, putting them in their historical context, is to be found in M. I. Artamonov, *Treasures from Scythian Tombs in the Hermitage Museum, Leningrad* (London, 1969).

The early decades of the twentieth century saw the publication of two seminal works, bringing together for the first time in readable compendia the considerable body of data that had accumulated by the beginning of the twentieth century: E. H. Minns, *Scythians and Greeks: A Survey of Ancient History and Archaeology on the North Coast of the Euxine* (Cambridge, 1913) and M. Rostovtzeff, *Iranians and Greeks in South Russia* (Oxford, 1922). The relationship of the two great contemporary scholars is examined in G. Bongard-Levin, 'E. H. Minns and M. I. Rostovtzeff: Glimpses of a Scythian Friendship', in D. Braund, *Scythians and Greeks: Cultural Interactions in Scythia, Athens and the Early Roman Empire (Sixth Century BC–First Century AD)* (Exeter, 2005), 13–32.

Among the many spectacular discoveries of the twentieth century the frozen tombs of Pazyryk must take pride of place. A full account by the excavator S. I. Rudenko was published in Russian in 1953 by the Academy of Sciences of the U.S.S.R. Fortunately for English readers it was translated by the British archaeologist M. W. Thompson and published as S. I. Rudenko, *Frozen Tombs of Siberia: The Pazyryk Burials of Iron Age Horsemen* (London, 1970). Although this is essentially a detailed archaeological report, it is surprisingly readable and full of fascinating insights into steppe culture. A much shorter introduction to the material is provided by the British Museum catalogue, *Frozen Tombs: The Culture and Art of the Ancient Tribes of Siberia* (London, 1978). The coverage is considerably extended in the more recent British Museum exhibition catalogue, Simpson and Pankova, *Scythians* (cited above), which focuses on material from the Pazyryk tombs but includes related finds. Work on other frozen tombs continues. The cemetery at Berel, Kazakhstan, first explored by Radlov in 1865 was the subject of a new campaign of excavation which began in 1998 and is briefly described in Z. S. Samashev, 'The Berel Kurgans: Some Results of Investigation', in S. Stark et al. (eds.), *Nomads and Networks: The Ancient Art and Culture of Kazakhstan* (Princeton, 2012), 30–49.

Of great importance to our understanding of the origin of the Scythian phenomena has been the excavation of two kurgans at Arzhan in the Tuva province of Siberia. Arzhan 1 has been fully published, in a German translation of the original Russian report, as M. P. Gryaznov, *Der Grosse Kurgan von Aržan in Tuva, Südsibirien* (Munich, 1984). Arzhan 2 is fully described in V. Čugunov, H. Parzinger, and A. Nagler (eds.), *Der skythenzeitliche Fürstenkurgan Aržan 2 in Tuva* (Mainz, 2010). The chronology of these two key tombs is fully discussed in G. I. Zaitseva et al., 'Chronology of Key Barrows belonging to Different Stages of the Scythian Period in Tuva (Arzhan-1 and Arzhan-2 Barrows)', *Radiocarbon*, 49 (2007), 645–58.

Other important discoveries include the tomb at Issyk, Kazakhstan, published in K. A. Akishev, *Kurgan Issyk: Iskusstvo sakov Kazakhstana* (in Russian) (Moscow, 1978) and the kurgan cemetery at Filippovka in the southern Ural steppe, summarized in A. K. Pshenichniuk, 'The Filippovka Kurgans in the Heart of the Eurasian Steppes', in J. Aruz et al. (eds.), *The Golden Deer of Eurasia: Scythian and Sarmatian Treasures from the Russian Steppes* (New York, 2000), 21–30. For an account of the more recent work see L. T. Yablonsky, 'New Excavations of the Early Nomadic Burial Ground at Filippovka (Southern Ural Region, Russia)', *American Journal of Archaeology*, 114 (2010), 129–43.

Finally to the question of terminology. The recognition that there is a cultural continuum extending from the Altai–Sayan Mountains to the Carpathians and beyond has led to much discussion concerning the appropriateness of the term Scythian when applied to the peoples of the entire region. Two papers help to explain the situation: V. A. Bashilov and L. T. Yablonsky, 'Introduction', in J. Davis-Kimball, V. A. Bashilov, and L. T. Yablonsky (eds.), *Nomads of the Eurasian Steppes in the Early Iron Age* (Berkeley, 1995), xi–xv and L. T. Yablonsky, 'Scythians and Saka: Ethnic Terminology and Archaeological Reality', in J. Aruz et al. (eds.), *The Golden Deer of Eurasia: Perspectives on the Steppe Nomads of the Ancient World* (New York, 2006), 24–31.

Chapter 2 The Scythians as Others saw Them

The historical sources dealing with Kimmerians and Scythians in Asia have been widely discussed. Three useful papers introducing the principal issues are: E. D. Phillips, 'The Scythian Domination in Western Asia: Its Record in History, Scripture and

Archaeology', *World Archaeology*, 4 (1972), 129–38; A. I. Ivantchik, 'The Scythians Rule over Asia: The Classical Tradition and the Historical Reality', in G. R. Tsetskhladze (ed.), *Ancient Greeks West and East* (Leiden, 1999), 497–520; and A. I. Ivantchik, 'Reconstructing Cimmerian and Early Scythian History: The Written Sources', in J. Aruz et al. (eds.), *The Golden Deer of Eurasia: Perspectives on the Steppe Nomads of the Ancient World* (New York, 2006), 146–53.

The interpretation of the available data is a very complex issue. Those who want to explore the many debates and uncertainties cannot do better than to consult A. I. Ivantchik, 'The Current State of the Cimmerian Problem', in *Ancient Civilizations from Scythia to Siberia*, 7 (2001), 307–40. This carefully argued paper has full references to the copious literature.

The Greek colonization of the Black Sea has generated a massive literature. The classic introductory work on Greek colonization, though now a little out of date, is J. Boardman, *The Greeks Overseas: Their Early Colonies and Trade* (new and enlarged edn., London, 1980); chapter 6 deals with the Black Sea. For a more recent assessment see G. R. Tsetskhladze, 'Greek Penetration of the Black Sea', in G. R. Tsetskhladze and F. de Angelis (eds.), *The Archaeology of Greek Colonization: Essays dedicated to Sir John Boardman* (Oxford, 1994), 111–35. The various Black Sea colonies are individually discussed in D. V. Grammenos and E. K. Petropoulos, *Ancient Greek Colonies in the Black Sea*, 2 vols. (Thessaloniki, 2003). A useful and well-illustrated discussion of Greek settlements in the Crimea is offered in T. L. Samoilova (ed.), *Ancient Greek Sites in the Crimea* (Kiev, 2004). The Greek city of Olbia is given detailed treatment in the various contributions published in D. Braund and S. D. Kryzhitskiy (eds.), *Classical Olbia and the Scythian World: From the Sixth Century BC to the Second Century AD* (Oxford, 2007) and in S. D. Kryzhitskiy, 'Olbia and the Scythians in the Fifth Century BC: The Scythian "Protectorate"', in D. Braund (ed.), *Scythians and Greeks: Cultural Interactions in Scythia, Athens and the Early Roman Empire (Sixth Century BC–First Century AD* (Exeter, 2005), 123–30.

Confrontation between Persians and Scythians (and Sakā) should best be viewed in the context of Persian expansionism. Three books help to provide the essential background: J. M. Cook, *The Persian Empire* (London, 1983); P. Briant, *From Cyrus to Alexander: A History of the Persian Empire* (Winona Lake, Ind., 2002); and L. Allen, *The Persian Empire: A History* (London, 2005). A very useful reference source is A. Kuhrt, *The Persian Empire: A Corpus of Sources from the Achaemenid Period* (London, 2013). The narrative of the campaign mounted by Darius against the European Scythians in given with all its vivid colour by Herodotus in Book iv of his *Histories*. As always there has been an ongoing debate about the reliability of the early accounts, especially that of Herodotus. Broadly there are two schools: those who consider his work to be a literary source fashioned by the topoi of the time and with little or no basis in fact and those who believe his accounts to be accurate and historical. Among the first school are D. Fehling, *Herodotus and his 'Sources': Citation, Invention, and Narrative Art* (rev. English edn., Leeds, 1989) and F. Hartog, *The Mirror of Herodotus* (rev. English edn., Berkeley, 2001). Both are roundly taken to task by W. Pritchett in his *The Liar School of Herodotos* (Amsterdam, 1993). The debate is nothing if not entertaining. A more down-to-earth assessment is provided in A. I. Ivantchik's paper, 'The Funeral of Scythian Kings: The Historical Reality and the Description of Herodotus (4, 71–72)', in L. Bonfante (ed.), *The Barbarians of Ancient Europe: Realities and Interactions* (Cambridge, 2011), 71–106, in which the author compares Herodotus' descriptions of royal funerals with the archaeological reality and is impressed by the precision of the correlation. Other interesting contributions to the debate include: J. G. F. Hind, 'The Black Sea: Between Asia and Europe (Herodotus' Approach to his Scythian Account)', in G. R. Tsetskhladze (ed.), *The Black Sea, Greece, Anatolia and Europe in the First Millennium BC* (Leuven, 2011), 77–93, which carefully dissects the structure of Herodotus' account; H. J. Kim, 'Herodotus' Scythians viewed from a Central Asian Perspective: Its Historicity and Significance', in *Ancient West and East*, 9 (2010), 115–34; and S. West, 'Herodotus and Olbia', in D. Braund and S. D. Kryzhitskiy (eds.), *Classical Olbia and the Scythian World* (cited above), 79–92.

Herodotus' description of the different groups of Scythians and their immediate neighbours is less easy to follow and to map onto archaeological reality, but attempts have been made by T. Taylor in his 'Thracians, Scythians, and Dacians, 800 BC–AD 300', in B. Cunliffe (ed.), *The Oxford Illustrated Prehistory of Europe* (Oxford, 1994), 389–90 and, in more detail, by I. Lebedynsky, *Les Scythes: les Scythes d'Europe et la période scythe dans les steppes d'Eurasie, VIIe–IIIe siècles* (2nd edn., Paris, 2010), 55–62.

The presence of Scythians in Athens, serving as a police force, provided the Greek urban elite with a source of amusement: they were foreigners and thus fair game for ridicule. These issues are discussed in B. Bäbler, 'Bobbies or Boobies? The Scythian Police Force in Classical Athens', in Braund (ed.), *Scythians and Greeks* (cited above), 114–22. The question of foreign archers depicted on Greek pottery is addressed in A. I. Ivantchik, 'Who were the "Scythian" Archers on Archaic Attic Vases?', in the same volume, 100–13. The same author returns to a discussion of the ethnic identity of the Scythian archers in a more lengthy treatment, '"Scythian" Archers on Archaic Attic Vases: Problems of Interpretation', in *Ancient Civilizations from Scythia to Siberia*, 12 (2006), 197–271. A corpus of the relevant material is provided in M. F. Vos, *Scythian Archers in Archaic Attic Vase Painting* (Groningen, 1963).

The theme of the Scythian 'other' is also explored in J. Porucznik, 'The Image of a "Drunken Scythian" in Greek Tradition', in *Proceedings of the 1st Annual International Interdisciplinary Conference* (2013), 710–14. That Scythians were regarded by some Greek

writers as 'noble savages' whose simple lifestyle was commendable is a theme developed in D. Braund, 'Greeks, Scythians and *Hippake* or "Reading Mare's-Cheese"', in G. Tsetskhladze (ed.), *Ancient Greeks West and East* (Leiden, 1999), 521–30. For the more elevating story of the Scythian philosopher, Anacharsis see C. Schubert, *Anacharsis der Weise: Nomade, Skythe, Grieche* (Tübingen, 2010).

The tombs of the Macedonian royal household excavated at Vergina are conveniently described in M. Andronikos, *Vergina: The Royal Tombs and the Ancient City* (Athens, 1987). The results of a new analysis of the cremation found in tomb II are given in T. G. Antikas and L. K. Wynn-Antikas, 'New Finds from the Cremains in Tomb II at Aegae point to Philip II and a Scythian Princess', *International Journal of Osteoarchaeology*, 26 (2016), 682–92.

The background to Ovid's exile in Tomis is explored in A. Radulescu, *Ovid in Exile* (Oxford, 2002). Ovid's poem *Tristia* (Sorrows) and other writings from his period in exile are translated and discussed in P. Green, *The Poems of Exile: 'Tristia' and 'The Black Sea Letters'* (Berkeley, 2005).

Chapter 3 Landscape with People

The world of the steppe is best appreciated by riding across it, but if this is not possible then begin by reading the descriptions of those who have. A delightful introduction is Anton Chekhov's novella, *The Steppe: The Story of a Journey*, originally published in 1888, a year after he had spent time travelling through the Ukrainian steppe to recover from overwork. A rather different work, but including lyrical passages about the steppe, is the German travel writer Johann Georg Kohl's account of his travels in Russia, *Russia and the Russians, in 1842*, first published in English in 1843. He was viewing the land at the time when tracts of virgin steppe were beginning to be ploughed up for agriculture.

To begin to understand the complexities of human interaction with the steppe landscape, A. M. Khazanov, *Nomads and the Outside World* (2nd edn., Madison, 1994) provides a powerful introduction, but it should be remembered that the first (Russian) edition was published in 1983 and there has been much work since which has challenged some of Khazanov's conclusions. Two books which provide broad-ranging and detailed studies of human communities in the steppe and adjacent ecozones in the Bronze Age can be recommended: P. L. Kohl, *The Making of Bronze Age Eurasia* (Cambridge, 2007) and M. D. Frachetti, *Pastoralist Landscapes and Social Interaction in Bronze Age Eurasia* (Berkeley, 2008). Together they provide the essential background to the region in which the Scythians were to develop in the first millennium BC.

The steppe is a fragile ecozone and slight changes of climate can have dramatic effects on the lifestyle of those who depend on it. A study of the impact of recent climatic fluctuations is provided by S. Begzsuren et al., 'Livestock Responses to Droughts and Severe Winter Weather in the Gobi Three Beauty National Park, Mongolia', *Journal of Arid Environments*, 59 (2004), 785–96. A series of papers exploring the effects of climate change on Eurasian societies in the past has been brought together in E. M. Scott, A. Y. Alekseev, and G. Zaitseva (eds.), *Impact of the Environment on Human Migration in Eurasia* (Dordrecht, 2005). Two specialist papers of direct relevance to the changes which saw the emergence of the Scythians are G. I. Zaitseva et al., 'Chronology and Possible Links between Climatic and Cultural Change during the First Millennium BC in Southern Siberia and Central Asia', *Radiocarbon*, 46/1 (2004), 259–76 and B. van Geel et al., 'Climate Change and the Expansion of Scythian Culture after 850 BC: A Hypothesis', *Journal of Archaeological Science*, 31 (2004), 1735–42. The suggestion that increased rainfall in the early thirteenth century AD may have been a cause of the rapid expansion of Mongol power is presented in M. Hvistendahl, 'Roots of Empire', *Science*, 337 (2012), 1596–9. There can be little doubt from these and other studies that minor fluctuations in climate in the steppe zone can have far-reaching effects on society. Excellent use of data of this kind is made by D. W. Anthony in his important book, *The Horse, The Wheel, and Language: How Bronze-Age Riders from the Eurasian Steppes Shaped the Modern World* (Princeton, 2007), which is essential reading for anyone wanting to trace the development of pastoral societies on the steppe from the fifth to the second millennium BC.

The horse features large in the story. D. Anthony's book, just mentioned, offers a thorough summary of the evidence of horse domestication up to the date of the book's publication, much of the crucial original research having been carried out by Anthony himself. Another important source is S. L. Olsen, 'Early Horse Domestication: Weighing the Evidence', in S. L. Olsen et al. (eds.), *Horses and Humans: The Evolution of Human–Equine Relationships* (Oxford, 2006), 81–113. More recent papers adding to the debate include: R. Bendrey, 'New Methods for the Identification of Evidence for Bitting on Horse Remains from Archaeological Sites', *Journal of Archaeological Science*, 34 (2007), 1036–50; A. K. Outram et al., 'The Earliest Horse Harnessing and Milking', *Science*, 323 (2009), 1332–5; and V. Warmuth et al., 'Reconstructing the Origin and Spread of Horse Domestication in the Eurasian Steppe', *Proceedings of the National Academy of Sciences*, 109/21 (2012), 8202–6.

The fascinating story of the strenuous attempts to re-establish herds of wild Przewalski's horses in Mongolia is told in I. Bouman and A. Groeneveld, *The History and Background of the Reintroduction of the Przewalski Horses in the Hustai National Park* (Boomdijk, 2008).

The impact of horse-riding on steppe society is discussed in: D. W. Anthony and D. R. Brown, 'The Secondary Products Revolution, Horse-Riding, and Mounted Warfare', *Journal of World Prehistory*, 24 (2011), 131–60; D. W. Anthony, 'The Prehistory of Scythian Cavalry: The Evolution of Fighting on Horseback', in J. Aruz et al. (eds.), *The Golden Deer of Eurasia: Perspectives on the Steppe Nomads of the Ancient World* (New York, 2006), 2–7; and B. K. Hanks, 'Mounted Warfare and its Sociopolitical Implications', in S. Stark et al. (eds.), *Nomads and Networks: The Ancient Art and Culture of Kazakhstan* (Princeton, 2012), 93–105.

The archaeology of the Late Bronze Age communities of the steppe is discussed in helpful detail in: Anthony, *The Horse, The Wheel, and Language* (cited above), Chapter 16; Frachetti, *Pastoralist Landscapes and Social Interaction in Bronze Age Eurasia* (cited above), Chapter 2; and L. Koryakova and A. V. Epimakhov, *The Urals and Western Siberia in the Bronze and Iron Ages* (Cambridge, 2007), 123–36. The economy of the Srubnaya culture is examined in K. P. Bunyatyan, 'Correlations between Agriculture and Pastoralism in the Northern Pontic Steppe Area during the Bronze Age', in M. Levine, C. Renfrew, and K. Boyle (eds.), *Prehistoric Steppe Adaptation and the Horse* (Cambridge, 2003), 269–86. A reader who wishes to explore the nature of the evidence used by archaeologists to build models of social and economic change can do no better than to consult the detailed report of a major fieldwork programme undertaken in the valley of the Samara, a tributary of the Volga, published in D. Anthony et al. (eds.), *A Bronze Age Landscape in the Russian Steppes: The Samara Valley Project* (Los Angeles, 2016). On the Pontic steppe the effects of climatic change on population distribution are introduced in S. V. Makhortykh, 'The Northern Black Sea Steppes in the Cimmerian Epoch', in E. M. Scott, A. Y. Alekseev, and G. Zaitseva (eds.), *Impact of the Environment on Human Migration in Eurasia* (Dordrecht, 2004), 35–44.

Chapter 4   Enter the Predatory Nomads

The cultural development in the Minusinsk Basin is of direct significance to the emergence of predatory nomads. The archaeology has been well studied and shows largely uninterrupted development from the time of the Andronovo culture in the seventeenth century BC to the end of the first millennium BC. The cultural sequence is reviewed in two important papers: S. Legrand, 'The Emergence of the Scythians: Bronze Age to Iron Age in South Siberia', *Antiquity*, 80 (2006), 843–59 and N. Bokovenko, 'The Emergence of the Tagar Culture', in the same volume, 860–79. The crucial work on climate change during this period is published in M. A. Koulkova, 'Applications of Geochemistry to Paleoenvironmental Reconstructions in Southern Siberia', in E. M. Scott, A. Y. Alekseev, and G. Zaitseva (eds.), *Impact of the Environment on Human Migration in Eurasia* (Dordrecht, 2004), 255–74. The hypothesis that climate change was a major factor in the spread of nomads from the Altai–Sayan to the west is outlined in N. Bokovenko, 'Migrations of Early Nomads of the Eurasian Steppe in a Context of Climate Changes', in Scott et al., *Impact of the Environment on Human Migration in Eurasia* (cited above), 21–33. A detailed study of the development of horse gear is provided in N. A. Bokovenko, 'The Origin of Horse Riding and the Development of Central Asian Nomadic Riding Harnesses', in J. Davis-Kimball et al. (eds.), *Kurgans, Ritual Sites, and Settlements: Eurasian Bronze and Iron Age* (Oxford, 2000), 304–10.

The kurgan cemetery of Arzhan in the Uyuk valley in Tuva has been examined in two excavations of outstanding importance. The kurgan of Arzhan 1 has been fully published in M. P. Grjaznov, *Der Grosskurgan von Aržan in Tuva, Südsibirien* (Munich, 1984), while Arzhan 2 is published in K. V. Čugunov, H. Parzinger, and A. Nagel (eds.), *Der skythenzeitliche Fürstenkurgan Aržan 2 in Tuva* (Mainz, 2010). For a comparative study of the horses found in the two kurgans see N. Bourova, 'Horse Remains from the Arzhan-1 and Arzhan-2 Scythian Monuments', in Scott et al., *Impact of the Environment on Human Migration in Eurasia* (cited above), 323–32. The chronology of the two burials is fully discussed in G. I. Zaitseva et al. (eds.), 'Chronology of Key Barrows belonging to Different Stages of the Scythian Period in Tuva (Arzhan-1 and Arzhan-2 Barrows)', *Radiocarbon*, 49 (2007), 645–58.

The contemporary situation on the Pontic steppe is briefly introduced in S. V. Makhortykh, 'The North Black Sea Steppes in the Cimmerian Epoch', in Scott et al., *Impact of the Environment on Human Migration in Eurasia* (cited above), 35–44. The same author's more substantial study is published in his *Kimmeriitsy na severom Kavkazej* (Kimmerians in the Northern Caucasus) (Kiev, 1994). The Pre-Scythian (Kimmerian) period in the Pontic region is treated in two useful papers: J. Bouzek, 'Cimmerians and Early Scythians: The Transition from Geometric to Orientalizing Style in the Pontic Area', in G. R. Tsetskhladze (ed.), *North Pontic Archaeology: Recent Discoveries and Studies* (Leiden, 2001), 33–44 and V. P. Vauchugov, 'The Demographic Situation in the Northwestern Part of the Black Sea Region in the 9th–7th Centuries BC', in the same volume, 45–52.

The most comprehensive consideration of the relationship of steppe nomads and the sedentary communities of Asia Minor and the adjacent Near East is in A. I. Ivantchik, *Kimmeriitsy Drevnevostochnye tsivilizatsii i stepnye Kochevniki v VIII–VII vekakh do n.é.* (Kimmerians: Ancient Near Eastern Civilizations and Steppe Nomads in the 8th–7th Centuries BC) (Moscow, 1996). A survey of the material culture of the period is presented in detail in the same author's *Kimmerier und Skythen: Kulturhistorische und chronologische Probleme der Archäologie der osteuropäischen Steppen und Kaukasiens in vor- und frühskythischer Zeit* (Moscow and Mainz, 2001), while in his 'The Current State of the Cimmerian Problem', *Ancient Civilizations from Scythia to Siberia*,

7 (2001), 307–39 he debates the different interpretations on offer. In another paper, 'Sinope et les Cimmériens', in the same journal, 16 (2010) 65–72 he explores one of the issues in detail.

The relevance of literary sources is considered in the same author's 'Reconstructing Cimmerian and Early Scythian History: The Written Sources', in J. Aruz et al. (eds.), *The Golden Deer of Eurasia: Perspectives on the Steppe Nomads of the Ancient World* (New York, 2006), 146–53. The involvement of Kimmerians or Scythians in the south Caucasus is also discussed in R. Rolle, 'Urartu und die Reiternomaden', *Saeculum*, 28 (1977), 291–340. The difficulty of using arrow typology in historical reconstruction is set out in O. W. Muscarella, 'Bronze Socketed Arrowheads and Ethnic Attribution', in J. Aruz et al. (eds.), *The Golden Deer of Eurasia: Perspective* (cited above), 154–9.

The question of the Pre-Scythian (Kimmerian) influence on Europe west of the Carpathians is complex. The material evidence is presented in some detail in J. Bouzek, 'Caucasus and Europe and the Cimmerian Problem', *Sborník Národního Muzea v Praze*, 39 (1983), 177–229 and more recently in J. Chochorowski, *Ekspansja Kimmeryjska na tereny Europy Środkowej* (Expansion of the Cimmerians into Central Europe) (Kraków, 1993). The Pre-Scythian, Mezöcsát group in the Carpathian Basin is introduced in E. Patek, 'Präskythische Gräberfelder in Ostungarn', in *Symposium zu Problemen der jüngeren Hallstattzeit in Mitteleurope* (Bratislava, 1974), 337–62. For a careful consideration of how the evidence may be interpreted, see C. Metzner-Nebelsick, 'Early Iron Age Pastoral Nomadism in the Great Hungarian Plain: Migration or Assimilation? The Thraco-Cimmerian Problem Revisited', in Davis-Kimball et al. (eds.), *Kurgans, Ritual Sites, and Settlements* (cited above), 160–84. The paper has copious references to the earlier literature.

Chapter 5 The Rise of the Pontic Steppe Scythians: 700–200 BC

There are few recent overviews of the Pontic steppe Scythians but R. Rolle, *The World of the Scythians* (London, 1989) is an excellent place to begin. Something of the richness and complexity of the evidence can be gleaned from a very useful compendium, J. Davis-Kimball, V. A. Bashilov, and L T. Yablonsky (eds.), *Nomads of the Eurasian Steppes in the Early Iron Age* (Berkeley, 1995), particularly Part I, which deals with the Scythians in the north Caucasus, south-eastern Europe, and the Crimea, and Part II, which considers the Sauromatae and Sarmatians, who are an essential part of the story. Although the texts are dense, they are copiously illustrated with vignettes of material culture and burial types.

The relationship of the Scythian nomads to events south of the Caucasus is explored in A. I. Ivantchik, 'The Scythian "Rule over Asia": The Classical Tradition and Historical Reality', in G. R. Tsetskhladze (ed.), *Ancient Greeks West and East* (Leiden, 1999), 479–520. For an earlier exploration of the evidence see E. D. Philips, 'The Scythian Domination in Western Asia: Its Record in History, Scripture and Archaeology', *World Archaeology*, 4 (1972), 129–38. The broader context is provided by A. I. Ivantchik, *Kimmerier und Skythen: Kulturhistorische und chronologische Probleme der Archäologie der osteuropäischen Steppen und Kaukasiens in vor- und frühskythischer Zeit* (Moscow and Mainz, 2001). More recent studies of significance include A. Hellmuth, 'The Chronological Setting of the So-Called Cimmerian and Early Scythian Material from Anatolia', *Ancient Near Eastern Studies*, 45 (2008), 102–22 and Ş. Dönmez, 'The Central Black Sea Region of Turkey during the Iron Age: The Local Cultures and Eurasian Horse Riding Nomads', in D. V. Grammenos and E. K. Petropoulos (eds.), *Ancient Greek Colonies in the Black Sea 2* (Oxford, 2007), 1207–20. Some of the issues raised in these last two papers are discussed in a very useful review article, G. R. Tsetskhladze, 'The Scythians: Three Essays', in G. R. Tsetskhladze (ed.), *The Black Sea, Greece, Anatolia and Europe in the First Millennium BC* (Leuven, 2011), 95–139. See, however, the review by A. Ivantchik in *Bryn Mawr Classical Review* 2013.03.36, bmcr/brynmawr.edu/2013/2013-03-36.html; accessed 18 Jan. 2019.

The impact of the Scythians returning from Asia Minor to the north Caucasus has been much debated; see, for example, G. Kossack, 'Von den Anfängen des skytho-iranischen Tierstils', in H. Franke (ed.), *Skythika* (Munich, 1987), 24–85. One revealing detailed study is C. Metdepenninghen, 'La Relation entre l'art urartéen au temps du roi Rusa II et les épées-*akinakès* de Kelermès et de Melgounov', *Iranica Antiqua*, 32 (1997), 109–36. The principal issues are well brought out in a thoughtful review of a detailed report on the Kelermes kurgan by L. K. Galanina, written by J. Boardman, in G. R. Tsetskhladze (ed.), *North Pontic Archaeology: Recent Discoveries and Studies* (Leiden, 2001), 449–51.

Helpful introductory accounts of the archaeology of the Scythians on the Pontic steppe will be found in G. R Tsetskhladze's 'The Scythians: Three Essays' paper noted above and in R. Rolle, 'The Scythians: Between Mobility, Tomb Architecture and Early Urban Structures', in L. Bonfante (ed.), *The Barbarians of Ancient Europe: Realities and Interactions* (Cambridge, 2011), 107–31. Issues of chronology are examined in detail in A. Y. Alekseev, *Xronografija Jevopejskoj Skifii VII–IV vv. do n.é.* (Chronology of European Scythians 7th–4th Century BC) (St Petersburg, 2003), while broader aspects of Scythian culture are discussed in N. A. Gavrilyuk, 'Social and Economic Issues in the Development of Steppe Scythia', in D. Braund and S. D. Kryzhitskiy (eds.), *Classical Olbia and the Scythian World: From the Sixth Century BC to the Second Century AD* (Oxford,

2007), 135–44 and in the same author's more detailed work, *Istoriya ekonomiki Stepnoi Skifii VI–III vv. do n.é.* (Economic History of Steppe Scythia, 6th–3rd Centuries BC) (Kiev, 1999).

A thoughtful introduction to the Sauromatians is given in T. Sulimirski, *The Sarmatians* (London, 1970), 39–53. For an extended treatment see four chapters in Davis-Kimball, Bashilov, and Yablonsky (eds.), *Nomads of the Eurasian Steppes in the Early Iron Age* (cited above): M. G. Moshkova, 'A Brief Review of the History of the Sauromatians and Sarmatian Tribes', 85–9; the same author's 'History of the Studies of the Sauromatian and Sarmatian Tribes', 91–6; V. V. Dvornichenko, 'Sauromatians and Sarmatians of the Eurasian Steppes: The Transitional Period from the Bronze Age', 101–4; and the same author's 'Sauromatian Culture', 105–16.

The literature on the interaction between Greeks and Scythians on the north Pontic interface is very considerable. The two classic works are E. H. Minns, *Scythians and Greeks: A Survey of the Ancient History and Archaeology on the North Coast of the Euxine from the Danube to the Caucasus* (Cambridge, 1913) and M. I. Rostovtzeff, *Iranians and Greeks in South Russia* (Oxford, 1922). The best brief introduction is provided in J. Boardman, *The Greeks Overseas: Their Early Colonies and Trade* (2nd edn., London, 1980), 238–66. The most comprehensive recent survey exploring the many complexities of the interaction is C. Meyer, *Greco-Scythian Art and the Birth of Eurasia: From Classical Antiquity to Russian Modernity* (Oxford, 2013). It is thoroughly referenced.

The early history of the kingdom of the Bosporus is reviewed in J. Hind, 'The Bosporan Kingdom', in D. M. Lewis et al. (eds.), *The Cambridge Ancient History*, vi: *The 4th Century BC* (Cambridge,1995), 476–511. Three articles dealing with different aspects of the Greek/Scythian engagement relevant to this chapter appear in D. Braund (ed.), *Scythians and Greeks: Cultural Interactions in Scythia, Athens and the Early Roman Empire (Sixth Century BC–First Century AD)* (Exeter, 2005): S. D. Kryzhitskiy, 'Olbia and the Scythians in the Fifth Century BC: The Scythian "Protectorate"', 123–30; V. Bylkova, 'The Lower Dnieper Region as an Area of Greek/Barbarian Interaction', 131–47; and A. A. Maslennikov, 'The Development of Graeco-Barbarian Contacts in the Chora of the European Bosphorus (Sixth–First Centuries)', 153–66.

The great inland market centres (*gorodišče*) are introduced in two general papers by R. Rolle, 'Royal Tombs and Hill Fortresses: New Perspectives on Scythian Life', in J. Aruz et al. (eds.), *The Golden Deer of Eurasia: Perspectives on the Steppe Nomads of the Ancient World* (New York, 2006), 168–81 and 'The Scythians: Between Mobility, Tomb Architecture and Early Urban Structures', in Bonfante (ed.), *The Barbarians of Ancient Europe* (cited above), 107–31. For more details of the fortification of Bel'sk see B. A. Shramko, *Bel'skoe gorodišče skifskoj epokhi (gorod Gelon)* (Bels'k Fortified Settlement of the Scythian Epoch (Gelon Town)) (Kiev, 1987) and R. Rolle, V. J. Murzin, and B. A. Shramko, 'Das

Burgwallsystem von Bel'sk (Ukraine). Eine frühe stadtartige Anlage im skythischen Landesinneren', *Hamburger Beiträge zur Archäologie*, 18 (1991), 57–84. The fortified settlement of Trakhtemirov is introduced in Y. V. Boltrik and E. E. Fialko, 'Trakhtemirov: A Fortified City Site on the Dnieper', in Braund and Kryzhitskiy (eds.), *Classical Olbia and the Scythian World* (cited above), 103–19. The most convenient source for the settlement of Kamenskoe is Rolle, *The World of the Scythians* (cited above), 119–22.

The literature on Scythian tombs is massive. Short but informative introductions appear in both of the papers by R. Rolle, referred to in the previous paragraph: 'Royal Tombs and Hill Fortresses: New Perspectives on Scythian Life' and 'The Scythians: Between Mobility, Tomb Architecture and Early Urban Structures', and in the relevant section of her book, *The World of the Scythians* (cited above). The same author has produced an invaluable corpus of the major kurgans, *Totenkult der Skythen*, Teil 1: *Das Steppengebiet* (Berlin, 1979). In a more recent paper M. Ochir-Goryaeva, 'The Scythian Tombs: Construction and Geographical Orientation', *European Journal of Archaeology*, 18 (2015), 477–96 has considered the structure of the tombs in terms of symbolism, with surprising results. An interesting discussion of the Greek influence on tomb construction is offered in G. R. Tsetskhladze, 'Who Built the Scythian and Thracian Royal and Elite Tombs?', *Oxford Journal of Archaeology*, 17 (1998), 55–92. A. I. Ivantchik's 'The Funeral of Scythian Kings: The Historical Reality and the Description of Herodotus (IV, 71–2)', in Bonfante (ed.), *The Barbarians of Ancient Europe* (cited above), 71–106 is a fascinating discussion relevant both here and in Chapter 11. M. I. Artamonov, *Treasures from Scythian Tombs in the Hermitage Museum, Leningrad* (London, 1969) focuses, as its title implies, on tomb contents but it also provides descriptions of the major tombs. Among the more recent publications of individual tombs are: B. M. Mozolevs'kyi, *Tovsta Mogila* (in Ukrainian) (Kiev, 1979); A. P. Mantsevich, *Kurgan Solokha* (in Russian) (Leningrad, 1987); L. K. Galanina, *Die Kurgane von Kelermes: 'Königsgräber' der frühskythischen Zeit* (Moscow, 1997); and R. Rolle, V. J. Murzin, and A. J. Alekseev, *Königskurgan Čertomlyk: Ein skythischer Grabhügel des 4. vorchristlichen Jahrhunderts* (Mainz, 1998). Identifying the occupants of royal tombs has been a temptation that few can resist. For a balanced consideration of the subject see A. Alekseev, 'Scythian Kings and "Royal Barrows" of the Fifth and Fourth Centuries BC: Modern Chronology and Interpretation', in Aruz et al. (eds.), *The Golden Deer of Eurasia: Perspectives* (cited above), 160–7.

Chapter 6   Crossing the Carpathians

Background reading for the pre-Scythian contact between the steppe and the Great Hungarian Plain and adjacent regions has already been given under Chapter 4

(pp. 368–70). These early contacts were followed by further movements of people in the Scythian period. The two seminal studies of Scythian-type material west of the Carpathians are M. Párducz, 'Problem des Skythenzeit im Karpatenbecken', *Acta Archaeologica Academiae Scientiarum Hungaricae*, 25 (1973), 27–63 and M. Dušek, 'Die Thraker im Karpatenbecken', *Slovenská Archeológia*, 22 (1974), 361–434. The archaeological evidence was assembled again and re-examined in J. Chochorowski, *Die Vekerzug-Kultur: Charakteristik der Funde* (Kraków, 1985) and further discussed in the context of possible movements of Scythians in the same author's 'Die Rolle der Vekerzug-Kultur (VK) im Rahmen der skythischen Einflüsse in Mitteleuropa', *Praehistorische Zeitschrift*, 60 (1985), 204–71. More recently the evidence has been reviewed in A. Pydyn, *Exchange and Cultural Interactions: A Study of Long-Distance Trade and Cross-Cultural Contacts in the Late Bronze Age and Early Iron Age in Central and Eastern Europe* (Oxford, 1999), 47–52. Two of the important Hungarian cemeteries are Szentes-Vekerzug and Ártánd. The first was reported by M. Párducz, in three parts, as 'Le Cimetière hallstattien de Szentes-Vekerzug', in *Acta Archaeologica Academiae Scientiarum Hungaricae*, 2 (1952), 143–72, 4 (1954), 25–91, and 6 (1955), 1–22. The excavations at Ártánd were reported by the same author in 'Graves from the Scythian Age of Ártánd (Hajdu-Bihar)', in the same journal, 17 (1965), 137–231. The cemetery at Chotin was published in M. Dušek, *Thrakisches Gräberfeld der Hallstattzeit in Chotin* (Bratislava, 1966). Evidence for horses of eastern type in Central Europe is considered in S. Bökönyi, 'Data on Iron Age Horses of Central and Eastern Europe', *American School of Prehistoric Research, Peabody Museum, Harvard University, Bulletin*, 25 (1968), 11–71. Scythian-type finds from the North European Plain are listed and discussed in Z. Bukowski, *The Scythian Influence in the Area of the Lusatian Culture* (Wrocław, 1977). The remarkable find from Witaszkowo (Vettersfelde) is described in the above, 197–204 and also in D. von Bothmer, 'The Vettersfelde Find', in Metropolitan Museum of Art, *From the Lands of the Scythians: Ancient Treasures from the Museums of the U.S.S.R., 3000 BC–100 BC* (New York, 1975), 153–5.

There is a considerable general literature on the Celts. For a broad introduction see B. Cunliffe, *The Ancient Celts* (2nd edn., Oxford, 2018). The classic work on Celtic art— the theme which concerns us here—is P. Jacobsthal, *Early Celtic Art* (Oxford, 1944; corrected edn., 1969). Jacobsthal was prepared to accept that eastern influences from Scythia and Persia were involved in the formative phases of Celtic art. Other writers are less convinced. For a brief discussion of these issues see R. and V. Megaw, *Celtic Art: From its Beginnings to the Book of Kells* (London, 1989; rev. edn., 2001), 65–9.

Chapter 7 Scythians in Central Asia: 700–200 BC

There is no easy way to approach the subject of the Scythian people of Central Asia but a short section in T. Sulimirski, *The Sarmatians* (London, 1970), 53–80 gives a broad survey of the question. The Sakā of Central Asia are covered in three chapters, all by L. T. Yablonsky, in J. Davis-Kimball, V. A. Bashilov, and L. T. Yablonsky (eds.), *Nomads of the Eurasian Steppe in the Early Iron Age* (Berkeley, 1995): 'Written Sources and the History of Archaeological Studies of the Sakā in Central Asia', 193–7; 'Material Culture of the Sakā and Historical Reconstruction', 201–39; and 'Some Ethnogenetical Hypotheses', 241–52. Together they provide the essential background data. For a shorter and updated overview see the same author's 'Scythians and Sakā: Ethnic Terminology and Archaeological Reality', in J. Aruz et al. (eds.), *The Golden Deer of Eurasia: Perspectives on the Steppe Nomads of the Ancient World* (New York, 2006), 24–31. The important issue of the relationship of the Central Asian nomads to the sedentary polities on their borders is considered in S. Stark, 'Nomads and Networks: Elites and their Connection to the Outside World', in S. Stark et al. (eds.), *Nomads and Networks: The Ancient Art and Culture of Kazakhstan* (Princeton, 2012), 107–38.

The cemetery of Filippovka is discussed in two papers by A. K. Pshenichniuk: 'The Filippovka Kurgans at the Heart of the Eurasian Steppes', in J. Aruz et al. (eds.), *The Golden Deer of Eurasia: Scythian and Sarmatian Treasures from the Russian Steppes* (New York, 2000), 21–30 and 'Burial Ritual of the Filippovka Kurgan in the Ural region', in Aruz et al. (eds.), *The Golden Deer of Eurasia: Perspectives* (cited above), 40–5. The more recent excavations are described by L. T. Yablonsky in 'New Excavations of the Early Nomadic Burial Ground at Filippovka (Southern Ural Region, Russia)', *American Journal of Archaeology*, 114 (2010), 129–43. The archaeological evidence for the desert-edge settlements is introduced in the papers of L. T. Yablonsky listed in the paragraph above. Evidence for settlement and burial in the Semirechye region of Kazakhstan is discussed in C. Chang, 'Cycles of Iron Age Mobility and Sedentism: Climate, Landscape and Material Culture in Southeastern Kazakhstan', in Stark et al. (eds.), *Nomads and Networks* (cited above), 140–51. The famous burial from Issyk in Kazakhstan is published in K. A. Akisev, *Kurgan Issyk: Iskusstvo sakov Kazakhstana* (Issyk Mound: Art of the Sakā in Kazakhstan) (Moscow, 1978).

The nomadic communities of the Altai–Sayan region have been extensively studied. A thorough overview of the material culture and burials is provided in four chapters by N. A. Bokovenko, in Davis-Kimball, Bashilov, and Yablonsky (eds.), *Nomads of the Eurasian Steppes in the Early Iron Age* (cited above): 'History of Studies and the Main Problem in the Archaeology of Southern Siberia during the Scythian period', 255–61;

'Tuva during the Scythian Period', 265–81; 'Scythian Culture in the Altai Mountains', 285–95; and 'The Tagar Culture in the Minusinsk Basin', 296–314. The same author provides an updated view of the Tagar culture in his paper 'The Emergence of the Tagar Culture', *Antiquity*, 80 (2006), 860–79.

By far the best account of the wonders of the Pazyryk cemetery is that written by the excavator, S. I. Rudenko, and carefully translated from the Russian by the archaeologist M. W. Thompson as *Frozen Tombs of Siberia: The Pazyryk Burials of Iron Age Horsemen* (London, 1970). It provides a meticulous account of the finds, written for the general reader but also of great value to the specialist. The first exhibition of material from Pazyryk and other tombs in the region held in Britain generated a useful catalogue with good introductory essays, *Frozen Tombs: The Culture and Art of the Ancient Tribes of Siberia* (London, 1978). A far more elaborate and brilliantly illustrated catalogue, prepared for a new exhibition nearly 40 years later, St J. Simpson and S. Pankova (eds.), *Scythians: Warriors of Ancient Siberia* (London, 2017) is essential reading. The date of the Pazyryk cemetery has been clarified by radiocarbon dating and the evidence is discussed in J. P. Mallory et al., 'The Date of Pazyryk', in K. Boyle, C. Renfrew, and M. Levine (eds.), *Ancient Interactions: East and West in Eurasia* (Cambridge, 2002), 199–213.

Other tombs, where the burial contents are preserved by the permafrost conditions, include the cemetery of Berel in Kazakhstan, details of which are provided in A. P. Gorbunov, Z. S. Samashev, and E. V. Severskii, *The Treasures of Frozen Burial Mounds of the Kazakh Altai: Materials of the Berel Burial Site* (in Russian and English) (Almaty, 2005) and Z. S. Samashev, 'The Berel Kurgans: Some Results of Investigations', in Stark et al. (eds.), *Nomads and Networks* (cited above), 31–49. The frozen tomb at Ak-Alakha on the Ukok plateau is reported in three papers by N. Polosmak: 'A Mummy Unearthed from the Pastures of Heaven', *National Geographic*, 186/4 (October, 1994), 80–103; 'The Burial of a Noble Pazyryk Woman', *Ancient Civilization from Scythia to Siberia*, 5 (1999), 125–65; and 'Ak-Alakh-3', in Simpson and Pankova (eds.), *Scythians* (cited above), 100–1.

The discovery and excavation of the frozen tombs have generated a range of specialist studies, some of which are of considerable general interest. Among them we may list: G. Argent, 'Do the Clothes make the Horse? Relationality, Roles and Statuses in Iron Age Inner Asia', *World Archaeology*, 42 (2010), 157–74; G. Azarpay, 'Some Classical and Near Eastern Motifs in the Art of Pazyryk', *Artibus Asiae*, 22 (1959), 313–39; J. Lerner; 'Some So-Called Achaemenid Objects from Pazyryk', *Source: Notes in the History of Art*, 10 (1991), 8–15; and K. S. Rubinson, 'The Textiles from Pazyryk: A Study in the Transfer and Transformation of Artistic Motifs', *Expedition*, 32 (1990), 49–60.

Chapter 8 Bodies Clothed in Skins

Classical sources, particularly Herodotus and Pseudo-Hippocrates, have much to say about the appearance, health, and clothing of the Scythians but one must remember that their observations, whether gathered from the field or through informants, would have been of people restricted to the Pontic steppe. Moreover, the way in which they chose to depict the Scythians would to some extent have been coloured by their prejudices about barbarians. Recent research on the human remains has given some fascinating insights into the health of the population. See, for example, M. Schultz et al., 'Oldest Known Case of Metastasizing Prostate Carcinoma Diagnosed in the Skeleton of a 2,700-Year-Old Scythian King from Arzhan (Siberia, Russia)', *International Journal of Cancer*, 121/12 (2007), 2591–5; M. Schultz et al., 'Die paläopathologische Untersuchungen erste Auswertungen einer bio-archäologischen Analyse', in K. Čugunov, H. Parzinger, and A. Nagler (eds.), *Der skythenzeitliche Fürstenkurgan Aržan 2 in Tuva* (Mainz, 2010), 296–302; and A. Y. Letyagin and A. A. Savelov, 'Life and Death of "the Altai Princess"', *Science First Hand*, 57/58 (2014), 117–37.

The evidence for dress comes from two principal sources: depictions on metal vessels and from the actual clothing preserved in the frozen tombs. For the former, the objects chosen for illustration in Gallery of Objects (pp. 331–51) offer the best examples. For the latter the most accessible source is S. I. Rudenko, *Frozen Tombs of Siberia: The Pazyryk Burials of Iron Age Horsemen* (London, 1970), augmented by the excellent illustrations and descriptions in St J. Simpson and S. Pankova (eds.), *Scythians: Warriors of Ancient Siberia* (London, 2017). The distribution of appliqué ornaments in graves, even when all traces of organic materials have rotted, can also give an indication of dress. See, for example, the elite person buried at Issyk described in K. A. Akisev, *Kurgan Issyk: Iskusstvo sakov Kazakhstana* (Issyk Mound: Art of the Sakā in Kazakhstan) (Moscow, 1978). A brief discussion of the strength and weaknesses of the various types of evidence for dress is offered in M. Gleba, 'You Are What You Wear: Scythian Costume as Identity', in M. Gleba, C. Munkholt, and M.-L. Nosch (eds.), *Dressing the Past* (Oxford, 2008), 13–28. Body tattoos are best displayed on the body from Pazyryk kurgan 2, described and discussed in Rudenko, *Frozen Tombs of Siberia* (cited above), 110–14. The apparatus used for inhaling the fumes of burning hemp is also described in Rudenko's book, pp. 284–5, as are the other comforts of home.

Evidence for social structure is referred to in the classical sources and is inherent in different styles of burial. The subject is discussed by A. I. Ivantchik in 'The Funeral of Scythian Kings: The Historical Reality and the Description of Herodotus (IV, 71–72)', in L. Bonfante (ed.), *The Barbarians of Ancient Europe: Realities and Interactions*

(Cambridge, 2011), 71–106 and by A. Y. Alekseyev, 'Scythian Kings and "Royal" Burial-Mounds of the Fifth and Fourth Centuries BC', in D. Braund (ed.), *Scythians and Greeks: Cultural Interactions in Scythia, Athens and the Early Roman Empire (Sixth Century BC–First Century AD)* (Exeter, 2005), 39–55.

That gender boundaries were fluid among the Scythians is explicitly stated by various classical observers, most notably Herodotus and Pseudo-Hippocrates. This theme and the role of women as warriors have been explored by a number of writers, most notably by J. Davis-Kimball in three papers: 'Burial Practices of Iranian Sarmatians', *Journal of Indo-European Studies. Monograph*, 23 (1995), 68–85; 'Sauro-Sarmatian Nomadic Women: New Gender Identities', *Journal of Indo-European Studies*, 25 (1997), 327–43; and 'Amazons, Priestesses and Other Women of State: Females in Eurasian Nomadic Societies', *Silk Road Art and Archaeology*, 5 (1998), 1–50. The theme is also considered in a wide-ranging paper by B. Hanks, 'Reconsidering Warfare, Status, and Gender in the Eurasian Steppe Iron Age', in K. M. Linduff and K. S. Rubinson (eds.), *Are All Warriors Male? Gender Roles on the Ancient Eurasian Steppe* (Lanham, Md., 2008), 15–34.

General accounts of everyday life and leisure are to be found in R. Rolle, *The World of the Scythians* (London, 1989), 92–117 and I. Lebedynsky, *Les Scythes: les Scythes d'Europe et la période scythe dans les steppes d'Eurasie, VIIe–IIIe siècles av. J.-C.* (2nd edn., Paris, 2010), 131–72. Rudenko, *Frozen Tombs of Siberia* (cited above) also has an excellent chapter (chapter 6) on life in the Altai. The importance of milk in the diet is discussed in fascinating detail in D. Braund, 'Greeks, Scythians and *Hippake*, or "Reading Mare's Cheese"', in G. R. Tsetskhladze (ed.), *Ancient Greeks West and East* (Leiden, 1999), 521–30.

Chapter 9   Bending the Bow

The theme of weapons and warfare is well catered for in several general works including R. Rolle, *The World of the Scythians* (London, 1989), 64–91 and I. Lebedynsky, *Les Scythes: les Scythes d'Europe et la période scythe dans les steppes d'Eurasie, VIIe–IIIe siècles av. J.-C.* (2nd edn., Paris, 2010), 187–210. Another good source is a small book devoted specifically to weapons and warfare: E. V. Cernenko, *The Scythians 700–300 BC* (Oxford, 1983). A briefer, but more up-to-date account is given in K. V. Chugunov, T. V. Rjabkova, and St J. Simpson, 'Mounted Warriors', in St J. Simpson and S. Pankova, *Scythians: Warriors of Ancient Siberia* (London, 2017), 194–255, a chapter which includes brilliant illustrations and full descriptions of relevant objects. For scenes of warriors with their weapons see the various vessels illustrated in Gallery of Objects above (pp. 329–51). For the all-important horses, bridles, and saddles there is no better introduction than S. I. Rudenko, *Frozen Tombs of Siberia: The Pazyryk Burials of Iron*

Age Horsemen (London, 1970), chapter 6. The Pazyryk saddles are again treated in E. V. Stepanova, 'Reconstruction of a Scythian Saddle from Pazyryk Barrow No. 3', *The Silk Road*, 14 (2016), 1–18. On horse riding see N. H. Bokovenko, 'The Origins of Horse Riding and the Development of Ancient Central Asian Nomad Riding Harnesses', in J. Davis-Kimball et al. (eds.), *Kurgans, Ritual Sites, and Settlements: Eurasian Bronze and Iron Age* (Oxford, 2000), 304–7.

Archery features large in discussion of Scythian warfare. Two useful sources are M. F. Vos, *Scythian Archers in Archaic Attic Vase-Painting* (Groningen, 1963) and G. Rausing, *The Bow: Some Notes on its Origin and Development* (Lund, 1967). Also of general interest is R. Miller, E. McEwen, and C. Bergman, 'Experimental Approaches to Ancient Near Eastern Archery', *World Archaeology*, 18 (1980), 178–95.

There is ample evidence of trauma resulting from battles. For a thorough overview providing an insight into the reality of battle see M. N. Daragan, 'Scythian Internecine Feuds', *Ancient Civilizations from Scythia to Siberia*, 22 (2016), 96–140. Other works include E. M. Murphy, *Iron Age Archaeology and Trauma from Aymyrlyg, South Siberia* (Oxford, 2003) and S. S. Tur et al., 'An Exceptional Case of Healed Vertebral Wound with Trapped Bronze Arrowhead: Analysis of a 7th–6th c. BC Individual from Central Kazakhstan', *International Journal of Osteoarchaeology*, 26/4 (2016), 740–6.

Helmets, possibly of Chinese origin, are discussed in K. S. Rubinson, 'Helmets and Mirrors: Markers of Social Transformation', in J. Aruz et al. (eds.), *The Golden Deer of Eurasia: Perspectives on the Steppe Nomads of the Ancient World* (New York, 2006), 32–9.

There has been little discussion of Scythian strategy and tactics in battle but the reader cannot do better than to turn to Herodotus' account of the Persian advance through Scythian territory in 513 BC (*Histories* iv). The use of the Scythian forces in support of Satyrus' claim for the kingdom of the Bosphorus two centuries later is described by Diodorus Siculus (*Histories* xx).

Finally, celebrating victory. For this we have to rely again on Herodotus (*Histories* iv), including his do-it-yourself account of scalping. Direct evidence for scalping comes from the body found in kurgan 2 at Pazyryk described in Rudenko, *Frozen Tombs of Siberia* (cited above), 221. The scalped head is graphically illustrated in Simpson and Pankova (eds.), *Scythians* (cited above), 106, with a description.

Chapter 10 Of Gods, Beliefs and Art

The origin myths, so succinctly laid out by Herodotus, have given rise to much discussion. Two papers by A. I. Ivantchik offer incisive analyses: 'Une légende sur l'origine des Scythes (Hdt. 4.5–7) et le problème des sources du *Scythicos logos* d'Hérodote', *Revue des études grecques*, 111 (1999), 169–89 and 'La Légend "grecque" sur l'origine des

Scythes (Hérodote 4.8–10)', in V. Fromentin and S. Gotteland (eds.), *Origines gentium* (Bordeaux, 2001), 207–20.

A comprehensive overview of Scythian religious beliefs is provided in D. Raev-skiy, *Scythian Mythology* (Sofia, 1993). The goddesses revered by the Scythians are discussed in Y. Ustinova, 'Snake-Limbed and Tendril-Limbed Goddesses in the Art and Mythology of the Mediterranean and Black Sea', in D. Braund (ed.), *Scythians and Greeks: Cultural Interactions in Scythia, Athens and the Early Roman Empire (Sixth Century BC–First Century AD)* (Exeter, 2005), 64–79 and is more fully treated in the same author's *The Supreme Gods of the Bosporan Kingdom: Celestial Aphrodite and the Most High God* (Leiden, 1999), 67–128. Other significant works are S. S. Bessonova, *Religioznye predstav-lenija skifov* (Scythian Religious Conceptions) (Kiev, 1983) and the same author's 'O kul'te oruzhiya u skifov' (Scythian Religious Conceptions), in E. V. Chernenko et al. (eds.), *Vooruzhenie skifov i sarmatov* (Scythians and Sarmatian Arms) (Kiev, 1984), 3–21. The imagery of the deities is well covered in E. Jacobson, *The Art of the Scythians: The Interpenetration of Culture at the Edge of the Hellenic World* (Leiden, 1995) and in the same author's 'The "Bird Woman", the "Birthing Woman" and the "Woman of the Ani-mals": A Consideration of the Female Image in the Petroglyphs of Ancient Central Asia', *Arts Asiatiques*, 52 (1997), 37–59. To put Scythian belief systems into the broader context of Iranian religion see G. Widengren, *Die Religionen Irans* (Stuttgart, 1965) and W. W. Malandra, *An Introduction to Ancient Iranian Religion: Readings from the Avesta and Achaemenid Inscriptions* (Minneapolis, 1983).

The most thorough treatment of the intermediary between the Scythians and their gods is D. Margreth, *Skythische Schamanen? Die Nachrichten über Enarees-Anarieis bei Herodot und Hippokrates* (Schaffhausen, 1993). For a much earlier, but no less important treatment, see K. Meuli, 'Scythica', *Hermes*, 70 (1935), 121–76. The broader questions of the relationship of shamanistic practices and Eurasian rock art are addressed in H.-P. Francfort, 'Central Asian Petroglyphs: Between Indo-Iranian and Shamanistic Interpretations', in C. Chippindale and P. S. C. Taçon (eds.), *The Archaeology of Rock Art* (Cambridge, 1998), 302–18. The rattles and bells often decorated with standing animals, which are likely to have been used in religious ceremonies, are discussed in exhaustive detail in K. Bakay, *Scythian Rattles in the Carpathian Basin and their Eastern Connections* (Budapest, 1971).

Scythian art is a vast topic. In this chapter we have restricted our discussion to animal art, which lies deeply rooted in the nomadic world. The subject was compre-hensively discussed in K. Jettmar, *Art of the Steppes: The Eurasian Animal Style* (London, 1967). In a classic work, now of historical interest, M. I. Rostovtzeff, *The Animal Style in South Russia and China* (Princeton, 1929), the author argued for an Iranian source for both eastern and western Eurasian animal art styles—a view now superseded by more recent discoveries in southern Siberia and Mongolia, notably the Bronze Age deer stones and the early animal-style items from Arzhan 1. For the Deer Stones see V. V. Volkov, *Olennye kamni Mongolii* (Deer Stones of Mongolia) (Moscow, 2002) and W. W. Fitzhugh, 'The Mongolian Deer Stone–Khirigsuur Complex: Dating and Organization of a Late Bronze Age Menagerie', in J. Bemmann et al. (eds.), *Current Archaeological Research in Mongolia* (Bonn, 2009), 183–99. The contribution of rock art to Scythian animal art is discussed in E. Jacobson, 'The Filippovka Deer: Inquiry into their North Asian Sources and Symbolic Significance', in J. Aruz et al. (eds.), *The Golden Deer of Eurasia: Perspectives on the Steppe Nomads of the Ancient World* (New York, 2006), 182–95. See also the same author's *The Deer Goddess of Ancient Siberia: A Study in the Ecology of Belief* (Leiden, 1993). Another view is offered in A. R. Kantorovich, '"Letiashchie" i lezhaschchie oleni v iskusstve zverinogo stila stepnoi Skifii' ('Flying' and Recumbent Deer in Animal-Style Art of the Scythian Steppes), *Istoriko-arkheologicheskii al'manakh* (Historico-Archaeological Almanac), 2 (1996), 46–59. For a thought-provoking discussion of flying-stag imagery in an adjacent region see T. Taylor, 'Flying Stags: Icons of Power in Thracian Art', in I. Hodder (ed.), *The Archaeology of Contextual Meaning* (Cambridge, 1987), 117–32. Similar structuralist themes are discussed in L. Schneider and P. Zazoff, 'Konstruktion und Recontrucktion: Zur Lesung thrakischer und skythischer Bilder', *Jahrbuch des Deutschen Archäologischen Instituts*, 109 (1994), 143–216.

Chapter 11 The Way of Death

Death as a 'rite of passage' was famously analysed in the seminal work of A. Van Gennep, *Les Rites de passage* (Paris, 1909), translated by M. B. Vizedom and G. L. Caffee, as *The Rites of Passage* (London, 1960, repr. 2010). It is essential reading for all archaeologists and will help the reader to understand the elaborate rituals adopted by the Scythians.

Any detailed consideration of Scythian burial practice must begin with the famous description of royal burials provided by Herodotus (*Hist.* iv. 71–2) and with the very careful analysis of the text in A. I. Ivantchik, 'The Funeral of Scythian Kings: The Historical Reality and the Description of Herodotus (IV, 71–72)', in L. Bonfante (ed.), *The Barbarians of Ancient Europe: Realities and Interactions* (Cambridge, 2011), 71–106. This important paper addresses many issues, not least the reliability of Herodotus as a source and the location of the royal burial ground in the land of the Gerrhi. For short general discussions of Scythian burials see R. Rolle, *The World of the Scythians* (London, 1989), 19–37 and I. Lebedynsky, *Les Scythes: les Scythes d'Europe et la période scythe dans les steppes d'Eurasie, VIIe–IIIe siècles av. J.-C.* (2nd edn., Paris, 2010), 229–50. Comprehensive treatments published in Russian include V. S. Ol'khovskiy, *Pogrebal'no-pominal'naya obryadnost' naseleniya stepnoy Skifii (VII–III vv. do n.é.)* (Burial and Wake Rites of the Population of the Scythian Steppe (7th–3rd Centuries BC)) (Moscow, 1991) and A. I. Alekseev et al. (eds.), *Élitnye kurgany stepeĭ Evrazii v skifo-sarmatskuiu épokhu* (Elite Barrows of the Eurasian Steppes during the Scytho-Sarmatian Period) (Moscow, 1994). A very useful corpus of tombs is brought together in R. Rolle, *Totenkult der Skythen, Teil 1: Das Steppengebiet* (Berlin, 1979). Symbolism inherent in tomb structure is explored in M. Ochir-Goryaeva, 'The Scythian Tombs: Construction and Geographical Orientation', *European Journal of Archaeology*, 18 (2015), 477–96.

The burials in the Altai–Sayan region are best approached through S. I. Rudenko, *Frozen Tombs of Siberia: The Pazyryk Burials of Iron Age Horsemen* (London, 1970) and E. F. Korolkova, 'Death and Burial', in St J. Simpson and S. Pankova (eds.), *Scythians: Warriors of Ancient Siberia* (London, 2017), 256–75, which places the evidence from the frozen tombs into its broader context.

For some recent publications of individual tombs see: R. Rolle, V. J. Murzin, and A. J. Alekseev, *Königskurgan Čertomlyk: Ein skythischer Gräbhugel des 4. vorschristlichen Jahrhunderts* (Mainz, 1998); A. P. Mantsevich, *Kurgan Solokha* (in Russian) (Leningrad, 1987); B. M. Mozolevs'kyi and S. V. Polin, *Kurgany skifskogo Gerrosa IV v. do n.é. (Babina, Vodyana i Soboleva Mogily)* (Tumuli of the Scythian Gerrhos of the Fourth Century BC (Babina, Vodyana, and Soboleva Mogila)) (Kiev, 2005); and L. Galanina, *Die Kurgane von Kelermes: Königsgräber der frühskythischen Zeit*, Steppenvölker Eurasiens (Moscow, 1997).

More specialist aspects of the burial rituals are dealt with in a variety of sources. For embalming see I. S. Kamenetskiy, 'O bal'zamirovanii umershikh tsarey u skifov' (About Embalming of the Dead Kings among the Scythians), *Istoriko-arkheologicheskiy al'manakh* (Historico-Archaeological Almanac), 1 (1995), 68–76. The *totenreiter* (death riders) found at Chertomlÿk are discussed in Rolle, Murzin, and Alekseev, *Königskurgan Čertomlyk* (cited above), 51. Herodotus' description of cannibalism among the Massagetae and Issedones has been taken to task in E. M. Murphy and J. P. Mallory, 'Herodotus and the Cannibals', *Antiquity*, 74 (2000), 388–94, who offer the hypothesis that Herodotus confused as cannibalism the de-fleshing of bodies for hygienic reasons, practised by pastoralists when a person died during the summer transhumance and they wished to bury the body later after they had returned to their winter camp.

Chapter 12 Scythians and the *Longue Durée*

The background to the development of pastoral nomadism in Eurasia up to the end of the Late Bronze Age is presented in D. W. Anthony, *The Horse, The Wheel, and Language: How Bronze-Age Riders from the Eurasian Steppes Shaped the Modern World* (Prince-

ton, 2007), while for a broader perspective, taking the story up to the Mongols, see B. Cunliffe, *By Steppe, Desert, and Ocean: The Birth of Eurasia* (Oxford, 2015). The power struggle in the Far East leading to the westerly migration of the Yuezhi and Wusun is thoroughly treated in X. Lin, 'Migration and Settlement of the Yuezhi-Kushan: Interaction and Interdependence of Nomadic and Sedentary Societies', *Journal of World History*, 12 (2001), 261–92 and C. G. R. Benjamin, *The Yuezhi: Origin, Migration and the Conquest of Northern Bactria* (Turnhout, 2007). For the cemetery of Tillya Tepe see V. I. Sarianidi, 'Ancient Bactria's Golden Hoard', in F. Hiebert and P. Cambon (eds.), *Afghanistan: Crossroads of the Ancient World* (London, 2011), 145–209.

The most accessible source on the Sarmatians in English is T. Sulimirski, *The Sarmatians* (London, 1970), which ranges wide, taking the story of the various nomadic groups from the sixth and fifth centuries to the time of the Alans and Huns. J. Harmatta, *Studies in the History and Language of the Sarmatians* (Szeged, 1970) offers a more focused account. For a more recent treatment, see L. Lebedynsky, *Les Sarmates: Amazones et lanciers cuirasses entre Ourai et Danube, VIIe siècle avant J.-C.–VIe siècle après J.-C.* (Paris, 2002). Something of the complexity of the archaeological data is shown by the various contributions (chapters 8–12), in J. Davis-Kimball, V. A. Bashilov, and L. T. Yablonsky (eds.), *Nomads of the Eurasian Steppes in the Early Iron Age* (Berkeley, 1995), 121–88. A critical view of the way in which the archaeological evidence has been interpreted is put forward in V. Mordviutseva, 'The Sarmatians: The Creation of Archaeological Evidence', in *Oxford Journal of Archaeology*, 32 (2013), 203–19. The engagement of the various Sarmatian tribes—the Iazyges and the Roxolani—with the Roman world is put into its historical context in A. Mócsy, *Pannonia and Upper Moesia: A History of the Middle Danube Provinces of the Roman Empire* (London, 1974). For the Alans in their steppe homeland see V. Kouznetsov and I. Lebedynsky, *Les Alains: Cavaliers des steppes, seigneurs du Caucase* (Paris, 1997) and S. G. Botalov, 'The Asian Migrations of the Alans in the 1st Century AD', *Ancient West and East*, 6 (2007), 135–60. The westerly migrations of Alans is presented in B. S. Bachrach, *A History of the Alans in the West: From their First Appearance in the Sources of Classical Antiquity through the Early Middle Ages* (Minneapolis, 1973). Among the many scholarly accounts of the Huns the most readable is E. A. Thompson, *The Huns* (rev. edn., Oxford, 1996). The survival of the culture and language of the Alans in the Caucasus contributing to that of the modern Ossetians is briefly summarized in Sulimirski, *The Sarmatians* (cited above), 197–202.

ILLUSTRATION SOURCES

Maps were produced by Phoenix Mapping.

The author and publishers wish to thank the following for their kind permission to reproduce the illustrations:

Chapter 1 opener and 1.12: Prisma Archivo/Alamy Stock Photo; **1.1** Private Collection/Pictorial Press Ltd/Alamy Stock Photo; **1.2** Jacob de Wilde, *Signa antiqua e museo Jacobi de Wilde* (Amsterdam, 1700). Heritage Image Partnership Ltd/Alamy Stock Photo; **1.3** Nicolas Witsen, *Noord en oost Tartaryen* (Second edition, Amsterdam, 1785); **1.4** SHM/photo by Vladimir Terebenin; **1.5** After J. Hayward, *The Cassell Atlas of World History* (Oxford, 1997), map 4.13; **1.6** SHM/photo by Vladimir Terebenin; **1.7** Royal College of Physicians of Edinburgh; image from A. Kohn & C. Mehlis, *Materialien zur Vorgeschichte des Menschen im östlichen Europa* (Jenufa, 1879); **1.8** Author: multiple sources; **1.9** Robert B. Haas Family Arts Library, Yale University; image from Drevnosti, *Gerodotovoi Skifii* (1866); **1.10** SHM; **1.11** SHM; **1.13** Древности Боспора Киммерийского / *Antiquités du Bospore Cimmérien* (St Petersburg 1854). Reproduced from M.I. Artamonov, *Treasures from Scythian Tombs* (London, 1969), pl. XIV; **1.14** Author: multiple sources; **1.15** Sputnik/TopFoto; **1.16** Sputnik/TopFoto; **1.17** S.I. Rudenko, *Frozen Tombs of Siberia*, Dent (London, 1970), pl. 27; **1.18** DeAgostini Picture Library/W. Buss/Bridgeman Images; **1.19** Author: multiple sources; **1.20** ITAR-TASS News Agency/Alamy Stock Photo.

Chapter 2 opener and 2.10: © The Trustees of the British Museum; **2.1** Author: multiple sources; **2.2** Author: multiple sources; **2.3** Author: multiple sources; **2.4** www.BibleLandPictures.com/Alamy Stock Photo; **2.5** SHM/photo by Vladimir Terebenin; **2.6** Author: multiple sources; **2.7** Author: multiple sources; **2.8** Photo © Vatican Museums. All rights reserved; **2.9** Su concessione del Ministero dei Beni e delle Attiv-

ità Culturali e del Turismo-Polo Museale della Toscana-Firenze; **2.11** Granger Historical Picture Archive/Alamy Stock Photo; **2.12** National Gallery, London/Mariano
Garcia/Alamy Stock Photo.

Chapter 3 opener and 3.1: Author; **3.2** Author: multiple sources; **3.3** Author using
selected information from D. Anthony, *The Horse, the Wheel and Language* (Princeton,
2007), fig. 11.6; **3.4** Author using information from D. Anthony (*op. cit.*), figs. 13.1 and
13.2; **3.5** Author; **3.6** Author: multiple sources; **3.7** After D. Anthony et al. (eds.), *A
Bronze Age Landscape in the Russian Steppes*, The Samara Valley Project (UCLA, 2016),
figs. 1.1 and 4.1; **3.8** After S. Legrand, 'The emergence of the Scythians: Bronze Age
to Iron Age in South Siberia', in *Antiquity* 80 (2006), 843–59, fig. 14.A; **3.9** After S.
Legrand (*op. cit.*), fig. 14.B; **3.10** After S. Legrand (*op. cit.*), fig. 2; **3.11** Bokovenko &
Legrand, 2000; **3.12** After S. Makhortykh, 'The northern Black Sea steppes in the
Cimmerian epoch', in E. Scott et al., (eds.), *Impact of the Environment on Human Migration
in Eurasia* (Dordrecht, 2004), 35–44, figs. 1 and 2.

Chapter 4 opener and 4.6: SHM/photo by Vladimir Terebenin; **4.1** Author using
information from N. Bokovenko, 'The emergence of the Tagar culture' in *Antiquity*
80 (2006), 850–79, fig. 1; **4.2** After N. Bokovenko (*op. cit.*), fig. 2; **4.3** N. Bokovenko
(*op. cit.*), fig. 10; **4.4** N. Bokovenko (*op. cit.*), fig. 11; **4.5** SHM/photo by Vladimir Terebenin; **4.7** SHM/photo by Vladimir Terebenin; **4.8** SHM/photo by Vladimir Terebenin;
4.9 iStock.com/DavorLovincic; **4.10** After N. Bokovenko (*op. cit.*), fig. 15; **4.11** Author
using data from V. V. Volkov, 'Early nomads in Mongolia' in J. Davis-Kimball et al.
(eds.), *Nomads of the Eurasian Steppes in the Early Iron Age* (Berkeley, 1995), map 19; **4.12**
After J. Bouzek, 'Cimmerians and early Scythians: the transition from geometric to
orientalising style in the Pontic Area' in G. Tsetskhladze (ed.), *North Pontic Archaeology* (Leiden, 2001), 33–44, fig. 1; **4.13** M.P. Grjaznov, *Der Grosskurgan von Aržan in Tuva,
Südsibirien* (Munich, 1984), fig 3; **4.14** M.P. Grjaznov (*op. cit.*), fig 6; **4.15** Archive of the
Institute for the History of Material Culture, St Petersburg. Photo by M Grjaznov; **4.16**
National Museum of Tuva, Kyzyl; **4.17** M.P. Grjaznov (*op. cit.*), Grjaznov and Mannai-
ool; **4.18** Eurasien-Abteilung, DAI; **4.19** Eurasien-Abteilung, DAI; **4.20** Author using
information selected from J. Bouzek (*op. cit.*), fig. 5; **4.21** After J. Bouzek (*op. cit.*), fig. 2.

Chapter 5 opener and 5.3b: SHM/photo by Vladimir Terebenin; **5.01** Author: multiple sources; **5.2a and b** SHM/photo by Vladimir Terebenin; **5.3a** SHM/photo by
Vladimir Terebenin; **5.4** After A.I. Malyukova, 'Scythians of Southeastern Europe' in
J. Davis-Kimball et al. (eds.), *Nomads of the Eurasian Steppes in the Early Iron Age* (Berkeley, 1995) 28–58, map 3; **5.5** Author: multiple sources; **5.6** Author: multiple sources;

5.7 Author: multiple sources; **5.8** Author: multiple sources; **5.9** Kamenskoe: after R. Rolle, *The World of the Scythians* (London, 1989), fig. 91; Trakhtemirov: after Y. Boltrik and E. Fialko, 'Trakhtemirov: a fortified city site on the Dnieper', in D. Brand and S. Kryzhitskiy (eds.), *Classical Olbia and the Scythian World: from the Sixth Century BC to the Second Century AD* (Oxford, 2007), fig. 14; **5.10** After R. Rolle (1989) (*op. cit.*), fig. 91; **5.11** US Geological Survey/Copernicus Sentinel/Science Photo Library; **5.12** Отчет археологической комиссии за / Report of the Archaeological Commission for 1904 (St Petersburg, 1907), from M.I. Artamonov, *Treasures from Scythian Tombs* (London, 1969), pl. I; **5.13** Tamara Talbot Rice, *The Scythians*, Thames & Hudson (1957), figs. 22 and 23; **5.14** After R. Rolle et al., Königskurgan Certomlyk. Ein skythischer Grabhügel des 4 vorchnstlichen Jahrhunderts (Mainz, 1988), fig. 25a; **5.15** After R. Rolle (1989) (*op. cit.*), fig. 16; **5.16** Отчет археологической комиссии за / Report of the Archaeological Commission for 1864, from M.I. Artamonov (*op. cit.*), pl. XV, after Gross; **5.17** Отчет археологической комиссии за / Report of the Archaeological Commission for 1864, from M.I. Artamonov (*op. cit.*), pl. XXIII, after Gross.

Chapter 6 opener and 6.16: SHM/photo by Vladimir Terebenin; **6.1** Jeff Schmaltz, MODIS Rapid Response Team, NASA/GSFC/Science Photo Library; **6.2** Author: multiple sources; **6.3** Author: using selected data from M. Parducz, 'Problem der Skythenzeit im Karpatenbecken', *Acta Archaeologica Academiae Scientiarum Hungancae* 25 (1973), 27–63 (kartes 1 and 2); **6.4** Author: using data from M. Parducz (*op. cit.*), karte 5; **6.5** © Hungarian National Museum; **6.6** © Hungarian National Museum; **6.7** After J. Chochorowski, 'Die Rolle des Vekerzug-Kultur im skythischen Einflüsse in Mitteleuropa', *Praehistorische Zeitschrift* 60 (1985), 204–71, fig. 5; **6.8** bpk/Antikensammlung, Staatliche Museen zu Berlin/Johannes Laurentius; **6.9** © The Trustees of the British Museum; **6.10** B. Cunliffe, *The Ancient Celts* (Oxford, 1997), fig. 95; **6.11** SHM/photo by Alexander Koksharov; **6.12** Landesmuseum Württemberg, P. Frankenstein/H. Zwietasch; **6.13** Commissioned by Thames & Hudson from Simon S.S. Driver. From Ruth and Vincent Megaw, *Celtic Art*, Thames & Hudson (2001), fig. 182; **6.14** Historisches Museum der Pfalz, Speyer. Photo by Peter Haag-Kirchner; **6.15** © The Trustees of the British Museum.

Chapter 7 opener and 7.4a: SHM/photo by Vladimir Terebenin; **7.1** Author: multiple sources; **7.2** Courtesy of the Oriental Institute of the University of Chicago; **7.3** SHM/photo by Vladimir Terebenin; **7.4b** SHM/photo by Vladimir Terebenin; **7.5** © The Trustees of the British Museum; **7.6** After A. Pshenichniuk, 'Burial ritual of the Filippovka Kurgan in the Ural region', in J. Aruz et al. (eds.), *The Golden Deer of Eurasia: Perspectives on the Steppe Nomads of the Ancient World* (New York, 2006), 40–5, figs. 3, 4,

7, and 8; **7.7** The work uses the results of scientific research, stored in archaeological funds of the Kuzeev Institute for Ethnological Studies of Ufa Federal Research Centre, Russian Academy of Sciences; **7.8** The work uses the results of scientific research, stored in archaeological funds of the Kuzeev Institute for Ethnological Studies of Ufa Federal Research Centre, Russian Academy of Sciences; **7.9** After L. Yablonsky, 'Scythians and Saka: ethnic terminology and archaeological reality' in J. Aruz et al. (*op. cit.*), 24–31, fig. 2; **7.10** Author: multiple sources; **7.11** Scientific-restoration laboratory 'Ostrov Krym', Almaty. Krym Altynbekov, 1996; **7.12** K. Akišev, *Kurgan Issyk* (Moscow, 1978); **7.13** K. Akišev (*op. cit.*); **7.14** After S. Rudenko (*op. cit.*), fig. 2; **7.15** © OUP; **7.16** K. Chugunov; **7.17a and b** S. Rudenko (*op. cit.*), figs 6 & 15; **7.18** Z. Samashev, "The Berel kurgans: some results of investigation', in S. Stark et al. (eds.), *Nomads and Networks* (Princeton, 2012), 31–49, fig. 2.3a; **7.19** Z. Samashev; **7.20** Z. Samashev; **7.21** Z. Samashev.

Chapter 8 opener and 8.3: SHM/photo by Vladimir Terebenin; **8.1** Marquand Library of Art and Archaeology, Princeton University. Photo by John Blazejewski. From Salomon Reinach, *Antiquités du Bosphore Cimmérien (1854) rééditées avec un commentaire nouveau et un index général des comptes rendus* (1892); **8.4** S. Rudenko (*op. cit.*), fig. 30; **8.5** SHM/photo by Vladimir Terebenin; **8.6a and b** S. Rudenko (*op. cit.*), figs 32 and 33; **8.7** SHM/photo by Vladimir Terebenin; **8.8** S. Rudenko (*op. cit.*), figs 32 and 33; **8.9** SHM/photo by Vladimir Terebenin; **8.10** Yevgeny Paletsky/Wikimedia Commons/CC-BY-SA-3.0; **8.11a and b** SHM/photo by Vladimir Terebenin; **8.12** SHM/photo by Vladimir Terebenin; **8.13** S. Rudenko (*op. cit.*), figs 23; **8.14** Tamara Talbot Rice (*op. cit.*), fig. 30; **8.15** SHM/photo by Alexander Koksharov; **8.16** Robert B. Haas Family Arts Library, Yale University: Drevnosti (*op. cit.*); **8.17a and b** Museum of Historical Treasures of Ukraine; **8.18** SHM/photo by Alexander Koksharov; **8.19** SHM/photo by Alexander Koksharov; **8.20** Museum of Historical Treasures of Ukraine; **8.21** SHM/photo by Vladimir Terebenin.

Chapter 9 opener and 9.4: SHM/photo by Vladimir Terebenin; **9.1a and b** SHM/photo by Vladimir Terebenin; **9.2** S. Rudenko (*op. cit.*), fig. 66; **9.3** SHM/photo by Vladimir Terebenin; **9.5** SHM/photo by Vladimir Terebenin; **9.6** S. Rudenko (*op. cit.*), fig. 87; **9.7** SHM/photo by Vladimir Terebenin; **9.8** Elena Stepanova, 'Horses' harnesses of the Nomads of Altai of the Scythian time' (based on material from the burial mounds of the Pazyryk culture) in the catalogue of an exhibition in Kazan, *Eurasian Nomads: On Their Way to the Empire* (St Petersburg, 2012), pp. 103–10, fig. 1 [Степанова Е. В. Конское снаряжение кочевников Алтая скифского времени (по материалам курганов Пазырыкской культуры), Кочевники Евразии на пути к империи:

Каталог выставки]; **9.9** After R. Rolle (1989) (*op. cit.*), fig. 39; **9.10** SHM/photo by Vladimir Terebenin; **9.11** SHM/photo by Daria Bobrova; **9.12** © The Trustees of the British Museum; **9.13** TimeLine Auctions Ltd; **9.14** SHM/photo by Vladimir Terebenin; **9.15** Museum of Historical Treasures of Ukraine; **9.16** SHM/photo by Vladimir Terebenin; **9.17** © The Trustees of the British Museum; **9.18a and b** SHM/photo by Vladimir Terebenin; **9.19** SHM/photo by Konstantin Sinyavskiy; **9.20** SHM/photo by Vladimir Terebenin; **9.21** SHM/photo by Vladimir Terebenin; **9.22** SHM/photo by Vladimir Terebenin; **9.23** National Historical and Ethnographic Reserve 'Pereiaslev' Ukraine. Photo by Igor Gaidaienko; **9.24** SHM/photo by Pavel Demidov; **9.25** Museum of Historical Treasures of Ukraine; **9.26** After R. Rolle (1989) (*op. cit.*), fig. 47 with additions; **9.27** SHM/photo by Konstantin Sinyavskiy; **9.28** After L. Galanina, *Kurdzhipskii Kurgan* (Leningrad, 1980).

Chapter 10 opener and 10.3: SHM/photo by Pavel Demidov; **10.1** SHM/photo by Vladimir Terebenin; **10.2** From S. Rudenko (*op. cit.*), fig 138; **10.4** SHM/photo by Vladimir Terebenin; **10.5** Museum of Historical Treasures of Ukraine; **10.6** SHM/photo by Vladimir Terebenin; **10.7** Museum of Historical Treasures of Ukraine; **10.8** SHM/photo by Vladimir Terebenin; **10.9** SHM/photo by Vladimir Terebenin; **10.10** SHM/photo by Vladimir Terebenin; **10.11** Museum of Historical Treasures of Ukraine; **10.12** After E. Jacobson, *The Art of the Scythians: the Interpretation of Cultures at the Edge of the Hellenic World* (Leiden, 1995), fig. 10.1; **10.13** SHM/photo by Vladimir Terebenin; **10.14** © Gary Tepfer. Reproduction courtesy Esther Jacobson-Tepfer; **10.15** SHM/photo by Vladimir Terebenin; **10.16** SHM/photo by Vladimir Terebenin; **10.17** SHM/photo by Vladimir Terebenin; **10.18** SHM/photo by Vladimir Terebenin; **10.19** SHM/photo by Vladimir Terebenin; **10.20** Museum of Historical Treasures of Ukraine; **10.21** Institute of Archaeology of the National Academy of Sciences of Ukraine, Kiev. © 2018 DeAgostini Picture Library/Scala, Florence; **10.22** After S. Rudenko (*op. cit.*), figs. 109, 111, and 113.

Chapter 11 opener and 11.10: National Historical and Ethnographic Reserve 'Pereiaslev' Ukraine. Photo by Igor Gaidaienko; **11.1** After A. Terenzhkin and B. Mozolevskiy, *Melitopolskiy Kurgans* (Kiev, 1988), fig. 61; **11.2** M.I. Artamonov, *Treasures from Scythian Tombs* (London, 1969), pl. VI; **11.3** M.I. Artamonov (*op. cit.*), pl. VII; **11.4** After R. Rolle, *Totenkult der Skythen Teil I* (Berlin, 1979); **11.5** S. Rudenko (*op. cit.*), pl. 19; **11.6** After R. Rolle (1979) (*op. cit.*); **11.7** S. Rudenko (*op. cit*), pl. 45; **11.8** Отчёт археологической комиссии за 1913–1915 годы. Петроград, 1918. Стр. 153 / Report of the Archaeological Commission for 1913–1915 (Petrograd, 1918), p. 153, from M.I. Artamonov (*op. cit.*), pl. VIII; **11.9** The Dean and Chapter of Hereford Cathedral and the Hereford Mappa Mundi Trust.

Chapter 12 opener and 12.7: SHM/photo by Vladimir Terebenin; **12.1** After B. Cunliffe, *By Steppe, Desert, and Ocean* (Oxford, 2016), fig. 7.11; **12.2** National Museum of Afghanistan, Kabul. Photo © MNΛΛG, Paris, Dist. RMN-Grand Palais/Thierry Ollivier; **12.3** Author: multiple sources including T. Sulimirski, *The Sarmatians* (London, 1970), fig. 41; **12.4** Author: multiple sources including T. Sulimirski (*op. cit.*), fig. 62; **12.5** Alinari/TopFoto; **12.6** © Grosvenor Museum, Cheshire West and Chester; **12.8** Author: multiple sources.

Gallery 1 SHM/photo by Vladimir Terebenin; **2** SHM/photo by Vladimir Terebenin; **3** Museum of Historical Treasures of Ukraine; **4** SHM/photo by Vladimir Terebenin; **5** SHM/photo by Vladimir Terebenin; **6** Museum of Historical Treasures of Ukraine; **7** SHM/photo by Konstantin Sinyavskiy; **8** Museum of Historical Treasures of Ukraine; **9** Institute of Archaeology of the National Academy of Sciences of Ukraine, Kiev. © 2018 DeAgostini Picture Library/Scala, Florence; **10** SHM/photo by Vladimir Terebenin.

Key: SHM = The State Hermitage Museum, St Petersburg. Photo © The State Hermitage Museum.

The publisher apologizes for any errors or omissions in the above list. If contacted, they will be pleased to rectify these at the earliest opportunity.

Picture Research by Sandra Assersohn

INDEX

Note: numbers in **bold** refer to
illustrations, maps, and diagrams.
For the benefit of digital users,
indexed terms that span two pages
(e.g., 52–3) may, on occasion,
appear on only one of those pages.

 391

coiled feline motif, Scythian 284–5, **285**

Colaxais 266

Colchis 30

copper mining 73

covered wagons, Scythian 211, **211**, 214–16, **215**

cremation graves, Hallstatt culture 159

Cyaxares, Median king 114, 259

Cyropolis, Persian garrison town 170

Cyrus the Great, Persian king 39–41, 44, 170, 175, 256, 262

Dacians 319, 320–2

daily life, Scythian 199–227

   Andrieis/Enarees (effeminates) 219–20, 268, 272, 273

   body tattooing 207–9, **208**, **209**, 265

   cannabis use 46, 210

   cheese making 222–4

   clean in body and mind 209–16

   covered wagons 211, **211**, 214–16, **215**

   dress and display 201–9, **202**, **203**, **204**

   furniture and cooking utensils 213, **213**, **214**

   gender fluidity 218–20

   goats and cattle 222

   hairstyles 211

   herd management and animal husbandry 220–2

   horse training 221, **221**

   hunting 225, **225**

   leather and wool working 207

   mare milking 222

   music 226, **226**, **227**

   permanent houses 212–13

   saunas 210

   sheep 222, **223**

   social structure 216–17

   wine 227

   women's skin cleaning 210–11

   work and play 220–7

   yurts and gers 211–12, **212**

Darius, Persian king 24, **40**, **41**, 41–3, 122, 175, 203, 231, 256

de Wilde, Jacob 2, **3**

death, burial, and ritual, Scythian 46, **46**, 291–309

   across the steppe 307–8

   burial grounds of the kings 293–5

   catacomb-style graves 139–41, **152**, 299–300, **299**

   consigned to the earth 300–4, **301**, **303**, **304**

   death riders 307

   displays of grief 297

   feasting 297, 306

   female companions 302

   gift giving 298

   preparing the body 295–6

   preparing the grave 298–300, **298**, **299**

   processions 297–8

   purifications 306

   raising the mound 304–6

   retainers 302

   ritual cannibalism 308–9, **308**

   ritual mutilation 297

   royal and aristocratic distinctions 295

   sarcophagi 300

   Scythian sources 292–3

   a year later 306–7

   see also horse sacrifice and burials

deer and stag motifs, Scythian 283, **284**

defended enclosures (*gorodišče*), Pontic steppe 22

   Bel'sk, Ukraine 22, 46, 129, **132**, 133–5, **133**

   Kamenskoe fortification, Ukraine 22, 129–31, **130**

deities, Scythian images of 276–82

Demidov, Alexis 6

Demosthenes 54

Diodorus Siculus 144, 258, 266

Dioskouroi cult 282

DNA evidence, Yamnaya culture 148

Dnepropetrovska ceremonial pole top, Ukraine **275**

'dragon-pairs' 162

dress and display, Scythian 201–9, **202**, **203**, **204**

Du Brux, Paul 332

Dugdamme/Lygdamis, Kimmerian king 33

Dutch East India Company 2

dzud, Mongolia 66

effeminate males ('female sickness'), *Andrieis*/Enarees 219–20, 272, 273

   and the hereditary priesthood 268

Eleusinian cult 143

Elizavetinskaya kurgans: six-wheeled wagon 304, **305**

Elizavetovskaya settlement, Don delta 127, **127**, 129, 131

   shaft graves 137–9

Enarees/*Andrieis* 219–20, 272, 273

   and the hereditary priesthood 268

Ephesus temple of Artemis 33, 35

Ephoros 48

Equus caballus 70

Equus hernionas (Onager) 70

Equus hydruntinus 70

Eumelus, Bosporan pretender 258

Eurasian steppe 61–82

   Atlantic wind systems and currents 64

   cereal cultivation (1800–1200 BC) 73–6

   climate 65–70